A COMPLETE BIOGRAPHY OF

Abraham Lincoln

By

Lord Charnwood

BOOKS

NEW DELHI (INDIA)

A COMPLETE BIOGRAPHY OF

Abraham Lincoln

By

Lord Charnwood

Published by

An Imprint of

MAANU GRAPHICS
(PUBLISHERS OF GENERAL BOOKS)
5FF, Ganpati Bhawan, 21 Ansari Road,
Darya Ganj, New Delhi-110002
Ph: 65285220, 64138266
E-mail : maanugraphics@yahoo.com
mgbooks.maanu@yahoo.com

Printed at : Satyam Enterprises, Delh

CONTENTS

PREFACE

Statesmen—even the greatest—have rarely won the same unquestioning recognition that falls to the great warriors or those supreme in science, art or literature. Not in their own lifetime and hardly to this day have the claims to supremacy of our own Oliver Cromwell, William III. and Lord Chatham rested on so sure a foundation as those of a Marlborough or a Nelson, a Newton, a Milton or a Hogarth. This is only natural. A warrior, a man of science, an artist or a poet are judged in the main by definite achievements, by the victories they have won over foreign enemies or over ignorance and prejudice, by the joy and enlightenment they have brought to the consciousness of their own and succeeding generations. For the statesman there is no such exact measure of greatness. The greater he is, the less likely is his work to be marked by decisive achievement which can be recalled by anniversaries or signalised by some outstanding event: the chief work of a great statesman rests in a gradual change of direction given to the policy of his people, still more in a change of the spirit within them. Again, the statesman must work with a rough and ready instrument. The soldier finds or makes his army ready to yield unhesitating obedience to his commands, the sailor animates his fleet with his own personal touch, and the great man in art, literature or science is master of his material, if he can master himself. The statesman cannot mould a heterogeneous people, as the men of a well-disciplined army or navy can be moulded, to respond to his call and his alone. He has to do all his work in a society of which a large part cannot see his object and another large part, as far as they do see it, oppose it. Hence his work at the best is often incomplete and he has to be satisfied with a rough average rather than with his ideal.

Lincoln, one of the few supreme statesmen of the last three centuries, was no exception to this rule. He was misunderstood and underrated in his lifetime, and even yet has hardly come to his own. For his place is among the great men of the earth. To them he belongs by right of his immense power of hard work, his unfaltering pursuit of what seemed to him right, and above all by that childlike directness and simplicity of vision which none but the greatest carry beyond their earliest years. It is fit that the first considered attempt by an Englishman to give a picture of Lincoln, the great hero of America's struggle for the noblest cause, should come at a time when we in England are passing through as fiery a trial for a cause we feel to be as noble. It is a time when we may learn much from Lincoln's failures and success, from his patience, his modesty, his serene optimism and his eloquence, so simple and so magnificent.

CHAPTER I

BOYHOOD OF LINCOLN

The subject of this memoir is revered by multitudes of his countrymen as the preserver of their commonwealth. This reverence has grown with the lapse of time and the accumulation of evidence. It is blended with a peculiar affection, seldom bestowed upon the memory of statesmen. It is shared to-day by many who remember with no less affection how their own fathers fought against him. He died with every circumstance of tragedy, yet it is not the accident of his death but the purpose of his life that is remembered.

Readers of history in another country cannot doubt that the praise so given is rightly given; yet any bare record of the American Civil War may leave them wondering why it has been so unquestioningly accorded. The position and task of the American President in that crisis cannot be understood from those of other historic rulers or historic leaders of a people; and it may seem as if, after that tremendous conflict in which there was no lack of heroes, some perverse whim had made men single out for glory the puzzled civil magistrate who sat by. Thus when an English writer tells again this tale, which has been well told already and in which there can remain no important new facts to disclose, he must endeavour to make clear to Englishmen circumstances and conditions which are familiar to Americans. He will incur the certainty that here and there his own perspective of American affairs and persons will be false, or his own touch unsympathetic.

He had better do this than chronicle sayings and doings which to him and to those for whom he writes have no significance. Nor should the writer shrink too timidly from the display of a partisanship which, on one side or the other, it would be insensate not to feel. The true obligation of impartiality is that he should conceal no fact which, in his own mind, tells against his views.

Abraham Lincoln, sixteenth President of the United States of America, was born on February 12, 1809, in a log cabin on a barren farm in the backwoods of Kentucky, about three miles west of a place called Hodgensville in what is now La Rue County.

Fifty years later when he had been nominated for the Presidency he was asked for material for an account of his early life. "Why," he said, "it is a great folly to attempt to make anything out of me or my early life. It can all be condensed into a single sentence; and that sentence you will find in Gray's 'Elegy': –

"'The short and simple annals of the poor.'

That's my life, and that's all you or anyone else can make out of it." His other references to early days were rare. He would repeat queer reminiscences of the backwoods to illustrate questions of state; but of his own part in that old life he spoke reluctantly and sadly. Nevertheless there was once extracted from him an awkward autobiographical fragment, and his friends have collected and recorded concerning his earlier years quite as much as is common in great men's biographies or can as a rule be reproduced with its true associations. Thus there are tales enough of the untaught student's perseverance, and of the boy giant's gentleness and prowess; tales, too, more than enough in proportion, of the fun which varied but did not pervade his existence, and of the young rustic's occasional and somewhat oafish pranks. But, in any conception we may form as to the growth of his mind and character, this fact must have its place, that to the man himself the thought of his early life was unattractive, void of self-content over the difficulties which he had conquered, and void of romantic fondness for vanished joys of youth.

Much the same may be said of his ancestry and family connections. Contempt for lowly beginnings, abhorrent as it is to any honest mind, would to Lincoln's mind have probably been inconceivable, but he lacked that interest in ancestry which is generally marked in his countrymen, and from talk of his nearer progenitors he seems to have shrunk with a positive sadness of which some causes will soon be apparent. Since his death it has been ascertained that in 1638 one Samuel Lincoln of Norwich emigrated to Massachusetts. Descent from him could be claimed by a prosperous family in Virginia, several of whom fought on the Southern side in the Civil War. One Abraham Lincoln, grandfather of the President and apparently a grandson of Samuel, crossed the mountains from Virginia in 1780 and settled his family in Kentucky, of which the nearer portions had recently been explored. One morning four years later he was at work near his cabin with Mordecai, Josiah, and Thomas, his sons, when a shot from the bushes near by brought him down.

Mordecai ran to the house, Josiah to a fort, which was close to them. Thomas, aged six, stayed by his father's body. Mordecai seized a gun and, looking through the window, saw an Indian in war paint stooping to pick up Thomas. He fired and killed the savage, and, when Thomas had run into the cabin, continued firing at others who appeared among the bushes. Shortly Josiah returned with soldiers from the fort, and the Indians ran off, leaving Abraham the elder dead. Mordecai, his heir-at-law, prospered. We hear of him long after as an old man of substance and repute in Western Illinois. He had decided views about Indians. The sight of a redskin would move him to strange excitement; he would disappear into the bushes with his gun, and his conscience as a son and a sportsman would not be satisfied till he had stalked and shot him. We are further informed that he was a "good old man." Josiah also moved to Illinois, and it is pleasant to learn that he also was a good old man, and, as became a good old man, prospered pretty well. But President Lincoln and his sister knew neither these excellent elders nor any other of their father's kin.

And those with whom the story of his own first twenty-one years is bound up invite almost as summary treatment. Thomas Lincoln never prospered like Mordecai and Josiah, and never seems to have left the impress of his goodness or of anything else on any man. But, while learning to carpenter under one Joseph Hanks, he married his employer's niece Nancy, and by her became the father first of a daughter Sarah, and four years later, at the farm near Hodgensville aforesaid, of Abraham, the future President. In 1816, after several migrations, he transported his household down the Ohio to a spot on the Indiana shore, near which the village of Gentryville soon sprang up. There he abode till Abraham was nearly twenty-one. When the boy was eight his mother died, leaving him in his sister's care; but after a year or so Thomas went back alone to Kentucky and, after brief wooing, brought back a wife, Sarah, the widow of one Mr. Johnston, whom he had courted vainly before her first marriage. He brought with her some useful additions to his household gear, and her rather useless son John Johnston. Relatives of Abraham's mother and other old neighbours – in particular John and Dennis Hanks – accompanied all the family's migrations.

Ultimately, in 1830, they all moved further west into Illinois. Meanwhile Abraham from an early age did such various tasks for his father or for neighbouring farmers as from time to time suited the father. When an older lad he was put for a while in charge of a ferry boat, and this led to the two great adventures of his early days, voyages with a cargo boat; and two mates down by river to New Orleans. The second and more memorable of these voyages was just after the migration to Illinois. He returned from it to a place called New Salem, in Illinois, some distance from his father's new farm, in expectation of work in a store which was about to be opened. Abraham, by this time, was of age, and in accordance with custom had been set free to shift for himself.

Each of these migrations was effected with great labour in transportation of baggage (sometimes in home-made boats), clearing of timber, and building; and Thomas Lincoln cannot have been wanting in the capacity for great exertions. But historians have been inclined to be hard on him. He seems to have been without sustained industry; in any case he had not much money sense and could not turn his industry to much account. Some hint that he drank, but it is admitted that most Kentucky men drank more. There are indications that he was a dutiful but ineffective father, chastising not too often or too much, but generally on the wrong occasion. He was no scholar and did not encourage his son that way; but he had a great liking for stories. He was of a peaceable and inoffensive temper, but on great provocation would turn on a bully with surprising and dire consequences. Old Thomas, after Abraham was turned loose, continued a migrant, always towards a supposed better farm further west, always with a mortgage on him. Abraham, when he was a struggling professional man, helped him with money as well as he could. We have his letter to the old man on his death-bed, a letter of genuine but mild affection with due words of piety. He explains that illness in his own household makes it impossible for him to pay a last visit to his father, and then, with that curious directness which is common in the families of the poor and has as a rule no sting, he remarks that an interview, if it had been possible, might have given more pain than pleasure to both. Everybody has insisted from the first how little Abraham took after his father, but more than one of the traits attributed to Thomas will certainly reappear.

Abraham, as a man, when for once he spoke of his mother, whom he very seldom mentioned, spoke with intense feeling for her motherly care. "I owe," he said, "everything that I am to her." It pleased him in this talk to explain by inheritance from her the mental qualities which distinguished him from the house of Lincoln, and from others of the house of Hanks. She was, he said, the illegitimate daughter of a Virginian gentleman, whose name he did not know, but from whom as he guessed the peculiar gifts, of which he could not fail to be conscious, were derived.

Sarah his sister was married at Gentryville to one Mr. Grigsby. The Grigsbys were rather great people, as people went in Gentryville. It is said to have become fixed in the boy's mind that the Grigsbys had not treated Sarah well; and this was the beginning of certain woes.

Sarah Bush Lincoln, his stepmother, was good to him and he to her. Above all she encouraged him in his early studies, to which a fretful housewife could have opposed such terrible obstacles. She lived to hope that he might not be elected President for fear that enemies should kill him, and she lived to have her fear fulfilled. His affectionate care over her continued to the end. She lived latterly with her son John Johnston. Abraham's later letters to this companion of his youth deserve to be looked up in the eight large volumes called his Works, for it is hard to see how a man could speak or act better to an impecunious friend who would not face his own troubles squarely. It is sad that the "ever your affectionate brother" of the earlier letters declines to "yours sincerely" in the last; but it is an honest decline of affection, for the man had proved to be cheating his mother, and Abraham had had to stop it.

Two of the cousinhood, Dennis Hanks, a character of comedy, and John Hanks, the serious and steady character of the connection, deserve mention. They and John Johnston make momentary reappearances again. Otherwise the whole of Abraham Lincoln's kindred are now out of the story. They have been disposed of thus hastily at the outset, not because they were discreditable or slight people, but because Lincoln himself when he began to find his footing in the world seems to have felt sadly that his family was just so much to him and no more. The dearest of his recollections attached to premature death; the next to chronic failure. Rightly or wrongly (and we know enough about heredity now to expect any guess as to its working in a particular case to be wrong) he attributed the best that he had inherited to a licentious connection and a nameless progenitor. Quite early he must have been intensely ambitious, and discovered in himself intellectual power; but from his twelfth year to his twenty-first there was hardly a soul to comprehend that side of him. This chill upon his memory unmistakably influenced the particular complexion of his melancholy. Unmistakably too he early learnt to think that he was odd, that his oddity was connected with his strength, that he might be destined to stand alone and capable of so standing.

The life of the farming pioneer in what was then the Far West afforded a fair prospect of laborious independence. But at least till Lincoln was grown up, when a time of rapid growth and change set in, it offered no hope of quickly gotten wealth, and it imposed severe hardship on all. The country was thickly wooded; the settler had before him at the outset heavy toil in clearing the ground and in building some rude shelter,—a house or just a "half-faced camp," that is, a shed with one side open to the weather such as that in which the Lincoln family passed their first winter near Gentryville. The site once chosen and the clearing once made, there was no such ease of cultivation or such certain fertility as later settlers found yet further west when the development of railways, of agricultural machinery, and of Eastern or European markets had opened out to cultivation the enormous stretches of level grass plain beyond the Mississippi.

Till population had grown a good deal, pioneer families were largely occupied in producing for themselves with their own hands what, in their hardy if not always frugal view, were the necessities and comforts of life. They had no Eastern market for their produce, for railways did not begin to be made till 1840, and it was many years before they crossed the Eastern mountains. An occasional cargo was taken on a flat-bottomed boat down the nearest creek, as a stream is called in America, into the Ohio and so by the innumerable windings of the Mississippi to New Orleans; but no return cargo could be brought up stream. Knives and axes were the most precious objects to be gained by trade; woollen fabrics were rare in the West, when Lincoln was born, and the white man and woman, like the red whom they had displaced, were chiefly dressed in deer skins. The woods abounded in game, and in the early stages of the development of the West a man could largely support himself by his gun. The cold of every winter is there great, and an occasional winter made itself long remembered, like the "winter of the deep snow" in Illinois, by the havoc of its sudden onset and the suffering of its long duration. The settling of a forest country was accompanied here as elsewhere by the occasional ravages of strange and destructive pestilences and the constant presence of malaria. Population was soon thick enough for occasional gatherings, convivial or religious, and in either case apt to be wild, but for long it was not thick enough for the life of most settlers to be other than lonely as well as hard.

Abraham Lincoln in his teens grew very fast, and by nineteen he was nearly six foot four. His weight was never quite proportionate to this. His ungainly figure, with long arms and large hands and relatively small development of chest, and the strange deep-cut lineaments of his face were perhaps the evidence of unfit (sometimes insufficient) food in these years of growth. But his muscular strength was great, and startling statistical tales are told of the weight he could lift and the force of his blows with a mallet or an axe. To a gentle and thoughtful boy with secret ambition in him such strength is a great gift, and in such surroundings most obviously so. Lincoln as a lad was a valuable workman at the varied tasks that came his way, without needing that intense application to manual pursuits which the bent of his mind made irksome to him. And he was a person of high consideration among the lads of his age and company. The manners of the people then settling in Indiana and Illinois had not the extreme ferocity for which Kentucky had earlier been famous, and which crops up here and there in frontier life elsewhere. All the same, as might naturally be supposed, they shared Plato's opinion that youths and men in the prime of life should settle their differences with their fists. Young Lincoln's few serious combats were satisfactorily decisive, and neither they nor his friendly wrestling bouts ended in the quarrels which were too common among his neighbours. Thus, for all his originality and oddity, he early grew accustomed to mix in the sort of company he was likely to meet, without either inward shrinking or the need of conscious self-assertion.

In one thing he stood aloof from the sports of his fellows. Most backwoodsmen were bred to the gun; he has told us that he shot a turkey when he was eight and never afterwards shot at all. There is an early tale of his protests against an aimless slaughter of mud turtles; and it may be guessed that the dislike of all killing, which gave him sore trouble later, began when he was young. Tales survive of his kindness to helpless men and animals. It marks the real hardness of his surroundings, and their hardening effect on many, that his exertions in saving a drunken man from death in the snow are related with apparent surprise. Some tales of his helping a pig stuck in a bog or a dog on an ice floe and the like seem to indicate a curious and lasting trait. These things seem not to have been done spontaneously, but on mature reflection after he had passed unheeding by. He grew to be a man of prompt action in circumstances of certain kinds; but generally his impulse was slow and not very sure. Taste and the minor sensibilities were a little deficient in him. As a lady once candidly explained to him, he was not ready with little gracious acts. But rare occasions, such as can arouse a passionate sense of justice, would kindle his slow, kind nature with a sudden fire.

The total amount of his schooling, at the several brief periods for which there happened to have been a school accessibleand facility to get to it, was afterwards computed by himself at something under twelve months. With this slight help distributed over the years from his eighth to his fifteenth birthday he taught himself to read, write, and do sums. The stories of the effort and painful shifts, by which great men accomplish this initial labour almost unhelped, have in all cases the same pathos, and have a certain sameness in detail. Having learnt to read he had the following books within his reach: the Bible, "Aesop's Fables," "Robinson Crusoe," the "Pilgrim's Progress," a "History of the United States," and Weems' "Life of Washington." Later on the fancy took him to learn the laws of his State, and he obtained the "Laws of Indiana." These books he did read, and read again, and pondered, not with any dreamy or purely intellectual interest, but like one who desires the weapon of learning for practical ends, and desires also to have patterns of what life should be. As already said, his service as a labourer could be considerable, and when something stirred his ambition to do a task quickly his energy could be prodigious. But "bone idle is what I called him," was the verdict long after of one, perhaps too critical, employer. "I found him," he said, "cocked up on a haystack with a book. 'What are you reading?' I said. 'I'm not reading, I'm studying,' says he. 'What are you studying?' says I. 'Law,' says he, as proud as Cicero. 'Great God Almighty!' said I." The boy's correction, "studying" for "reading," was impertinent, but probably sound. To be equally sound, we must reckon among his educational facilities the abundant stories which came his way in a community which, however unlettered, was certainly not dull-spirited; the occasional newspaper; the rare lectures or political meetings; the much more frequent religious meetings, with preachers who taught a grim doctrine, but who preached with vigour and sometimes with the deepest sincerity; the hymns often of great emotional power over a simple congregation—Cowper's "There is a fountain filled with blood," is one recorded favourite among them; the songs, far other than hymns, which Dennis Hanks and his other mates would pick up or compose; and the practice in rhetoric and the art of exposition, which he unblushingly afforded himself before audiences of fellow labourers who welcomed the jest and the excuse for stopping work. The achievement of the self-taught man remains wonderful, but, if he surmounts his difficulties at all, some of his limitations may turn to sheer advantage. There is some advantage merely in being driven to make the most of few books; great advantage in having one's choice restricted by circumstances to good books; great advantage too in the consciousness of untrained faculty which leaves a man capable in mature life of deliberately undertaking mental discipline.

Along with the legends and authentic records of his self-training, signs of an ambition which showed itself early and which was from the first a clean and a high ambition, there are also other legends showing Lincoln as a naughty boy among naughty boys. The selection here made from these lacks refinement, and the reader must note that this was literally a big, naughty boy, not a man who had grown stiff in coarseness and ill-nature. First it must be recalled that Abraham bore a grudge against the Grigsbys, an honourable grudge in its origin and perhaps the only grudge he ever bore. There had arisen from this a combat, of which the details might displease the fastidious, but which was noble in so far that Abraham rescued a weaker combatant who was over-matched. But there ensued something more displeasing, a series of lampoons by Abraham, in prose and a kind of verse. These were gross and silly enough, though probably to the taste of the public which he then addressed, but it is the sequel that matters. In a work called "The First Chronicles of Reuben," it is related how Reuben and Josiah, the sons of Reuben Grigsby the elder, took to themselves wives on the same day. By local custom the bridal feast took place and the two young couples began their married careers under the roof of the bridegrooms' father. Moreover, it was the custom that, at a certain stage in the celebrations, the brides should be escorted to their chambers by hired attendants who shortly after conducted the bridegrooms thither. On this occasion some sense of mischief afoot disturbed the heart of Mrs. Reuben Grigsby the elder, and, hastening upstairs, just after the attendants had returned, she cried out in a loud voice and to the great consternation of all concerned, "Why, Reuben, you're in bed with the wrong wife!" The historian who, to the manifest annoyance of Lincoln's other biographers, has preserved this and much other priceless information, infers that Abraham, who was not invited to the feast, had plotted this domestic catastrophe and won over the attendants to his evil purpose. This is not a certain inference, nor is it absolutely beyond doubt that the event recorded in "The First Chronicles of Reuben" ever happened at all. What is certain is that these Chronicles themselves, composed in what purports to be the style of Scripture, were circulated for the joint edification of the proud race of Grigsby and of their envious neighbours in the handwriting of Abraham Lincoln, then between seventeen and eighteen. Not without reason does an earlier manuscript of the same author conclude, after several correct exercises in compound subtraction, with the distich: –

"Abraham Lincoln, his hand and pen,
He will be good, but God knows when."

Not to be too solemn about a tale which has here been told for the whimsical fancy of its unseemliness and because it is probably the worst that there is to tell, we may here look forward and face the well-known fact that the unseemliness in talk of rough, rustic boys flavoured the great President's conversation through life. It is well to be plain about this. Lincoln was quite without any elegant and sentimental dissoluteness, such as can be attractively portrayed. His life was austere and seems to have been so from the start. He had that shy reverence for womanhood which is sometimes acquired as easily in rough as in polished surroundings and often quite as steadily maintained. The testimony of his early companions, along with some fragments of the boy's feeble but sincere attempts at verse, shows that he acquired it young. But a large part of the stories and pithy sayings for which he was famous wherever he went, but of which when their setting is lost it is impossible to recover the enjoyment, were undeniably coarse, and naturally enough this fact was jarring to some of those in America who most revered him. It should not really be hard, in any comprehensive view of his character and the circumstances in which it unfolded itself, to trace in this bent of his humour something not discordant with the widening sympathy and deepening tenderness of his nature. The words of his political associate in Illinois, Mr. Leonard Swett, afterwards Attorney-General of the United States, may suffice. He writes: "Almost any man, who will tell a very vulgar story, has, in a degree, a vulgar mind. But it was not so with him; with all his purity of character and exalted morality and sensibility, which no man can doubt, when hunting for wit he had no ability to discriminate between the vulgar and refined substances from which he extracted it. It was the wit he was after, the pure jewel, and he would pick it up out of the mud or dirt just as readily as from a parlour table." In any case his best remembered utterances of this order, when least fit for print, were both wise and incomparably witty, and in any case they did not prevent grave gentlemen, who marvelled at them rather uncomfortably, from receiving the deep impression of what they called his pure-mindedness.

One last recollection of Lincoln's boyhood has appealed, beyond any other, to some of his friends as prophetic of things to come. Mention has already been made of his two long trips down the Mississippi. With the novel responsibilities which they threw on him, and the novel sights and company which he met all the way to the strange, distant city of New Orleans, they must have been great experiences. Only two incidents of them are recorded. In the first voyage he and his mates had been disturbed at night by a band of negro marauders and had had a sharp fight in repelling them, but in the second voyage he met with the negro in a way that to him was more memorable. He and the young fellows with him saw, among the sights of New Orleans, negroes chained, maltreated, whipped and scourged; they came in their rambles upon a slave auction where a fine mulatto girl was being pinched and prodded and trotted up and down the room like a horse to show how she moved, that "bidders might satisfy themselves," as the auctioneer said, of the soundness of the article to be sold. John Johnston and John Hanks and Abraham Lincoln saw these sights with the unsophisticated eyes of honest country lads from a free State. In their home circle it seems that slavery was always spoken of with horror. One of them had a tenacious memory and a tenacious will. "Lincoln saw it," John Hanks said long after, and other men's recollections of Lincoln's talk confirmed him—"Lincoln saw it; his heart bled; said nothing much, was silent. I can say, knowing it, that it was on this trip that he formed his opinion of slavery. It ran its iron into him then and there, May, 1831. I have heard him say so often." Perhaps in other talks old John Hanks dramatised his early remembrances a little; he related how at the slave auction Lincoln said, "By God, boys, let's get away from this. If ever I get a chance to hit that thing, I'll hit it hard."

The youth, who probably did not express his indignation in these prophetic words, was in fact chosen to deal "that thing" a blow from which it seems unlikely to recover as a permitted institution among civilised men, and it is certain that from this early time the thought of slavery never ceased to be hateful to him. Yet it is not in the light of a crusader against this special evil that we are to regard him. When he came back from this voyage to his new home in Illinois he was simply a youth ambitious of an honourable part in the life of the young country of which he was proud. We may regard, and he himself regarded, the liberation of the slaves, which will always be associated with his name, as a part of a larger work, the restoration of his country to its earliest and noblest tradition, which alone gave permanence or worth to its existence as a nation.

CHAPTER II

THE GROWTH OF THE AMERICAN NATION

1. The Formation of a National Government.

It is of course impossible to understand the life of a politician in another country without study of its conditions and its past. In the case of America this study is especially necessary, not only because the many points of comparison between that country and our own are apt to conceal profound differences of customs and institutions, but because the broader difference between a new country and an old is in many respects more important than we conceive. But in the case of Lincoln there is peculiar reason for carrying such a study far back. He himself appealed unceasingly to a tradition of the past. In tracing the causes which up to his time had tended to conjoin the United States more closely and the cause which more recently had begun to threaten them with disruption, we shall be examining the elements of the problem with which it was his work in life to deal.

The "Thirteen United States of America" which in 1776 declared their independence of Great Britain were so many distinct Colonies distributed unevenly along 1,300 miles of the Atlantic coast. These thirteen Colonies can easily be identified on the map when it is explained that Maine in the extreme north was then an unsettled forest tract claimed by the Colony of Massachusetts, that Florida in the extreme south belonged to Spain, and that Vermont, which soon after asserted its separate existence, was a part of the State of New York. Almost every one of these Colonies had its marked peculiarities and its points of antagonism as against its nearest neighbours; but they fell into three groups. We may broadly contrast the five southernmost, which included those which were the richest and of which in many ways the leading State was Virginia, with the four (or later six) northernmost States known collectively as New England. Both groups had at first been colonised by the same class, the smaller landed gentry of England with a sprinkling of well-to-do traders, though the South received later a larger number of poor and shiftless immigrants than the North, and the North attracted a larger number of artisans. The physical conditions of the South led to the growth of large farms, or "plantations" as they were called, and of a class of large proprietors; negro slaves thrived there and were useful in the cultivation of tobacco, indigo, rice, and later of cotton. The North continued to be a country of small farms, but its people turned also to fishery and to commerce, and the sea carrying trade became early its predominant interest, yielding place later on to manufacturing industries. The South was attached in the main, though by no means altogether, to the Church of England; New England owed its origin to successive immigrations of Puritans often belonging to the Congregational or Independent body; with the honourable exception of Rhode Island these communities showed none of the liberal and tolerant Spirit which the Independents of the old country often developed; they manifested, however, the frequent virtues as well as the occasional defects of the Puritan character. The middle group of Colonies were of more mixed origin; New York and New Jersey had been Dutch possessions, Delaware was partly Swedish, Pennsylvania had begun as a Quaker settlement but included many different elements; in physical and economic conditions they resembled on the whole New England, but they lacked, some of them conspicuously, the Puritan discipline, and had a certain cosmopolitan character. Though there were sharp antagonisms among the northern settlements, and the southern settlements were kept distinct by the great distances between them, the tendency of events was to soften these minor differences. But it greatly intensified one broad distinction which marked off the southern group from the middle and the northern groups equally.

Nevertheless, before independence was thought of there were common characteristics distinguishing Americans from English people. They are the better worth an attempt to note them because, as a historian of America wrote some years ago, "the typical American of 1900 is on the whole more like his ancestor of 1775 than is the typical Englishman." In all the Colonies alike the conditions of life encouraged personal independence. In all alike they also encouraged a special kind of ability which may be called practical rather than thorough—that of a workman who must be competent at many tasks and has neither opportunity nor inducement to become perfect at one; that of the scientific man irresistibly drawn to inventions which shall make life less hard; that of the scholar or philosopher who must supply the new community's need of lawyers and politicians.

On the other hand, many of the colonists' forefathers had come to their new home with distinct aspirations for a better ordering of human life than the old world allowed, and it has frequently been noticed that Americans from the first have been more prone than their kinsmen in England to pay homage to large ideal conceptions. This is a disposition not entirely favourable to painstaking and sure-footed reform. The idealist American is perhaps too ready to pay himself with fine words, which the subtler and shyer Englishman avoids and rather too readily sets down as insincere in others. Moreover, this tendency is quite consistent with the peculiar conservatism characteristic of America. New conditions in which tradition gave no guidance called forth great inventive powers and bred a certain pride in novelty. An American economist has written in a sanguine humour, "The process of transplanting removes many of the shackles of custom and tradition which retard the progress of older countries. In a new country things cannot be done in the old way, and therefore they are probably done in the best way." But a new country is always apt to cling with tenacity to those old things for which it still has use; and a remote and undeveloped country does not fully share the continual commerce in ideas which brings about change (and, in the main, advance) in the old world. The conservatism which these causes tend to produce has in any case been marked in America. Thus, as readers of Lowell are aware, in spite of the ceaseless efflorescence of the modern slang of America, the language of America is in many respects that of an older England than ours, and the like has all along been true of important literature, and still more of oratory, in America. Moreover, as the sentences which have just been quoted may suggest, the maxim that has once hit the occasion, or the new practice or expedient once necessitated by the conditions of the moment, has been readily hallowed as expressing the wisdom of the ages. An Englishman will quote Burke as he would quote Demosthenes or Plato, but Americans have been apt to quote their elder statesmen as they would quote the Bible. In like manner political practices of accidental origin—for instance, that a representative should be an inhabitant of the place he represents—acquire in America something like the force of constitutional law.

In this connection we must recall the period at which the earliest settlers came from England, and the political heritage which they consequently brought with them. This heritage included a certain aptitude for local government, which was fostered in the south by the rise of a class of large landowners and in the north by the Congregational Church system. It included also a great tenacity of the subject's rights as against the State—the spirit of Hampden refusing payment of ship-money—and a disposition to look on the law and the Courts as the bulwarks of such rights against Government. But it did not include—and this explains the real meaning of the War of Independence—any sort of feeling of allegiance to a Parliament which represented Great Britain only, and which had gained its position even in Great Britain since the fathers of Virginia and Massachusetts left home. Nor did it include—and this was of great importance in its influence on the form of the Constitution—any real understanding of or any aptitude for the English Parliamentary Government, under which the leaders of the legislative body and the advisers of the Crown in its executive functions are the same men, and under which the elected persons, presumed for the moment to represent the people, are allowed for that moment an almost unfettered supremacy.

Thus there was much that made it easy for the Colonies to combine in the single act of repudiating British sovereignty, yet the characteristics which may be ascribed to them in common were not such as inclined them or fitted them to build up a great new unity.

The Colonies, however, backed up by the British Government with the vigour which Chatham imparted to it, had acted together against a common danger from the French. When the States, as we must now call them, acted together against the British Government they did so in name as "United States," and they shortly proceeded to draw up "Articles of Confederation and Perpetual Union." But it was union of a feeble kind. The separate government of each State, in its internal affairs, was easy to provide for; representative institutions always existed, and no more change was needed than to substitute elected officers for the Governors and Councillors formerly appointed by the Crown. For the Union a Congress was provided which was to represent all the States in dealings with the outside world, but it was a Government with no effective powers except such as each separate State might independently choose to lend it. It might wage war with England, but it could not effectually control or regularly pay the military service of its own citizens; it might make a treaty of peace with England, but it could not enforce on its citizens distasteful obligations of that treaty. Such an ill-devised machine would have worked well enough for a time, if the Union Government could have attached to itself popular sentiments of honour and loyalty. But the sentiments were not there; and it worked badly.

When once we were reconciled to a defeat which proved good for us, it became a tradition among English writers to venerate the American Revolution. Later English historians have revolted from this indiscriminate veneration. They insist on another side of the facts: on the hopelessness of the American cause but for the commanding genius of Washington and his moral authority, and for the command which France and Spain obtained of the seas; on the petty quarrelsomeness with which the rights of the Colonists were urged, and the meanly skilful agitation which forced on the final rupture; on the lack of sustained patriotic effort during the war; on the base cruelty and dishonesty with which the loyal minority were persécuted and the private rights guaranteed by the peace ignored. It does not concern us to ascertain the precise justice in this displeasing picture; no man now regrets the main result of the Revolution, and we know that a new country is a new country, and that there was much in the circumstances of the war to encourage indiscipline and ferocity. But the fact that there is cause for such an indictment bears in two ways upon our present subject.

In the first place, there has been a tendency both in England and in America to look at this history upside down. The epoch of the Revolution and the Constitution has been regarded as a heroic age—wherein lived the elder Brutus, Mucius Scaevola, Claelia and the rest—to be followed by almost continuous disappointment, disillusionment and decline. A more pleasing and more bracing view is nearer to the historic truth. The faults of a later time were largely survivals, and the later history is largely that of growth though in the face of terrific obstacles and many influences that favoured decay. The nobility of the Revolution in the eighteenth century may be rated higher or lower, but in the Civil War, in which the elder brothers of so many men now living bore their part, the people of the North and of the South alike displayed far more heroic qualities.

In the second place, the War of Independence and of the Revolution lacked some of the characteristics of other national uprisings. It was not a revolt against grievous oppression or against a wholly foreign domination, but against a political system which the people mildly résented and which only statesmen felt to be pernicious and found to be past cure. The cause appealed to far-seeing political aspiration and appealed also to turbulent and ambitious spirits and to whatever was present of a merely revolutionary temper, but the ordinary law-abiding man who minded his own business was not greatly moved one way or the other in his heart.

The subsequent movement which, in a few years after independence was secured, gave the United States a national and a working Constitution was altogether the work of a few, to which popular movement contributed nothing. Of popular aspiration for unity there was none. Statesmen knew that the new nation or group of nations lay helpless between pressing dangers from abroad and its own financial difficulties. They saw clearly that they must create a Government of the Union which could exercise directly upon the individual American citizen an authority like that of the Government of his own State. They did this, but with a reluctant and half-convinced public opinion behind them.

The makers of the Constitution earned in a manner the full praise that has ever since been bestowed on them. But they did not, as it has often been suggested they did, create a sort of archetype and pattern for all Governments that may hereafter partake of a federal character. Nor has the curious machine which they devised—with its balanced opposition between two legislative chambers, between the whole Legislature and the independent executive power of the President, between the governing power of the moment and the permanent expression of the people's will embodied in certain almost unalterable laws—worked conspicuously better than other political constitutions. The American Constitution owes its peculiarities partly to the form which the State Governments had naturally taken, and partly to sheer misunderstanding of the British Constitution, but much more to the want at the time of any strong sense of national unity and to the existence of a good deal of dislike to all government whatsoever. The sufficient merit of its founders was that of patient and skilful diplomatists, who, undeterred by difficulties, found out the most satisfactory settlement that had a chance of being accepted by the States.

So the Colonies, which in 1776 had declared their independence of Great Britain under the name of the United States of America, entered in 1789 into the possession of machinery of government under which their unity and independence could be maintained.

It will be well at once to describe those features of the Constitution which it will be necessary for us later to bear in mind. It is generally known that the President of the United States is an elected officer—elected by what operates, though intended to act otherwise, as a popular vote. During the four years of his office he might roughly be said to combine the functions of the King in this country and those of a Prime Minister whose cabinet is in due subjection to him. But that description needs one very important qualification. He wields, with certain slight restrictions, the whole executive power of government, but neither he nor any of his ministers can, like the ministers of our King, sit or speak in the Legislature, nor can he, like our King, dissolve that Legislature. He has indeed a veto on Acts of Congress, which can only be overridden by a large majority in both Houses. But the executive and the legislative powers in America were purposely so constituted as to be independent of each other to a degree which is unknown in this country.

It is perhaps not very commonly understood that President and Congress alike are as strictly fettered in their action by the Constitution as a limited liability company is by its Memorandum of Association. This Constitution, which defines both the form of government and certain liberties of the subject, is not unalterable, but it can be altered only by a process which requires both the consent of a great majority in Congress or alternatively of a great majority of the legislatures of the distinct States composing the Union, and also ratification of amendments by three-fourths of the several States. Thus we shall have to notice later that a "Constitutional Amendment" abolishing slavery became a terror of the future to many people in the slave States, but remained all the time an impossibility in the view of most people in the free States.

We have, above all things, to dismiss from our minds any idea that the Legislature of a State is subordinate to the Congress of the United States, or that a State Governor is an officer under the President. The Constitution of the Union was the product of a half-developed sense of nationality. Under it the State authority (in the American sense of "State") and the Union or Federal authority go on side by side working in separate spheres, each subject to Constitutional restrictions, but each in its own sphere supreme. Thus the State authority is powerless to make peace or war or to impose customs duties, for those are Federal matters. But the Union authority is equally powerless, wherever a State authority has been constituted, to punish ordinary crime, to promote education, or to regulate factories. In particular, by the Constitution as it stood till after the Civil War, the Union authority was able to prohibit the importation of slaves from abroad after the end of 1807, but had no power to abolish slavery itself in any of the States.

Further, Congress had to be constituted in such a manner as to be agreeable to the smaller States which did not wish to enter into a Union in which their influence would be swamped by their more populous neighbours. Their interest was secured by providing that in the Senate each State should have two members and no more, while in the House of Representatives the people of the whole Union are represented according to population. Thus legislation through Congress requires the concurrence of two forces which may easily be opposed, that of the majority of American citizens and that of the majority of the several States. Of the two chambers, the Senate, whose members are elected for six years, and to secure continuity do not all retire at the same time, became as time went on, though not at first, attractive to statesmen of position, and acquired therefore additional influence.

Lastly, the Union was and is still the possessor of Territories not included in any State, and in the Territories, whatever subordinate self-government they might be allowed, the Federal authority has always been supreme and uncontrolled in all matters. But as these Territories have become more settled and more populated, portions of them have steadily from the first been organised as States and admitted to the Union. It is for Congress to settle the time of their admission and to make any conditions in regard to their Constitutions as States. But when once admitted as States they have thenceforward the full rights of the original States. Within all the Territories, while they remained under its jurisdiction it lay with Congress to determine whether slavery should be lawful or not, and, when any portion of them was ripe for admission to the Union as a State, Congress could insist that the new State's Constitution should or should not prohibit slavery. When the Constitution of the Union was being settled, slavery was the subject of most careful compromise; but in any union formed between slave States and free, a bitter root of controversy must have remained, and the opening through which controversy actually returned was provided by the Territories.

On all other matters the makers of the Constitution had in the highest temper of statesmanship found a way round seemingly insuperable difficulties. The whole attitude of "the fathers" towards slavery is a question of some consequence to a biographer of Lincoln, and we shall return to it in a little while.

2. Territorial Expansion.

A machine of government had been created, and we are shortly to consider how it was got to work. But the large dominion to be governed had to be settled, and its area was about to undergo an enormous expansion. It will be convenient at this point to mark the stages of this development.

The thirteen Colonies had, when they first revolted, definite western boundaries, the westernmost of them reaching back from the sea-board to a frontier in the Alleghany Mountains. But at the close of the war Great Britain ceded to the United States the whole of the inland country up to the Mississippi River. Virginia had in the meantime effectively colonised Kentucky to the west of her, and for a time this was treated as within her borders. In a similar way Tennessee had been settled from North and South Carolina and was treated as part of the former. Virginia had also established claims by conquest north of the Ohio River in what was called the North-West Territory, but these claims and all similar claims of particular States in unsettled or half-settled territory were shortly before or shortly after the adoption of the Constitution ceded to the Union Government. But the dominions of that Government soon received a vast accession. In 1803, by a brave exercise of the Constitutional powers which he was otherwise disposed to restrict jealously, President Jefferson bought from Napoleon I. the great expanse of country west of the Mississippi called Louisiana. This region in the extreme south was no wider than the present State of Louisiana, but further north it widened out so as to take in the whole watershed of the Missouri and its tributaries, including in the extreme north nearly all the present State of Montana. In 1819 Florida was purchased from Spain, and that country at the same time abandoned its claims to a strip of coastland which now forms the sea-board of Alabama and Mississippi.

Such was the extent of the United States when Lincoln began his political life. In the movement of population by which this domain was being settled up, different streams may be roughly distinguished. First, there was from 1780 onwards a constant movement of the poorer class and of younger sons of rich men from the great State of Virginia and to some extent from the Carolinas into Kentucky and Tennessee, whence they often shifted further north into Indiana and Illinois, or sometimes further west into Missouri. It was mainly a movement of single families or groups of families of adventurous pioneers, very sturdy, and very turbulent. Then there came the expansion of the great plantation interest in the further South, carrying with it as it spread, not occasional slaves as in Kentucky and Tennessee, but the whole plantation system. This movement went not only directly westward, but still more by the Gulf of Mexico and up the Mississippi, into the State of Louisiana, where a considerable French population had settled, the State of Mississippi, and later into Missouri. Later still came the westward movement from the Northern States. The energies of the people in these States had at first been to great extent absorbed by sea-going pursuits and the subjugation of their own rugged soil, so that they reached western regions like Illinois rather later than did the settlers from States further south. Ultimately, as their manufactures grew, immigration from Europe began its steady flow to these States, and the great westward stream, which continuing in our days has filled up the rich lands of the far North-West, grew in volume. But want of natural timber and other causes hindered the development of the fertile prairie soil in the regions beyond the upper Mississippi, till the period of railway development, which began about 1840. was far advanced. Illinois was Far West in

1830, Iowa and Minnesota continued to be so in 1860. The Northerners, when they began to move westward, came in comparatively large numbers, bringing comparatively ordered habits and the full machinery of outward civilisation with them. Thus a great social change followed upon their arrival in the regions to which only scattered pioneers such as the Lincolns had previously penetrated. In Illinois, with which so much of our story is bound up, the rapidity of that change may be estimated from the fact that the population of that State multiplied sevenfold between the time when Lincoln settled there and the day when he left it as President.

The concluding stages by which the dominions of the United States came to be as we know them were: the annexation by agreement in 1846 of the Republic of Texas, which had separated itself from Mexico and which claimed besides the great State of Texas a considerable territory reaching north-west to the upper portions of the Arkansas River; the apportionment to the Union by a delimitation treaty with Great Britain in 1846 of the Oregon Territory, including roughly the State of that name and the rest of the basin of the Columbia River up to the present frontier—British Columbia being at the same time apportioned to Great Britain; the conquest from Mexico in 1848 of California and a vast mountainous tract at the back of it; the purchase from Mexico of a small frontier strip in 1853; and the acquisition at several later times of various outlying dependencies which will in no way concern us.

3. The Growth of the Practice and Traditions of the Union Government.

We must turn back to the internal growth of the new united nation. When the Constitution had been formed and the question of its acceptance by the States had been at last settled, and when Washington had been inaugurated as the first President under it, a wholly new conflict arose between two parties. led by two Ministers in the President's Cabinet, Alexander Hamilton and

Thomas Jefferson. Both were potent and remarkable men, Hamilton in all senses a great man. These two men, for all their antagonism, did services to their country, without which the vigorous growth of the new nation would not have been possible.

The figure of Alexander Hamilton, then Secretary of the Treasury (ranked by Talleyrand with Fox and Napoleon as one of the three great men he had known), must fascinate any English student of the period. If his name is not celebrated in the same way in the country which he so eminently served, it is perhaps because in his ideas, as in his origin, he was not strictly American. As a boy, half Scotch, half French Huguenot, from the English West Indian island of Nevis, he had been at school in New York when his speeches had some real effect in attaching that city to the cause of Independence. He had served brilliantly in the war, on Washington's staff and with his regiment. He had chivalrously defended, as an advocate and in other ways, the Englishmen and loyalists against whose cause he fought. He had induced the great central State of New York to accept the Constitution, when the strongest local party would have rejected it and made the Union impossible. As Washington's Secretary of the Treasury he organised the machinery of government, helped his chief to preserve a strong, upright and cautious foreign policy at the critical point of the young Republic's infancy, and performed perhaps the greatest and most difficult service of all in setting the disordered finances of the country upon a sound footing. In early middle age he ended a life, not flawless but admirable and lovable, in a duel, murderously forced upon him by one Aaron Burr. This man, who was an elegant profligate, with many graces but no public principle, was a claimant to the Presidency in opposition to Hamilton's greatest opponent, Jefferson; Hamilton knowingly incurred a feud which must at the best have been dangerous to him, by unhesitatingly throwing his weight upon the side of Jefferson, his own ungenerous rival. The details of his policy do not concern us, but the United States could hardly have endured for many years without the passionate sense of the need of government and the genius for actual administration with which Hamilton set the new nation on its way. Nevertheless—so do gifts differ—the general spirit which has on the whole informed the American nation and held it together was neither respected nor understood by him. His party, called the Federalists, because they claimed to stand for a strong and an efficient Federal Government, did not survive him long. It is of interest to us here only because, with its early disappearance, there ceased for ever to be in America any party whatsoever which in any sense represented aristocratic principles or leanings.

The fate of Jefferson's party (at first called Republican but by no means to be confused with the Republican party which will concern us later) was far different, for the Democratic party, represented by the President of the United States at this moment, claims to descend from it in unbroken apostolic succession. But we need not pause to trace the connecting thread between them, real as it is, for parties are not to be regarded as individuals. Indeed the personality of Thomas Jefferson, Secretary of State in Washington's Cabinet, impressed itself, during his life and long after, upon all America more than that of any other man. Democrats to-day have described Lincoln, who by no means belonged to their party, as Jefferson's spiritual heir; and Lincoln would have welcomed the description.

No biographer has achieved an understanding presentment of Jefferson's curious character, which as presented by unfriendly critics is an unpleasing combination of contrasting elements. A tall and active fellow, a good horseman and a good shot, living through seven years of civil war, which he had himself heralded in, without the inclination to strike a blow; a scholar, musician, and mathematician, without delicacy, elevation, or precision of thought or language; a man of intense ambition, without either administrative capacity or the courage to assert himself in counsel or in debate; a dealer in philanthropic sentiment, privately malignant and vindictive. This is not as a whole a credible portrait; it cannot stand for the man as his friends knew him; but there is evidence for each feature of it, and it remains impossible for a foreigner to think of Jefferson and not compare him to his disadvantage with the antagonist whom he eclipsed. By pertinacious industry, however, working chiefly through private correspondence, he constructed a great party, dominated a nation, and dominated it mainly for good. For the rapid and complete triumph of Jefferson's party over its opponents signifies a very definite and lasting conversion of the main stream of American public opinion to what may be called the sane element in the principles of the French Revolution. At the time when he set himself to counterwork Hamilton, American statesmanship was likely to be directed only to making Government strong and to ensuring the stability of the business world; for reaction against the bloody absurdities that had happened in France was strong in America, and in English thought, which still had influence in America, it was all-powerful. Against this he asserted an intense belief in the value of freedom, in the equal claim of men of all conditions to the consideration of government, and in the supreme importance to government of the consenting mind of the governed. And he made this sense so definitely a part of the national stock of ideas that, while the older-established principles of strong and sound government were not lost to sight, they were consciously rated as subordinate to the principles of liberty.

It must not be supposed that the ascendency thus early acquired by what may be called liberal opinions in America was a matter merely of setting some fine phrases in circulation, or of adopting, as was early done in most States, a wide franchise and other external marks of democracy. We may dwell a little longer on the unusual but curiously popular figure of Jefferson, for it illustrates the spirit with which the commonwealth became imbued under his leadership. He has sometimes been presented as a man of flabby character whose historical part was that of intermediary between impracticable French "philosophes" and the ruffians and swindlers that Martin Chuzzlewit encountered, who were all "children of liberty," and whose "boastful answer to the Despot and the Tyrant was that their bright home was in the Settin' Sun." He was nothing of the kind. His judgment was probably unsound on the questions of foreign policy on which as Secretary of State he differed from Washington, and he leaned, no doubt, to a jealous and too narrow insistence upon the limits set by the Constitution to the Government's power. But he and his party were emphatically right in the resistance which they offered to certain needless measures of coercion. As President, though he was not a great President, he suffered the sensible course of administration originated by his opponent to continue undisturbed, and America owed to one bold and far-seeing act of his the greatest of the steps by which her territory was enlarged. It is, however, in the field of domestic policy, which rested with the States and with which a President has often little to do, that the results of his principles must be sought. Jefferson was a man who had worked unwearyingly in Virginia at sound, and what we should now call conservative, reforms, establishing religious toleration, reforming a preposterous land law, seeking to provide education for the poor, striving unsuccessfully for a sensible scheme of gradual emancipation of the slaves. In like manner his disciples after him, in their several States, devoted themselves to the kind of work in removing manifest abuses and providing for manifest new social needs in which English reformers like Romilly and Bentham, and the leaders of the first reformed Parliament, were to be successful somewhat later. The Americans who so exasperated Dickens vainly supposed themselves to be far ahead of England in much that we now consider essential to a well-ordered nation. But there could have been no answer to Americans of Jefferson's generation if they had made the same claim.

It is with this fact in mind that we should approach the famous words of Jefferson which echoed so long with triumphant or reproachful sound in the ears of Americans and to which long after Lincoln was to make a memorable appeal. The propaganda which he carried on when the Constitution had been adopted was on behalf of a principle which he had enunciated as a younger man when he drafted the Declaration of Independence. That document is mainly a rehearsal of the colonists' grievances, and is as strictly lawyerlike and about as fair or unfair as the arguments of a Parliamentarian under Charles I. But the argumentation is prefaced with these sounding words: "We hold these truths to be self-evident: – that all men are created equal; that they are endowed by their Creator with certain unalienable rights; that among these are life, liberty and the pursuit of happiness. That to secure these rights, governments are instituted among men, deriving their just powers from the consent of the governed." Few propositions outside the Bible have offered so easy a mark to the shafts of unintelligently clever criticism.

Jefferson, when he said that "all men are created equal," and the Tory Dr. Johnson, when he spoke of "the natural equality of man," used a curious eighteenth century phrase, of which a Greek scholar can see the origin; but it did not mean anything absurd, nor, on the other hand, did it convey a mere platitude. It should not be necessary to explain, as Lincoln did long after, that Jefferson did not suppose all men to be of equal height or weight or equally wise or equally good. He did, however, contend for a principle of which one elementary application is the law which makes murder the same crime whatever be the relative positions of the murderer and the murdered man. Such a law was indeed firmly rooted in England before Jefferson talked of equality, but it amazed the rest of Europe when the House of Lords hanged a peer for the murder of his servant. There are indefinitely many further ways in which men who are utterly unequal had best be treated as creatures equally entitled to the consideration of government and of their neighbours. It is safer to carry this principle too far than not to carry it far enough. If Jefferson had expressed this and his cognate principle of liberty with scientific precision, or with the full personal sincerity with which a greater man like Lincoln expressed it, he would have said little from which any Englishman to-day would dissent. None the less he would have enunciated a doctrine which most Governments then existing set at naught or proscribed, and for which Hamilton and the prosperous champions of independence who supported him had no use.

The Declaration of Independence was not a very candid State paper, and the popularity Jefferson afterwards created for its sentiments was not wholly free from humbug. Many men were more ready to think themselves the equals of Washington or Hamilton in the respects in which they were not so, than to think a negro their own equal in the respects in which he was. The boundless space and untrammelled conditions of the new world made liberty and equality in some directions highly attainable ideals, so much so that they seemed to demand little effort or discipline. The patriotic orators under whom Lincoln sat in his youth would ascribe to the political wisdom of their great democracy what was really the result of geography. They would regard the extent of forest and prairie as creditable to themselves, just as some few Englishmen have regarded our location upon an island.

This does not, however, do away with the value of that tradition of the new world which in its purest and sincerest form became part and parcel of Lincoln's mind. Jefferson was a great American patriot. In his case insistence on the rights of the several States sprang from no half-hearted desire for a great American nation; he regarded these provincial organisations as machinery by which government and the people could be brought nearer together; and he contributed that which was most needed for the evolution of a vigorous national life. He imparted to the very recent historical origin of his country, and his followers imparted to its material conditions, a certain element of poetry and the felt presence of a wholesome national ideal. The patriotism of an older country derives its glory and its pride from influences deep rooted in the past, creating a tradition of public and private action which needs no definite formula. The man who did more than any other to supply this lack in a new country, by imbuing its national consciousness—even its national cant—with high aspiration, did—it may well be—more than any strong administrator or constructive statesman to create a Union which should thereafter seem worth preserving.

4. The Missouri Compromise.

No sober critic, applying to the American statesmen of the first generation the standards which he would apply to their English contemporaries, can blame them in the least because they framed their Constitution as best they could and were not deterred by the scruples which they felt about slavery from effecting a Union between States which, on all other grounds except their latent difference upon slavery, seemed meant to be one. But many of these men had set their hands in the Declaration of Independence to the most unqualified claim of liberty and equality for all men and proceeded, in the Constitution, to give nineteen years' grace to "that most detestable sum of all villainies," as Wesley called it, the African slave trade, and to impose on the States which thought slavery wrong the dirty work of restoring escaped slaves to captivity. "Why," Dr. Johnson had asked, "do the loudest yelps for liberty come from the drivers of slaves?" We are forced to recognise, upon any study of the facts, that they could not really have made the Union otherwise than as they did; yet a doubt presents itself as to the general soundness and sincerity of their boasted notions of liberty. Now, later on we shall have to understand the policy as to slavery on behalf of which Lincoln stepped forward as a leader. In his own constantly reiterated words it was a return to the position of "the fathers," and, though he was not a professional historian, it concerns us to know that there was sincerity at least in his intensely historical view of politics. We have, then, to see first how "the fathers" – that is, the most considerable men among those who won Independence and made the Constitution – set out with a very honest view on the subject of slavery, but with a too comfortable hope of its approaching end, which one or two lived to see frustrated; secondly, how the men who succeeded them were led to abandon such hopes and content themselves with a compromise as to slavery which they trusted would at least keep the American nation in being.

Among those who signed the Declaration of Independence there were presumably some of Dr. Johnson's "yelpers." It mattered more that there were sturdy people who had no idea of giving up slavery and probably did not relish having to join in protestations about equality. Men like Jefferson ought to have known well that their associates in South Carolina and Georgia in particular did not share their aspirations – the people of Georgia indeed were recent and ardent converts to the slave system. But these sincere and insincere believers in slavery were the exceptions; their views did not then seem to prevail even in the greatest of the slave States, Virginia. Broadly speaking, the American opinion on this matter in 1775 or in 1789 had gone as far ahead of English opinion, as English opinion had in turn gone ahead of American, when, in 1833, the year after the first Reform Bill, the English people put its hand into its pocket and bought out its own slave owners in the West Indies. The British Government had forced several of the American Colonies to permit slavery against their will, and only in 1769 it had vetoed, in the interest of British trade, a Colonial enactment for suppressing the slave trade. This was sincerely felt as a part, though a minor part, of the grievance against the mother country. So far did such views prevail on the surface that a Convention of all the Colonies in 1774 unanimously voted that "the abolition of domestic slavery is the greatest object of desire in those Colonies where it was unhappily introduced in their infant state. But previous to the enfranchisement of the slaves in law, it is necessary to exclude all further importation from Africa." It was therefore very commonly assumed when, after an interval of war which suspended such reforms, Independence was achieved, that slavery was a doomed institution.

Those among the "fathers" whose names are best known in England, Washington, John Adams, Jefferson, Madison, Franklin, and Hamilton, were all opponents of slavery. These include the first four Presidents, and the leaders of very different schools of thought. Some of them, Washington and Jefferson at least, had a few slaves of their own. Washington's attitude to his slaves is illustrated by a letter which he wrote to secure the return of a black attendant of Mrs. Washington's who had run away (a thing which he had boasted could never occur in his household); the runaway was to be brought back if she could be persuaded to return; her master's legal power to compel her was not to be used. She was in fact free, but had foolishly left a good place; and there is no reason to suppose that it was otherwise with Jefferson's slaves. Jefferson's theory was vehemently against slavery. In old age he gave up hope in the matter and was more solicitous for union than for liberty, but this was after the disappointment of many efforts. In these efforts he had no illusory notion of equality; he wrote in 1791, when he had been defeated in the attempt to carry a measure of gradual emancipation in Virginia: "Nobody wishes more than I do to see such proofs as you exhibit, that Nature has given to our black brothers talents equal to those of the other colours of men, and that the appearance of a want of them is owing mainly to the degraded condition of their existence, both in Africa and America. I can add with truth, that nobody wishes more ardently to see a good system commenced for raising the condition both of their body and mind to what it ought to be, as fast as the imbecility of their present existence and other circumstances, which cannot be neglected, will permit."

When he felt at last that freedom was not making way, his letters, by which his influence was chiefly exercised, abounded in passionate regrets. "I tremble for my country," he wrote, "when I think of the negro and remember that God is just." But if he is judged not by his sentiments, or even by his efforts, but by what he accomplished, this rhetorical champion of freedom did accomplish one great act, the first link as it proved in the chain of events by which slavery was ultimately abolished. In 1784 the North-West Territory, as it was called, was ceded by Virginia to the old Congress of the days before the Union. Jefferson then endeavoured to pass an Ordinance by which slavery should be excluded from all territory that might ever belong to Congress. In this indeed he failed, for in part of the territory likely to be acquired slavery was already established, but the result was a famous Ordinance of 1787, by which slavery was for ever excluded from the soil of the North-West Territory itself, and thus, when they came into being, the States of Ohio, Indiana, Illinois, Michigan, and Wisconsin found themselves congenitally incapable of becoming slave States.

The further achievements of that generation in this matter were considerable. It must of course be understood that the holding of slaves and the slave trade from Africa were regarded as two distinct questions. The new Congress abolished the slave trade on the first day on which the Constitution allowed it to do so, that is, on January 1, 1808. The mother country abolished it just about the same time. But already all but three of the States had for themselves abolished the slave trade in their own borders. As to slavery itself, seven of the original thirteen States and Vermont, the first of the added States, had abolished that before 1805. These indeed were Northern States, where slavery was not of importance, but in Virginia there was, or had been till lately, a growing opinion that slavery was not economical, and, with the ignorance common in one part of a country of the true conditions in another part, it was natural to look upon emancipation as a policy which would spread of itself. At any rate it is certain fact that the chief among the men who had made the Constitution had at that time so regarded it, and continued to do so. Under this belief and in the presence of many pressing subjects of interest the early movement for emancipation in America died down with its work half finished. But before this happy belief expired an economic event had happened which riveted slavery upon the South. In 1793 Eli Whitney, a Yale student upon a holiday in the South, invented the first machine for cleaning cotton of its seeds. The export of cotton jumped from 192,000 lbs. in 1791 to 6,000,000 lbs. in 1795. Slave labour had been found, or was believed, to be especially economical in cotton growing. Slavery therefore rapidly became the mainstay of wealth and of the social system in South Carolina and throughout the far South; and in a little while the baser sort of planters in Virginia discovered that breeding slaves to sell down South was a very profitable form of stock-raising.

We may pass to the year 1820, when an enactment was passed by Congress which for thirty-four years thereafter might be regarded as hardly less fundamental than the Constitution itself. Up till then nine new States had been added to the original thirteen. It was repugnant to principles still strong in the North that these States should be admitted to the Union with State Constitutions which permitted slavery. On the other hand, it was for two reasons important to the chief slave States, that they should be. They would otherwise be closed to Southern planters who wished to migrate to unexhausted soil carrying with them the methods of industry and the ways of life which they understood. Furthermore, the North was bound to have before long a great preponderance of population, and if this were not neutralised by keeping the number of States on one side and the other equal there would be a future political danger to slavery. Up to a certain point the North could with good conscience yield to the South in this matter, for the soil of four of the new slave States had been ceded to the Union by old slave States and slave-holders had settled freely upon it; and in a fifth, Louisiana, slavery had been safeguarded by the express stipulations of the treaty with France, which applied to that portion, though no other, of the territory then ceded. Naturally, then, it had happened, though without any definite agreement, that for years past slave States and free States had been admitted to the Union in pairs. Now arose the question of a further portion of the old French territory, the present State of Missouri. A few slave-holders with their slaves had in fact settled there, but no distinct claims on behalf of slavery could be alleged. The Northern Senators and members of Congress demanded therefore that the Constitution of Missouri should provide for the gradual extinction of slavery there. Naturally there arose a controversy which sounded to the aged Jefferson like "a fire-bell in the night" and revealed for the first time to all America a deep rift in the Union. The Representatives of the South eventually carried their main point with the votes of several Northern men, known to history as the "Dough-faces," who all lost their seats at the next election. Missouri was admitted as a slave State, Maine about the same time as a free State; and it was enacted that thereafter in the remainder of the territory that had been bought from France slavery should be unlawful north of latitude 36 degrees 30 minutes, while by tacit agreement permitted south of it.

This was the Missouri Compromise. The North regarded it at first as a humiliation, but learnt to point to it later as a sort of Magna Carta for the Northern territories. The adoption of it marks a point from which it became for thirty-four years the express ambition of the principal American statesmen and the tacit object, of every party manager to keep the slavery question from ever becoming again a burning issue in politics. The collapse of it in 1854 was to prove the decisive event in the career of Abraham Lincoln, aged 11 when it was passed.

5. Leaders, Parties, and Tendencies in Lincoln's Youth.

Just about the year 1830, when Lincoln started life in Illinois, several distinct movements in national life began or culminated. They link themselves with several famous names.

The two leaders to whom, as a young politician, Lincoln owed some sort of allegiance were Webster and Clay, and they continued throughout his long political apprenticeship to be recognised in most of America as the great men of their time. Daniel Webster must have been nearly a great man. He was always passed over for the Presidency. That was not so much because of the private failings which marked his robust and generous character, as because in days of artificial party issues, when vital questions are dealt with by mere compromise, high office seems to belong of right to men of less originality. If he was never quite so great as all America took him to be, it was not for want of brains or of honesty, but because his consuming passion for the Union at all costs led him into the path of least apparent risk to it. Twice as Secretary of State (that is, chiefly, Foreign Minister) he showed himself a statesman, but above all he was an orator and one of those rare orators who accomplish a definite task by their oratory. In his style he carried on the tradition of English Parliamentary speaking, and developed its vices yet further; but the massive force of argument behind gave him his real power. That power he devoted to the education of the people in a feeling for the nation and for its greatness. As an advocate he had appeared in great cases in the Supreme Court. John Marshall, the Chief Justice from 1801 to 1835, brought a great legal mind of the higher type to the settlement of doubtful points in the Constitution, and his statesmanlike judgments did much both to strengthen the United States Government and to gain public confidence for it. It was a memorable work, for the power of the Union Government, under its new Constitution, lay in the grip of the Courts. The pleading of the young Webster contributed much to this. Later on Webster, and a school of followers, of whom perhaps we may take "our Elijah Pogram" to have been one, used ceremonial occasions, on which Englishmen only suffer the speakers, for the purpose of inculcating their patriotic doctrine, and Webster at least was doing good. His greatest speech, upon an occasion to which we shall shortly come, was itself an event. Lincoln found in it as inspiring a political treatise as many Englishmen have discovered in the speeches and writings of Burke.

Henry Clay was a slighter but more attractive person. He was apparently the first American public man whom his countrymen styled "magnetic," but a sort of scheming instability caused him after one or two trials to be set down as an "impossible" candidate for the Presidency. As a dashing young man from the West he had the chief hand in forcing on the second war with Great Britain, from 1812 to 1814, which arose out of perhaps insufficient causes and ended in no clear result, but which, it is probable, marked a stage in the growth of loyalty to America. As an older man he was famed as an "architect of compromises," for though he strove for emancipation in his own State, Kentucky, and dreamed of a great scheme for colonising the slaves in Africa, he was supremely anxious to avert collision between North and South, and in this respect was typical of his generation. But about 1830 he was chiefly known as the apostle of what was called the "American policy." This was a policy which aimed at using the powers of the national Government for the development of the boundless resources of the country. Its methods comprised a national banking system, the use of the money of the Union on great public works, and a protective tariff, which it was hoped might chiefly operate to encourage promising but "infant" industries and to tax the luxuries of the rich. Whatever may have been the merits of this policy, which made some commotion for a few years, we can easily understand that it appealed to the imagination of young Lincoln at a time of keen political energy on his part of which we have but meagre details.

A third celebrity of this period, in his own locality a still more powerful man, was John Caldwell Calhoun, of South Carolina. He enjoyed beyond all his contemporaries the fame of an intellectual person. Lincoln conceded high admiration to his concise and penetrating phrases. An Englishwoman, Harriet Martineau, who knew him, has described him as "embodied intellect." He had undoubtedly in full measure those negative tides to respect which have gone far in America to ensure praise from the public and the historians; for he was correct and austere, and, which is more, kindly among his family and his slaves. He is credited, too, with an observance of high principle in public life, which it might be difficult to illustrate from his recorded actions. But the warmer-blooded Andrew Jackson set him down as "heartless, selfish, and a physical coward," and Jackson could speak generously of an opponent whom he really knew. His intellect must have been powerful enough, but it was that of a man who delights in arguing, and delights in elaborate deductions from principles which he is too proud to revise; a man, too, who is fearless in accepting conclusions which startle or repel the vulgar mind; who is undisturbed in his logical processes by good sense, healthy sentiment, or any vigorous appetite for truth. Such men have disciples who reap the disgrace which their masters are apt somehow to avoid; they give the prestige of wisdom and high thought to causes which could not otherwise earn them. A Northern soldier came back wounded in 1865 and described to the next soldier in the hospital Calhoun's monument at Charleston. The other said: "What you saw is not the real monument, but I have seen it. It is the desolated, ruined South. . . . That is Calhoun's real monument."

This man was a Radical, and known as the successor of Jefferson, but his Radicalism showed itself in drawing inspiration solely from the popular catchwords of his own locality. He adored the Union, but it was to be a Union directed by distinguished politicians from the South in a sectional Southern interest. He did not originate, but he secured the strength of orthodoxy and fashion to a tone of sentiment and opinion which for a generation held undisputed supremacy in the heart of the South. Americans might have seemed at this time to be united in a curiously exultant national self-consciousness, but though there was no sharp division of sections, the boasted glory of the one America meant to many planters in the South the glory of their own settled and free life with their dignified equals round them and their often contented dependents under them. Plain men among them doubtless took things as they were, and, without any particular wish to change them, did not pretend they were perfect. But it is evident that in a widening circle of clever young men in the South the claim of some peculiar virtue for Southern institutions became habitual in the first half of the nineteenth century.

Their way of life was beautiful in their eyes. It rested upon slavery. Therefore slavery was a good thing. It was wicked even to criticise it, and it was weak to apologise for it or to pretend that it needed reformation. It was easy and it became apparently universal for the different Churches of the South to prostitute the Word of God in this cause. Later on crude notions of evolution began to get about in a few circles of advanced thought, and these lent themselves as easily to the same purpose. Loose, floating thoughts of this kind might have mattered little. Calhoun, as the recognised wise man of the old South, concentrated them and fastened them upon its people as a creed. Glorification of "our institution at the South" became the main principle of Southern politicians, and any conception that there may ever have been of a task for constructive statesmanship, in solving the negro problem, passed into oblivion under the influence of his revered reasoning faculty.

But, of his dark and dangerous sort, Calhoun was an able man. He foresaw early that the best weapon of the common interest of the slave States lay in the rights which might be claimed for each individual State against the Union. The idea that a discontented State might secede from the Union was not novel—it had been mooted in New England, during the last war against Great Britain, and, curiously enough, among the rump of the old Federalist party, but it was generally discounted. Calhoun first brought it into prominence, veiled in an elaborate form which some previous South Carolinian had devised. The occasion had nothing to do with slavery. It concerned Free Trade, a very respectable issue, but so clearly a minor issue that to break up a great country upon it would have gone beyond the limit of solemn frivolity, and Calhoun must be taken to have been forging an implement with which his own section of the States could claim and extort concessions from the Union. A protective tariff had been passed in 1828. The Southern States, which would have to pay the protective duties but did not profit by them, disliked it. Calhoun and others took the intelligible but too refined point, that the powers of Congress under the Constitution authorised a tariff for revenue but not a tariff for a protective purpose. Every State, Calhoun declared, must have the Constitutional right to protect itself against an Act of Congress which it deemed unconstitutional. Let such a State, in special Convention, "nullify" the Act of Congress. Let Congress then, unless it compromised the matter, submit its Act to the people in the form of an Amendment to the Constitution. It would then require a three-fourths majority of all the States to pass the obnoxious Act. Last but not least, if the Act was passed, the protesting State had,

Calhoun claimed, the right to secede from the Union.

Controversy over this tariff raged for fully four years, and had a memorable issue. In the course of 1830 the doctrine of "nullification" and "secession" was discussed in the Senate, and the view of Calhoun was expounded by one Senator Hayne. Webster answered him in a speech which he meant should become a popular classic, and which did become so. He set forth his own doctrine of the Union and appealed to national against State loyalty in the most influential oration that was perhaps ever made. "His utterance," writes President Wilson, "sent a thrill through all the East and North which was unmistakably a thrill of triumph. Men were glad because of what he had said. He had touched the national self-consciousness, awakened it, and pleased it with a morning vision of its great tasks and certain destiny." Later there came in the President, the redoubtable Andrew Jackson, the most memorable President between Jefferson and Lincoln. He said very little—only, on Jefferson's birthday he gave the toast, "Our Federal Union; it must be preserved."

But when in 1832, in spite of concessions by Congress, a Convention was summoned in South Carolina to "nullify" the tariff, he issued the appropriate orders to the United States Army, in case such action was carried out, and it is understood that he sent Calhoun private word that he would be the first man to be hanged for treason. Nullification quietly collapsed. The North was thrilled still more than by Webster's oratory, and as not a single other State showed signs of backing South Carolina, it became thenceforth the fixed belief of the North that the Union was recognised as in law indissoluble, as Webster contended it was. None the less the idea of secession had been planted, and planted in a fertile soil.

General Andrew Jackson, whose other great achievements must now be told, was not an intellectual person, but his ferocious and, in the literal sense, shocking character is refreshing to the student of this period. He had been in his day the typical product of the West—a far wilder West than that from which Lincoln later came. Originally a lawyer, he had won martial fame in fights with Indians and in the celebrated victory over the British forces at New Orleans. He was a sincere Puritan; and he had a courtly dignity of manner; but he was of arbitrary and passionate temper, and he was a sanguinary duellist. His most savage duels, it should be added, concerned the honour of a lady whom he married chivalrously, and loved devotedly to the end. The case that can be made for his many arbitrary acts shows them in some instances to have been justifiable, and shows him in general to have been honest.

When in 1824 Jackson had expected to become President, and, owing to proceedings which do not now matter, John Quincy Adams, son of a former President, and himself a remarkable man, was made President instead of him, Jackson resolved to overthrow the ruling class of Virginian country gentlemen and Boston city magnates which seemed to him to control Government, and to call into life a real democracy. To this end he created a new party, against which of course an opposition party arose.

Neither of the new parties was in any sense either aristocratic or democratic. "The Democracy," or Democratic party, has continued in existence ever since, and through most of Lincoln's life ruled America. In trying to fix the character of a party in a foreign country we cannot hope to be exact in our portraiture. At the first start, however, this party was engaged in combating certain tendencies to Government interference in business. It was more especially hostile to a National Bank, which Jackson himself regarded as a most dangerous form of alliance between the administration and the richest class. Of the growth of what may be called the money power in American politics he had an intense, indeed prophetic, dread. Martin Van Buren, his friend and successor, whatever else he may have been, was a sound economist of what is now called the old school, and on a financial issue he did what few men in his office have done, he deliberately sacrificed his popularity to his principles. Beyond this the party was and has continued prone, in a manner which we had better not too clearly define, to insist upon the restrictions of the Constitution, whether in the interest of individual liberty or of State rights. This tendency was disguised at the first by the arbitrary action of Jackson's own proceedings, for Jackson alone among Presidents displayed the sentiments of what may be called a popular despot. Its insistence upon State rights, aided perhaps by its dislike of Protection, attracted to it the leading politicians of the South, who in the main dominated its counsels, though later on they liked to do it through Northern instruments. But it must not in the least be imagined that either party was Northern or Southern; for there were many Whigs in the South, and very many Democrats in the North. Moreover, it should be clearly grasped, though it is hard, that among Northern Democrats insistence on State rights did not involve the faintest leaning towards the doctrine of secession; on the contrary a typical Democrat would believe that these limitations to the power of the Union were the very things that gave it endurance and strength. Slavery, moreover, had friends and foes in both parties. If we boldly attempted to define the prevailing tone of the Democrats we might say that, while they and their opponents expressed loyalty to the Union and the Constitution, the Democrats would be prone to lay the emphasis upon the Constitution. Whatever might be the case with an average Whig, a man like Lincoln would be stirred in his heart by the general spirit of the country's institutions, while the typical Democrat of that time would dwell affectionately on the legal instruments and formal maxims in which that spirit was embodied.

Of the Whigs it is a little harder to speak definitely, nor is it very necessary, for in two only out of seven Presidential elections did they elect their candidate, and in each case that candidate then died, and in 1854 they perished as a party utterly and for ever. Just for a time they were identified with the "American policy" of Clay. When that passed out of favour they never really attempted to formulate any platform, or to take permanently any very definite stand. They nevertheless had the adherence of the ablest men of the country, and, as an opposition party to a party in power which furnished much ground for criticism, they possessed an attraction for generous youth.

The Democrats at once, and the Whigs not long after them, created elaborate party machines, on the need of which Jackson insisted as the only means of really giving influence to the common people. The prevailing system and habit of local self-government made such organisation easy. Men of one party in a township or in a county assembled, formulated their opinions, and sent delegates with instructions, more or less precise, to party conventions for larger areas, these would send delegates to the State Convention and these in turn to the National Convention of the Party. The party candidates for the Presidency, as well as for all other elective positions, were and are thus chosen, and the party "platform" or declaration of policy was and is thus formulated. Such machinery, which in England is likely always to play a less important part, has acquired an evil name. At the best there has always been a risk that a "platform" designed to detach voters from the opposite party will be an insincere and eviscerated document, by which active public opinion is rather muzzled than expressed. There has been a risk too that the "available" candidate should be some blameless nonentity, to whom no one objects, and whom therefore no one really wants. But it must be observed that the rapidity with which such organisation was taken up betokened the prevalence of a widespread and keen interest in political affairs.

The days of really great moneyed interests and of corruption of the gravest sort were as yet far distant, but one demoralising influence was imposed upon the new party system by its author at its birth. Jackson, in his perpetual fury, believed that office holders under the more or less imaginary ruling clique that had held sway were a corrupt gang, and he began to turn them out. He was encouraged to extend to the whole country a system which had prevailed in New York and with which Van Buren was too familiar. "To the victors belong the spoils," exclaimed a certain respectable Mr. Marcy. A wholesale dismissal of office holders large and small, and replacement of them by sound Democrats, soon took place. Once started, the "spoils system" could hardly be stopped.

Thenceforward there was a standing danger that the party machine would be in the hands of a crew of jobbers and dingy hunters after petty offices. England, of course, has had and now has practices theoretically as indefensible, but none possessing any such sinister importance. It is hard, therefore, for us to conceive how little of really vicious intent was necessary to set this disastrous influence going. There was no trained Civil Service with its unpartisan traditions. In the case of offices corresponding to those of our permanent heads of departments it seemed reasonable that the official should, like his chief the Minister concerned, be a person in harmony with the President. As to the smaller offices – the thousands of village postmasterships and so forth – one man was likely to do the work as well as another; the dispossessed official could, in the then condition of the country, easily find another equally lucrative employment; "turn and turn about" seemed to be the rule of fair play.

There were now few genuine issues in politics. Compromise on vital questions was understood to be the highest statesmanship. The Constitution itself, with its curious system of checks and balances, rendered it difficult to bring anything to pass. Added to this was a party system with obvious natural weaknesses, infected from the first with a dangerous malady. The political life, which lay on the surface of the national life of America, thus began to assume an air of futility, and, it must be added, of squalor. Only, Englishmen, recollecting the feebleness and corruption which marked their aristocratic government through a great part of the eighteenth century, must not enlarge their phylacteries at the expense of American democracy. And it is yet more important to remember that the fittest machinery for popular government, the machinery through which the real judgment of the people will prevail, can only by degrees and after many failures be devised. Popular government was then young, and it is young still.

So much for the great world of politics in those days. But in or about 1830 a Quaker named Lundy had, as Quakers used to say, "a concern" to walk 125 miles through the snow of a New England winter and speak his mind to William Lloyd Garrison. Garrison was a poor man who, like Franklin, had raised himself as a working printer, and was now occupied in philanthropy. Stirred up by Lundy, he succeeded after many painful experiences, in gaol and among mobs, in publishing in Boston on January 1, 1831, the first number of the Liberator. In it he said: "I shall strenuously contend for the immediate enfranchisement of our slave population. I will be as hard as truth and as uncompromising as justice.

I will not equivocate; I will not excuse; I will not retreat a single inch; and I will be heard." This was the beginning of the new Abolitionist movement. The Abolitionists, in the main, were impracticable people; Garrison in the end proved otherwise. Under the existing Constitution, they had nothing to propose but that the free States should withdraw from "their covenant with death and agreement with hell" – in other words, from the Union, – whereby they would not have liberated one slave. They included possibly too many of that sort who would seek salvation by repenting of other men's sins. But even these did not indulge this propensity at their ease, for by this time the politicians, the polite world, the mass of the people, the churches (even in Boston), not merely avoided the dangerous topic; they angrily proscribed it. The Abolitionists took their lives in their hands, and sometimes lost them. Only two men of standing helped them: Channing, the great preacher, who sacrificed thereby a fashionable congregation; and Adams, the sour, upright, able ex-President, the only ex-President who ever made for himself an after-career in Congress. In 1852 a still more potent ally came to their help, a poor lady, Mrs. Beecher Stowe, who in that year published "Uncle Tom's Cabin," often said to have influenced opinion more than any other book of modern times. Broadly speaking, they accomplished two things. If they did not gain love in quarters where they might have looked for it, they gained the very valuable hatred of their enemies; for they goaded Southern politicians to fury and madness, of which the first symptom was their effort to suppress Abolitionist petitions to Congress. But above all they educated in their labour of thirty years a school of opinion, not entirely in agreement with them but ready one day to revolt with decision from continued complicity in wrong.

6. Slavery and Southern Society.

In the midst of this growing America, a portion, by no means sharply marked off, and accustomed to the end to think itself intensely American, was distinguished by a peculiar institution. What was the character of that institution as it presented itself in 1830 and onwards?

Granting, as many slave holders did, though their leaders always denied it, that slavery originated in foul wrongs and rested legally upon a vile principle, what did it look like in its practical working? Most of us have received from two different sources two broad but vivid general impressions on this subject, which seem hard to reconcile but which are both in the main true. On the one hand, a visitor from England or the North, coming on a visit to the South, or in earlier days to the British West Indies, expecting perhaps to see all the horror of slavery at a glance, would be, as a young British officer once wrote home, "most agreeably undeceived as to the situation of these poor people." He would discern at once that a Southern gentleman had no more notion of using his legal privilege to be cruel to his slave than he himself had of overdriving his old horse. He might easily on the contrary find quite ordinary slave owners who had a very decided sense of responsibility in regard to their human chattels. Around his host's house, where the owner's children, petted by a black nurse, played with the little black children or with some beloved old negro, he might see that pretty aspect of "our institution at the South," which undoubtedly created in many young Southerners as they grew up a certain amount of genuine sentiment in favour of slavery. Riding wider afield he might be struck, as General Sherman was, with the contentment of the negroes whom he met on the plantations. On enquiry he would learn that the slave in old age was sure of food and shelter and free from work, and that as he approached old age his task was systematically diminished. As to excessive toil at any time of life, he would perhaps conclude that it was no easy thing to drive a gang of Africans really hard. He would be assured, quite incorrectly, that the slave's food and comfort generally were greater than those of factory workers in the North, and, perhaps only too truly, that his privations were less than those of the English agricultural labourer at that time. A wide and careful survey of the subject was made by Frederick Law Olmsted, a New York farmer, who wrote what but for their gloomy subject would be among the best books of travel. He presents to us the picture of a prevailingly sullen, sapless, brutish life, but certainly not of acute misery or habitual oppression. A Southerner old enough to remember slavery would probably not question the accuracy of his details, but would insist, very likely with truth, that there was more human happiness there than an investigator on such a quest would readily discover. Even on large plantations in the extreme South, where the owner only lived part of the year, and most things had to be left to an almost always unsatisfactory overseer, the verdict of the observer was apt to be "not so bad as I expected."

On the other hand, many of us know Longfellow's grim poem of the Hunted Negro. It is a true picture of the life led in the Dismal Swamps of Virginia by numbers of skulking fugitives, till the industry of negro-hunting, conducted with hounds of considerable value, ultimately made their lairs untenable. The scenes in the auction room where, perhaps on the death or failure of their owner, husbands and wives, parents and children, were constantly being severed, and negresses were habitually puffed as brood mares; the gentleman who had lately sold his half-brother, to be sent far south, because he was impudent; the devilish cruelty with which almost the only recorded slave insurrection was stamped out; the chase and capture and return in fetters of slaves who had escaped north, or, it might be, of free negroes in their place; the advertisements for such runaways, which Dickens collected, and which described each by his scars or mutilations; the systematic slave breeding, for the supply of the cotton States, which had become a staple industry of the once glorious Virginia; the demand arising for the restoration of the African slave trade—all these were realities. The Southern people, in the phrase of President Wilson, "knew that their lives were honourable, their relations with their slaves humane, their responsibility for the existence of slavery amongst them remote"; they burned with indignation when the whole South was held responsible for the occasional abuses of slavery. But the harsh philanthropist, who denounced them indiscriminately, merely dwelt on those aspects of slavery which came to his knowledge or which he actually saw on the border line.

And the occasional abuses, however occasional, were made by the deliberate choice of Southern statesmanship an essential part of the institution. Honourable and humane men in the South scorned exceedingly the slave hunter and the slave dealer. A candid slave owner, discussing "Uncle Tom's Cabin," found one detail flagrantly unfair; the ruined master would have had to sell his slaves to the brute, Legree, but for the world he would not have shaken hands with him. "Your children," exclaimed Lincoln, "may play with the little black children, but they must not play with his" – the slave dealer's, or the slave driver's, or the slave hunter's. By that fact alone, as he bitingly but unanswerably insisted, the whole decent society of the South condemned the foundation on which it rested.

It is needless to discuss just how dark or how fair American slavery in its working should be painted. The moderate conclusions which are quite sufficient for our purpose are uncontested. First, this much must certainly be conceded to those who would defend the slave system, that in the case of the average slave it was very doubtful whether his happiness (apart from that of future generations) could be increased by suddenly turning him into a free man working for a wage; justice would certainly have demanded that the change should be accompanied by other provisions for his benefit. But, secondly, on the refractory negro, more vicious, or sometimes, one may suspect, more manly than his fellows, the system was likely to act barbarously. Thirdly, every slave family was exposed to the risk, on such occasions as the death or great impoverishment of its owner, of being ruthlessly torn asunder, and the fact that negroes often rebounded or seemed to rebound from sorrows of this sort with surprising levity does not much lessen the horror of it. Fourthly, it is inherent in slavery that its burden should be most felt precisely by the best minds and strongest characters among the slaves. And, though the capacity of the negroes for advancement could not then and cannot yet be truly measured, yet it existed, and the policy of the South shut the door upon it. Lastly, the system abounded in brutalising influences upon a large number of white people who were accessory to it, and notoriously it degraded the poor or "mean whites," for whom it left no industrial opening, and among whom it caused work to be despised.

There is thus no escape from Lincoln's judgment: "If slavery is not wrong, nothing is wrong." It does not follow that the way to right the wrong was simple, or that instant and unmitigated emancipation was the best way. But it does follow that, failing this, it was for the statesmen of the South to devise a policy by which the most flagrant evils should be stopped, and, however cautiously and experimentally, the raising of the status of the slave should be proceeded with. It does not follow that the people who, on one pretext or another, shut their eyes to the evil of the system, while they tried to keep their personal dealing humane, can be sweepingly condemned by any man. But it does follow that a deliberate and sustained policy which, neglecting all reform, strove at all costs to perpetuate the system and extend it to wider regions, was as criminal a policy as ever lay at the door of any statesmen. And this, in fact, became the policy of the South.

"The South" meant, for political purposes, the owners of land and slaves in the greater part of the States in which slavery was lawful. The poor whites never acquired the political importance of the working classes in the North, and count for little in the story. Some of the more northerly slave States partook in a greater degree of the conditions and ideas of the North and were doubtfully to be reckoned with the South. Moreover, there is a tract of mountainous country, lying between the Atlantic seaboard and the basin of the Mississippi and extending southwards to the borders of Georgia and Alabama, of which the very vigorous and independent inhabitants were and are in many ways a people apart, often cherishing to this day family feuds which are prosecuted in the true spirit of the Icelandic Sagas.

The South, excluding these districts, was predominantly Democratic in politics, and its leaders owed some allegiance to the tradition of Radicals like Jefferson. But it was none the less proud of its aristocracy and of the permeating influence of aristocratic manners and traditions. A very large number of Southerners felt themselves to be ladies and gentlemen, and felt further that there were few or none like them among the "Yankee" traders of the North. A claim of that sort is likely to be aggressively made by those who have least title to make it, and, as strife between North and South grew hotter, the gentility of the latter infected with additional vulgarity the political controversy of private life and even of Congress. But, as observant Northerners were quite aware, these pretensions had a foundation of fact. An Englishman, then or now, in chance meetings with Americans of either section, would at once be aware of something indefinable in their bearing to which he was a stranger; but in the case of the Southerner the strangeness would often have a positive charm, such as may be found also among people of the Old World under southern latitudes and relatively primitive conditions. Newly-gotten and ill-carried wealth was in those days (Mr. Olmsted, of New York State, assures us) as offensive in the more recently developed and more prosperous parts of the South as in New York City itself; and throughout the South sound instruction and intellectual activity were markedly lacking – indeed, there is no serious Southern literature by which we can check these impressions of his. Comparing the masses of moderately well-to-do and educated people with whom he associated in the North and in the South, he finds them both free from the peculiar vulgarity which, we may be pained to know, he had discovered among us in England; he finds honesty and dishonesty in serious matters of conduct as prevalent in one section as in the other; he finds the Northerner better taught and more alert in mind; but he ascribes to him an objectionable quality of "smartness," a determination to show you that he is a stirring and pushing fellow, from which the Southerner is wholly free; and he finds that the Southerner has derived from home influences and from boarding schools in which the influence of many similar homes is concentrated, not indeed any great refinement, but a manner which is "more true, more quiet, more modestly self-assured, more dignified." This advantage, we are to understand, is diffused over a comparatively larger class than in England. Beyond this he discerns in a few parts of the South and notably in South Carolina a somewhat inaccessible, select society, of which the nucleus is formed by a few (incredibly few) old Colonial families which have not gone under, and which altogether is so small that some old gentlewomen can enumerate all the members of it. Few as they are, these form "unquestionably a wealthy and remarkably generous, refined, and accomplished first class, clinging with some pertinacity, although with too evident an effort, to the traditional manners and customs of an established gentry."

No doubt the sense of high breeding, which was common in the

South, went beyond mere manners; it played its part in making the struggle of the Southern population, including the "mean whites," in the Civil War one of the most heroic, if one of the most mistaken, in which a whole population has ever been engaged; it went along with integrity and a high average of governing capacity among public men; and it fitted the gentry of the South to contribute, when they should choose, an element of great value to the common life of America. As it was, the South suffered to the full the political degeneration which threatens every powerful class which, with a distinct class interest of its own, is secluded from real contact with competing classes with other interests and other ideas. It is not to be assumed that all individual Southerners liked the policy which they learnt to support in docile masses. But their very qualities of loyalty made them the more ready, under accepted and respected leaders, to adopt political aims and methods which no man now recalls without regret.

The connection between slavery and politics was this; as population slowly grew in the South, and as the land in the older States became to some extent exhausted, the desire for fresh territory in which cultivation by slaves could flourish became stronger and stronger. This was the reason for which the South became increasingly aware of a sectional interest in politics. In all other respects the community of public interests, of business dealings, and of general intercourse was as great between North and South as between East and West. It is certain that throughout the South, with the doubtful exception of South Carolina, political instinct and patriotic pride would have made the idea of separation intolerable upon any ground except that of slavery. In regard to this matter of dispute a peculiar phenomenon is to be observed. The quarrel grew not out of any steady opposition between North and South, but out of the habitual domination of the country by the South and the long-continued submission of the North to that domination.

For the North had its full share of blame for the long course of proceedings which prepared the coming tragedy, and the most impassioned writers on the side of the Union during the Civil War have put that blame highest. The South became arrogant and wrong-headed, and no defence is possible for the chief acts of Southern policy which will be recorded later; but the North was abject. To its own best sons it seemed to have lost both its conscience and its manhood, and to be stifled in the coils of its own miserable political apparatus. Certainly the prevailing attitude of the Northern to the Southern politicians was that of truckling. And Southerners who went to Washington had a further reason for acquiring a fatal sense of superiority to the North. The tradition of popular government which maintained itself in the South caused men who were respected, in private life, and were up to a point capable leaders, who were, in short, representative, to be sent to Congress and to be kept there. The childish perversion of popular government which took hold of the newer and more unsettled population in the North led them to send to Congress an ever-changing succession of unmeritable and sometimes shady people. The eventual stirring of the mind of the North which so closely concerns this biography was a thing hard to bring about, and to the South it brought a great shock of surprise.

7. Intellectual Development.

No survey of the political movements of this period should conclude without directing attention to something more important, which cannot be examined here. In the years from 1830 till some time after the death of Lincoln, America made those contributions to the literature of our common language which, though neither her first nor her last, seemed likely to be most permanently valued. The learning and literature of America at that time centred round Boston and Harvard University in the adjacent city of Cambridge, and no invidious comparison is intended or will be felt if they, with their poets and historians and men of letters at that time, with their peculiar atmosphere, instinct then and now with a life athletic, learned, business-like and religious, are taken to show the dawning capacities of the new nation. No places in the United States exhibit more visibly the kinship of America with England, yet in none certainly can a stranger see more readily that America is independent of the Old World in something more than politics. Many of their streets and buildings would in England seem redolent of the past, yet no cities of the Eastern States played so large a part in the development, material and mental, of the raw and vigorous West. The limitations of their greatest writers are in a manner the sign of their achievement. It would have been contrary to all human analogy if a country, in such an early stage of creation out of such a chaos, had put forth books marked strongly as its own and yet as the products of a mature national mind. It would also have been surprising if since the Civil War the rush of still more appalling and more complex practical problems had not obstructed for a while the flow of imaginative or scientific production. But the growth of those relatively early years was great. Boston had been the home of a loveless Christianity; its insurrection in the War of Independence had been soiled by shifty dealing and mere acidity; but Boston from the days of Emerson to those of Phillips Brooks radiated a temper and a mental force that was manly, tender, and clean. The man among these writers about whose exact rank, neither low nor very high among poets, there can be least dispute was Longfellow. He might seem from his favourite subjects to be hardly American; it was his deliberately chosen task to bring to the new country some savour of things gentle and mellow caught from the literature of Europe. But, in the first place, no writer could in the detail of his work have been more racy of that New England countryside which lay round his home; and, in the second place, no writer could have spoken more unerringly to the ear of the whole wide America of which his home was a little part. It seems strange to couple the name of this mild and scholarly man with the thought of that crude Western world to which we must in a moment pass.

But the connection is real and vital. It is well shown in the appreciation written of him and his fellows by the American writer who most violently contrasts with him, Walt Whitman.

A student of American history may feel something like the experience which is common among travellers in America. When they come home they cannot tell their friends what really interested them. Ugly things and very dull things are prominent in their story, as in the tales of American humorists. The general impression they convey is of something tiresomely extensive, distractingly miscellaneous, and yet insufferably monotonous. But that is not what they mean. They had better not seek to express themselves by too definite instances. They will be understood and believed when they say that to them America, with its vast spaces from ocean to ocean, does present itself as one country, not less worthy than any other of the love which it has actually inspired; a country which is the home of distinctive types of manhood and womanhood, bringing their own addition to the varying forms in which kindness and courage and truth make themselves admirable to mankind. The soul of a single people seems to be somewhere present in that great mass, no less than in some tiny city State of antiquity. Only it has to struggle, submerged evermore by a flood of newcomers, and defeated evermore by difficulties quite unlike those of other lands; and it struggles seemingly with undaunted and with rational hope.

Americans are fond of discussing Americanism. Very often they select as a pattern of it Abraham Lincoln, the man who kept the North together but has been pronounced to have been a Southerner in his inherited character. Whether he was so typical or not, it is the central fact of this biography that no man ever pondered more deeply in his own way, or answered more firmly the question whether there was indeed an American nationality worth preserving.

CHAPTER III

LINCOLN'S EARLY CAREER

1. Life at New Salem.

From this talk of large political movements we have to recall ourselves to a young labouring man with hardly any schooling, naturally and incurably uncouth, but with a curious, quite modest, impulse to assert a kindly ascendency over the companions whom chance threw in his way, and with something of the gift, which odd, shy people often possess, for using their very oddity as a weapon in their struggles. In the conditions of real equality which still prevailed in a newly settled country it is not wonderful that he made his way into political life when he was twenty-five, but it was not till twenty years later that he played an important part in events of enduring significance.

Thus the many years of public activity with which we are concerned in this and the following chapter belong rather to his apprenticeship than to his life's work; and this apprenticeship at first sight contrasts more strongly with his fame afterwards than does his boyhood of poverty and comparatively romantic hardship. For many poor boys have lived to make a great mark on history, but as a rule they have entered early on a life either of learning or of adventure or of large business. But the affairs in which Lincoln early became immersed have an air of pettiness, and from the point of view of most educated men and women in the Eastern States or in Europe, many of the associates and competitors of his early manhood, to whom he had to look up as his superiors in knowledge, would certainly have seemed crude people with a narrow horizon. Indeed, till he was called upon to take supreme control of very great matters, Lincoln must have had singularly little intercourse either with men versed in great affairs or with men of approved intellectual distinction. But a mind too original to be subdued to its surroundings found much that was stimulating in this time when Illinois was beginning rapidly to fill up. There were plenty of men with shrewd wits and robust character to be met with, and the mental atmosphere which surrounded him was one of keen interest in life. Lincoln eventually stands out as a surprising figure from among the other lawyers and little politicians of Illinois, as any great man does from any crowd, but some tribute is due to the undistinguished and historically uninteresting men whose generous appreciation gave rapid way to the poor, queer youth, and ultimately pushed him into a greater arena as their selected champion.

In 1831, at the age of twenty-two, Lincoln, returning from his New Orleans voyage, settled in New Salem to await the arrival of his patron, Denton Offutt, with the goods for a new store in which Lincoln was to be his assistant. The village itself was three years old. It never got much beyond a population of one hundred, and like many similar little towns of the West it has long since perished off the earth. But it was a busy place for a while, and, contrary to what its name might suggest, it aspired to be rather fast. It was a cock-fighting and whisky-drinking society into which Lincoln was launched. He managed to combine strict abstinence from liquor with keen participation in all its other diversions. One departure from total abstinence stands alleged among the feats of strength for which he became noted. He hoisted a whisky barrel, of unspecified but evidently considerable content, on to his knees in a squatting posture and drank from the bunghole. But this very arduous potation stood alone. Offutt was some time before he arrived with his goods, and Lincoln lived by odd jobs. At the very beginning one Mentor Graham, a schoolmaster officiating in some election, employed him as a clerk, and the clerk seized the occasion to make himself well known to New Salem as a story-teller. Then there was a heavy job at rail-splitting, and another job in navigating the Sangamon River. Offutt's store was at last set up, and for about a year the assistant in this important establishment had valuable opportunities of conversation with all New Salem. He had also leisure for study. He had mentioned to the aforesaid Mentor Graham his "notion to study English grammar," and had been introduced to a work called "Kirkham's Grammar," which by a walk of some miles he could borrow from a neighbour. This he would read, lying full length on the counter with his head on a parcel of calico. At other odd times he would work away at arithmetic. Offutt's kindly interest procured him distinction in another field. At Clary's Grove, near New Salem, lived a formidable set of young ruffians, over whose somewhat disguised chivalry of temper the staid historian of Lincoln's youth becomes rapturous. They were given to wrecking the store of any New Salem tradesman who offended them; so it shows some spirit in Mr. Denton Offutt that he backed his Abraham Lincoln to beat their Jack Armstrong in a wrestling match. He did beat him; moreover, some charm in the way he bore himself made him thenceforth not hated but beloved of Clary's Grove in general, and the Armstrongs in particular. Hannah Armstrong, Jack's wife, thereafter mended and patched his clothes for him, and, years later, he had the satisfaction, as their unfeed advocate, of securing the acquittal of their son from a charge of murder, of which there is some reason to hope he may not have been guilty. It is, by the way, a relief to tell that there once was a noted wrestling match in which Lincoln was beaten; it is characteristic of the country that his friends were sure there was foul play, and characteristic of him that he indignantly denied it.

Within a year Offutt's store, in the phrase of the time, "petered out," leaving Lincoln shiftless. But the victor of Clary's Grove, with his added mastery of "Kirkham's Grammar," was now ripe for public life. Moreover, his experience as a waterman gave him ideas on the question, which then agitated his neighbours, whether the Sangamon River could be made navigable. He had a scheme of his own for doing this; and in the spring of 1832 he wrote to the local paper a boyish but modest and sensible statement of his views and ambitions, announcing that he would be a candidate in the autumn elections for the State Legislature.

Meanwhile he had his one experience of soldiering. The Indian chief, Black Hawk, who had agreed to abide west of the Mississippi, broke the treaty and led his warriors back into their former haunts in Northern Illinois. The Governor of the State called for volunteers, and Lincoln became one. He obtained the elective rank of captain of his company, and contrived to maintain some sort of order in that, doubtless brave, but undisciplined body. He saw no fighting, but he could earn his living for some months, and stored up material for effective chaff in Congress long afterwards about the military glory which General Cass's supporters for the Presidency wished to attach to their candidate. His most glorious exploit consisted in saving from his own men a poor old friendly Indian who had fallen among them. A letter of credentials, which the helpless creature produced, was pronounced a forgery and he was about to be hanged as a spy, when Lincoln appeared on the scene, "swarthy with resolution and rage," and somehow terrified his disorderly company into dropping their prey.

The war ended in time for a brief candidature, and a supporter of his at the time preserved a record of one of his speeches. His last important speech will hereafter be given in full for other reasons; this may be so given too, for it is not a hundred words long: "Fellow Citizens, I presume you all know who I am. I am humble Abraham Lincoln. I have been solicited by many friends to become a candidate for the Legislature. My politics are short and sweet like the old woman's dance. I am in favour of a national bank. I am in favour of the internal improvement system and a high protective tariff. These are my sentiments and political principles. If elected, I shall be thankful; if not, it will be all the same."

To this succinct declaration of policy may be added from his earlier letter that he advocated a law against usury, and laws for the improvement of education. The principles of the speech are those which the new Whig party was upholding against the Democrats under Jackson (the President) and Van Buren.

Lincoln's neighbours, like the people of Illinois generally, were almost entirely on the side of the Democrats. It is interesting that however he came by his views, they were early and permanently fixed on the side then unpopular in Illinois; and it is interesting that though, naturally, not elected, he secured very nearly the whole of the votes of his immediate neighbourhood.

The penniless Lincoln was now hankering to become a lawyer, though with some thoughts of the more practicable career of a blacksmith. Unexpectedly, however, he was tempted into his one venture, singularly unsuccessful, in business. Two gentlemen named Herndon, cousins of a biographer of Lincoln's, started a store in New Salem and got tired of it. One sold his share to a Mr. Berry, the other sold his to Lincoln. The latter sale was entirely on credit—no money passed at the time, because there was no money. The vendor explained afterwards that he relied solely on Lincoln's honesty. He had to wait a long while for full payment, but what is known of storekeeping in New Salem shows that he did very well for himself in getting out of his venture as he did. Messrs. Berry and Lincoln next acquired, likewise for credit, the stock and goodwill of two other storekeepers, one of them the victim of a raid from Clary's Grove. The senior partner then applied himself diligently to personal consumption of the firm's liquid goods; the junior member of the firm was devoted in part to intellectual and humorous converse with the male customers, but a fatal shyness prevented him from talking to the ladles. For the rest, he walked long distances to borrow books, got through Gibbon and through Rollin's "History of the World," began his study of Blackstone, and acquired a settled habit of reading novels. So business languished. Early in 1833 Berry and Lincoln sold out to another adventurer. This also was a credit transaction. The purchaser without avoidable delay failed and disappeared. Berry then died of drink, leaving to Lincoln the sole responsibility for the debts of the partnership. Lincoln could with no difficulty and not much reproach have freed himself by bankruptcy. As a matter of fact, he ultimately paid everything, but it took him about fifteen years of striving and pinching himself.

Lincoln is one of the many public characters to whom the standing epithet "honest" became attached; in his case the claim to this rested originally on the only conclusive authority, that of his creditors. But there is equally good authority, that of his biographer, William Herndon, for many years his partner as a lawyer, that "he had no money sense." This must be understood with the large qualification that he meant to pay his way and, unlike the great statesmen of the eighteenth century in England, did pay it. But, though with much experience of poverty in his early career, he never developed even a reasonable desire to be rich. Wealth remained in his view "a superfluity of the things one does not want." He was always interested in mathematics, but mainly as a discipline in thinking, and partly, perhaps, in association with mechanical problems of which he was fond enough to have once in his life patented an invention. The interest never led him to take to accounts or to long-sighted financial provisions. In later days, when he received a payment for his fees, his partner's share would be paid then and there; and perhaps the rent would be paid, and the balance would be spent at once in groceries and other goods likely to be soon wanted, including at long intervals, when the need was very urgent, a new hat.

These are amiable personal traits, but they mark the limitations of his capacity as a statesman. The chief questions which agitated the Illinois Legislature were economic, and so at first were the issues between Whigs and Democrats in Federal policy. Lincoln, though he threw himself into these affairs with youthful fervour, would appear never to have had much grasp of such matters. "In this respect alone," writes an admirer, "I have always considered Mr. Lincoln a weak man." It is only when (rarely, at first) constitutional or moral issues emerge that his politics become interesting. We can guess the causes which attached him to the Whigs. As the party out of power, and in Illinois quite out of favour, they had doubtless some advantage in character. As we have seen, the greatest minds among American statesmen of that day, Webster and Clay, were Whigs. Lincoln's simple and quite reasonable, if inconclusive, argument for Protection, can be found among his speeches of some years later. And schemes of internal development certainly fired his imagination.

After his failure in business Lincoln subsisted for a while on odd jobs for farmers, but was soon employed as assistant surveyor by John Calhoun, then surveyor of the county. This gentleman, who had been educated as a lawyer but "taught school in preference," was a keen Democrat, and had to assure Lincoln that office as his assistant would not necessitate his desertion of his principles. He was a clever man, and Lincoln remembered him long after as the most formidable antagonist he ever met in debate. With the help, again, of Mentor Graham, Lincoln soon learned the surveyor's business. He continued at this work till he was able to start as a lawyer, and there is evidence that his surveys of property were done with extreme accuracy. Soon he further obtained the local Postmastership. This, the only position except the Presidency itself which he ever held in the Federal Government, was not onerous, for the mails were infrequent; he "carried the office around in his hat"; we are glad to be told that "his administration gave satisfaction." Once calamity threatened him; a creditor distrained on the horse and the instruments necessary to his surveyorship; but Lincoln was reputed to be a helpful fellow, and friends were ready to help him; they bought the horse and instruments back for him. To this time belongs his first acquaintance with some writers of unsettling tendency, Tom Paine, Voltaire, and Volney, who was then recognised as one of the dangerous authors. Cock-fights, strange feats of strength, or of usefulness with axe or hammer or scythe, and a passion for mimicry continue. In 1834 he became a candidate again. "Can't the party raise any better material than that?" asked a bystander before a speech of his; after it, he exclaimed that the speaker knew more than all the other candidates put together. This time he was elected, being then twenty-five, and thereafter he was returned for three further terms of two years. Shortly before his second election in 1836 the State capital was removed to Springfield, in his own county. There in 1837 Lincoln fixed his home. He had long been reading law in his curious, spasmodically concentrated way, and he had practised a little as a "pettifogger," that is, an unlicensed practitioner in the inferior courts. He had now obtained his license and was very shortly taken into partnership by an old friend in Springfield.

2. In the Illinois Legislature.

Here his youth may be said to end. Springfield was a different place from New Salem. There were carriages in it, and ladles who studied poetry and the fashions. There were families from Virginia and Kentucky who were conscious of ancestry, while graver, possibly more pushing, people from the North-eastern States, soon to outnumber them, were a little inclined to ridicule what they called their "illusory ascendency." There was a brisk competition of churches, and mutual improvement societies such as the "Young Men's Lyceum" had a rival claim to attention with races and cock-fights.

And it was an altered Abraham Lincoln that came to inhabit Springfield. Arriving a day or two before his first law partnership was settled he came into the shop of a thriving young tradesman, Mr. Joshua Speed, to ask about the price of the cheapest bedding and other necessary articles. The sum for which Lincoln, who had not one cent, would have had to ask, and would have been readily allowed, credit, was only seventeen dollars. But this huge prospect of debt so visibly depressed him that Speed instantly proposed an arrangement which involved no money debt. He took him upstairs and installed him – Western domestic arrangements were and are still simple – as the joint occupant of his own large bed. "Well, Speed, I'm moved," was the terse acknowledgment.

Speed was to move him later by more precious charity. We are concerned for the moment with what moved Speed. "I looked up at him," said he, long after, "and I thought then, as I think now, that I never saw so gloomy and melancholy a face in my life." The struggle of ambition and poverty may well have been telling on Lincoln; but besides that a tragical love story (shortly to be told) had left a deep and permanent mark; but these influences worked, we may suppose, upon a disposition quite as prone to sadness as to mirth. His exceedingly gregarious habit, drawing him to almost any assembly of his own sex, continued all his life; but it alternated from the first with a habit of solitude or abstraction, the abstraction of a man who, when he does wish to read, will read intently in the midst of crowd or noise, or walking along the street. He was what might unkindly be called almost a professional humorist, the master of a thousand startling stories, delightful to the hearer, but possibly tiresome in written reminiscences, but we know too well that gifts of this kind are as compatible with sadness as they certainly are with deadly seriousness.

The Legislature of Illinois in the eight years from 1834 to 1842, in which Lincoln belonged to it, was, though not a wise, a vigorous body. In the conditions which then existed it was not likely to have been captured as the Legislatures of wilder and more thinly-peopled States have sometimes been by a disreputable element in the community, nor to have subsided into the hands of the dull mechanical class of professional politicians with which, rightly or wrongly, we have now been led to associate American State Government. The fact of Lincoln's own election suggests that dishonest adventurers might easily have got there, but equally suggests that a very different type of men prevailed. "The Legislature," we are told, "contained the youth and blood and fire of the frontier." Among the Democrats in the Legislature was Stephen Douglas, who was to become one of the most powerful men in the United States while Lincoln was still unknown; and several of Lincoln's Whig colleagues were afterwards to play distinguished or honourable parts in politics or war. We need not linger over them, but what we know of those with whom he had any special intimacy makes it entirely pleasant to associate him with them.

After a short time in which, like any sensible young member of an assembly, he watched and hardly ever spoke, Lincoln soon made his way among these men, and in 1838 and 1840 the Whig members – though, being in a minority, they could not elect him – gave him their unanimous votes for the Speakership of the Assembly. The business which engrossed the Legislature, at least up to 1838, was the development of the natural resources of the State. These were great. It was natural that railways, canals and other public works to develop them should be pushed forward at the public cost. Other new countries since, with less excuse because with greater warning from experience, have plunged in this matter, and, though the Governor protested, the Illinois Legislature, Whigs and Democrats, Lincoln and every one else, plunged gaily, so that, during the collapse which followed, Illinois, though, like Lincoln himself, it paid its debts in the end, was driven in 1840 to suspend interest payments for several years.

Very little is recorded of Lincoln's legislative doings. What is related chiefly exhibits his delight in the game of negotiation and combination by which he and the other members for his county, together known as "the Long Nine," advanced the particular projects which pleased their constituents or struck their own fancy. Thus he early had a hand in the removal of the capital from Vandalia to Springfield in his own county. The map of Illinois suggests that Springfield was a better site for the purpose than Vandalia and at least as good as Jacksonville or Peoria or any of its other competitors. Of his few recorded speeches one concerns a proposed inquiry into some alleged impropriety in the allotment of shares in the State Bank. It is certainly the speech of a bold man; it argues with remarkable directness that whereas a committee of prominent citizens which had already inquired into this matter consisted of men of known honesty, the proposed committee of the Legislators, whom he was addressing, would consist of men who, for all he knew, might be honest, and, for all he knew, might not.

The Federal politics of this time, though Lincoln played an active local part in the campaigns of the Whig party, concern us little. The Whigs, to whom he did subordinate service, were, as has been said, an unlucky party. In 1840, in the reaction which extreme commercial depression created against the previously omnipotent Democrats, the Whig candidate for the Presidency was successful. This was General Harrison, a respected soldier of the last war, who was glorified as a sort of Cincinnatus and elected after an outburst of enthusiastic tomfoolery such as never before or since rejoiced the American people. But President Harrison had hardly been in office a month when he died. Some say he was worried to death by office seekers, but a more prosaic cause, pneumonia, can also be alleged. It is satisfactory that this good man's grandson worthily filled his office forty-eight years after, but his immediate successor was of course the Vice-President, Tyler, chosen as an influential opponent of the last Democrat Presidents, but not because he agreed with the Whigs. Cultivated but narrow-minded, highly independent and wholly perverse, he satisfied no aspiration of the Whigs and paved the way effectually for the Democrat who succeeded him.

Throughout these years Lincoln was of course working at law, which became, with the development of the country, a more arduous and a more learned profession. Sessions of the Legislature did not last long, and political canvasses were only occasional. If Lincoln was active in these matters he was in many other directions, too, a keen participator in the keen life of the society round him. Nevertheless politics as such, and apart from any large purpose to be achieved through them, had for many years a special fascination for him. For one thing he was argumentative in the best sense, with a passion for what the Greeks sometimes called "dialectic"; his rare capacity for solitary thought, the most marked and the greatest of his powers, went absolutely hand in hand with the desire to reduce his thoughts to a form which would carry logical conviction to others. Further, there can be no doubt – and such a combination of tastes, though it seems to be uncommon, is quite intelligible – that the somewhat unholy business of party management was at first attractive to him. To the end he showed no intuitive comprehension of individual men. His sincere friendly intention, the unanswerable force of an argument, the convincing analogy veiled in an unseemly story, must take their chance of suiting the particular taste of Senator Sherman or General McClellan; but any question of managing men in the mass – will a given candidate's influence with this section of people count for more than his unpopularity with that section? and so on – involved an element of subtle and long-sighted calculation which was vastly congenial to him. We are to see him hereafter applying this sort of science on a grand scale and for a great end. His early discipline in it is a dull subject, interesting only where it displays, as it sometimes does, the perfect fairness with which this ambitious man could treat his own claims as against those of a colleague and competitor.

In forming any judgment of Lincoln's career it must, further, be realised that, while he was growing up as a statesman, the prevailing conception of popular government was all the time becoming more unfavourable to leadership and to robust individuality. The new party machinery adopted by the Democrats under Jackson, as the proper mode of securing government by the people, induced a deadly uniformity of utterance; breach of that uniformity was not only rash, but improper. Once in early days it was demanded in a newspaper that "all candidates should show their hands." "Agreed," writes Lincoln, "here's mine"; and then follows a young man's avowal of advanced opinions; he would give the suffrage to "all whites who pay taxes or bear arms, by no means excluding females." Disraeli, who was Lincoln's contemporary, throve by exuberances quite as startling as this, nor has any English politician found it damaging to be bold. On this occasion indeed (in 1836) Lincoln was far from damaging himself; the Whigs had not till a few years later been induced, for self-preservation, to copy the Democratic machine. But it is striking that the admiring friend who reports this declaration, "too audacious and emphatic for the statesmen of a later day," must carefully explain how it could possibly suit the temper of a time which in a few years passed away. Very soon the question whether a proposal or even a sentiment was timely or premature came to bulk too large in the deliberations of Lincoln's friends. The reader will perhaps wonder later whether such considerations did not bulk too largely in Lincoln's own mind. Was there in his statesmanship, even in later days when he had great work to do, an element of that opportunism which, if not actually base, is at least cheap? Or did he come as near as a man with many human weaknesses could come to the wise and nobly calculated opportunism which is not merely the most beneficent statesmanship, but demands a heroic self-mastery?

The main interest of his doings in Illinois politics and in Congress is the help they may give in penetrating his later mind. On the one hand, it is certain that Lincoln trained himself to be a great student of the fitting opportunity. He evidently paid very serious attention to the counsels of friends who would check his rasher impulses. One of his closest associates insists that his impulsive judgment was bad, and he probably thought so himself. It will be seen later that the most momentous utterance he ever made was kept back through the whole space of two years of crisis at the instance of timid friends. It required not less courage and was certainly more effective when at last it did come out. The same great capacity for waiting marks any steps that he took for his own advancement. Indeed it was a happy thing for him and for his country that his character and the whole cast of his ideas and sympathies were of a kind to which the restraint imposed on an American politician was most congenial and to which therefore it could do least harm. He was to prove himself a patient man in other ways as well as this. On many things, perhaps on most, the thoughts he worked out in his own mind diverged very widely from those of his neighbours, but he was not in the least anxious either to conceal or to obtrude them. His social philosophy as he expressed it to his friends in these days was one which contemplated great future reforms—abolition of slavery and a strict temperance policy were among them. But he looked for them with a sort of fatalistic confidence in the ultimate victory of reason, and saw no use and a good deal of harm in premature political agitation for them. "All such questions," he is reported to have said, "must find lodgment with the most enlightened souls who stamp them with their approval. In God's own time they will be organised into law and thus woven into the fabric of our institutions." This seems a little cold-blooded, but perhaps we can already begin to recognise the man who, when the time had fully come, would be on the right side, and in whom the evil which he had deeply but restrainedly hated would find an appallingly wary foe.

But there were crucial instances which test sufficiently whether this wary politician was a true man or not. The soil of Illinois was free soil by the Ordinance of 1787, and Congress would only admit it to the Union as a free State. But it had been largely peopled from the South. There had been much agitation against this restriction; prevailing sentiment to a late date strongly approved of slavery; it was at Alton in Illinois that, in 1836, Elijah Lovejoy, an Abolitionist publisher, had been martyred by the mob which had failed to intimidate him. In 1837, when the bold agitation of the Abolitionists was exciting much disapproval, the

Illinois Legislature passed resolutions condemning that agitation and declaring in soothing tones the constitutional powerlessness of Congress to interfere with slavery in the Southern States. Now Lincoln himself—whether for good reasons or bad must be considered later—thoroughly disapproved of the actual agitation of the Abolitionists; and the resolutions in question, but for one merely theoretical point of law and for an unctuous misuse of the adjective "sacred," contained nothing which he could not literally have accepted. The objection to them lay in the motive which made it worth while to pass them. Lincoln drew up and placed on the records of the House a protest against these resolutions. He defines in it his own quite conservative opinions; he deprecates the promulgation of Abolition doctrines; but he does so because it "tends rather to increase than abate the evils" of slavery; and he lays down "that the institution of slavery is founded on both injustice and bad policy." One man alone could he induce to sign this protest with him, and that man was not seeking re-election.

By 1842 Lincoln had grown sensibly older, and a little less ready, we may take it, to provoke unnecessary antagonism. Probably very old members of Free Churches are the people best able to appreciate the daring of the following utterance. Speaking on Washington's birthday in a Presbyterian church to a temperance society formed among the rougher people of the town and including former drunkards who desired to reform themselves, he broke out in protest against the doctrine that respectable persons should shun the company of people tempted to intemperance. "If," he said, "they believe as they profess that Omnipotence condescended to take upon Himself the form of sinful man, and as such die an ignominious death, surely they will not refuse submission to the infinitely lesser condescension, for the temporal and perhaps eternal salvation of a large, erring, and unfortunate class of their fellow creatures! Nor is the condescension very great. In my judgment such of us as have never fallen victims have been spared more from the absence of appetite than from any mental or moral superiority over those who have. Indeed, I believe, if we take habitual drunkards as a class, that their heads and their hearts will bear an advantageous comparison with those of any other class." It proved, at a later day, very lucky for America that the virtuous Lincoln, who did not drink strong drink—nor, it is sad to say, smoke, nor, which is all to the good, chew—did feel like that about drunkenness; But there was great and loud wrath. "It's a shame," said one, "that he should be permitted to abuse us so in the house of the Lord." It is certain that in this sort of way he did himself a good deal of injury as an aspiring politician. It is also the fact that he continued none the less persistently in a missionary work conceived in a spirit none the less Christian because it shocked many pious people.

3. Marriage.

The private life of Lincoln continued, and for many years increasingly, to be equally marked by indiscriminate sociability and brooding loneliness. Comfort and the various influences which may be associated with the old-fashioned American word "elegance" seem never to enter into it. What is more, little can be discerned of positive happiness in the background of his life, as the freakish elasticity of his youth disappeared and, after a certain measure of marked success, the further objects of his ambition though not dropped became unlikely of attainment and seemed, we may guess, of doubtful value. All along he was being moulded for endurance rather than for enjoyment.

Nor, though his children evidently brought him happiness, does what we know of his domesticities and dearest affections weaken this general impression. When he married he had gone through a saddening experience. He started on manhood with a sound and chivalrous outlook on women in general, and a nervous terror of actual women when he met them. In New Salem days he absented himself from meals for the whole time that some ladies were staying at his boarding house. His clothes and his lack of upbringing must have weighed with him, besides his natural disposition. None the less, of course he fell in love. Miss Ann Rutledge, the daughter of a store and tavern keeper from Kentucky with whom Lincoln was boarding in 1833, has been described as of exquisite beauty; some say this is over-stated, but speak strongly of her grace and charm. A lady who knew her gives these curiously collocated particulars: "Miss Rutledge had auburn hair, blue eyes, fair complexion. She was pretty, slightly slender, but in everything a good-hearted young woman. She was about five feet two inches high, and weighed in the neighbourhood of a hundred and twenty pounds. She was beloved by all who knew her. She died as it were of grief. In speaking of her death and her grave Lincoln once said to me, 'My heart lies buried there.'" The poor girl, when Lincoln first came courting to her, had passed through a grievous agitation. She had been engaged to a young man, who suddenly returned to his home in the Eastern States, after revealing to her, with some explanation which was more convincing to her than to her friends, that he had been passing under an assumed name. It seems that his absence was strangely prolonged, that for a long time she did not hear from him, that his letters when they did come puzzled her, that she clung to him long, but yielded at last to her friends, who urged their very natural suspicions upon her.

It is further suggested that there was some good explanation of his conduct all the while, and that she learnt this too late when actually engaged to Lincoln. However that may be, shortly after her engagement to Lincoln she fell seriously ill, insisted, as she lay ill, on a long interview with Lincoln alone, and a day or two later died. This was in 1835, when he was twenty-six. It is perhaps right to say that one biographer throws doubt on the significance of this story in Lincoln's life. The details as to Ann Rutledge's earlier lover are vague and uncertain. The main facts of Lincoln's first engagement and almost immediate loss of his betrothed are quite certain; the blow would have been staggering enough to any ordinary young lover and we know nothing of Lincoln which would discredit Mr. Herndon's judgment that its effect on him was both acute and permanent. There can be no real doubt that his spells of melancholy were ever afterwards more intense, and politer biographers should not have suppressed the testimony that for a time that melancholy seemed to his friends to verge upon insanity. He always found good friends, and, as was to happen again later, one of them, Mr. Bowline Greene, carried him off to his own secluded home and watched him carefully.

He said "the thought that the snows and rains fell upon her grave filled him with indescribable grief." Two years later he told a fellow-legislator that "although he seemed to others to enjoy life rapturously, yet when alone he was so overcome by mental depression, he never dared to carry a pocket-knife." Later still Greene, who had helped him, died, and Lincoln was to speak over his grave. For once in his life he broke down entirely; "the tears ran down his yellow and shrivelled cheeks. . . . After repeated efforts he found it impossible to speak and strode away sobbing."

The man whom a grief of this kind has affected not only intensely, but morbidly, is almost sure, before its influence has faded, to make love again, and is very likely to do so foolishly. Miss Mary Owens was slightly older than Lincoln. She was a handsome woman; commanding, but comfortable. In the tales of Lincoln's love stories, much else is doubtfully related, but the lady's weight is in each case stated with assurance, and when she visited her sister in New Salem in 1836 Mary Owens weighed one hundred and fifty pounds. There is nothing sad in her story; she was before long happily married—not to Lincoln—and she long outlived him. But Lincoln, who had seen her on a previous visit and partly remembered her, had been asked, perhaps in jest, by her sister to marry her if she returned, and had rashly announced half in jest that he would. Her sister promptly fetched her, and he lingered for some time in a half-engaged condition, writing her reasonable, conscientious, feeble letters, in which he put before her dispassionately the question whether she could patiently bear "to see without sharing . . . a lot of flourishing about in carriages, . . . to be poor without the means of hiding your poverty," and assuring her that "I should be much happier with you than the way I am, provided I saw no signs of discontent in you." Whether he rather wished to marry her but felt bound to hold her free, or distinctly wished not to marry her but felt bound not to hold himself free, he probably was never sure. The lady very wisely decided that he could not make her happy, and returned to Kentucky. She said he was deficient in the little courteous attentions which a woman's happiness requires of her husband. She gave instances long after to prove her point; but she always spoke of him with friendship and respect as "a man with a heart full of human kindness and a head full of common sense."

Rather unluckily, Lincoln, upon his rejection or release, relieved his feelings in a letter about Miss Owens to one of the somewhat older married ladies who were kind to him, the wife of one of his colleagues. She ought to have burnt his letter, but she preserved it to kindle mild gossip after his death. It is a burlesque account of his whole adventure, describing, with touches of very bad taste, his disillusionment with the now maturer charms of Miss Owens when her sister brought her back to New Salem, and making comedy of his own honest bewilderment and his mingled relief and mortification when she at last refused him. We may take it as evidence of the natural want of perception and right instinctive judgment in minor matters which some who knew and loved him attribute to him. But, besides that, the man who found relief in this ill-conceived exercise of humour was one in whom the prospect of marriage caused some strange and pitiful perturbation of mind.

This was in 1838, and a year later Mary Todd came from Kentucky to stay at Springfield with her brother-in-law Ninian Edwards, a legislator of Illinois and a close ally of Lincoln's. She was aged twenty-one, and her weight was one hundred and thirty pounds. She was well educated, and had family connections which were highly esteemed. She was pleasant in company, but somewhat imperious, and she was a vivacious talker. When among the young men who now became attentive in calling on the Edwards's Lincoln came and sat awkwardly gazing on Miss Todd, Mrs. Edwards appears to have remarked that the two were not suited to each other. But an engagement took place all the same. As to the details of what followed, whether he or she was the first to have doubts, and whether, as some say, the great Stephen Douglas appeared on the scene as a rival and withdrew rather generously but too late, is uncertain. But Lincoln composed a letter to break off his engagement. He showed it to Joshua Speed, who told him that if he had the courage of a man he would not write to her, but see her and speak. He did so. She cried. He kissed and tried to comfort her. After this Speed had to point out to him that he had really renewed his engagement. Again there may be some uncertainty whether on January 1, 1841, the bridal party had actually assembled and the bridegroom after long search was found by his friends wandering about in a state which made them watch day and night and keep knives from him. But it is quite certain from his letters that in some such way on "the fatal 1st of January, 1841," he broke down terribly. Some weeks later he wrote to his partner: "Whether I shall ever be better I cannot tell; I awfully forebode I shall not. To remain as I am is impossible. I must die or be better, as it appears to me." After a while Speed was able to remove him to his own parents' home in Kentucky, where he and his mother nursed him back to mental life.

Then in the course of 1841 Speed himself began to contemplate marriage, and Speed himself had painful searchings of heart, and Lincoln's turn came to show a sureness of perception in his friend's case that he wholly lacked in his own. "I know," he writes, "what the painful point with you is . . . it is an apprehension that you do not love her as you should. What nonsense! How came you to court her? But you say you reasoned yourself into it. What do you mean by that? Was it not that you found yourself unable to reason yourself out of it? Did you not think, and partly form the purpose, of courting her the first time you ever saw or heard of her? What had reason to do with it at that early stage?" A little later the lady of Speed's love falls ill. Lincoln writes: "I hope and believe that your present anxiety about her health and her life must and will for ever banish those horrid doubts which I know you sometimes felt as to the truth of your affection for her. . . . Perhaps this point is no longer a question with you, and my pertinacious dwelling upon it is a rude intrusion upon your feelings.

If so, you must pardon me. You know the hell I have suffered upon that point, and how tender I am upon it." When he writes thus it is no surprise to hear from him that he has lost his hypochondria, but it may be that the keen recollection of it gives him excessive anxieties for Speed. On the eve of the wedding he writes: "You will always hereafter be on ground that I have never occupied, and consequently, if advice were needed, I might advise wrong. I do fondly hope, however, that you will never need comfort from abroad. I incline to think it probable that your nerves will occasionally fail you for a while; but once you get them firmly graded now, that trouble is over for ever. If you went through the ceremony calmly or even with sufficient composure not to excite alarm in any present, you are safe beyond question, and in two or three months, to say the most, will be the happiest of men." Soon he is reassured and can "feel somewhat jealous of both of you now. You will be so exclusively concerned with one another that I shall be forgotten entirely. I shall feel very lonesome without you." And a little later: "It cannot be told how it thrills me with joy to hear you say you are far happier than you ever expected to be. I know you too well to suppose your expectations were not at least sometimes extravagant, and if the reality exceeds them all, I say, 'Enough, dear Lord.'" And here follows what might perhaps have been foreseen: "Your last letter gave me more pleasure than the total sum of all that I have received since the fatal 1st of January, 1841. Since then it seems to me I should have been entirely happy but for the never absent idea that there is still one unhappy whom I have contributed to make so. That kills my soul. I cannot but reproach myself for even wishing to be happy while she is otherwise." Very significantly he has inquired of friends how that one enjoyed a trip on the new railway cars to Jacksonville, and—not being like Falkland in "The Rivals"—praises God that she has enjoyed it exceedingly.

This was in the spring of 1842. Some three months later he writes again to Speed: "I must gain confidence in my own ability to keep my resolves when they are made. In that ability I once prided myself as the only chief gem of my character. That gem I lost how and where you know too well. I have not regained it, and until I do I cannot trust myself in any matter of much importance. I believe now that, had you understood my case at the time as well as I understood yours afterwards, by the aid you would have given me I should have sailed through clear. . . . I always was superstitious. I believe God made me one of the instruments of bringing Fanny and you together, which union I have no doubt He had fore-ordained. Whatever He designs for me He will do. 'Stand still and see the salvation of the Lord,' is my text just now. If, as you say, you have told Fanny all, I should have no objection to her seeing this letter. I do not think I can come to Kentucky this season. I am so poor and make so little headway in the world that I drop back in a month of idleness as much as I gain in a year's sowing." At last in the autumn of that year Lincoln addresses to Speed a question at once so shrewd and so daringly intimate as perhaps no other man ever asked of his friend. "The immense sufferings you endured from the first days of September till the middle of February" (the date of Speed's wedding) "you never tried to conceal from me, and I well understood. You have now been the husband of a lovely woman nearly eight months. That you are happier now than the day you married her I well know. . . . But I want to ask a close question! 'Are you in _feeling_ as well as in _judgment_ glad you are married as you are?' From anybody but me this would be an impudent question, not to be tolerated, but I know you will pardon it in me. Please answer it quickly, as I am impatient to know."

Speed remained in Kentucky; Lincoln was too poor for visits of pleasure; and Speed was not a man who cared for political life; but the memorials, from which the above quotations have been taken, of Lincoln's lasting friendship with Speed and his kind mother, who gave Lincoln a treasured Bible, and his kind young wife, who made her husband's friend her own, and whose violet, dropped into her husband's letter to him just as he was sealing it, was among the few flowers that Lincoln ever appreciated, throw the clearest light that we can anywhere obtain on the inner mind of Lincoln.

As may have been foreseen, Mary Todd and he had met again on a friendly footing. A managing lady is credited with having brought about a meeting between them, but evidently she did not do it till Lincoln was at least getting desirous to be managed. He was much absorbed at this time in law business, to which since his breakdown he had applied himself more seriously. It was at this period too that his notable address on temperance was given. Soon after his meetings with Miss Todd began again he involved himself in a complication of a different kind. He had written, partly, it seems, for the young lady's amusement, some innocent if uninteresting political skits relating to some question about taxes. This brought on him an unexpected challenge from a fiery but diminutive revenue official, one Colonel Shields, a prominent Democratic politician. Lincoln availed himself of the right of the challenged to impose ridiculous conditions of combat, partly no doubt in fun, but with the sensible object also of making sure that he could disarm his antagonist with no risk of harm to the little man. The tangled controversy which ensued as to how and by whose fault the duel eventually fell through has nothing in it now, but the whole undignified business seems to have given Lincoln lasting chagrin, and worried him greatly at a time when it would have been well that he should be cheerful. At last on November 4, 1842, when Lincoln was nearly thirty-three, he was safely married. The wedding, held, according to the prevailing custom, in a private house, was an important function, for it was the first Episcopalian wedding that good society in Springfield had witnessed. Malicious fortune brought in a ludicrous incident at the last moment, for when in the lawyerlike verbiage of the then American Prayer-Book the bridegroom said, "With this ring I thee endow with all my goods, chattels, lands and tenements," old Judge Brown of the Illinois Supreme Court, who had never heard the like, impatiently broke in, "God Almighty, Lincoln! The statute fixes all that."

There is more than the conventional reason for apology for pressing the subject a little further. Nothing very illuminating can be said as to the course of Lincoln's married life, but much has already been made public about it which, though it cannot be taken as reaching to the heart of the matter, is not properly to be dismissed as mere gossip. Mrs. Lincoln, it is clear, had a high temper—the fact that, poor woman! after her husband had been murdered by her side, she developed clear symptoms of insanity, may or may not, for all we are entitled to know, be relevant in this regard. She was much younger than her husband, and had gone through a cruel experience for him. Moreover, she had proper ambitions and was accustomed to proper conventional refinements; so her husband's exterior roughness tried her sorely, not the less we may be sure because of her real pride in him. Wife and tailor combined could not, with any amount of money, have dressed him well. Once, though they kept a servant then, Lincoln thought it friendly to open the door himself in his shirt sleeves when two most elegant ladies came to call. On such occasions, and doubtless on other occasions of less provocation, Mrs. Lincoln's high temper was let loose. It seems pretty certain, too, that he met her with mere forbearance, sad patience, and avoidance of conflict. His fellow lawyers came to notice that he stayed away from home on circuit when all the rest of them could go home for a day or two. Fifteen years after his wedding he himself confessed to his trouble, not disloyally, but in a rather moving remonstrance with some one who had felt intolerably provoked by Mrs. Lincoln. There are slight indications that occasions of difficulty and pain to Lincoln happened up to the end of his life. On the other hand, there are slight indications that common love for their children helped to make the two happier, and there are no indications at all of any approach to a serious quarrel. All that is told us may be perfectly true and not by any means have justified the pity that some of Lincoln's friends were ready to feel for him. It is difficult to avoid suspecting that Lincoln's wife did not duly like his partner and biographer, Mr. Herndon, who felt it his duty to record so many painful facts and his own possibly too painful impression from them. On the other side, Mr. Herndon makes it clear that in some respects Mrs. Lincoln was an admirable wife for her husband. She faced the difficulties of their poverty with spirit and resolution. Testimony from other sources to her graceful hospitality abounds. More than this, from the very first she believed in his powers. It seems she had the discernment to know, when few others can have done so, how far greater he was than his rival Douglas. It was Herndon's belief, in days when he and Mrs. Lincoln were the two persons who saw most of him, that she sustained his just ambition, and that at the most critical moment of his personal career she had the courage to make him refuse an attractive appointment which must have ruined it. The worst that we are told with any certainty amounts to this, that like the very happily married writer of "Virginibus Puerisque," Lincoln discovered that marriage is "a field of battle and not a bed of roses" – a battle in which we are forced to suspect that he did not play his full part.

We should perhaps be right in associating his curious record, of right and high regard for women and inefficiency where a particular woman's happiness depended on him, with the belief in Woman Suffrage, which he early adopted and probably retained. Be that as it may, this part of his story points to something which runs through his whole character, something which perhaps may be expressed by saying that the natural bias of his qualities was towards the negative side. We hear, no doubt, of occasions when his vigour was instant and terrible—like that of Hamlet on the ship for England; but these were occasions when the right or the necessity of the case was obvious. We have seen him also firm and absolutely independent where his conviction had already been thought out. Where there was room for further reflection, for patiently waiting on events, or for taking counsel of wise friends, manly decision had not come easily to him. He had let a third person almost engage him to Miss Owens. Once in this relation to her, he had let it be the woman's part and not the man's to have decision enough for the two. Speed had to tell him that he must face Miss Todd and speak to her, and Speed again had to make clear to him what the effect of his speaking had been. In time he decided what he thought his own feelings were, but it was by inference from the feelings of Speed.

Lastly, it seems, the troubles of his married life were met by mere patience and avoidance. All this, of course, concerned a side of life's affairs in regard to which his mind had suffered painful shocks; but it shows the direction of his possible weakness and his possible strength in other things. It falls in with a trait which he himself noted in one of the letters to Speed: "I have no doubt," he writes, "it is the peculiar misfortune of both you and me to dream dreams of Elysium far exceeding all that anything earthly can realise." All such men have to go through deep waters; but they do not necessarily miss either success or happiness in the end. Lincoln's life may be said to have tested him by the test which Mr. Kipling states in his lines about Washington:—

"If you can dream—and not make dreams your master;

If you can think—and not make thoughts your aim."

He was to prove that he could do this; it is for the following pages to show in how high a degree. Meanwhile one thing should already be clear about him. No shrewd judge of men could read his letters to Speed with care and not feel that, whatever mistakes this man might commit, fundamentally he was worthy of entire trust. That, as a matter of fact, is what, to the end of his life, Speed and all the men who knew him and an ever widening circle of men who had to judge by more casual impressions did feel about Lincoln. Whatever was questionable in his private or public acts, his own explanation, if he happened to give one, would be taken by them as the full and naked truth, and, if there was no known explanation, it remained to them an irrebuttable presumption that his main intention was right.

CHAPTER IV

LINCOLN IN CONGRESS AND IN RETIREMENT

1. The Mexican War and Lincoln's Work in Congress.

Lincoln had ceased before his marriage to sit in the Illinois Legislature. He had won sufficient standing for his ambition to aim higher; a former law partner of his was now in Congress, and he wished to follow. But he had to submit to a few years' delay of which the story is curious and honourable. His rivals for the representation of his own constituency were two fellow Whigs, Baker and Hardin, both of whom afterwards bore distinguished parts in the Mexican war and with both of whom he was friendly. Somewhat to his disgust at a party gathering in his own county in 1843, Baker was preferred to him. A letter of his gives a shrewd account of the manoeuvres among members of various Churches which brought this about; it is curiously careful not to overstate the effect of these influences and characteristically denies that Baker had part in them. To make the thing harder, he was sent from this meeting to a convention, for the whole constituency, with which the nomination lay, and his duty, of course, was to work for Baker. Here it became obvious that Hardin would be chosen; nothing could be done for Baker at that time, but Lincoln, being against his will there in Baker's interests, took an opportunity in the bargaining that took place to advance Baker's claim, to the detriment of his own, to be Hardin's successor two years later.

By some perverse accident notes about details of party management fill a disproportionate space among those letters of Lincoln's which have been preserved, but these reveal that, with all his business-like attention to the affairs of his very proper ambition, he was able throughout to illuminate dull matters of this order with action of singular disinterestedness. After being a second time postponed, no doubt to the advantage of his law business, he took his seat in the House of Representatives at Washington for two years in the spring of 1847. Two short sessions can hardly suffice for mastering the very complicated business of that body. He made hardly any mark. He probably learned much and was able to study at leisure the characters of his brother politicians. He earned the valuable esteem of some, and seems to have passed as a very pleasant, honest, plain specimen of the rough West. Like others of the younger Congressmen, he had the privilege of breakfasting with Webster. His brief career in the House seems to have disappointed him, and it certainly dissatisfied his constituents. The part that he played may impress us more favourably than it did them, but, slight as it was, it requires a historical explanation.

Mexico had detached itself from Spain in 1826, and in 1833 the province of Texas detached itself from Mexico. Texas was largely peopled by immigrants from the States, and these had grievances. One of them was that Mexico abolished slavery, but there was real misgovernment as well, and, among other cruel incidents of the rebellion which followed, the massacre of rebels at the Alamo stamped itself on American memory. The Republic of Texas began to seek annexation to the United States in 1839, but there was opposition in the States and there were difficulties with Mexico and other Governments. At last in 1845, at the very close of his term of office, President Tyler got the annexation pushed through in defiance of the Whigs who made him President. Mexico broke off diplomatic relations, but peace could no doubt have been preserved if peace had been any object with the new President Polk or with the Southern leaders whose views he represented. They had set their eyes upon a further acquisition, larger even than Texas—California, and the whole of the territories, still belonging to Mexico, to the east of it. It is not contested, and would not have been contested then, that the motive of their policy was the Southern desire to win further soil for cultivation by slaves. But there was no great difficulty in gaining some popularity for their designs in the North. Talk about "our manifest destiny" to reach the Pacific may have been justly described by Parson Wilbur as "half on it ign'ance and t'other half rum," but it is easy to see how readily it might be taken up, and indeed many Northerners at that moment had a fancy of their own for expansion in the North-West and were not over-well pleased with Polk when, in 1846, he set the final seal upon the settlement with Great Britain of the Oregon frontier.

When he did this Polk had already brought about his own war. The judgment on that war expressed at the time in the first "Biglow Papers" has seldom been questioned since, and there seldom can have been a war so sternly condemned by soldiers—Grant amongst others—who fought in it gallantly. The facts seem to have been just as Lincoln afterwards recited them in Congress. The Rio Grande, which looks a reasonable frontier on a map, was claimed by the United States as the frontier of Texas. The territory occupied by the American settlers of Texas reached admittedly up to and beyond the River Nueces, east of the Rio Grande. But in a sparsely settled country, where water is not abundant, the actual border line, if there be any clear line, between settlement from one side and settlement from the other will not for the convenience of treaty-makers run along a river, but rather for the convenience of the settlers along the water-parting between two rivers. So Mexico claimed both banks of the Rio Grande and Spanish settlers inhabited both sides. Polk ordered General Zachary Taylor, who was allowed no discretion in the matter, to march troops right up to the Rio Grande and occupy a position commanding the encampment of the Mexican soldiers there. The Mexican commander, thus threatened, attacked. The

Mexicans had thus begun the war. Polk could thus allege his duty to prosecute it. When the whole transaction was afterwards assailed his critics might be tempted to go, or represented as going, upon the false ground that only Congress can constitutionally declare war—that is, of course, sanction purely offensive operations. Long, however, before the dispute could come to a head, the brilliant successes of General Taylor and still more of General Scott, with a few trained troops against large undisciplined numbers, put all criticism at a disadvantage. The City of Mexico was occupied by Scott in September, 1847, and peace, with the cession of the vast domain that had been coveted, was concluded in May, 1848.

War having begun, the line of the Whig opposition was to vote supplies and protest as best they might against the language endorsing Polk's policy which, in the pettiest spirit of political manoeuvre, was sometimes incorporated in the votes. In this Lincoln steadily supported them. One of his only two speeches of any length in Congress was made on the occasion of a vote of this kind in 1848. The subject was by that time so stale that his speech could hardly make much impression, but it appears to-day an extraordinarily clear, strong, upright presentment of the complex and unpopular case against the war. His other long speech is elevated above buffoonery by a brief, cogent, and earnest passage on the same theme, but it was a frank piece of clowning on a licensed occasion. It was the fashion for the House when its own dissolution and a Presidential election were both imminent to have a sort of rhetorical scrimmage in which members on both sides spoke for the edification of their own constituencies and that of Buncombe. The Whigs were now happy in having "diverted the war-thunder against the Democrats" by running for the Presidency General Taylor, a good soldier who did not know whether he was a Whig or a Democrat, but who, besides being a hero of the war, was inoffensive to the South, for he lived in Louisiana and had slaves of his own. It is characteristic of the time that the Democrats, in whose counsels the Southern men prevailed, now began a practice of choosing Northern candidates, and nominated General Cass of Michigan, whose distinction had not been won in war. The Democratic Congressmen in this debate made game of the Whigs, with their war-hero, and seem to have carried a crude manner of pleasantry pretty far when Lincoln determined to show them that they could be beaten at that game. He seems to have succeeded admirably, with a burlesque comparison, too long to quote, of General Cass's martial exploits with his own, and other such-like matter enhanced by the most extravagant Western manner and delivery.

Anyone who reads much of the always grave and sometimes most moving orations of Lincoln's later years may do well to turn back to this agreeable piece of debating-society horse-play. But he should then turn a few pages further back to Lincoln's little Bill for the gradual and compensated extinction of slavery in the District of Columbia, where Washington stands. He introduced this of his own motion, without encouragement from Abolitionist or Non-Abolitionist, accompanying it with a brief statement that he had carefully ascertained that the representative people of the district privately approved of it, but had no right to commit them to public support of it. It perished, of course. With the views which he had long formed and continued to hold about slavery, very few opportunities could in these years come to him of proper and useful action against it. He seized upon these opportunities not less because in doing so he had to stand alone.

His career as a Congressman was soon over. There was no movement to re-elect him, and the Whigs now lost his constituency. His speeches and his votes against the Mexican war offended his friends. Even his partner, the Abolitionist, Mr. Herndon, whose further acquaintance we have to make, was too much infected with the popularity of a successful war to understand Lincoln's plain position or to approve of his giving votes which might seem unpatriotic. Lincoln wrote back to him firmly but sadly. Persuaded as he was that political action in advance of public sentiment was idle, resigned and hardened as we might easily think him to many of the necessities of party discipline, it evidently caused him naive surprise that, when he was called upon for a definite opinion, anybody should expect him, as he candidly puts it, to "tell a lie."

As a retiring Congressman he was invited to speak in several places in the East on behalf of Taylor's candidature; and after

Taylor's election claimed his right as the proper person to be consulted, with certain others, about Government appointments in Illinois. Taylor carried out the "spoils system" with conscientious thoroughness; as he touchingly said, he had thought over the question from a soldier's point of view, and could not bear the thought that, while he as their chief enjoyed the Presidency, the private soldiers in the Whig ranks should not get whatever was going. Lincoln's attitude in the matter may be of interest. To take an example, he writes to the President, about the postmastership in some place, that he does not know whether the President desires to change the tenure of such offices on party grounds, and offers no advice; that A is a Whig whose appointment is much desired by the local Whigs, and a most respectable man; that B, also a Whig, would in Lincoln's judgment be a somewhat better but not so popular subject for appointment; that C, the present postmaster, is a Democrat, but is on every ground, save his political party, a proper person for the office. There was an office which he himself desired, it was that of "Commissioner of the General Land Office," a new office in Washington dealing with settlement on Government lands in the West.

He was probably well suited to it; but his application was delayed by the fact that friends in Illinois wanted the post too; a certain Mr. Butterfield (a lawyer renowned for his jokes, which showed, it is said, "at least a well-marked humorous intention") got it; and then it fell to the lot of the disappointed Lincoln to have to defend Butterfield against some unfair attack. But a tempting offer was made him, that of the Governorship of Oregon Territory, and he wavered before refusing to take work which would, as it happened, have kept him far away when the opportunity of his life came. It was Mrs. Lincoln who would not let him cut himself off so completely from politics. As for himself, it is hard to resist the impression that he was at this time a tired man, disappointed as to the progress of his career and probably also disappointed and somewhat despondent about politics and the possibilities of good service that lay open to politicians. It may be that this was partly the reason why he was not at all aroused by the crisis in American politics which must now be related.

2. California and the Compromise of 1850.

It has been said that the motive for the conquests from Mexico was the desire for slave territory. The attractive part of the new dominion was of course California. Arizona and New Mexico are arid regions, and the mineral wealth of Nevada was unknown. The peacefully acquired region of Oregon, far north, need not concern us, but Oregon became a free State in 1859. Early in the war a struggle began between Northerners and Southerners (to a large extent independent of party) in the Senate and the House as to whether slavery should be allowed in the conquered land or not. David Wilmot, a Northern Democratic Congressman, proposed a proviso to the very first money grant connected with the war, that slavery should be forbidden in any territory to be annexed. The "Wilmot Proviso" was proposed again on every possible occasion; Lincoln, by the way, sturdily supported it while in Congress; it was always voted down. Cass proposed as a solution of all difficulties that the question of slavery should be left to the people of the new Territories or States themselves. The American public, apt as condensing an argument into a phrase, dismissed Cass's principle for the time being with the epithet "squatter sovereignty." Calhoun and his friends said it was contrary to the Constitution that an American citizen should not be free to move with his property, including his slaves, into territory won by the Union. The annexation was carried out, and the question of slavery was unsettled. Then events took a surprising turn.

In the winter of 1848 gold was discovered in California. Throughout 1849 gold-seekers came pouring in from every part of the world. This miscellaneous new people, whose rough ways have been more celebrated in literature than those of any similar crowd, lived at first in considerable anarchy, but they determined without delay to set up some regular system of government. In the course of 1849 they elected a Convention to draw up a State

Constitution, and to the astonishment of all the States the Convention unanimously made the prohibition of slavery part of that Constitution. There was no likelihood that, with a further influx of settlers of the same sort, this decision of California would alter. Was California to be admitted as a State with this Constitution of its own choice, which the bulk of the people of America approved?

To politicians of the school now fully developed in the South there seemed nothing outrageous in saying that it should be refused admission. To them Calhoun's argument, which regarded a citizen's slave as his chattel in the same sense as his hat or walking-stick, seemed the ripe fruit of logic. It did not shock them in the least that they were forcing the slave system on an unwilling community, for were not the Northerners prepared to force the free system? A prominent Southern Senator, talking with a Northern colleague a little later, said triumphantly: "I see how it is. You may force freedom as much as you like, but we are to beware how we force slavery," and was surprised that the Northerner cheerfully accepted this position. It is necessary to remember throughout the following years that, whatever ordinary Southerners thought in private, their whole political action was now based on the assumption that slavery, as it was, was an institution which no reasonable man could think wrong.

Zachary Taylor, unlike Harrison, the previous hero of the Whigs, survived his inauguration by sixteen months. He was no politician at all, but placed in the position of President, for which fairness and firmness were really the greatest qualifications, he was man enough to rely on his own good sense. He had come to Washington under the impression that the disputes which raged there were due to the aggressiveness of the North; a very little time there convinced him of the contrary. Slave-owner as he was, the claim of the South to force slavery on California struck him as an arrogant pretension, and so far as matters rested with him, he was simply not to be moved by it. He sent a message to Congress advising the admission of California with the constitution of its own choice. When, as we shall shortly see, the great men of the Senate thought the case demanded conciliation and a great scheme of compromise, he resolutely disagreed; he used the whole of his influence against their compromise, and it is believed with good reason that he would have put his veto as President on the chief measure in which the compromise issued. If he had lived to carry out his policy, it seems possible that there would have been an attempt to execute the threats of secession which were muttered—this time in Virginia. But it is almost certain that at that time, and with the position which he occupied, he would have been able to quell the movement at once. There is nothing to suggest that Taylor was a man of any unusual gifts of intellect, but he had what we may call character, and it was the one thing wanting in political life at the time. The greatest minds in American politics, as we shall see, viewed the occasion otherwise, but, in the light of what followed, it seems a signal and irreparable error that, when the spirit of aggression rising in the South had taken definite shape in a demand which was manifestly wrongful, it was bought off and not met with a straightforward refusal. Taylor died in the course of 1850 and Vice-President Millard Fillmore, of New York, succeeded him. Fillmore had an appearance of grave and benign wisdom which led a Frenchman to describe him as the ideal ruler of a Republic, but he was a pattern of that outwardly dignified, yet nerveless and heartless respectability, which was more dangerous to America at that period than political recklessness or want of scruple.

The actual issue of the crisis was that the admission of California was bought from the South by large concessions in other directions. This was the proposal of Henry Clay, who was now an old man anxious for the Union, but had been a lover of such compromises ever since he promoted the Missouri Compromise thirty years ago; but, to the savage indignation of some of his Boston admirers, Webster used the whole force of his influence and debating power in support of Clay. The chief concessions made to the South were two. In the first place Territorial Governments were set up in New Mexico and Utah (since then the home of the Mormons) without any restriction on slavery. This concession was defended in the North on the ground that it was a sham, because the physical character of those regions made successful slave plantations impossible there. But it was, of course, a surrender of the principle which had been struggled for in the Wilmot Proviso during the last four years; and the Southern leaders showed the clearness of their limited vision by valuing it just upon that ground. There had been reason for the territorial concessions to slavery in the past generation because it was established in the territories concerned; but there was no such reason now. The second concession was that of a new Federal law to ensure the return of fugitive slaves from the free States. The demand for this was partly factitious, for the States in the far South, which were not exposed to loss of slaves, were the most insistent on it, and it would appear that the Southern leaders felt it politic to force the acceptance of the measure in a form which would humiliate their opponents. There is no escape from the contention, which Lincoln especially admitted without reserve, that the enactment of an effective Act of this sort was, if demanded, due under the provisions of the Constitution; but the measure actually passed was manifestly defiant of all principles of justice. It was so framed as almost to destroy the chance which a lawfully free negro might have of proving his freedom, if arrested by the professional slave-hunters as a runaway. It was the sort of Act which a President should have vetoed as a fraud upon the Constitution. Thus over and above the objection, now plain, to any compromise, the actual compromise proposed was marked by flagrant wrong. But it was put through by the weight of Webster and Clay.

This event marks the close of a period. It was the last achievement of Webster and Clay, both of whom passed away in 1852 in the hope that they had permanently pacified the Union. Calhoun, their great contemporary, had already died in 1850, gloomily presaging and lamenting the coming danger to the Union which was so largely his own creation. For a while the cheerful view of Webster and Clay seemed better justified. There had been angry protest in the North against the Fugitive Slave Law; there was some forcible resistance to arrests of negroes; and some States passed Protection of Liberty Acts of their own to impede the Federal law in its working. But the excitement, which had flared up suddenly, died down as suddenly. In the Presidential election of 1852 Northerners generally reflected that they wanted quiet and had an instinct, curiously falsified, that the Democratic party was the more likely to give it them. The Whigs again proposed a hero, General Scott, a greater soldier than Taylor, but a vainer man, who mistakenly broke with all precedent and went upon the stump for himself. The President who was elected, Franklin Pierce of New Hampshire, a friend of Hawthorne, might perhaps claim the palm among the Presidents of those days, for sheer, deleterious insignificance. The favourite observation of his contemporaries upon him was that he was a gentleman, but his convivial nature made the social attractiveness of Southern circles in Washington overpowering to any brain or character that he may have possessed. A new generation of political personages now came to the front. Jefferson Davis of Mississippi, a man of force and considerable dignity, began to take the leading part in the powerful group of Southern Senators; Stephen Douglas, of Illinois, rapidly became the foremost man of the Democratic party generally; William Seward, late Governor of New York, and Salmon Chase, a Democrat, late Governor of Ohio, had played a manful part in the Senate in opposition to Webster and Clay and their compromise. From this time on we must look on these two, joined a little later by Charles Sumner, of Massachusetts, as the obvious leaders in the struggle against slavery which was shortly to be renewed, and in which Lincoln's part seemed likely to remain a humble one.

3. Lincoln in Retirement.

Whether Seward and Chase and the other opponents of the Compromise were right, as it now seems they were, or not, Lincoln was not the man who in the unlooked-for crisis of 1850 would have been likely to make an insurrectionary stand against his old party-leader Clay, and the revered constitutional authority of Webster. He had indeed little opportunity to do so in Illinois, but his one recorded speech of this period, an oration to a meeting of both parties on the death of Clay in 1852, expresses approval of the Compromise. This speech, which is significant of the trend of his thoughts at this time, does not lend itself to brief extracts because it is wanting in the frankness of his speeches before and after. A harsh reference to Abolitionists serves to disguise the fact that the whole speech is animated by antagonism to slavery. The occasion and the subject are used with rather disagreeable subtlety to insinuate opposition to slavery into the minds of a cautious audience. The speaker himself seems satisfied with the mood of mere compromise which had governed Clay in this matter, or rather perhaps he is twisting Clay's attitude into one of more consistent opposition to slavery than he really showed. In any case we can be quite sure that the moderate and subtle but intensely firm opinion with which a little later Lincoln returned to political strife was the product of long and deep and anxious thought during the years from 1849 to 1854. On the surface it did not go far beyond the condemnation of slavery and acceptance of the Constitution which had guided him earlier, nor did it seem to differ from the wide-spread public opinion which in 1854 created a new party; but there was this difference that Lincoln had by then looked at the matter in all its bearings, and prepared his mind for all eventualities. We shall find, and need not be surprised to find, that he who now hung back a little, and who later moved when public opinion moved, later still continued to move when public opinion had receded.

What we know of these years of private life is mainly due to Mr. William Herndon, the young lawyer already quoted, whom he took into partnership in 1845, and who kept on the business of the firm in Springfield till Lincoln's death. This gentleman was, like Boswell, of opinion that a great man is not best portrayed as a figure in a stained-glass window. He had lived with Lincoln, groaned under his odd ways, and loved them, for sixteen years before his Presidency, and after his death he devoted much research, in his own memory and those of many others, to the task of substituting for Lincoln's aureole the battered tall hat, with valuable papers stuck in its lining, which he had long contemplated with reverent irritation. Mr. Herndon was not endowed with Boswell's artistic gift for putting his materials together, perhaps because he lacked that delicacy and sureness of moral perception which more than redeemed Boswell's absurdities. He succeeded on the whole in his aim, for the figure that more or less distinctly emerges from the litter of his workshop is lovable; but in spite of all Lincoln's melancholy, the dreariness of his life, sitting with his feet on the table in his unswept and untidy office at Illinois, or riding on circuit or staying at ramshackle western inns with the Illinois bar, cannot have been so unrelieved as it is in Mr. Herndon's presentation. And Herndon overdid his part. He ferreted out petty incidents which he thought might display the acute Lincoln as slightly too acute, when for all that can be seen Lincoln acted just as any sensible man would have acted. But the result is that, in this part of his life especially, Lincoln's way of living was subjected to so close a scrutiny as few men have undergone.

Herndon's scrutiny does not reveal the current of his thoughts either on life generally or on the political problem which hereafter was to absorb him. It shows on the contrary, and the recollections of his Presidency confirm it, that his thought on any important topic though it might flash out without disguise in rare moments of intimacy, usually remained long unexpressed. His great sociability had perhaps even then a rather formidable side to it. He was not merely amusing himself and other people, when he chatted and exchanged anecdotes far into the night; there was an element, not ungenial, of purposeful study in it all. He was building up his knowledge of ordinary human nature, his insight into popular feeling, his rather slow but sure comprehension of the individual men whom he did know. It astonished the self-improving young Herndon that the serious books he read were few and that he seldom seemed to read the whole of them—though with the Bible, Shakespeare, and to a less extent Burns, he saturated his mind. The few books and the great many men were part of one study. In so far as his thought and study turned upon politics it seems to have led him soon to the conclusion that he had for the present no part to play that was worth playing. By 1854, as he said himself, "his profession as a lawyer had almost superseded the thought of politics in his mind." But it does not seem that the melancholy sense of some great purpose unachieved or some great destiny awaiting him ever quite left him. He must have felt that his chance of political fame was in all appearance gone, and would have liked to win himself a considerable position and a little (very little) money as a lawyer; but the study, in the broadest sense, of which these years were full, evidently contemplated a larger education of himself as a man than professional keenness, or any such interest as he had in law, will explain. Middle-aged and from his own point of view a failure, he was set upon making himself a bigger man.

In some respects he let himself be. His exterior oddities never seem to have toned down much; he could not be taught to introduce tidiness or method into his office; nor did he make himself an exact lawyer; a rough and ready familiarity with practice and a firm grasp of larger principles of law contented him without any great apparatus of learning. His method of study was as odd as anything else about him; he could read hard and commit things to memory in the midst of bustle and noise; on the other hand, since reading aloud was his chosen way of impressing what he read on his own mind, he would do it at all sorts of times to the sore distraction of his partner. When his studies are spoken of, observation and thought on some plan concealed in his own mind must be taken to have formed the largest element in these studies. There was, however, one methodic discipline, highly commended of old but seldom perhaps seriously pursued with the like object by men of forty, even self-taught men, which he did pursue. Some time during these years he mastered the first six Books of Euclid. It would probably be no mere fancy if we were to trace certain definite effects of this discipline upon his mind and character. The faculty which he had before shown of reducing his thought on any subject to the simplest and plainest terms possible, now grew so strong that few men can be compared with him in this. He was gaining, too, from some source, what the ancient geometers would themselves have claimed as partly the product of their study: the plain fact and its plain consequences were not only clear in calm hours of thought, but remained present to him, felt and instinctive, through seasons of confusion, passion, and dismay. His life in one sense was very full of companionship, but it is probable that in his real intellectual interests he was lonely. To Herndon, intelligently interested in many things, his master's mind, much as he held it in awe, seemed chillingly unpoetic – which is a curious view of a mind steeped in Shakespeare and Burns. The two partners had been separately to Niagara. Herndon was anxious to know what had been Lincoln's chief impression, and was pained by the reply, "I wondered where all that water came from," which he felt showed materialism and insensibility. Lincoln's thought had, very obviously, a sort of poetry of its own, but of a vast and rather awful kind. He had occasionally written verses of his own a little before this time; sad verses about a friend who had become a lunatic, wondering that he should be allowed to outlive his mind while happy young lives passed away, and sad verses about a visit to old familiar fields in Indiana, where he wandered brooding, as he says,

"Till every sound appears a knell,
And every spot a grave."

They are not great poetry; but they show a correct ear for verse, and they are not the verses of a man to whom any of the familiar forms of poetic association were unusual. They are those of a man in whom the habitual undercurrent of thought was melancholy.

Apart from these signs and the deep, humorous delight which he evidently took in his children, there may be something slightly forbidding in this figure of a gaunt man, disappointed in ambition and not even happy at home, rubbing along through a rather rough crowd, with uniform rough geniality and perpetual jest; all the while in secret forging his own mind into an instrument for some vaguely foreshadowed end. But there are two or three facts which stand out certain and have to be taken account of in any image we may be tempted to form of him. In the first place, his was no forbidding figure at the time to those who knew him; a queer and a comic figure evidently, but liked, trusted, and by some loved; reputed for honest dealing and for kindly and gentle dealing; remarked too by some at that time, as before and ever after, for the melancholy of his face in repose; known by us beyond doubt to have gone through great pain; known lastly among his fellows in his profession for a fire of anger that flashed out only in the presence of cruelty and wrong.

His law practice, which he pursued with energy, and on which he was now, it seems, prepared to look as his sole business in life, fitted in none the less well with his deliberately adopted schemes of self-education. A great American lawyer, Mr. Choate, assures us that at the Illinois bar in those days Lincoln had to measure himself against very considerable men in suits of a class that required some intellect and training. And in his own way he held his own among these men. A layman may humbly conjecture that the combination in one person of the advocate and the solicitor must give opportunities of far truer intellectual training than the mere advocate can easily enjoy. The Illinois advocate was not all the time pleading the cause which he was employed to plead, and which if it was once offered to him it was his duty to accept; he was the personal adviser of the client whose cause he pleaded, and within certain limits he could determine whether the cause was brought at all, and if so whether he should take it up himself or leave it to another man. The rule in such matters was elastic and practice varied. Lincoln's practice went to the very limit of what is permissible in refusing legal aid to a cause he disapproved. Coming into court he discovered suddenly some fact about his case which was new to him but which would probably not have justified an English barrister in throwing up his brief. The case was called; he was absent; the judge sent to his hotel and got back a message: "Tell the judge I'm washing my hands." One client received advice much to this effect: "I can win your case; I can get you $600. I can also make an honest family miserable. But I shall not take your case, and I shall not take your fee. One piece of advice I will give you gratis: Go home and think seriously whether you cannot make $600 in some honest way."

And this habit of mind was beyond his control. Colleagues whom he was engaged to assist in cases agreed that if a case lost his sympathy he became helpless and useless in it. This, of course, was not the way to make money; but he got along and won a considerable local position at the bar, for his perfect honesty in argument and in statement of fact was known to have won the confidence of the judges, and a difficult case which he thought was right elicited the full and curious powers of his mind. His invective upon occasion was by all accounts terrific. An advocate glanced at Lincoln's notes for his speech, when he was appearing against a very heartless swindler and saw that they concluded with the ominous words, "Skin Defendant." The vitriolic outburst which occurred at the point thus indicated seems to have been long remembered by the Illinois bar. To a young man who wished to be a lawyer yet shrunk from the profession lest it should necessarily involve some dishonesty Lincoln wrote earnestly and wisely, showing him how false his impression of the law was, but concluding with earnest entreaty that he would not enter the profession if he still had any fear of being led by it to become a knave.

One of his cases is interesting for its own sake, not for his part in it. He defended without fee the son of his old foe and friend Jack Armstrong, and of Hannah, who mended his breeches, on a charge of murder. Six witnesses swore that they had seen him do the deed about 11 P.M. on such and such a night. Cross-examined: They saw it all quite clearly; they saw it so clearly because of the moonlight. The only evidence for the defence was an almanac. There had been no moon that night. Another case is interesting for his sake. Two young men set up in a farm together, bought a waggon and team from a poor old farmer, Lincoln's client, did not pay him, and were sued. They had both been just under twenty-one when they contracted the debt, and they were advised to plead infancy. A stranger who was present in Court described afterwards his own indignation as the rascally tale was unfolded, and ABRAHAM LINCOLNhis greater indignation as he watched the locally famous Mr. Lincoln, lying back in his seat, nodding complacently and saying, "I reckon that's so," as each of the relevant facts was produced, and the relevant Statute read and expounded. At last, as the onlooker proceeded to relate, the time came for Lincoln to address the jury, with whom, by Illinois law, the issue still rested. Slowly he disengaged his long, lean form from his seat, and before he had got it drawn out to its height he had fixed a gaze of extraordinary benevolence on the two disgraceful young defendants and begun in this strain: "Gentlemen of the Jury, are you prepared that these two young men shall enter upon life and go through life with the stain of a dishonourable transaction for ever affixed to them," and so forth at just sufficient length and with just enough of Shakespearean padding about honour. The result with that emotional and probably irregular Western court is obvious, and the story concludes with the quite credible assertion that the defendants themselves were relieved. Any good jury would, of course, have been steeled against the appeal, which might have been expected, to their compassion for a poor and honest old man. A kind of innocent and benign cunning has been the most engaging quality in not a few great characters. It is tempting, though at the risk of undue solemnity, to look for the secret of Lincoln's cunning in this instance. We know from copybooks and other sources that these two young men, starting on the down grade with the help of their blackguardly legal adviser, were objects for pity, more so than the man who was about to lose a certain number of dollars. Lincoln, as few other men would have done, felt a certain actual regret for them then and there; he felt it so naturally that he knew the same sympathy could be aroused, at least in twelve honest men who already wished they could find for the plaintiff. It has often been remarked that the cause of his later power was a knowledge of the people's mind which was curiously but vitally bound up with his own rectitude.

Any attempt that we may make to analyse a subtle character and in some respects to trace its growth is certain to miss the exact mark. But it is in any case plain that Abraham Lincoln left political life in 1849, a praiseworthy self-made man with good sound views but with nothing much to distinguish him above many other such, and at a sudden call returned to political life in 1854 with a touch of something quite uncommon added to those good sound views.

4. The Repeal of the Missouri Compromise.

The South had become captive to politicians, personally reputable and of some executive capacity, who had converted its natural prejudice into a definite doctrine which was paradoxical and almost inconceivably narrow, and who, as is common in such instances of perversion and fanaticism, knew hardly any scruple in the practical enforcement of their doctrine. In the North, on the other hand, though there were some few politicians who were clever and well-intentioned, public opinion had no very definite character, and public men generally speaking were flabby. At such a time the sheer adventurer has an excellent field before him and perhaps has his appointed use.

Stephen Douglas, who was four years younger than Lincoln, had come to Illinois from the Eastern States just about the time when Lincoln entered the Legislature. He had neither money nor friends to start with, but almost immediately secured, by his extraordinary address in pushing himself, a clerkship in the Assembly. He soon became, like Lincoln, a lawyer and a legislator, but was on the Democratic side. He rapidly soared into regions beyond the reach of Lincoln, and in 1847 became a Senator for Illinois, where he later became Chairman of the Committee on Territories, and as such had to consider the question of providing for the government of the districts called Kansas and Nebraska, which lay west and north-west of Missouri, and from which slavery was excluded by the Missouri Compromise. He was what in England is called a "Jingo," and was at one time eager to fight this country for the possession of what is now British Columbia. His short figure gave an impression of abounding strength and energy which obtained him the nickname of "the little Giant." With no assignable higher quality, and with the blustering, declamatory, shamelessly fallacious and evasive oratory of a common demagogue, he was nevertheless an accomplished Parliamentarian, and imposed himself as effectively upon the Senate as he did upon the people of Illinois and the North generally. He was, no doubt, a remarkable man, with the gift of attracting many people. A political opponent has described vividly how at first sight he was instantly repelled by the sinister and dangerous air of Douglas' scowl; a still stronger opponent, but a woman, Mrs. Beecher Stowe, seems on the contrary to have found it impossible to hate him. What he now did displayed at any rate a sporting quality.

In the course of 1854 Stephen Douglas while in charge of an inoffensive Bill dealing with the government of Kansas and Nebraska converted it into a form in which it empowered the people of Kansas at any time to decide for themselves whether they would permit slavery or not, and in express terms repealed the Missouri Compromise. With the easy connivance of President Pierce and the enthusiastic support of the Southerners, and by some extraordinary exercise of his art as demagogue and

Parliamentarian, he triumphantly ran this measure through.

Just how it came about seems to be rather obscure, but it is easy to conjecture his motives. Trained in a school in which scruple or principle were unknown and the man who arrives is the great man, Douglas, like other such adventurers, was accessible to visions of a sort. He cared nothing whether negroes were slaves or not, and doubtless despised Northern and Southern sentiment on that subject equally; as he frankly said once, on any question between white men and negroes he was on the side of the white men, and on any question between negroes and crocodiles he would be on the side of the negroes. But he did care for the development of the great national heritage in the West, that subject of an easy but perfectly wholesome patriotic pride with which we are familiar. It must have been a satisfaction to him to feel that North and South would now have an equal chance in that heritage, and also that the white settlers in the West would be relieved of any restriction on their freedom. None the less his action was to the last degree reckless. The North had shown itself ready in 1850 to put up with a great deal of quiet invasion of its former principle, but to lay hands upon the sacred letter of the Act in which that principle was enshrined was to invite exciting consequences.

The immediate consequences were two-fold. In the first place Southern settlers came pouring into Kansas and Northern settlers in still larger numbers (rendered larger still by the help of an emigration society formed in the North-East for that purpose) came pouring in too. It was at first a race to win Kansas for slavery or for freedom. When it became apparent that freedom was winning easily, the race turned into a civil war between these two classes of immigrants for the possession of the Territorial government, and this kept on its scandalous and bloody course for three or four years.

In the second place there was a revolution in the party system. The old Whig party, which, whatever its tendencies, had avoided having any principle in regard to slavery, now abruptly and opportunely expired. There had been an attempt once before, and that time mainly among the Democrats, to create a new "Free-soil Party," but it had come to very little. This time a permanent fusion was accomplished between the majority of the former Whigs in the North and a numerous secession from among the Northern Democrats. They created the great Republican party, of which the name and organisation have continued to this day, but of which the original principle was simply and solely that there should be no further extension of slavery upon territory present or future of the United States. It naturally consisted of Northerners only. This was of course an ominous fact, and caused people, who were too timid either to join the Republicans or turn Democrat, to take refuge in another strange party, formed about this time, which had no views about slavery. This was the "American" party, commonly called the "Know-Nothing" party from its ridiculous and objectionable secret organisation. Its principle was dislike of foreign immigrants, especially such as were Roman Catholics. To them ex-President Fillmore, protesting against "the madness of the times" when men ventured to say yes or no on a question relating to slavery, fled for comfort, and became their candidate for the Presidency at the next election.

It was in 1854 that Lincoln returned to political life as one of the founders of the Republican party. But it will be better at once to deal with one or two later events with which he was not specially concerned. The Republicans chose as their Presidential candidate in 1856 an attractive figure, John Fremont, a Southerner of French origin, who had conducted daring and successful explorations in Oregon, had some hand (perhaps a very important hand) in conquering California from Mexico, and played a prominent part in securing California for freedom. The Southern Democrats again secured a Northern instrument in James Buchanan of Pennsylvania, an elderly and very respectable man, who was understood to be well versed in diplomatic and official life. He was a more memorable personage than Pierce. A great chorus of friendly witnesses to his character has united in ascribing all his actions to weakness.

Buchanan was elected; but for a brand-new party the Republicans had put up a very good fight, and they were in the highest of spirits when, shortly after Buchanan's Inauguration in 1857, a staggering blow fell upon them from an unexpected quarter. This was nothing less than a pronouncement by the Chief Justice and a majority of Justices in the Supreme Court of the United States, that the exclusion of slavery from any portion of the Territories, and therefore, of course, the whole aim and object of the Republicans, was, as Calhoun had contended eight or ten years before, unconstitutional.

Dred Scott was a Missouri slave whose misfortunes it is needless to compassionate, since, after giving his name to one of the most famous law cases in history, he was emancipated with his family by a new master into whose hands he had passed. Some time before the Missouri Compromise was repealed he had been taken by his master into Minnesota, as a result of which he claimed that he became, by virtue of the Missouri Compromise, a free man. His right to sue his master in a Federal Court rested on the allegation that he was now a citizen of Missouri, while his master was a citizen of another State. There was thus a preliminary question to be decided, Was he really a citizen, before the question, Was he a freeman, could arise at all. If the Supreme Court followed its established practice, and if it decided against his citizenship, it would not consider the question which interested the public, that of his freedom.

Chief Justice Roger Taney may be seen from the refined features of his portrait and the clear-cut literary style of his famous judgment to have been a remarkable man. He was now eighty-three, but in unimpaired intellectual vigour. In a judgment, with which five of his colleagues entirely concurred and from which only two dissented, he decided that Dred Scott was not a citizen, and went on, contrary to practice, to pronounce, in what was probably to be considered as a mere _obiter dictum_, that Dred Scott was not free, because the Missouri Compromise had all along been unconstitutional and void. Justices McLean and Curtis, especially the latter, answered Taney's arguments in cogent judgments, which it seems generally to be thought were right. Many lawyers thought so then, and so did the prudent Fillmore. This is one of the rare cases where a layman may have an opinion on a point of law, for the argument of Taney was entirely historical and rested upon the opinion as to negroes and slavery which he ascribed to the makers of the Constitution and the authors of the Declaration of Independence. On the question of Scott's citizenship he laid down that these men had hardly counted Africans as human at all, and used words such as "men," "persons," "citizens" in a sense which necessarily excluded the negro. We have seen already that he was wrong—the Southern politician who called the words of the Declaration of Independence "a self-evident lie" was a sounder historian than Taney; but an amazing fact is to be added: the Constitution, whose authors, according to Taney, could not conceive of a negro as a citizen, was actually the act of a number of States in several of which negroes were exercising the full rights of citizens at the time. It would be easy to bring almost equally plain considerations to bear against the more elaborate argument of Taney that the Missouri Compromise was unconstitutional, but it is enough to say this much: the first four Presidents—that is, all the Presidents who were in public life when the Constitution was made—had all acted unhesitatingly upon the belief that Congress had the power to allow or forbid slavery in the Territories. The fifth, John Quincy Adams, when he set his hand to Acts involving this principle, had consulted before doing so the whole of his Cabinet on this constitutional point and had signed such legislation with the full concurrence of them all. Even Polk had acted later upon the same view. The Dred Scott judgment would thus appear to show the penetrating power at that time of an altogether fantastic opinion.

The hope, which Taney is known to have entertained, that his judgment would compose excited public opinion, was by no means fulfilled. It raised fierce excitement. What practical effect would hereafter be given to the opinion of six out of the nine judges in that Court might depend on many things. But to the Republicans, who appealed much to antiquity, it was maddening to be thus assured that their whole "platform" was unconstitutional. In the long run, there seems to be no doubt that Taney helped the cause of freedom. He had tried to make evident the personal sense of compassion for "these unfortunate people" with which he contemplated the opinion that he ascribed to a past generation; but he failed to do this, and instead he succeeded in imparting to the supposed Constitutional view of the slave, as nothing but a chattel, a horror which went home to many thousands of the warm-hearted men and women of his country.

For the time, however, the Republicans were deeply depressed, and a further perplexity shortly befell them. An attempt, to which we must shortly return, was made to impose the slave system on Kansas against the now unmistakable will of the majority there. Against this attempt Douglas, in opposition to whom the Republican party had been formed, revolted to his lasting honour, and he now stood out for the occasion as the champion of freedom. It was at this late period of bewilderment and confusion that the life-story of Abraham Lincoln became one with the life-story of the American people.

CHAPTER V

THE RISE OF LINCOLN

1. Lincoln's Return to Public Life.

We possess a single familiar letter in which Lincoln opened his heart about politics. It was written while old political ties were not yet quite broken and new ties not quite knit, and it was written to an old and a dear friend who was not his political associate. We may fittingly place it here, as a record of the strong and conflicting feelings out of which his consistent purpose in this crisis was formed.

"24 August, 1855.

"To JOSHUA SPEED.

"You know what a poor correspondent I am. Ever since I received your very agreeable letter of the 22nd I have been intending to write you an answer to it. You suggest that in political action, now, you and I would differ. I suppose we would; not quite so much, however, as you may think. You know I dislike slavery, and you fully admit the abstract wrong of it. So far there is no cause of difference. But you say that sooner than yield your legal right to the slave, especially at the bidding of those who are not themselves interested, you would see the Union dissolved. I am not aware that any one is bidding you yield that right; very certainly I am not. I leave that matter entirely to yourself. I also acknowledge your rights and my obligations under the Constitution in regard to your slaves. I confess I hate to see the poor creatures hunted down and caught and carried back to their stripes and unrequited toil; but I bite my lips and keep quiet. In 1841 you and I had together a tedious low-water trip on a steamboat from Louisville to St. Louis. You may remember, as I well do, that from Louisville to the mouth of the Ohio there were on board ten or a dozen slaves shackled together with irons. That sight was a continual torment to me, and I see something like it every time I touch the Ohio or any other slave border. It is not fair for you to assume that I have no interest in a thing which has, and continually exercises, the power to make me miserable. You ought rather to appreciate how much the great body of the Northern people do crucify their feelings, in order to maintain their loyalty to the Constitution and the Union. I do oppose the extension of slavery because my judgment and feelings so prompt me, and I am under no obligations to the contrary. If for this you and I must differ, differ we must. . . .

"You say that if Kansas fairly votes herself a free State, as a Christian you will rejoice at it. All decent slave holders talk that way and I do not doubt their candour. But they never vote that way. Although in a private letter or conversation you will express your preference that Kansas shall be free, you will vote for no man for Congress who would say the same thing publicly. No such man could be elected from any district in a slave State. . . . The slave breeders and slave traders are a small, odious and detested class among you; and yet in politics they dictate the course of all of you, and are as completely your masters as you are the masters of your own negroes.

"You inquire where I now stand. That is a disputed point. I think I am a Whig; but others say there are no Whigs, and that I am an Abolitionist. When I was at Washington I voted for the Wilmot Proviso as good as forty times; and I never heard of any one attempting to un-Whig me for that. I now do no more than oppose the extension of slavery. I am not a Know-Nothing, that is certain. How could I be? How can any one who abhors the oppression of negroes be in favour of degrading classes of white people? Our progress in degeneracy appears to me pretty rapid. As a nation we began by declaring that 'all men are created equal.' We now practically read it, 'all men are created equal, except negroes.' When the Know-Nothings get control, it will read, 'all men are created equal, except negroes and foreigners and Catholics.' When it comes to this, I shall prefer emigrating to some country where they make no pretence of loving liberty – to Russia, for instance, where despotism can be taken pure, and without the base alloy of hypocrisy.

"Mary will probably pass a day or two in Louisville in October. My kindest regards to Mrs. Speed. On the leading subject of this letter I have more of her sympathy than I have of yours; and yet let me say I am "Your friend forever,

"A. LINCOLN."

The shade of doubt which this letter suggests related really to the composition of political parties and the grouping of political forces, not in the least to the principles by which Lincoln's own actions would be guided. He has himself recorded that the repeal of the Missouri Compromise meant for him the sudden revival in a far stronger form of his interest in politics, and, we may add, of his political ambition. The opinions which he cherished most deeply demanded no longer patience but vehement action. The faculties of political organisation and of popular debate, of which he enjoyed the exercise, could now be used for a purpose which satisfied his understanding and his heart.

From 1854 onwards we find Lincoln almost incessantly occupied, at conventions, at public meetings, in correspondence, in secret consultation with those who looked to him for counsel, for the one object of strengthening the new Republican movement in his own State of Illinois, and, so far as opportunity offered, in the neighbouring States. Some of the best of his reported and the most effective of his unreported speeches were delivered between 1854 and 1858. Yet as large a part of his work in these years was done quietly in the background, and it continued to be his fate to be called upon to efface himself.

It is unnecessary to follow in any detail the labours by which he became a great leader in Illinois. It may suffice to pick out two instances that illustrate the ways of this astute, unselfish man. The first is very trifling and shows him merely astute. A Springfield newspaper called the _Conservative_ was acquiring too much influence as the organ of moderate and decent opinion that acquiesced in the extension of negro slavery. The Abolitionist, Mr. Herndon, was a friend of the editor. One day he showed Lincoln an article in a Southern paper which most boldly justified slavery whether the slaves were black or white. Lincoln observed what a good thing it would be if the pro-slavery papers of Illinois could be led to go this length. Herndon ingeniously used his acquaintance with the editor to procure that he should reprint this article with approval. Of course that promising journalistic venture, the _Conservative_, was at once ruined by so gross an indiscretion. This was hard on its confiding editor, and it is not to Lincoln's credit that he suggested or connived at this trick. But this trumpery tale happens to be a fair illustration of two things. In the first place a large part of Lincoln's activity went in the industrious and watchful performance of services to his cause, very seldom as questionable but constantly as minute as this, and in making himself as in this case confidant and adviser to a number of less notable workers. In the second place a biographer must set forth if he can the materials for the severest judgment on his subject, and in the case of a man whose fame was built on his honesty, but who certainly had an aptitude for ingenious tricks and took a humorous delight in them, this duty might involve a tedious examination of many unimportant incidents. It may save such discussion hereafter to say, as can safely be said upon a study of all the transactions in his life of which the circumstances are known, that this trick on the editor of the _Conservative_ marks the limit of Lincoln's deviation from the straight path. Most of us might be very glad if we had really never done anything much more dishonest.

Our second tale of this period is much more memorable. In 1856 the term of office of one of the Senators for Illinois came to an end; and there was a chance of electing an opponent of Douglas. Those of the Republicans of Illinois who were former Whigs desired the election of Lincoln, but could only secure it by the adhesion of a sufficient number of former Democrats and waverers. United States Senators were elected by the Legislatures of their own States through a procedure similar to that of the Conclave of Cardinals which elects a Pope; if there were several candidates and no one of them had an absolute majority of the votes first cast, the candidate with most votes was not elected; the voting was repeated, perhaps many times, till some one had an absolute majority; the final result was brought about by a transfer of votes from one candidate to another in which the prompt and cunning wire-puller had sometimes a magnificent opportunity for his skill. In this particular contest there were many ballots, and Lincoln at first led. His supporters were full of eager hope. Lincoln, looking on, discerned before any of them the setting in of an under-current likely to result in the election of a supporter of Douglas. He discerned, too, that the surest way to prevent this was for the whole of his friends immediately to go over to the Democrat, Lyman Trumbull, who was a sound opponent of slavery. He sacrificed his own chance instantly by persuading his supporters to do this. They were very reluctant, but he overbore them; one, a very old friend, records that he never saw him more earnest and decided. The same friend records, what is necessary to the appreciation of Lincoln's conduct, that his personal disappointment and mortification at his failure were great. Lincoln, it will be remembered, had acted just in this way when he sought election to the House of Representatives; he was to repeat this line of conduct in a manner at least as striking in the following year. Minute criticism of his action in many matters becomes pointless when we observe that his managing shrewdness was never more signally displayed than it was three times over in the sacrifice of his own personal chances.

For four years, it is to be remembered, the activity and influence of which we are speaking were of little importance beyond the boundaries of Illinois. It is true that at the Republican Convention in 1856 which chose Fremont as its candidate for the Presidency, Lincoln was exposed for a moment to the risk (for so it was to be regarded) of being nominated for the Vice-Presidency; but even his greatest speech was not noticed outside Illinois, and in the greater part of the Northern States his name was known to comparatively few and to them only as a local notability of the West. But in the course of 1858 he challenged the attention of the whole country. There was again a vacancy for a Senator for Illinois. Douglas was the sole and obvious candidate of the Democrats. Lincoln came forward as his opponent. The elections then pending of the State Legislature, which in its turn would elect a Senator, became a contest between Lincoln and Douglas. In the autumn of that year these rival champions held seven joint debates before mass meetings in the open air at important towns of Illinois, taking turns in the right of opening the debate and replying at its close; in addition each was speaking at meetings of his own at least once a day for three months. At the end of it all Douglas had won his seat in the Senate, and Lincoln had not yet gained recognition among the Republican leaders as one of themselves. Nevertheless the contest between Lincoln and Douglas was one of the decisive events in American history, partly from the mere fact that at that particular moment any one opposed Douglas at all; partly from the manner in which, in the hearing of all America, Lincoln formulated the issue between them; partly from the singular stroke by which he deliberately ensured his own defeat and certain further consequences.

2. The Principles and the Oratory of Lincoln.

We can best understand the causes which suddenly made him a man of national consequence by a somewhat close examination of the principles and the spirit which governed all his public activity from the moment of the repeal of the Missouri Compromise. The new Republican party which then began to form itself stood for what might seem a simple creed; slavery must be tolerated where it existed because the Constitution and the maintenance of the Union required it, but it must not be allowed to extend beyond its present limits because it was fundamentally wrong. This was what most Whigs and many Democrats in the North had always held, but the formulation of it as the platform of a party, and a party which must draw its members almost entirely from the North, was bound to raise in an acute form questions on which very few men had searched their hearts. Men who hated slavery were likely to falter and find excuses for yielding when confronted with the danger to the Union which would arise. Men who loved the Union might in the last resort be ready to sacrifice it if they could thereby be rid of complicity with slavery, or might be unwilling to maintain it at the cost of fratricidal war. The stress of conflicting emotions and the complications of the political situation were certain to try to the uttermost the faith of any Republican who was not very sure just how much he cared for the Union and how much for freedom, and what loyalty to either principle involved. It was the distinction of Lincoln—a man lacking in much of the knowledge which statesmen are supposed to possess, and capable of blundering and hesitation about details—first, that upon questions like these he was free from ambiguity of thought or faltering of will, and further, that upon his difficult path, amid bewildering and terrifying circumstances, he was able to take with him the minds of very many very ordinary men.

In a slightly conventional memorial oration upon Clay, Lincoln had said of him that "he loved his country, partly because it was his own country, and mostly because it was a free country." He might truly have said the like of himself. To him the national unity of America, with the Constitution which symbolised it, was the subject of pride and of devotion just in so far as it had embodied and could hereafter more fully embody certain principles of permanent value to mankind. On this he fully knew his own inner mind. For the preservation of an America which he could value more, say, than men value the Argentine Republic, he was to show himself better prepared than any other man to pay any possible price. But he definitely refused to preserve the Union by what in his estimation would have been the real surrender of the principles which had made Americans a distinct and self-respecting nation.

Those principles he found in the Declaration of Independence. Its rhetorical inexactitude gave him no trouble, and must not, now that its language is out of fashion, blind us to the fact that the founders of the United States did deliberately aspire to found a commonwealth in which common men and women should count for more than elsewhere, and in which, as we might now phrase it, all authority must defer somewhat to the interests and to the sentiments of the under dog. "Public opinion on any subject," he said, "always has a 'central idea' from which all its minor thoughts radiate. The 'central idea' in our public opinion at the beginning was, and till recently has continued to be, 'the equality of man'; and, although it has always submitted patiently to whatever inequality seemed to be a matter of actual necessity, its constant working has been a steady and progressive effort towards the practical equality of all men." The fathers, he said again, had never intended any such obvious untruth as that equality actually existed, or that any action of theirs could immediately create it; but they had set up a standard to which continual approximation could be made.

So far as white men were concerned such approximation had actually taken place; the audiences Lincoln addressed were fully conscious that very many thousands had found in the United States a scope to lead their own lives which the traditions and institutions no less than the physical conditions of their former countries had denied them. There was no need for him to enlarge on this fact; but there are repeated indications of the distaste and alarm with which he witnessed a demand that newcomers from Europe, or some classes of them, should be accorded lesser privileges than they had enjoyed.

But notions of freedom and equality as applied to the negroes presented a real difficulty. "There is," said Lincoln, "a natural disgust in the minds of nearly all white people at the idea of an indiscriminate amalgamation of the white and black men." (We might perhaps add that as the inferior race becomes educated and rises in status it is likely itself to share the same disgust.) Lincoln himself disliked the thought of intermarriage between the races. He by no means took it for granted that equality in political power must necessarily and properly follow upon emancipation. Schemes for colonial settlement of the negroes in Africa, or for gradual emancipation accompanied by educational measures, appealed to his sympathy. It was not given him to take a part in the settlement after the war, and it is impossible to guess what he would have achieved as a constructive statesman; but it is certain that he would have proceeded with caution and with the patience of sure faith; and he had that human sympathy with the white people of the South, and no less with the slaves themselves, which taught him the difficulty of the problem. But difficult as the problem was, one solution was certainly wrong, and that was the permanent acquiescence in slavery. If we may judge from reiteration in his speeches, no sophism angered him quite so much as the very popular sophism which defended slavery by presenting a literal equality as the real alternative to it. "I protest against the counterfeit logic which says that since I do not want a negro woman for my slave I must necessarily want her for my wife. I may want her for neither. I may simply let her alone. In some respects she is certainly not my equal. But in her natural right to eat the bread which she has earned by the sweat of her brow, she is my equal and the equal of any man."

The men who had made the Union had, as Lincoln contended, and in regard to most of them contended justly, been true to principle in their dealing with slavery. "They yielded to slavery," he insists, "what the necessity of the case required, and they yielded nothing more." It was, as we know, impossible for them in federating America, however much they might hope to inspire the new nation with just ideas, to take the power of legislating as to slavery within each existing State out of the hands of that State. Such power as they actually possessed of striking at slavery they used, as we have seen and as Lincoln recounted in detail, with all promptitude and almost to its fullest extent. They reasonably believed, though wrongly, that the natural tendency of opinion throughout the now freed Colonies with principles of freedom in the air would work steadily towards emancipation. "The fathers," Lincoln could fairly say, "place slavery, where the public mind could rest in the belief that it was in the course of ultimate extinction." The task for statesmen now was "to put slavery back where the fathers placed it."

Now this by no means implied that slavery in the States which now adhered to it should be exposed to attack from outside, or the slave owner be denied any right which he could claim under the Constitution, however odious and painful it might be, as in the case of the rendition of fugitive slaves, to yield him his rights. "We allow," says Lincoln, "slavery to exist in the slave States, not because it is right, but from the necessities of the Union. We grant a fugitive slave law because it is so 'nominated in the bond'; because our fathers so stipulated – had to – and we are bound to carry out this agreement." And the obligations to the slave owners and the slave States, which this original agreement and the fundamental necessities of the Union involved, must be fulfilled unswervingly, in spirit as well as in the letter. Lincoln was ready to give the slave States any possible guarantee that the Constitution should not be altered so as to take away their existing right of self-government in the matter of slavery. He had remained in the past coldly aloof from the Abolitionist propaganda when Herndon and other friends tried to interest him in it, feeling, it seems, that agitation in the free States against laws which existed constitutionally in the slave States was not only futile but improper. With all his power he dissuaded his more impulsive friends from lending any aid to forcible and unlawful proceedings in defence of freedom in Kansas. "The battle of freedom," he exclaims in a vehement plea for what may be called moderate as against radical policy, "is to be fought out on principle. Slavery is violation of eternal right. We have temporised with it from the necessities of our condition; but as sure as God reigns and school children read, that black foul lie can never be consecrated into God's hallowed truth." In other words, the sure way and the only way to combat slavery lay in the firm and the scrupulous assertion of principles which would carry the reason and the conscience of the people with them; the repeal of the prohibition of slavery in the Territories was a defiance of such principles, but so too in its way was the disregard by Abolitionists of the rights covenanted to the slave States. This side of Lincoln's doctrine is apt to jar upon us. We feel with a great American historian that the North would have been depraved indeed if it had not bred Abolitionists, and it requires an effort to sympathise with Lincoln's rigidly correct feeling – sometimes harshly expressed and sometimes apparently cold. It is not possible to us, as it was to him a little later, to look on John Brown's adventure merely as a crime. Nor can we wonder that, when he was President and Civil War was raging, many good men in the North mistook him and thought him half-hearted, because he persisted in his respect for the rights of the Slave

States so long as there seemed to be a chance of saving the Union in that way. It was his primary business, he then said, to save the Union if he could; "if I could save the Union by emancipating all the slaves I would do so; if I could save it by emancipating none of them, I would do it; if I could save it by emancipating some and not others, I would do that too." But, as in the letter at the beginning of this chapter he called Speed to witness, his forbearance with slavery cost him real pain, and we shall misread both his policy as President and his character as a man if we fail to see that in the bottom of his mind he felt this forbearance to be required by the very same principles which roused him against the extension of the evil. Years before, he had written to an Abolitionist correspondent that respect for the rights of the slave States was due not only to the Constitution but, "as it seems to me, in a sense to freedom itself." Negro slavery was not the only important issue, nor was it an isolated issue. What really was in issue was the continuance of the nation "dedicated," as he said on a great occasion, "to the proposition that all men are equal," a nation founded by the Union of self-governing communities, some of which lagged far behind the others in applying in their own midst the elementary principles of freedom, but yet a nation actuated from its very foundation in some important respects by the acknowledgment of human rights.

The practical policy, then, on which his whole efforts were concentrated consisted in this single point – the express recognition of the essential evil of slavery by the enactment that it should not spread further in the Territories subject to the Union. If slavery were thus shut up within a ring fence and marked as a wrong thing which the Union as a whole might tolerate but would not be a party to, emancipation in the slave States would follow in course of time. It would come about, Lincoln certainly thought, in a way far better for the slaves as well as for their masters, than any forced liberation. He was content to wait for it. "I do not mean that when it takes a turn towards ultimate extinction, it will be in a day, nor in a year, nor in two years. I do not suppose that in the most peaceful way ultimate extinction would occur in less than a hundred years at least, but that it will occur in the best way for both races in God's own good time I have no doubt." If we wonder whether this policy, if soon enough adopted by the Union as a whole, would really have brought on emancipation in the South, the best answer is that, when the policy did receive national sanction by the election of Lincoln, the principal slave States themselves instinctively recognised it as fatal to slavery.

For the extinction of slavery he would wait; for a decision on the principle of slavery he would not. It was idle to protest against agitation of the question. If politicians would be silent that would not get rid of "this same mighty deep-seated power that somehow operates on the minds of men, exciting them and stirring them up in every avenue of society – in politics, in religion, in literature, in morals, in all the manifold relations of life." The stand, temperate as it was, that he advocated against slavery should be taken at once and finally. The difference, of which people grown accustomed to slavery among their neighbours thought little, between letting it be in Missouri, which they could not help, and letting it cross the border into Kansas, which they could help, appeared to Lincoln the whole tremendous gulf between right and wrong, between a wise people's patience with ills they could not cure and a profligate people's acceptance of evil as their good. And here there was a distinction between Lincoln and many Republicans, which again may seem subtle, but which was really far wider than that which separated him from the Abolitionists. Slavery must be stopped from spreading into Kansas not because, as it turned out, the immigrants into Kansas mostly did not want it, but because it was wrong, and the United States, where they were free to act, would not have it. The greatest evil in the repeal of the Missouri Compromise was the laxity of public tone which had made it possible. "Little by little, but steadily as man's march to the grave, we have been giving up the old faith for the new faith."

Formerly some deference to the "central idea" of equality was general and in some sort of abstract sense slavery was admitted to be wrong.

Now it was boldly claimed by the South that "slavery in the abstract was right." All the most powerful influences in the country, "Mammon" (for "the slave property is worth a billion dollars"), "fashion, philosophy," and even "the theology of the day," were enlisted in favour of this opinion. And it met with no resistance. "You yourself may detest slavery; but your neighbour has five or six slaves, and he is an excellent neighbour, or your son has married his daughter, and they beg you to help save their property, and you vote against your interests and principle to oblige a neighbour, hoping your vote will be on the losing side." And again "the party lash and the fear of ridicule will overawe justice and liberty; for it is a singular fact, but none the less a fact and well known by the most common experience, that men will do things under the terror of the party lash that they would not on any account or for any consideration do otherwise; while men, who will march up to the mouth of a loaded cannon without shrinking, will run from the terrible name of 'Abolitionist,' even when pronounced by a worthless creature whom they with good reason despise." And so people in the North, who could hardly stomach the doctrine that slavery was good, yet lapsed into the feeling that it was a thing indifferent, a thing for which they might rightly shuffle off their responsibility on to the immigrants into Kansas. This feeling that it was indifferent Lincoln pursued and chastised with special scorn. But the principle of freedom that they were surrendering was the principle of freedom for themselves as well as for the negro. The sense of the negro's rights had been allowed to go back till the prospect of emancipation for him looked immeasurably worse than it had a generation before. They must recognise that when, by their connivance, they had barred and bolted the door upon the negro, the spirit of tyranny which they had evoked would then "turn and rend them." The "central idea" which had now established itself in the intellect of the Southern was one which favoured the enslavement of man by man "apart from colour." A definite choice had to be made between the principle of the fathers, which asserted certain rights for all men, and that other principle against which the fathers had rebelled and of which the "divine right of kings" furnished Lincoln with his example. In what particular manner the white people would be made to feel the principle of tyranny when they had definitely "denied freedom to others" and ceased to "deserve it for themselves" Lincoln did not attempt to say, and perhaps only dimly imagined. But he was as convinced as any prophet that America stood at the parting of the ways and must choose now the right principle or the wrong with all its consequences.

The principle of tyranny presented itself for their choice in a specious form in Douglas' "great patent, everlasting principle of 'popular sovereignty.'" This alleged principle was likely, so to say, to take upon their blind side men who were sympathetic to the impatience of control of any crowd resembling themselves but not sympathetic to humanity of another race and colour. The claim to some divine and indefeasible right of sovereignty overriding all other considerations of the general good, on the part of a majority greater or smaller at any given time in any given area, is one which can generally be made to bear a liberal semblance, though it certainly has no necessary validity. Americans had never before thought of granting it in the case of their outlying and unsettled dominions; they would never, for instance, as Lincoln remarked, have admitted the claim of settlers like the Mormons to make polygamy lawful in the territory they occupied. In the manner in which it was now employed the proposed principle could, as Lincoln contended, be reduced to this simple form "that, if one man chooses to enslave another, no third man shall have the right to object."

It is impossible to estimate how far Lincoln foresaw the strain to which a firm stand against slavery would subject the Union. It is likely enough that those worst forebodings for the Union, which events proved to be very true, were confined to timid men who made a practice of yielding to threats. Lincoln appreciated better than many of his fellows the sentiment of the South, but it is often hard for men, not in immediate contact with a school of thought which seems to them thoroughly perverse, to appreciate its pervasive power, and Lincoln was inclined to stake much upon the hope that reason will prevail. Moreover, he had a confidence in the strength of the Union which might have been justified if his predecessor in office had been a man of ordinary firmness. But it is not to be supposed that any undue hopefulness, if he felt it, influenced his judgment. He was of a temper which does not seek to forecast what the future has to show, and his melancholy prepared him well for any evil that might come. Two things we can say with certainty of his aim and purpose. On the one hand, as has already been said, whatever view he had taken of the peril to the Union he would never have sought to avoid the peril by what appeared to him a surrender of the principle which gave the Union its worth. On the other hand, he must always have been prepared to uphold the Union at whatever the cost might prove to be. To a man of deep and gentle nature war will always be hateful, but it can never, any more than an individual death, appear the worst of evils. And the claim of the Southern States to separate from a community which to him was venerable and to form a new nation, based on slavery and bound to live in discord with its neighbors, did not appeal to him at all, though in a certain literal sense it was a claim to liberty. His attitude to any possible movement for secession was defined four years at least before secession came, in words such as it was not his habit to use without full sense of their possible effect or without much previous thought. They were quite simple: "We won't break up the Union, and you shan't."

Such were the main thoughts which would be found to animate the whole of Lincoln's notable campaign, beginning with his first encounter with Douglas in 1855 and culminating in his prolonged duel with him in the autumn of 1858. It is unnecessary here to follow the complexities, especially in regard to the Dred Scott judgments, through which the discussion wandered. It is now worth few men's while to do more than glance at two or three of his speeches at that period; his speeches in the formal Lincoln-Douglas debates, except the first, are not the best of them. A scientific student of rhetoric, as the art by which man do actually persuade crowds, might indeed do well to watch closely the use by Douglas and Lincoln of their respective weapons, but for most of us it is an unprofitable business to read reiterated argument, even though in beautiful language, upon points of doubt that no longer trouble us. Lincoln does not always show to advantage; later readers have found him inferior in urbanity to Douglas, of whom he disapproved, while Douglas probably disapproved of no man; his speeches are, of course, not free either from unsound arguments or from the rough and tumble of popular debate; occasionally he uses hackneyed phrases; but it is remarkable that a hackneyed or a falsely sentimental phrase in Lincoln comes always as a lapse and a surprise. Passages abound in these speeches which to almost any literate taste are arresting for the simple beauty of their English, a beauty characteristic of one who had learned to reason with Euclid and learned to feel and to speak with the authors of the Bible. And in their own kind they were a classic and probably unsurpassed achievement. Though Lincoln had to deal with a single issue demanding no great width of knowledge, it must be evident that the passions aroused by it and the confused and shifting state of public sentiment made his problem very subtle, and it was a rare profundity and sincerity of thought which solved it in his own mind. In expressing the result of thought so far deeper than that of most men, he achieved a clearness of expression which very few writers, and those among the greatest, have excelled. He once during the Presidential election of 1856 wrote to a supporter of Fillmore to persuade him of a proposition which must seem paradoxical to anyone not deeply versed in American institutions, namely, that it was actually against Fillmore's interest to gain votes from Fremont in Illinois. He demonstrated his point, but he was not always judicious in his way of addressing solemn strangers, and in his rural manner he concludes his letter, "the whole thing is as simple as figuring out the weight of three small hogs," and this inelegant sentence conveys with little exaggeration one especial merit of his often austerely graceful language. Grave difficulties are handled in a style which could arouse all the interest of a boy and penetrate the understanding of a case-hardened party man.

But if in comparison with the acknowledged masterpieces of our prose we rank many passages in these speeches very high—and in fact the men who have appreciated them most highly have been fastidious scholars—we shall not yet have measured Lincoln's effort and performance. For these are not the compositions of a cloistered man of letters, they are the outpourings of an agitator upon the stump. The men who think hard are few; few of them can clothe their thought in apt and simple words; very, very few are those who in doing this could hold the attention of a miscellaneous and large crowd. Popular government owes that comparative failure, of which in recent times we have taken perhaps exaggerated notice, partly to the blindness of the polite world to the true difficulty and true value of work of this kind; and the importance which Roman education under the Empire gave to rhetoric was the mark not of deadness, but of the survival of a manly public spirit. Lincoln's wisdom had to utter itself in a voice which would reach the outskirts of a large and sometimes excited crowd in the open air. It was uttered in strenuous conflict with a man whose reputation quite overshadowed his; a person whose extraordinary and good-humoured vitality armed him with an external charm even for people who, like Mrs. Beecher Stowe, detested his principles; an orator whose mastery of popular appeal and of resourceful and evasive debate was quite unhampered by any weakness for the truth. The utterance had to be kept up day after day and night after night for a quarter of a year, by a man too poor to afford little comforts, travelling from one crowded inn to another, by slow trains on a railway whose officials paid little attention to him, while his more prosperous and distinguished rival could travel in comfort and comparative magnificence. The physical strain of electioneering, which is always considerable, its alternation of feverish excitement with a lassitude that, after a while, becomes prevailing and intense, were in this case far greater and more prolonged than in any other instance recorded of English or probably of American statesmen. If, upon his sudden elevation shortly afterwards, Lincoln was in a sense an obscure man raised up by chance, he was nevertheless a man who had accomplished a heroic labour.

On the whole the earthen vessel in which he carried his treasure of clear thought and clean feelings appears to have enhanced its flavour.

There was at any rate nothing outward about him that aroused the passion of envy. A few peculiarly observant men were immediately impressed with his distinction, but there is no doubt that to the ordinary stranger he appeared as a very odd fish. "No portraits that I have ever seen," writes one, "do justice to the awkwardness and ungainliness of his figure." Its movements when he began to speak rather added to its ungainliness, and, though to a trained actor his elocution seemed perfect, his voice when he first opened his mouth surprised and jarred upon the hearers with a harsh note of curiously high pitch. But it was the sort of oddity that arrests attention, and people's attention once caught was apt to be held by the man's transparent earnestness. Soon, as he lost thought of himself in his subject, his voice and manner changed; deeper notes, of which friends record the beauty, rang out, the sad eyes kindled, and the tall, gaunt figure, with the strange gesture of the long, uplifted arms, acquired even a certain majesty. Hearers recalled afterwards with evident sincerity the deep and instantaneous impression of some appeal to simple conscience, as when, "reaching his hands towards the stars of that still night," he proclaimed, "in some things she is certainly not my equal, but in her natural right to eat the bread that she has earned with the sweat of her brow, she is my equal, and the equal of Judge Douglas, and the equal of any man." Indeed, upon a sympathetic audience, already excited by the occasion, he could produce an effect which the reader of his recorded speeches would hardly believe. Of his speech at an early state convention of the Republican party there is no report except that after a few sentences every reporter laid down his pen for the opposite of the usual reason, and, as he proceeded, "the audience arose from their chairs and with pale faces and quivering lips pressed unconsciously towards him." And of his speech on another similar occasion several witnesses seem to have left descriptions hardly less incongruous with English experience of public meetings. If we credit him with these occasional manifestations of electric oratory—as to which it is certain that his quiet temperament did at times blaze out in a surprising fashion—it is not to be thought that he was ordinarily what could be called eloquent; some of his speeches are commonplace enough, and much of his debating with Douglas is of a drily argumentative kind that does honour to the mass meetings which heard it gladly. But the greatest gift of the orator he did possess; the personality behind the words was felt. "Beyond and above all skill," says the editor of a great paper who heard him at Peoria, "was the overwhelming conviction imposed upon the audience that the speaker himself was charged with an irresistible and inspiring duty to his fellow men."

One fact about the method of his speaking is easily detected. In debate, at least, he had no use for perorations, and the reader who looks for them will often find that Lincoln just used up the last few minutes in clearing up some unimportant point which he wanted to explain only if there was time for it. We associate our older Parliamentary oratory with an art which keeps the hearer pleasedly expectant rather than dangerously attentive, through an argument which if dwelt upon might prove unsubstantial, secure that it all leads in the end to some great cadence of noble sound. But in Lincoln's argumentative speeches the employment of beautiful words is least sparing at the beginning or when he passes to a new subject. It seems as if he deliberately used up his rhetorical effects at the outset to put his audience in the temper in which they would earnestly follow him and to challenge their full attention to reasoning which was to satisfy their calmer judgment. He put himself in a position in which if his argument were not sound nothing could save his speech from failure as a speech. Perhaps no standing epithet of praise hangs with such a weight on a man's reputation as the epithet "honest." When the man is proved not to be a fraud, it suggests a very mediocre virtue. But the method by which Lincoln actually confirmed his early won and dangerous reputation of honesty was a positive and potent performance of rare distinction. It is no mean intellectual and spiritual achievement to be as honest in speech with a crowd as in the dearest intercourse of life. It is not, of course, pretended that he never used a fallacious argument or made an unfair score—he was entirely human. But this is the testimony of an Illinois political wire-puller to Lincoln: "He was one of the shrewdest politicians in the State. Nobody had more experience in that way. Nobody knew better what was passing in the minds of the people. Nobody knew better how to turn things to advantage politically." And then he goes on—and this is really the sum of what is to be said of his oratory: "He could not cheat people out of their votes any more than he could out of their money."

3. Lincoln against Douglas.

It has now to be told how the contest with Douglas which concluded Lincoln's labours in Illinois affected the broad stream of political events in America as a whole. Lincoln, as we know, was still only a local personage; Illinois is a State bigger than Ireland, but it is only a little part and was still a rather raw and provincial part of the United States; but Douglas had for years been a national personage, for a time the greatest man among the Democrats, and now, for a reason which did him honour, he was in disgrace with many of his party and on the point of becoming the hero of all moderate Republicans.

We need not follow in much detail the events of the great political world. The repeal of the Missouri Compromise threw it into a ferment, which the continuing disorders in Kansas were in themselves sufficient to keep up. New great names were being made in debate in the Senate; Seward, the most powerful opponent of the repeal of the Missouri Compromise, kept his place as the foremost man in the Republican party not by consistency in the stand that he made, but by his mastery of New York political machinery; Sumner of Massachusetts, the friend of John Bright, kept up a continual protest for freedom in turgid, scholarly harangues, which caught the spirit of Cicero's Philippics most successfully in their personal offensiveness. Powerful voices in literature and the Press were heard upon the same side – the New York Tribune_, edited by Horace Greeley, acquired, as far as a paper in so large a country can, a national importance. Broadly it may be said that the stirring intellect of America old and young was with the Republicans – it is a pleasant trifle to note that Longfellow gave up a visit to Europe to vote for Fremont as President, and we know the views of Motley and of Lowell and of Darwin's fellow labourer Asa Gray. But fashion and that better and quite different influence, the tone of opinion prevailing in the pleasantest society, inclined always to the Southern view of every question, and these influences were nowhere more felt than among Washington politicians. A strong and respectable group of Southern Senators, of whom Jefferson Davis was the strongest, were the real driving power of the administration. Convivial President Pierce and doting President Buchanan after him were complaisant to their least scrupulous suggestions in a degree hardly credible of honourable men who were not themselves Southerners.

One famous incident of life in Congress must be told to explain the temper of the times. In 1856, during one of the many debates that arose out of Kansas, Sumner recited in the Senate a speech conscientiously calculated to sting the slave-owning Senators to madness. Sumner was a man with brains and with courage and rectitude beyond praise, set off by a powerful and noble frame, but he lacked every minor quality of greatness. He would not call his opponent in debate a skunk, but he would expend great verbal ingenuity in coupling his name with repeated references to that animal's attributes. On this occasion he used to the full both the finer and the most exquisitely tasteless qualities of his eloquence. This sort of thing passed the censorship of many excellent Northern men who would lament Lincoln's lack of refinement; and though from first to last the serious provocation in their disputes lay in the set policy of the Southern leaders, it ought to be realised that they, men who for the most part were quite kind to their slaves and had long ago argued themselves out of any compunction about slavery, were often exposed to intense verbal provocation. Nevertheless, what followed on Sumner's speech is terribly significant of the depravation of Southern honour.

Congressman Preston Brooks, of South Carolina, had an uncle in the Senate; South Carolina, and this Senator in particular, had been specially favoured with self-righteous insolence in Sumner's speech. A day or so later the Senate had just risen and Sumner sat writing at his desk in the Senate chamber in a position in which he could not quickly rise. Brooks walked in, burning with piety towards his State and his uncle, and in the presence, it seems, of Southern Senators who could have stopped him, beat Sumner on the head with a stick with all his might. Sumner was incapacitated by injuries to his spine for nearly five years. Brooks, with a virtuous air, explained in Congress that he had caught Sumner in a helpless attitude because if Sumner had been free to use his superior strength he, Brooks, would have had to shoot him with his revolver. It seems to be hardly an exaggeration to say that the whole South applauded Brooks and exulted. Exuberant Southerners took to challenging Northern men, knowing well that their principles compelled them to refuse duels, but that the refusal would still be humiliating to the North. Brooks himself challenged Burlingame, a distinguished Congressman afterwards sent by Lincoln as Minister to China, who had denounced him. Burlingame accepted, and his second arranged for a rifle duel at a wild spot across the frontier at Niagara. Brooks then drew back; he alleged, perhaps sincerely, that he would have been murdered on his way through the Northern States, but Northern people were a little solaced. The whole disgusting story contains only one pleasant incident. Preston Brooks, who, after numbers of congratulations, testimonials, and presentations, died within a year of his famous exploit, had first confessed himself tired of being a hero to every vulgar bully in the South!

Now, though this dangerous temper burned steadily in the South, and there were always sturdy Republicans ready to provoke it, and questions arising out of slavery would constantly recur to disturb high political circles, it is not to be imagined that opinion in the North, the growing and bustling portion of the States, would remain for years excited about the repeal of the Missouri Compromise. In 1857 men's minds were agitated by a great commercial depression and collapse of credit, and in 1858 there took place one of the most curious (for it would seem to have deserved this cold description) of evanescent religious revivals. Meanwhile, by 1857 the actual bloodshed in Kansas had come to an end under the administration of an able Governor; the enormous majority of settlers in Kansas were now known to be against slavery and it was probably assumed that the legalisation of slavery could not be forced upon them. Prohibition of slavery there by Congress thus began to seem needless, and the Dred Scott judgments raised at least a grave doubt as to whether it was possible. Thus enthusiasm for the original platform of the Republicans was cooling down, and to the further embarrassment of that party, when towards the end of 1857 the Southern leaders attempted a legislative outrage, the great champion of the Northern protest was not a Republican, but Douglas himself.

A Convention had been elected in Kansas to frame a State Constitution. It represented only a fraction of the people, since, for some reason good or bad, the opponents of slavery did not vote in the election. But it was understood that whatever Constitution was framed would be submitted to the popular vote. The Convention framed a Constitution legalising slavery, and its proposals came before Congress backed by the influence of Buchanan. Under them the people of Kansas were to vote whether they would have this Constitution as it stood, or have it with the legalisation of slavery restricted to the slaves who had then been brought into the territory. No opportunity was to be given them of rejecting the Constitution altogether, though Governor Walker, himself in favor of slavery, assured the President that they wished to do so. Ultimately, by way of concession to vehement resistance, the majority in Congress passed an Act under which the people in Kansas were to vote simply for or against the slavery Constitution as it stood, only—if they voted for it, they as a State were to be rewarded with a large grant of public lands belonging to the Union in their territory. Eventually the Kansas people, unmoved by this bribe, rejected the Constitution by a majority of more than 11,000 to 1,800. Now, the Southern leaders, three years before, had eagerly joined with Douglas to claim a right of free choice for the Kansas people. The shamelessness of this attempt to trick them out of it is more significant even than the tale of Preston Brooks. There was no hot blood there; the affair was quietly plotted by respected leaders of the South. They were men in many ways of character and honour, understood by weak men like Buchanan to represent the best traditions of American public life. But, as they showed also in other instances that cannot be related here, slavery had become for them a sacred cause which hallowed almost any means. It is essential to remember this in trying to understand the then political situation.

Douglas here behaved very honourably. He, with his cause of popular sovereignty, could not have afforded to identify himself with the fraud on Kansas, but he was a good enough trickster to have made his protest safely if he had cared to do so. As it was he braved the hatred of Buchanan and the fury of his Southern friends by instant, manly, courageous, and continued opposition. It may therefore seem an ungracious thing that, immediately after this, Lincoln should have accepted the invitation of his friends to oppose Douglas' re-election. To most of the leading Republicans out of Illinois it seemed altogether unwise and undesirable that their party, which had seemed to be losing ground, should do anything but welcome Douglas as an ally. Of these Seward indeed went too far for his friends, and in his sanguine hope that it would work for freedom was ready to submit to the doctrine of "popular sovereignty"; but, except the austere Chase, now Governor of Ohio, who this once, but unfortunately not again, was whole-heartedly with Lincoln, the Republican leaders in the East, and great Republican journals, like the Tribune, declared their wish that Douglas should be re-elected. Why, then, did Lincoln stand against him?

It has often been suggested that his personal feelings towards Douglas played some part in the matter, though no one thinks they played the chief part. Probably they did play a part, and it is a relief to think that Lincoln thoroughly gratified some minor feelings in this contest. Lincoln no doubt enjoyed measuring himself against other men; and it was galling to his ambition to have been so completely outstripped by a man inferior to him in every power except that of rapid success. He had also the deepest distrust for Douglas as a politician, thinking that he had neither principle nor scruple, though Herndon, who knew, declares he neither distrusted nor had cause to distrust Douglas in his professional dealings as a lawyer. He had, by the way, one definite, if trifling, score to wipe off. After their joint debate at Peoria in 1855 Douglas, finding him hard to tackle, suggested to Lincoln that they should both undertake to make no more speeches for the present.

Lincoln oddly assented at once, perhaps for no better reason than a ridiculous difficulty, to which he once confessed, in refusing any request whatever. Lincoln of course had kept this agreement strictly, while Douglas had availed himself of the first temptation to break it. Thus on all grounds we may be sure that Lincoln took pleasure in now opposing Douglas. But to go further and say that the two men cordially hated each other is probably to misread both. There is no necessary connection between a keen desire to beat a man and any sort of malignity towards him. That much at least may be learned in English schools, and the whole history of his dealing with men shows that in some school or other Lincoln had learned it very thoroughly. Douglas, too, though an unscrupulous, was not, we may guess, an ungenerous man.

But the main fact of the matter is that Lincoln would have turned traitor to his rooted convictions if he had not stood up and fought Douglas even at this moment when Douglas was deserving of some sympathy. Douglas, it must be observed, had simply acted on his principle that the question between slavery and freedom was to be settled by local, popular choice; he claimed for the white men of Kansas the fair opportunity of voting; given that, he persistently declared, "I do not care whether slavery be voted up or voted down." In Lincoln's settled opinion this moral attitude of indifference to the wrongfulness of slavery, so long as respect was had to the liberties of the privileged race, was, so to say, treason to the basic principle of the American Commonwealth, a treason which had steadily been becoming rife and upon which it was time to stamp.

There can be no doubt of his earnestness about this. But the Republican leaders, honourably enough, regarded this as an unpractical line to take, and indeed to the political historian this is the most crucial question in American history. Nobody can say that civil war would or would not have occurred if this or that had been done a little differently, but Abraham Lincoln, at this crisis of his life, did, in pursuance of his peculiarly cherished principle, forge at least a link in the chain of events which actually precipitated the war. And he did it knowing better than any other man that he was doing something of great national importance, involving at least great national risk. Was he pursuing his principles, moderate as they were in the original conception, with fanaticism, or at the best preferring a solemn consistency of theory to the conscientious handling of facts not reducible to theory? As a question of practical statesmanship in the largest sense, how did matters really stand in regard to slavery and to the relations between South and North, and what was Lincoln's idea of "putting slavery back where the fathers placed it" really worth?

Herndon in these days went East to try to enlist the support of the great men for Lincoln. He found them friendly but immovable. Editor Horace Greeley said to him: "The Republican standard is too high; we want something practical." This, we may be pretty sure, stiffened Lincoln's back, as a man with a cause that he cared for, and, for that matter, as a really shrewd manager in a party which he thought stood for something. It reveals the flabbiness which the Northerners were in danger of making a governing tradition of policy. The wrongfulness of any extension of slavery might be loudly asserted in 1854, but in 1858, when it no longer looked as if so great an extension of it was really imminent, there was no harm in shifting towards some less provocative principle on which more people at the moment might agree. Confronted with Northern politicians who would reason in this fashion stood a united South whose leaders were by now accustomed to make the Union Government go which way they chose and had no sort of disposition to compromise their principle in the least. "What," as Lincoln put it in an address given, not long after his contest with Douglas, at the Cooper Institute in New York, "what do you think will content the South?" "Nothing," he answered, "but an acknowledgment that slavery is right." "Holding as they do that slavery is morally right and socially elevating, they cannot cease to demand a full national recognition of it, as a legal right and a social blessing. Nor can we justifiably withhold this on any ground save our conviction that slavery is wrong." That being so, there was no use, he said, in "groping about for some middle ground between right and wrong," or in "a policy of 'don't care' on a question about which all true men do care." And there is ample evidence that he understood rightly the policy of the South. It is very doubtful whether any large extension of cultivation by slave labour was economically possible in Kansas or in regions yet further North, but we have seen to what lengths the Southern leaders would go in the attempt to secure even a limited recognition of slavery as lawful in a new State. They were not succeeding in the business of the Kansas Constitution. But they had a very good prospect of a far more important success. The celebrated dicta of Chief Justice Taney and other judges in the Dred Scott case had not amounted to an actual decision, nor if they had would a single decision have been irreversible. Whether the principle of them should become fixed in American Constitutional law depended (though this could not be openly said) on whether future appointments to the Supreme Court were to be made by a President who shared Taney's views; whether the executive action of the President was governed by the same views; and on the subtle pressure which outside opinion does exercise, and in this case had surely exercised, upon judicial minds. If the simple principle that the right to a slave is just one form of the ordinary right to property once became firmly fixed in American jurisprudence it is hard to see how any laws prohibiting slavery could have continued to be held constitutional except in States which were free States when the Constitution was adopted. Of course, a State like New York where slaves were industrially useless would not therefore have been filled with slave plantations, but, among a loyally minded people, the tradition which reprobated slavery would have been greatly weakened.

The South would have been freed from the sense that slavery was a doomed institution. If attempts to plant slavery further in the West with profit failed, there was Cuba and there was Central America, on which filibustering raids already found favour in the South, and in which the national Government might be led to adopt schemes of conquest or annexation. Moreover, it was avowed by leaders like Jefferson Davis that though it might be impracticable to hope for the repeal of the prohibition of the slave trade, at least some relaxation of its severity ought to be striven for, in the interest of Texas and New Mexico and of possible future Territories where there might be room for more slaves. Such were the views of the leaders whose influence preponderated with the present President and in the main with the present Congress. When Lincoln judged that a determined stand against their policy was required, and further that no such stand could be possible to a party which had embraced Douglas with his principle, "I care not whether slavery be voted up or voted down," there is no doubt now that he was right and the great body of Republican authority opposed to him wrong.

When Lincoln and his friends in Illinois determined to fight Douglas, it became impossible for the Republican party as a whole to fall far behind them. This was in itself at that crisis an important thing. Lincoln added greatly to its importance by the opening words in the first speech of his campaign. They were the most carefully prepared words that he had yet spoken, and the most momentous that he had spoken till now or perhaps ever spoke. There is nothing in them for which what has been said of the situation and of his views will not have prepared us, and nothing which thousands of men might not have said to one another in private for a year or two before. But the first public avowal by a responsible man in trenchant phrase, that a grave issue has been joined upon which one party or the other must accept entire defeat, may be an event of great and perilous consequence.

He said: "If we could first know where we are and whither we are tending, we could better judge what to do and how to do it. We are now far into the fifth year since a policy was initiated with the avowed object, and confident promise, of putting an end to slavery agitation. Under the operation of that policy, that agitation has not only not ceased, but has constantly augmented. In my opinion it will not cease until a crisis shall have been reached and passed. 'A house divided against itself cannot stand.' I believe this Government cannot endure permanently half slave and half free. I do not expect the Union to be dissolved—I do not expect the house to fall—but I do expect that it will cease to be divided. It will become all one thing or all the other. Either the opponents of slavery will arrest the further spread of it and place it where the public mind shall rest in the belief that it is in course of ultimate extinction, or its advocates will push it forward till it shall become lawful alike in all the States, old as well as new—North as well as South."

It may perhaps be said that American public opinion has in the past been very timid in facing clear-cut issues. But, as has already been observed, an apt phrase crystallising the unspoken thought of many is even more readily caught up in America than anywhere else; so, though but few people in States at a distance paid much attention to the rest of the debates, or for a while again to Lincoln, the comparison of the house divided against itself produced an effect in the country which did not wear out. In this whole passage, moreover, Lincoln had certainly formulated the question before the nation more boldly, more clearly, more truly than any one before. It is impossible to estimate such influences precisely, but this was among the speeches that rank as important actions, and the story, most characteristic of the speaker, which lay behind it, is worth relating in detail. Lincoln had actually in a speech in 1856 declared that the United States could not long endure half slave and half free. "What in God's name," said some friend after the meeting, "could induce you to promulgate such an opinion?" "Upon my soul," he said, "I think it is true," and he could not be argued out of this opinion. Finally the friend protested that, true or not, no good could come of spreading this opinion abroad, and after grave reflection Lincoln promised not to utter it again for the present. Now, in 1858, having prepared his speech he read it to Herndon. Herndon questioned whether the passage on the divided house was politic. Lincoln said: "I would rather be defeated with this expression in my speech, and uphold and discuss it before the people, than be victorious without it." Once more, just before he delivered it, he read it over to a dozen or so of his closest supporters, for it was his way to discuss his intentions fully with friends, sometimes accepting their advice most submissively and sometimes disregarding it wholly. One said it was "ahead of its time," another that it was a "damned fool utterance." All more or less strongly condemned it, except this time Herndon, who, according to his recollection, said, "It will make you President." He listened to all and then addressed them, we are told, substantially as follows: "Friends, this thing has been retarded long enough. The time has come when these sentiments should be uttered; and if it is decreed that I should go down because of this speech, then let me go down linked to the truth—let me die in the advocacy of what is just and right." Rather a memorable pronouncement of a candidate to his committee; and the man who records it is insistent upon every little illustration he can find both of Lincoln's cunning and of his ambition.

Lincoln did go down in this particular contest. Many friends wrote and reproved him after this "damned fool utterance," but his defeat was not, after all, attributed to that. All the same he did himself assure his defeat, and he did it with extraordinary skill, for the purpose of ensuring that the next President should be a Republican President, though it is impossible he should at that time have counted upon being himself that Republican. Each candidate had undertaken to answer set questions which his opponent might propound to him. And great public attention was paid to the answers to these interrogatories. The Dred Scott judgments created a great difficulty for Douglas; he was bound to treat them as right; but if they were right and Congress had no power to prohibit slavery in a Territory, neither could a Territorial Legislature with authority delegated by Congress have that power; and, if this were made clear, it would seem there was an end of that free choice of the people in the Territories of which Douglas had been the great advocate. Douglas would use all his evasive skill in keeping away from this difficult point. If, however, he could be forced to face it Lincoln knew what he would say. He would say that slavery would not be actually unlawful in a Territory, but would never actually exist in it if the Territorial Legislature chose to abstain, as it could, from passing any of the laws which would in practice be necessary to protect slave property. By advocating this view Douglas would fully reassure those of his former supporters in Illinois who puzzled themselves on the Dred Scott case, but he would infuriate the South. Lincoln determined to force Douglas into this position by the questions which he challenged him to answer. When he told his friends of his ambition, they all told him he would lose his election.

"Gentlemen," said Lincoln, "I am killing larger game; if Douglas answers, he can never be President, and the battle of 1860 is worth a hundred of this." The South was already angry with Douglas for his action over the Kansas Constitution, but he would have been an invincible candidate for the South to support in 1860, and it must have told in his favour that his offence then had been one of plain honesty. But in this fresh offence the Southern leaders had some cause to accuse him of double dealing, and they swore he should not be President.

A majority of the new Illinois Legislature returned Douglas to the Senate. Lincoln, however, had an actual majority of the votes of the whole State. Probably also he had gained a hold on Illinois for the future out of all proportion to the actual number of votes then given against the popular Douglas, and above all he had gathered to him a band of supporters who had unbounded belief in him. But his fall for the moment was little noticed or regretted outside Illinois, or at any rate in the great Eastern States, to which

Illinois was, so to speak, the provinces and he a provincial attorney. His first words in the campaign had made a stir, but the rest of his speeches in these long debates could not be much noticed at a distance. Douglas had won, and the presumption was that he had proved himself the better man. Lincoln had performed what, apart from results, was a work of intellectual merit beyond the compass of any American statesman since Hamilton; moreover, as can now be seen, there had been great results; for, first, the young Republican party had not capitulated and collapsed, and, then, the great Democratic party, established in power, in indifference, and in complicity with wrong, was split clean in two. But these were not results that could be read yet awhile in election figures. Meanwhile the exhausted Lincoln reconciled himself for the moment to failure. As a private man he was thoroughly content that he could soon work off his debt for his election expenses, could earn about 500 pounds a year, and be secure in the possession of the little house and the 2,000 pounds capital which was "as much as any man ought to have." As a public man he was sadly proud that he had at least "said some words which may bear fruit after I am forgotten."

Persistent melancholy and incurable elasticity can go together, and they make a very strong combination. The tone of resignation had not passed away from his comparatively intimate letters when he was writing little notes to one political acquaintance and another inciting them to look forward to the fun of the next fight.

4. John Brown.

For the next few months the excitements of the great political world concern this biography little. There was strife between Davis and Douglas in the Senate. At a meeting strong against slavery, Seward regained courage from the occasion and roused the North with grave and earnest words about the "irrepressible conflict." The "underground railway," or chain of friendly houses by which fugitive slaves were stealthily passed on to Canada, became famous. Methodist professors riotously attempted to rescue an arrested fugitive at Oberlin. A Southern grand jury threw out the bill of indictment against a slave-trading crew caught red-handed. In California Democrats belonging to what was nicknamed "the chivalry" forced upon Senator Broderick, a literally democratic Irishman and the bravest of the Democrats who stood out for fair treatment to Kansas, a duel in which he might fairly be said to have been murdered. The one event which demands more than allusion was the raid and the death of John Brown.

John Brown, in whom Puritan religion, as strict as that of his ancestors on the _Mayflower_, put forth gentler beauties of character than his sanguinary mission may suggest, had been somewhat of a failure as a scientific farmer, but as a leader of fighting men in desperate adventure only such men as Drake or Garibaldi seem to have excelled him. More particularly in the commotions in Kansas he had led forays, slain ruthlessly, witnesses dry-eyed the deaths of several of his tall, strong sons, and as a rule earned success by cool judgment—all, as he was absolutely sure, at the clear call of God. In October, 1859—how and with whose help the stroke was prepared seems to be a question of some mystery—John Brown, gathering a little band of Abolitionists and negroes, invaded the slave States and seized the United States arsenal at Harper's Ferry in Virginia. In the details, which do not matter, of this tiny campaign, John Brown seems, for the first time in his life, to have blundered badly. This was the only thing that lay upon his conscience towards the last. What manner of success he can have expected does not appear; most likely he had neither care nor definite expectation as to the result. The United States troops under Robert Lee, soon to be famous, of course overcame him quickly. One of his prisoners describes how he held out to the last; a dead son beside him; one hand on the pulse of a dying son, his rifle in the other. He was captured, desperately wounded. Southerners could not believe the fact that Brown had not contemplated some hideous uprising of slaves against their wives and children, but he only wished to conquer them with the sword of the Lord and of Gideon, quietly freeing slaves as he went. So naturally there was talk of lynching, but the Virginian gentlemen concerned would not have that. Governor Wise, of Virginia, had some talk with him and justified his own high character rather than Brown's by the estimate he gave of him in a speech at Richmond. Brown was hanged. "Stonewall" Jackson, a brother fanatic, if that is the word, felt the spectacle "awful," as he never felt slaughter in battle, and "put up a prayer that if possible Brown might be saved." "So perish all foes of the human race," said the officer commanding on the occasion, and the South generally felt the like.

A little before his death Brown was asked: "How do you justify your acts?" He said: "I think, my friend, you are guilty of a great wrong against God and humanity—I say it without wishing to be offensive—and it would be perfectly right for any one to interfere with you so far as to free those you wilfully and wickedly hold in bondage. I think I did right, and that others will do right who interfere with you at any time and at all times." In a conversation still later, he is reported to have concluded: "I wish to say furthermore that you had better—all you people at the South—prepare yourselves for a settlement of this question, that must come up for settlement sooner than you are prepared for it. You may dispose of me very easily. I am nearly disposed of now. But this question is still to be settled—this negro question I mean. The end of that is not yet." To a friend he wrote that he rejoiced like Paul because he knew like Paul that "if they killed him, it would greatly advance the cause of Christ."

Lincoln, who regarded lawlessness and slavery as twin evils, could only say of John Brown's raid: "That affair, in its philosophy, corresponds with the many attempts related in history at the assassination of kings and emperors. An enthusiast broods over the oppression of a people till he fancies himself commissioned by Heaven to liberate them. He ventures the attempt, which ends in little else than his own execution. Orsini's attempt on Louis Napoleon and John Brown's attempt at Harper's Ferry were, in their philosophy, precisely the same." Seward, it must be recorded, spoke far more sympathetically of him than Lincoln; and far more justly, for there is a flaw somewhere in this example, as his chief biographer regards it, of "Mr. Lincoln's common-sense judgment." John Brown had at least left to every healthy-minded Northern boy a memory worth much in the coming years of war and, one hopes, ever after. He had well deserved to be the subject of a song which, whatever may be its technical merits as literature, does stir. Emerson took the same view of him as the song writer, and Victor Hugo suggested as an epitaph for him: "Pro Christo sicut Christus." A calmer poet, Longfellow, wrote in his diary on Friday, December 2, 1859, the day when Brown was hanged: "This will be a great day in our history, the date of a new revolution, quite as much needed as the old one. Even now, as I write, they are leading old John Brown to execution in Virginia for attempting to rescue slaves. This is sowing the wind to reap the whirlwind, which will soon come."

Any one who is interested in Lincoln is almost forced to linger over the contrasting though slighter character who crossed the stage just before he suddenly took the principal part upon it. Men like John Brown may be fitly ranked with the equally rare men who, steering a very different course, have consistently acted out the principles of the Quakers, constraining no man whether by violence or by law, yet going into the thick of life prepared at all times to risk all. All such men are abnormal in the sense that most men literally could not put life through on any similar plan and would be wrong and foolish to try. The reason is that most men have a wider range of sympathy and of intellect than they. But the common sense of most of us revolts from any attitude of condemnation or condescension towards them; for they are more disinterested than most of us, more single-minded, and in their own field often more successful. With a very clear conscience we refuse to take example from these men whose very defects have operated in them as a special call; but undoubtedly most of us regard them with a warmth of sympathy which we are slow to accord to safer guides. We turn now from John Brown, who saw in slavery a great oppression, and was very angry, and went ahead slaying the nearest oppressor and liberating—for some days at least—the nearest slave, to a patient being, who, long ago in his youth, had boiled with anger against slavery, but whose whole soul now expressed itself in a policy of deadly moderation towards it: "Let us put back slavery where the fathers placed it, and there let it rest in peace." We are to study how he acted when in power. In almost every department of policy we shall see him watching and waiting while blood flows, suspending judgment, temporising, making trial of this expedient and of that, adopting in the end, quite unthanked, the measure of which most men will say, when it succeeds, "That is what we always said should be done." Above all, in that point of policy which most interests us, we shall witness the long postponement of the blow that killed negro slavery, the steady subordination of this particular issue to what will not at once appeal to us as a larger and a higher issue. All this provoked at the time in many excellent and clever men dissatisfaction and deep suspicion; they longed for a leader whose heart visibly glowed with a sacred passion; they attributed his patience, the one quality of greatness which after a while everybody might have discerned in him, not to a self-mastery which almost passed belief, but to a tepid disposition and a mediocre if not a low level of desire. We who read of him to-day shall not escape our moments of lively sympathy with these grumblers of the time; we shall wish that this man could ever plunge, that he could ever see red, ever commit some passionate injustice; we shall suspect him of being, in the phrase of a great philosopher, "a disgustingly well-regulated person," lacking that indefinable quality akin to the honest passions of us ordinary men, but deeper and stronger, which alone could compel and could reward any true reverence for his memory. These moments will recur but they cannot last. A thousand little things, apparent on the surface but deeply significant; almost every trivial anecdote of his boyhood, his prime, or his closing years; his few recorded confidences; his equally few speeches made under strong emotion; the lineaments of his face described by observers whom photography corroborated; all these absolutely forbid any conception of Abraham Lincoln as a worthy commonplace person fortunately fitted to the requirements of his office at the moment, or as merely a "good man" in the negative and disparaging sense to which that term is often wrested. It is really evident that there were no frigid perfections about him at all; indeed the weakness of some parts of his conduct is so unlike what seems to be required of a successful ruler that it is certain some almost unexampled quality of heart and mind went to the doing of what he did.

There is no need to define that quality. The general wisdom of his statesmanship will perhaps appear greater and its not infrequent errors less the more fully the circumstances are appreciated. As to the man, perhaps the sense will grow upon us that this balanced and calculating person, with his finger on the pulse of the electorate while he cracked his uncensored jests with all comers, did of set purpose drink and refill and drink again as full and fiery a cup of sacrifice as ever was pressed to the lips of hero or of saint.

5. The Election of Lincoln.

Unlooked-for events were now raising Lincoln to the highest place which his ambition could contemplate. His own action in the months that followed his defeat by Douglas cannot have contributed much to his surprising elevation, yet it illustrates well his strength and his weakness, his real fitness, now and then startlingly revealed, for the highest position, and the superficial unfitness which long hid his capacity from many acute contemporaries.

In December, 1859, he made a number of speeches in Kansas and elsewhere in the West, and in February, 1860, he gave a memorable address in the Cooper Institute in New York before as consciously intellectual an audience as could be collected in that city, proceeding afterwards to speak in several cities of New England. His appearance at the Cooper Institute, in particular, was a critical venture, and he knew it. There was natural curiosity about this untutored man from the West. An exaggerated report of his wit prepared the way for probable disappointment. The surprise which awaited his hearers was of a different kind; they were prepared for a florid Western eloquence offensive to ears which were used to a less spontaneous turgidity; they heard instead a speech with no ornament at all, whose only beauty was that it was true and that the speaker felt it. The single flaw in the Cooper Institute speech has already been cited, the narrow view of Western respectability as to John Brown. For the rest, this speech, dry enough in a sense, is an incomparably masterly statement of the then political situation, reaching from its far back origin to the precise and definite question requiring decision at that moment. Mr. Choate, who as a young man was present, set down of late years his vivid recollection of that evening. "He appeared in every sense of the word like one of the plain people among whom he loved to be counted. At first sight there was nothing impressive or imposing about him; his clothes hung awkwardly on his giant frame; his face was of a dark pallor without the slightest tinge of colour; his seamed and rugged features bore the furrows of hardship and struggle; his deep-set eyes looked sad and anxious; his countenance in repose gave little evidence of the brilliant power which raised him from the lowest to the highest station among his countrymen; as he talked to me before the meeting he seemed ill at ease." We know, as a fact, that among his causes of apprehension, he was for the first time painfully conscious of those clothes. "When he spoke," proceeds Mr. Choate, "he was transformed; his eye kindled, his voice rang, his face shone and seemed to light up the whole assembly. For an hour and a half he held his audience in the hollow of his hand. His style of speech and manner of delivery were severely simple. What Lowell called 'the grand simplicities of the Bible,' with which he was so familiar, were reflected in his discourse. . . . It was marvellous to see how this untutored man, by mere self-discipline and the chastening of his own spirit, had outgrown all meretricious arts, and found his way to the grandeur and strength of absolute simplicity."

The newspapers of the day after this speech confirm these reverent reminiscences. On this, his first introduction to the cultivated world of the East, Lincoln's audience were at the moment and for the moment conscious of the power which he revealed. The Cooper Institute speech takes the plain principle that slavery is wrong, and draws the plain inference that it is idle to seek for common ground with men who say it is right. Strange but tragically frequent examples show how rare it is for statesmen in times of crisis to grasp the essential truth so simply. It is creditable to the leading men of New York that they recognised a speech which just at that time urged this plain thing in sufficiently plain language as a very great speech, and had an inkling of great and simple qualities in the man who made it. It is not specially discreditable that very soon and for a long while part of them, or of those who were influenced by their report, reverted to their former prejudices in regard to Lincoln. When they saw him thrust by election managers into the Presidency, very few indeed of what might be called the better sort believed, or could easily learn, that his great qualities were great enough to compensate easily for the many things he lacked. This specially grotesque specimen of the wild West was soon seen not to be of the charlatan type; as a natural alternative he was assumed to be something of a simpleton. Many intelligent men retained this view of him throughout the years of his trial, and, only when his triumph and tragic death set going a sort of Lincoln myth, began to recollect that "I came to love and trust him even before I knew him," or the like. A single speech like this at the Cooper Institute might be enough to show a later time that Lincoln was a man of great intellect, but it could really do little to prepare men in the East for what they next heard of him.

Already a movement was afoot among his friends in Illinois to secure his nomination for the Presidency at the Convention of the Republican party which was to be held in Chicago in May. Before that Convention could assemble it had become fairly certain that whoever might be chosen as the Republican candidate would be President of the United States, and signs were not wanting that he would be faced with grave peril to the Union. For the Democratic party, which had met in Convention at Charleston in April, had proceeded to split into two sections, Northern and Southern. This memorable Convention was a dignified assembly gathered in a serious mood in a city of some antiquity and social charm. From the first, however, a latent antipathy between the Northern and the Southern delegates made itself felt. The Northerners, predisposed to a certain deference towards the South and prepared to appreciate its graceful hospitality, experienced an uneasy sense that they were regarded as social inferiors. Worse trouble than this appeared when the Convention met for its first business, the framing of the party platform. Whether the position which Lincoln had forced Douglas to take up had precipitated this result or not, dissension between Northern and Southern Democrats on the subject of slavery had already manifested itself in Congress, and in the party Convention the division became irreparable.

Douglas, it will be remembered, had started with the principle that slavery in the Territories formed a question for the people of each territory to decide; he had felt bound to accept the doctrine underlying the Dred Scott judgments, according to which slavery was by the Constitution lawful in all territories; pressed by Lincoln, he had tried to reconcile his original position with this doctrine by maintaining that while slavery was by the Constitution lawful in every Territory it was nevertheless lawful for a Territorial Legislature to make slave-owning practically impossible. In framing a declaration of the party principles as to slavery the Southern delegates in the Democratic Convention aimed at meeting this evasion. With considerable show of logic they asserted, in the party platform which they proposed, not merely the abstract rightfulness and lawfulness of slavery, but the duty of Congress itself to make any provision that might be necessary to protect it in the Territories. To this the Northern majority of the delegates could not consent; they carried an amendment declaring merely that they would abide by any decision of the Supreme Court as to slavery. Thereupon the delegates, not indeed of the whole South but of all the cotton-growing States except Georgia, withdrew from the Convention. The remaining delegates were, under the rules of the Convention, too few to select a candidate for the Presidency, and the Convention adjourned, to re-assemble at Baltimore in June. Eventually, after attempts at reunion and further dissensions, two separate Democratic Conventions at Baltimore, a Northern and a Southern, nominated, as their respective candidates, Stephen Douglas, the obvious choice with whom, if the Southerners had cared to temporise further, a united Democratic party could have swept the polls, and John C. Breckinridge of Kentucky, a gentleman not otherwise known than as the standard bearer on this great occasion of the undisguised and unmitigated claims of the slave owners.

Thus it was that the American Democratic party forfeited power for twenty-four years, divided between the consistent maintenance of a paradox and the adroit maintenance of inconsistency. Another party in this election demands a moment's notice. A Convention of delegates, claiming to represent the old Whigs, met also at Baltimore and declared merely that it stood for "the Constitution of the country, the union of the States, and the enforcement of the laws." They nominated for the Presidency John Bell of Tennessee, and for the Vice-Presidency Edward Everett. This latter gentleman was afterwards chosen as the orator of the day at the ceremony on the battlefield of Gettysburg when Lincoln's most famous speech was spoken. He was a travelled man and a scholar; he was Secretary of State for a little while under Fillmore, and dealt honestly and firmly with the then troublous question of Cuba. His orations deserve to be looked at, for they are favourable examples of the eloquence which American taste applauded, and as such they help to show how original Lincoln was in the simpler beauty of his own simpler diction. In justice to the Whigs, let it be noted that they declared for the maintenance of the Union, committing themselves with decision on the question of the morrow; but it was a singular platform that resolutely and totally ignored the only issue of the day. Few politicians can really afford to despise either this conspicuously foolish attempt to overcome a difficulty by shutting one's eyes to it, or the more plausible proposal of the Northern Democrats to continue temporising with a movement for slavery in which they were neither bold enough nor corrupted enough to join. The consequences, now known to us, of a determined stand against the advance of slavery were instinctively foreseen by these men, and they cannot be blamed for shrinking from them. Yet the historian now, knowing that those consequences exceeded in terror all that could have been foreseen, can only agree with the judgment expressed by Lincoln in one of his Kansas speeches: "We want and must have a national policy as to slavery which deals with it as being a wrong. Whoever would prevent slavery becoming national and perpetual yields all when he yields to a policy which treats it either as being right, or as being a matter of indifference." The Republican party had been founded upon just this opinion.

Electoral victory was now being prepared for it, not because a majority was likely yet to take so resolute a view, but because its effective opponents were divided between those who had gone the length of calling slavery right and those who strove to treat it as indifferent. The fate of America may be said to have depended in the early months of 1860 on whether the nominee of the Republican party was a man who would maintain its principles with irresolution, or with obstinacy, or with firm moderation.

When it had first been suggested to Lincoln in the course of 1859 that he might be that nominee he said, "I do not think myself fit for the Presidency." This was probably his sincere opinion at the moment, though perhaps the moment was one of dejection. In any case his opinion soon changed, and though it is not clear whether he encouraged his friends to bring his name forward, we know in a general way that when they decided to do so he used every effort of his own to help them. We must accept without reserve Herndon's reiterated assertion that Lincoln was intensely ambitious; and, if ambition means the eager desire for great opportunities, the depreciation of it, which has long been a commonplace of literature, and which may be traced back to the Epicureans, is a piece of cant which ought to be withdrawn from currency, and ambition, commensurate with the powers which each man can discover in himself, should be frankly recognised as a part of Christian duty. In judging him to be the best man for the Presidency, Lincoln's Illinois friends and he himself formed a very sensible judgment, but they did so in flagrant contradiction to many superficial appearances. This candidate for the chief magistracy at a critical time of one of the great nations of the world had never administered any concern much larger than that post office that he once "carried around in his hat." Of the several other gentlemen whose names were before the party there was none who might not seem greatly to surpass him in experience of affairs. To one of them, Seward, the nomination seemed to belong almost of right. Chase and Seward both were known and dignified figures in that great assembly the Senate. Chase was of proved rectitude and courage, Seward of proved and very considerable ability. Chase had been Governor of Ohio, Seward of New York State; and the position of Governor in a State—a State it must be remembered is independent in almost the whole of what we call domestic politics—is strictly analogous to the position of President in the Union, and, especially in a great State, is the best training ground for the Presidency. But beyond this, Seward, between whom and Lincoln the real contest lay, had for some time filled a recognised though unofficial position as the leader of his party. He had failed, as has been seen in his dealings with Douglas, in stern insistence upon principle, but the failure was due rather to his sanguine and hopeful temper than to lack of courage. On the whole from the time when he first stood up against Webster in the discussions of 1850, when Lincoln was both silent and obscure, he had earned his position well.

Hereafter, as Lincoln's subordinate, he was to do his country first-rate service, and to earn a pure fame as the most generously loyal subordinate to a chief whom he had thought himself fit to command. We happen to have ample means of estimating now all Lincoln's Republican competitors; we know that none of the rest were equal to Seward; and we know that Seward himself, if he had had his way, would have brought the common cause to ruin. Looking back now at the comparison which Lincoln, when he entered into the contest, must have drawn between himself and Seward—for of the rest we need not take account—we can see that to himself at least and some few in Illinois he had now proved his capacities, and that in Seward's public record, more especially in his attitude towards Douglas, he had the means of measuring Seward. In spite of the far greater experience of the latter he may have thought himself to be his superior in that indefinable thing—the sheer strength of a man. Not only may he have thought this; he must have known it. He had shown his grasp of the essential facts when he forced the Republican party to do battle with Douglas and the party of indifference; he showed the same now when, after long years of patience and self-discipline, he pushed himself into Seward's place as the Republican leader.

All the same, what little we know of the methods by which he now helped his own promotion suggests that the people who then and long after set him down as a second-rate person may have had a good deal to go upon. A kind friend has produced a letter which he wrote in March, 1860, to a Kansas gentleman who desired to be a delegate to the Republican Convention, and who offered, upon condition, to persuade his fellow delegates from Kansas to support Lincoln. Here is the letter: "As to your kind wishes for myself, allow me to say I cannot enter the ring on the money basis—first because in the main it is wrong; and secondly

I have not and cannot get the money. I say in the main the use of money is wrong; but for certain objects in a political contest the use of some is both right and indispensable. With me, as with yourself, this long struggle has been one of great pecuniary loss. I now distinctly say this: If you shall be appointed a delegate to Chicago I will furnish one hundred dollars to bear the expenses of the trip." The Kansas gentleman failed to obtain the support of the Kansas delegates as a body for Lincoln. Lincoln none the less held to his promise of a hundred dollars if the man came to Chicago; and, having, we are assured, much confidence in him, took the earliest opportunity of appointing him to a lucrative office, besides consulting him as to other appointments in Kansas. This is all that we know of the affair, but our informant presents it as one of a number of instances in which Lincoln good-naturedly trusted a man too soon, and obstinately clung to his mistake. As to the appointment, the man had evidently begun by soliciting money in a way which would have marked him to most of us as a somewhat unsuitable candidate for any important post; and the payment of the hundred dollars plainly transgresses a code both of honour and of prudence which most politicians will recognise and which should not need definition. To say, as Lincoln probably said to himself, that there is nothing intrinsically wrong in a moderate payment for expenses to a fellow worker in a public cause, whom you believe to have sacrificed much, is to ignore the point, indeed several points. Lincoln, hungry now for some success in his own unrewarded career, was tempted to a small manoeuvre by which he might pick up a little support; he was at the same time tempted, no less, to act generously (according to his means) towards a man who, he readily believed, had made sacrifices like his own. He was not the man to stand against this double temptation.

Petty lapses of this order, especially when the delinquent may be seen to hesitate and excuse himself, are more irritating than many larger and more brazen offences, for they give us the sense of not knowing where we are. When they are committed by a man of seemingly strong and high character, it is well to ask just what they signify. Some of the shrewdest observers of Lincoln, friendly and unfriendly, concur in their description of the weaknesses of which this incident may serve as the example, weaknesses partly belonging to his temperament, but partly such as a man risen from poverty, with little variety of experience and with no background of home training, stands small chance of escaping. For one thing his judgment of men and how to treat them was as bad in some ways as it was good in others. His own sure grasp of the largest and commonest things in life, and his sober and measured trust in human nature as a whole, gave him a rare knowledge of the mind of the people in the mass. So, too, when he had known a man long, or been with him or against him in important transactions, he sometimes developed great insight and sureness of touch; and, when the man was at bottom trustworthy, his robust confidence in him was sometimes of great public service. But he had no gift of rapid perception and no instinctive tact or prudence in regard to the very numerous and very various men with whom he had slight dealings on which he could bestow no thought. This is common with men who have risen from poverty; if they have not become hard and suspicious, they are generally obtuse to the minor indications by which shrewd men of education know the impostor, and they are perversely indulgent to little meannesses in their fellows which they are incapable of committing themselves. In Lincoln this was aggravated by an immense good-nature—as he confessed, he could hardly say "no";—it was an obstinate good-nature, which found a naughty pleasure in refusing to be corrected; and if it should happen that the object of his weak benevolence had given him personal cause of offence, the good-nature became more incorrigible than ever. Moreover, Lincoln's strength was a slow strength, shown most in matters in which elementary principles of right or the concentration of intense thought guided him. Where minor and more subtle principles of conduct should have come in, on questions which had not come within the range of his reflection so far and to which, amidst his heavy duties, he could not spare much cogitation, he would not always show acute perception, and, which is far worse, he would often show weakness of will. The present instance may be ever so trifling, yet it does relate to the indistinct and dangerous borderland of political corruption. It need arouse no very serious suspicions. Mr. Herndon, whose pertinacious researches unearthed that Kansas gentleman's correspondence, and who is keenly censorious of Lincoln's fault, in the upshot trusts and reveres Lincoln. And the massive testimony of his keenest critics to his honesty quite decides the matter. But Lincoln had lived in a simple Western town, not in one of the already polluted great cities; he was a poor man himself and took the fact that wealth was used against him as a part of the inevitable drawbacks of his lot; and it is certain that he did not clearly take account of the whole business of corruption and jobbery as a hideous and growing peril to America. It is certain too that he lacked the delicate perception of propriety in such matters, or the strict resolution in adhering to it on small occasions, which might have been possessed by a far less honest man. The severest criticisms which Lincoln afterwards incurred were directed to the appointments which he made; we shall see hereafter that he had very solid reasons for his general conduct in such matters; but it cannot be said with conviction that he had that horror of appointment on other grounds than merit which enlightens, though it does not always govern, more educated statesmen. His administration would have been more successful, and the legacy he left to American public life more bountiful, if his traditions, or the length of his day's work, had allowed him to be more careful in these things. As it is he was not commended to the people of America and must not be commended to us by the absence of defects as a ruler or as a man, but by the qualities to which his defects belonged. An acute literary man wrote of Lincoln, when he had been three years in office, these remarkable words: "You can't help feeling an interest in him, a sympathy and a kind of pity; feeling, too, that he has some qualities of great value, yet fearing that his weak points may wreck him or may wreck something. His life seems a series of wise, sound conclusions, slowly reached, oddly worked out, on great questions with constant failures in administration of detail and dealings with individuals." It was evidently a clever man who wrote this; he would have been a wise man if he had known that the praise he was bestowing on Lincoln was immeasurably greater than the blame.

So the natural prejudice of those who welcomed Lincoln as a prophet in the Cooper Institute but found his candidature for the Presidency ridiculous, was not wholly without justification. His partisans, however—also not unjustly—used his humble origin for all it was worth. The Republicans of Illinois were assembled at Decatur in preparation for the Chicago Convention, when, amid tumultuous cheers, there marched in old John Hanks and another pioneer bearing on their shoulders two long fence rails labelled: "Two rails from a lot made by Abraham Lincoln and John Hanks in the Sangamon Bottom in the year 1830." "Gentlemen," said Lincoln, in response to loud calls, "I suppose you want to know something about those things. Well, the truth is, John Hanks and I did make rails in the Sangamon Bottom. I don't know whether we made those rails or not; fact is, I don't think they are a credit to the makers. But I do know this: I made rails then, and I think I could make better ones than these now." It is unnecessary to tell of the part those rails were to play in the coming campaign. It is a contemptible trait in books like that able novel "Democracy," that they treat the sentiment which attached to the "Rail-splitter" as anything but honourable.

The Republican Convention met at Chicago in circumstances of far less dignity than the Democratic Convention at Charleston. Processions and brass bands, rough fellows collected by Lincoln's managers, rowdies imported from New York by Seward's, filled the streets with noise; and the saloon keepers did good business. Yet the actual Convention consisted of grave men in an earnest mood. Besides Seward and Chase and Lincoln, Messrs. Cameron of Pennsylvania and Bates of Missouri, of whom we shall hear later, were proposed for the Presidency. So also were Messrs. Dayton and Collamer, politicians of some repute; and McLean, of the Supreme Court, had some supporters. The prevalent expectation in the States was that Seward would easily secure the nomination, but it very soon appeared in the Convention that his opponents were too strong for that. Several ballots took place; there were the usual conferences and bargainings, which probably affected the result but little; Lincoln's managers, especially Judge David Davis, afterwards of the Supreme Court, were shrewd people; Lincoln had written to them expressly that they could make no bargain binding on him, but when Cameron was clearly out of the running they did promise Cameron's supporters a place in Lincoln's Cabinet, and a similar promise was made for one Caleb Smith. The delegates from Pennsylvania went on to Lincoln; then those of Ohio; and before long his victory was assured. A Committee of the Convention, some of them sick at heart, was sent to bear the invitation to Lincoln. He received them in his little house with a simple dignity which one of them has recorded; and as they came away one said, "Well, we might have chosen a handsomer article, but I doubt whether a better."

On the whole, if we can put aside the illusion which besets us, who read the preceding history if at all in the light of Lincoln's speeches, and to whom his competitors are mere names, this was the most surprising nomination ever made in America. Other Presidential candidates have been born in poverty, but none ever wore the scars of poverty so plainly; others have been intrinsically more obscure, but these have usually been chosen as bearing the hall-mark of eminent prosperity or gentility. Lincoln had indeed at this time displayed brilliant ability in the debates with Douglas, and he had really shown a statesman's grasp of the situation more than any other Republican leader. The friends in Illinois who put him forward—men like David Davis, who was a man of distinction himself—did so from a true appreciation of his powers. But this does not seem to have been the case with the bulk of the delegates from other States. The explanation given us of their action is curious. The choice was not the result of merit; on the other hand, it was not the work of the ordinary wicked wire-puller, for what may be called the machine was working for Seward. The choice was made by plain representative Americans who set to themselves this question: "With what candidate can we beat Douglas?" and who found the answer in the prevalence of a popular impression, concerning Lincoln and Seward, which was in fact wholly mistaken. There was, it happens, earnest opposition to Seward among some Eastern Republicans on the good ground that he was a clean man but with doubtful associates. This opposition could not by itself have defeated him. What did defeat him was his reputation at the moment as a very advanced Republican who would scare away the support of the weaker brethren. He was, for instance, the author of the alarming phrase about "irrepressible conflict," and he had spoken once, in a phrase that was misinterpreted, about "a higher law than the Constitution."

Lincoln had in action taken a far stronger line than Seward; he was also the author of the phrase about the house divided against itself; but then, besides the fact that Lincoln was well regarded just where Douglas was most popular, Lincoln was a less noted man than Seward and his stronger words occasioned less wide alarm. So, to please those who liked compromise, the Convention rejected a man who would certainly have compromised, and chose one who would give all that moderation demanded and die before he yielded one further inch. Many Americans have been disposed to trace in the raising up of Lincoln the hand of a Providence protecting their country in its worst need. It would be affectation to set their idea altogether aside; it is, at any rate, a memorable incident in the history of a democracy, permeated with excellent intentions but often hopelessly subject to inferior influences, that at this critical moment the fit man was chosen on the very ground of his supposed unfitness.

The result of the contest between the four Presidential candidates was rendered almost a foregone conclusion by the decision of the Democrats. Lincoln in deference to the usual and seemly procedure took no part in the campaign, nor do his doings in the next months concern us. Seward, to his great honour, after privately expressing his bitter chagrin at the bestowal of what was his due upon "a little Illinois attorney," threw himself whole-heartedly into the contest, and went about making admirable speeches. On the night of November 6, Lincoln sat alone with the operator in the telegraph box at Springfield, receiving as they came in the results of the elections of Presidential electors in the various States. Long before the returns were complete his knowledge of such matters made him sure of his return, and before he left that box he had solved in principle, as he afterwards declared, the first and by no means least important problem of his Presidency, the choice of a Cabinet.

The victory was in one aspect far from complete. If we look not at the votes in the Electoral College with which the formal choice of President lay, but at the popular votes by which the electors were returned, we shall see that the new President was elected by a minority of the American people. He had a large majority over Douglas, but if Douglas had received the votes which were given for the Southern Democrat, Breckinridge, he would have had a considerable majority over Lincoln, though the odd machinery of the Electoral College would still have kept him out of the Presidency. In another aspect it was a fatally significant victory. Lincoln's votes were drawn only from the Northern States; he carried almost all the free States and he carried no others. For the first time in American history, the united North had used its superior numbers to outvote the South. This would in any case have caused great vexation, and the personality of the man chosen by the North aggravated it. The election of Lincoln was greeted throughout the South with a howl of derision.

CHAPTER VI

SECESSION

1. The Case of the South against the Union.

The Republicans of the North had given their votes upon a very clear issue, but probably few of them had fully realised how grave a result would follow. Within a few days of the election of Lincoln the first step in the movement of Secession had been taken, and before the new President entered upon his duties it was plain that either the dissatisfied States must be allowed to leave the Union or the Union must be maintained by war.

Englishmen at that time and since have found a difficulty in grasping the precise cause of the war that followed. Of those who were inclined to sympathise with the North, some regarded the war as being simply about slavery, and, while unhesitatingly opposed to slavery, wondered whether it was right to make war upon it; others, regarding it as a war for the Union and not against slavery at all, wondered whether it was right to make war for a Union that could not be peaceably maintained. Now it is seldom possible to state the cause of a war quite candidly in a single sentence, because as a rule there are on each side people who concur in the final rupture for somewhat different reasons. But, in this case, forecasting a conclusion which must be examined in some detail, we can state the cause of war in a very few sentences. If we ask first what the South fought for, the answer is: the leaders of the South and the great mass of the Southern people had a single supreme and all-embracing object in view, namely, to ensure the permanence and, if need be, the extension of the slave system; they carried with them, however, a certain number of Southerners who were opposed or at least averse to slavery, but who thought that the right of their States to leave the Union or remain in it as they chose must be maintained. If we ask what the North fought for, the answer is: A majority, by no means overwhelming, of the Northern people refused to purchase the adhesion of the South by conniving at any further extension of slavery, and an overwhelming majority refused to let the South dissolve the Union for slavery or for any other cause.

The issue about slavery, then, became merged in another issue, concerning the Union, which had so far remained in the background. The first thing that must be grasped about it is the total difference of view which now existed between North and South in regard to the very nature of their connection. The divergence had taken place so completely and in the main so quietly that each side now realised with surprise and indignation that the other held an opposite opinion. In the North the Union was regarded as constituting a permanent and unquestionable national unity from which it was flat rebellion for a State or any other combination of persons to secede. In the South the Union appeared merely as a peculiarly venerable treaty of alliance, of which the dissolution would be very painful, but which left each State a sovereign body with an indefeasible right to secede if in the last resort it judged that the painful necessity had come. In a few border States there was division and doubt on this subject, a fact which must have helped to hide from each side the true strength of opinion on the other. But, setting aside these border States, there were in the North some who doubted whether it was expedient to fight for the Union, but none of any consequence who doubted that it was constitutionally correct; and there were in the South men who insisted that no occasion to secede had arisen, but these very men, when outvoted in their States, maintained most passionately the absolute right of secession.

The two sides contended for two contrary doctrines of constitutional law. It is natural when parties are disputing over a question of political wisdom and of moral right that each should claim for its contention if possible the sanction of acknowledged legal principle. So it was with the parties to the English Civil War, and the tendency to regard matters from a legal point of view is to this day deeply engrained in the mental habits of America. But North and South were really divided by something other than legal opinion, a difference in the objects to which their feelings of loyalty and patriotism were directed. This difference found apt expression in the Cabinet of President Buchanan, who of course remained in office between the election of Lincoln in November and his inauguration in March. General Cass of Michigan had formerly stood for the Presidency with the support of the South, and he held Cabinet office now as a sympathiser with the South upon slavery, but he was a Northerner. "I see how it is," he said to two of his colleagues; "you are a Virginian, and you are a South Carolinian; I am not a Michigander, I am an American."

In a former chapter the creation of the Union and the beginnings of a common national life have been traced in outline. Obstacles to the Union had existed both in the North and in the South, and, after it had been carried, the tendency to threaten disruption upon some slight conflict of interest had shown itself in each. But a proud sense of single nationality had soon become prevalent in both, and in the North nothing whatever had happened to set back this growth, for the idea which Lowell had once attributed to his Hosea Biglow of abjuring Union with slave owners was a negligible force. Undivided allegiance to the Union was the natural sentiment of citizens of Ohio or Wisconsin, States created by the authority of the Union out of the common dominion of the Union. It had become, if anything, more deeply engrained in the original States of the North, for their predominant occupation in commerce would tend in this particular to give them larger views. The pride of a Boston man in the Commonwealth of Massachusetts was of the same order as his pride in the city of

Boston; both were largely pride in the part which Boston and Massachusetts had taken in making the United States of America. Such a man knew well that South Carolina had once threatened secession, but, for that matter, the so-called Federalists of New England had once threatened it. The argument of Webster in the case of South Carolina was a classic, and was taken as conclusive on the question of legal right. The terser and more resonant declaration of President Jackson, a Southerner, and the response to it which thrilled all States, South or North, outside South Carolina, had set the seal to Webster's doctrines. There had been loud and ominous talk of secession lately; it was certainly not mere bluster; Northerners in the main were cautious politicians and had been tempted to go far to conciliate it. But if the claim of Southern States were put in practice, the whole North would now regard it not as a respectable claim, but as an outrage.

It is important to notice that the disposition to take this view did not depend upon advanced opinions against slavery. Some of the most violent opponents of slavery would care relatively little about the Constitution or the Union; they would at first hesitate as to whether a peaceful separation between States which felt so differently on a moral question like slavery was not a more Christian solution of their difference than a fratricidal war. On the other hand, men who cared little about slavery, and would gladly have sacrificed any convictions they had upon that matter for the sake of the Union, were at first none the less vehement in their anger at an attack upon the Union. There is, moreover, a more subtle but still important point to be observed in this connection. Democrats in the North inclined as a party to stringent and perhaps pedantically legal views of State rights as against the rights of the Union; but this by no means necessarily meant that they sympathised more than Republicans with the claim to dissolve the Union. They laid emphasis on State rights merely because they believed that these would be a bulwark against any sort of government tyranny, and that the large power which was reserved to the local or provincial authorities of the States made the government of the nation as a whole more truly expressive of the will of the whole people. They now found themselves entangled (as we shall see) in curious doubts as to what the Federal Government might do to maintain the Union, but they had not the faintest doubt that the Union was meant to be maintained. The point which is now being emphasised must not be misapprehended; differences of sentiment in regard to slavery, in regard to State rights, in regard to the authority of Government, did, as the war went on and the price was paid, gravely embarrass the North; but it was a solid and unhesitating North which said that the South had no right to secede.

Up to a certain point the sense of patriotic pride in the Union had grown also in the South. It was fostered at first by the predominant part which the South played in the political life of the country. But for a generation past the sense of a separate interest of the South had been growing still more vigorously. The political predominance of the South had continued, but under a standing menace of downfall as the North grew more populous and the patriotism which it at first encouraged had become perverted into an arrogantly unconscious feeling that the Union was an excellent thing on condition that it was subservient to the South. The common interest of the Southern States was slavery; and, when the Northerners had become a majority which might one day dominate the Federal Government, this common interest of the slave States found a weapon at hand in the doctrine of the inherent sovereignty of each individual State. This doctrine of State sovereignty had come to be held as universally in the South as the strict Unionist doctrine in the North, and held with as quiet and unshakable a confidence that it could not be questioned. It does not seem at all strange that the State, as against the Union, should have remained the supreme object of loyalty in old communities like those of South Carolina and Virginia, abounding as they did in conservative influences which were lacking in the North. But this provincial loyalty was not in the same sense a natural growth in States like Alabama or Mississippi. These, no less than Indiana and Illinois, were the creatures of the Federal Congress, set up within the memory of living men, with arbitrary boundaries that cut across any old lines of division. There was, in fact, no spontaneous feeling of allegiance attaching to these political units, and the doctrine of their sovereignty had no use except as a screen for the interest in slavery which the Southern States had in common. But Calhoun, in a manner characteristic of his peculiar and dangerous type of intellect, had early seen in a view of State sovereignty, which would otherwise have been obsolete, the most serviceable weapon for the joint interests of the Southern States. In a society where intellectual life was restricted, his ascendency had been great, though his disciples had, reasonably enough, thrown aside the qualifications which his subtle mind had attached to the right of secession. Thus in the Southern States generally, even among men most strongly opposed to the actual proposal to secede, the real or alleged constitutional right of a State to secede if it chose now passed unquestioned and was even regarded as a precious liberty.

It is impossible to avoid asking whether on this question of constitutional law the Northern opinion or the Southern opinion was correct. (The question was indeed an important question in determining the proper course of procedure for a President when confronted with secession, but it must be protested that the moral right and political wisdom of neither party in the war depended mainly, if at all, upon this legal point. It was a question of the construction which a court of law should put upon a document which was not drawn up with any view to determining this point.) If we go behind the Constitution, which was then and is now in force, to the original document of which it took the place, we shall find it entitled "Articles of Confederation and Perpetual Union," but we shall not find any such provisions as men desirous of creating a stable and permanent federal government might have been expected to frame. If we read the actual Constitution we shall find no word distinctly implying that a State could or could not secede. As to the real intention of its chief authors, there can be no doubt that they hoped and trusted the Union would prove indissoluble, and equally little doubt that they did not wish to obtrude upon those whom they asked to enter into it the thought that this step would be irrevocable. For the view taken in the South there is one really powerful argument, on which Jefferson Davis insisted passionately in the argumentative memoirs with which he solaced himself in old age. It is that in several of the States, when the Constitution was accepted, public declarations were made to the citizens of those States by their own representatives that a State might withdraw from the Union. But this is far from conclusive. No man gets rid of the obligation of a bond by telling a witness that he does not mean to be bound;

the question is not what he means, but what the party with whom he deals must naturally take him to mean. Now the Constitution of the United States upon the face of it purports to create a government able to take its place among the other governments of the world, able if it declares war to wield the whole force of its country in that war, and able if it makes peace to impose that peace upon all its subjects. This seems to imply that the authority of that government over part of the country should be legally indefeasible. It would have been ridiculous if, during a war with Great Britain, States on the Canadian border should have had the legal right to secede, and set up a neutral government with a view to subsequent reunion with Great Britain. The sound legal view of this matter would seem to be: that the doctrine of secession is so repugnant to the primary intention with which the national instrument of government was framed that it could only have been supported by an express reservation of the right to secede in the Constitution itself.

The Duke of Argyll, one of the few British statesmen of the time who followed this struggle with intelligent interest, briefly summed up the question thus: "I know of no government in the world that could possibly have admitted the right of secession from its own allegiance." Oddly enough, President Buchanan, in his Message to Congress on December 4, put the same point not less forcibly.

But to say – as in a legal sense we may – that the Southern States rebelled is not necessarily to say that they were wrong. The deliberate endeavour of a people to separate themselves from the political sovereignty under which they live and set up a new political community, in which their national life shall develop itself more fully or more securely, must always command a certain respect. Whether it is entitled further to the full sympathy and to the support or at least acquiescence of others is a question which in particular cases involves considerations such as cannot be foreseen in any abstract discussion of political theory. But, speaking very generally, it is a question in the main of the worth which we attribute on the one hand to the common life to which it is sought to give freer scope, and on the other hand to the common life which may thereby be weakened or broken up. It sometimes seems to be held that when a decided majority of the people whose voices can be heard, in a more or less defined area, elect to live for the future under a particular government, all enlightened men elsewhere would wish them to have their way. If any such principle could be accepted without qualification, few movements for independence would ever have been more completely justified than the secession of the Southern States. If we set aside the highland region of which mention has already been made, in the six cotton-growing States which first seceded, and in several of those which followed as soon as it was clear that secession would be resisted, the preponderance of opinion in favour of the movement was overwhelming. This was not only so among the educated and governing portions of society, which were interested in slavery. While the negroes themselves were unorganised and dumb and made no stir for freedom, the poorer class of white people, to whom the institution of slavery was in reality oppressive, were quite unconscious of this; the enslavement of the negro appeared to them a tribute to their own dignity, and their indiscriminating spirit of independence responded enthusiastically to the appeal that they should assert themselves against the real or fancied pretensions of the North. So large a statement would require some qualification if we were here concerned with the life of a Southern leader; and there was of course a brief space, to be dealt with in this chapter, in which the question of secession hung in the balance, and it is true in this, as in every case, that the men who gave the initial push were few. But, broadly speaking, it is certain that the movement for secession was begun with at least as general an enthusiasm and maintained with at least as loyal a devotion as any national movement with which it can be compared. And yet to-day, just fifty-one years after the consummation of its failure, it may be doubted whether one soul among the people concerned regrets that it failed.

English people from that time to this have found the statement incredible; but the fact is that this imposing movement, in which rich and poor, gentle and simple, astute men of state and pious clergymen, went hand in hand to the verge of ruin and beyond, was undertaken simply and solely in behalf of slavery. Northern writers of the time found it so surprising that they took refuge in the theory of conspiracy, alleging that a handful of schemers succeeded, by the help of fictitious popular clamour and intimidation of their opponents, in launching the South upon a course to which the real mind of the people was averse. Later and calmer historical survey of the facts has completely dispelled this view; and the English suspicion, that there must have been some cause beyond and above slavery for desiring independence, never had any facts to support it. Since 1830 no exponent of Southern views had ever hinted at secession on any other ground than slavery; every Southern leader declared with undoubted truth that on every other ground he prized the Union; outside South Carolina every Southern leader made an earnest attempt before he surrendered the Union cause to secure the guarantees he thought sufficient for slavery within the Union. The Southern statesman (for the soldiers were not statesmen) whose character most attracts sympathy now was Alexander Stephens, the Vice-President of the Southern Confederacy, and though he was the man who persisted longest in the view that slavery could be adequately secured without secession, he was none the less entitled to speak for the South in his remarkable words on the Constitution adopted by the Southern Confederacy: "The new Constitution has put at rest for ever all the agitating questions relating to our peculiar institution, African slavery. This was the immediate cause of the late rupture and present revolution. The prevailing ideas entertained by Jefferson and most of the leading statesmen at the time of the old Constitution were that the enslavement of the African was wrong in principle socially, morally, and politically. Our new government is founded upon exactly the opposite idea; its foundations are laid, its corner stone rests, upon the great truth that the negro is not the equal of the white man; that slavery—subordination to the white man—is his natural and normal condition. This, our new government, is the first in the history of the world based upon this great physical, philosophical, and moral truth. The great objects of humanity are best attained when there is conformity to the Creator's laws and decrees." Equally explicit and void of shame was the Convention of the State of Mississippi. "Our position," they declared, "is thoroughly identified with slavery."

It is common to reproach the Southern leaders with reckless folly.

They tried to destroy the Union, which they really valued, for the sake of slavery, which they valued more; they in fact destroyed slavery; and they did this, it is said, in alarm at an imaginary danger. This is not a true ground of reproach to them. It is true that the danger to slavery from the election of Lincoln was not immediately pressing. He neither would have done nor could have done more than to prevent during his four years of office any new acquisition of territory in the slave-holding interest, and to impose his veto on any Bill extending slavery within the existing territory of the Union. His successor after four years might or might not have been like-minded. He did not seem to stand for any overwhelming force in American politics; there was a majority opposed to him in both Houses of Congress; a great majority of the Supreme Court, which might have an important part to play, held views of the Constitution opposed to his; he had been elected by a minority only of the whole American people. Why could not the Southern States have sat still, secure that no great harm would happen to their institution for the present, and hoping that their former ascendency would come back to them with the changing fortunes of party strife? This is an argument which might be expected to have weighed with Southern statesmen if each of them had been anxious merely to keep up the value of his own slave property for his own lifetime, but this was far from being their case.

It is hard for us to put ourselves at the point of view of men who could sincerely speak of their property in negroes as theirs by the "decree of the Creator"; but it is certain that within the last two generations trouble of mind as to the rightfulness of slavery had died out in a large part of the South; the typical Southern leader valued the peculiar form of society under which he lived and wished to hand it on intact to his children's children. If their preposterous principle be granted, the most extreme among them deserve the credit of statesmanlike insight for having seen, the moment that Lincoln was elected, that they must strike for their institution now if they wished it to endure. The Convention of South Carolina justly observed that the majority in the North had voted that slavery was sinful; they had done little more than express this abstract opinion, but they had done all that. Lincoln's administration might have done apparently little, and after it the pendulum would probably have swung back. But the much-talked-of swing of the pendulum is the most delusive of political phenomena; America was never going to return to where it was before this first explicit national assertion of the wrongfulness of slavery had been made. It would have been hard to forecast how the end would come, or how soon; but the end was certain if the Southern States had elected to remain the countrymen of a people who were coming to regard their fundamental institution with growing reprobation. Lincoln had said, "This government cannot endure permanently, half slave and half free." Lincoln was right, and so from their own point of view, that of men not brave or wise enough to take in hand a difficult social reform, were the leaders who declared immediately for secession.

In no other contest of history are those elements in human affairs on which tragic dramatists are prone to dwell so clearly marked as in the American Civil War. No unsophisticated person now, except in ignorance as to the cause of the war, can hesitate as to which side enlists his sympathy, or can regard the victory of the North otherwise than as the costly and imperfect triumph of the right. But the wrong side – emphatically wrong – is not lacking in dignity or human worth; the long-drawn agony of the struggle is not purely horrible to contemplate; there is nothing that in this case makes us reluctant to acknowledge the merits of the men who took arms in the evil cause. The experience as to the relations between superior and inferior races, which is now at the command of every intelligent Englishman, forbids us to think that the inferiority of the negro justified slavery, but it also forbids us to fancy that men to whom the relation of owner to slave had become natural must themselves have been altogether degraded. The men upon the Southern side who can claim any special admiration were simple soldiers who had no share in causing the war; among the political leaders whom they served, there was none who stands out now as a very interesting personality, and their chosen chief is an unattractive figure; but we are not to think of these authors of the war as a gang of hardened, unscrupulous, corrupted men. As a class they were reputable, public-spirited, and religious men; they served their cause with devotion and were not wholly to blame that they chose it so ill. The responsibility for the actual secession does not rest in an especial degree on any individual leader. Secession began rather with the spontaneous movement of the whole community of South Carolina, and in the States which followed leading politicians expressed rather than inspired the general will. The guilt which any of us can venture to attribute for this action of a whole deluded society must rest on men like Calhoun, who in a previous generation, while opinion in the South was still to some extent unformed, stifled all thought of reform and gave the semblance of moral and intellectual justification to a system only susceptible of a historical excuse.

The South was neither base nor senseless, but it was wrong. To some minds it may not seem to follow that it was well to resist it by war, and indeed at the time, as often happens, people took up arms with greater searchings of heart upon the right side than upon the wrong. If the slave States had been suffered to depart in peace they would have set up a new and peculiar political society, more truly held together than the original Union by a single avowed principle; a nation dedicated to the inequality of men. It is not really possible to think of the free national life which they could thus have initiated as a thing to be respected and preserved. Nor is it true that their choice for themselves of this dingy freedom was no concern of their neighbours. We have seen how the slave interest hankered for enlarged dominion; and it is certain that the Southern Confederacy, once firmly established, would have been an aggressive and disturbing power upon the continent of America. The questions of territorial and other rights between it and the old Union might have been capable of satisfactory settlement for the moment, or they might have proved as insoluble as Lincoln thought they were. But, at the best, if the States which adhered to the old Union had admitted the claim of the first seceding States to go, they could only have retained for themselves an insecure existence as a nation, threatened at each fresh conflict of interest or sentiment with a further disruption which could not upon any principle have been resisted. The preceding chapters have dwelt with iteration upon the sentiments which had operated to make Americans a people, and on the form and the degree in which those sentiments animated the mind of Lincoln. Only so perhaps can we fully appreciate for what the people of the North fought. It is inaccurate, though not gravely misleading, to say that they fought against slavery. It would be wholly false to say that they fought for mere dominion. They fought to preserve and complete a political unity nobly conceived by those who had done most to create it, and capable, as the sequel showed, of a permanent and a healthy continuance.

And it must never be forgotten, if we wish to enter into the spirit which sustained the North in its struggle, that loyalty for Union had a larger aspect than that of mere allegiance to a particular authority. Vividly present to the mind of some few, vaguely but honestly present to the mind of a great multitude, was the sense that even had slavery not entered into the question a larger cause than that of their recent Union was bound up with the issues of the war. The Government of the United States had been the first and most famous attempt in a great modern country to secure government by the will of the mass of the people. If in this crucial instance such a Government were seen to be intolerably weak, if it was found to be at the mercy of the first powerful minority which seized a worked-up occasion to rebel, what they had learnt to think the most hopeful agency for the uplifting of man everywhere would for ages to come have proved a failure. This feeling could not be stronger in any American than it was in Lincoln himself. "It has long been a question," he said, "whether any Government which is not too strong for the liberties of the people can be strong enough to maintain itself." There is one marked feature of his patriotism, which could be illustrated by abundance of phrases from his speeches and letters, and which the people of several countries of Europe can appreciate to-day. His affection for his own country and its institutions is curiously dependent upon a wider cause of human good, and is not a whit the less intense for that. There is perhaps no better expression of this widespread feeling in the North than the unprepared speech which he delivered on his way to become President, in the Hall of Independence at Philadelphia, in which the Declaration of Independence had been signed. "I have never," he said, "had a feeling politically that did not spring from the sentiments embodied in the Declaration of Independence. I have often pondered over the dangers which were incurred by the men who assembled here and framed and adopted that

Declaration of Independence. I have pondered over the toils that were endured by the officers and soldiers of the army who achieved that independence. I have often inquired of myself what great principle or idea it was that kept the Confederacy so long together. It was not the mere matter of separation of the colonies from the motherland, it was the sentiment in the Declaration of Independence which gave liberty, not alone to the people of this country, but I hope to the world, for all future time. It was that which gave promise that in due time the weight would be lifted from the shoulders of all men."

2. The Progress of Secession.

So much for the broad causes without which there could have been no Civil War in America. We have now to sketch the process by which the fuel was kindled. It will be remembered that the President elected in November does not enter upon his office for nearly four months. For that time, therefore, the conduct of government lay in the hands of President Buchanan, who, for all his past subserviency to Southern interests, believed and said that secession was absolutely unlawful. Several members of his Cabinet were Southerners who favoured secession; but the only considerable man among them, Cobb of Georgia, soon declared that his loyalty to his own State was not compatible with his office and resigned; and, though others, including the Secretary for War, hung on to their position, it does not appear that they influenced Buchanan much, or that their somewhat dubious conduct while they remained was of great importance. Black, the Attorney-General, and Cass, the Secretary of State, who, however, resigned when his advice was disregarded, were not only loyal to the Union, but anxious that the Government should do everything that seemed necessary in its defence. Thus this administration, hitherto Southern in its sympathies, must be regarded for its remaining months as standing for the Union, so far as it stood for anything. Lincoln meanwhile had little that he could do but to watch events and prepare. There was, nevertheless, a point in the negotiations which took place between parties at which he took on himself a tremendous responsibility and at which his action was probably decisive of all that followed.

The Presidential election took place on November 6, 1860. On November 10 the Legislature of South Carolina, which had remained in session for this purpose, convened a specially elected Convention of the State to decide upon the question of secession. Slave owners and poor whites, young and old, street rabble, persons of fashion, politicians and clergy, the whole people of this peculiar State, distinguished in some marked respects even from its nearest neighbours, received the action of the Legislature with enthusiastic but grave approval. It was not till December 20 that the Convention could pass its formal "Ordinance of Secession," but there was never for a moment any doubt as to what it would do. The question was what other States would follow the example of South Carolina. There ensued in all the Southern States earnest discussion as to whether to secede or not, and in the North, on which the action of South Carolina, however easily it might have been foretold, came as a shock, great bewilderment as to what was to be done. As has been said, there was in the South generally no disposition to give up Southern claims, no doubt as to the right of secession, and no fundamental and overriding loyalty to the Union, but there was a considerable reluctance to give up the Union and much doubt as to whether secession was really wise; there was in the North among those who then made themselves heard no doubt whatever as to the loyalty due to the Union, but there was, apart from previous differences about slavery, every possible variety and fluctuation of opinion as to the right way of dealing with States which should secede or rebel. In certain border States, few in number but likely to play an important part in civil war, Northern and Southern elements were mingled. Amid loud and distracted discussion, public and private, leaders of the several parties and of the two sections of the country conducted earnest negotiations in the hope of finding a peaceable settlement, and when Congress met, early in December, their debates took a formal shape in committees appointed by the Senate and by the House.

Meanwhile the President was called upon to deal with the

problem presented for the Executive Government of the Union by the action of South Carolina. It may be observed that if he had given his mind to the military measures required to meet the possible future, the North, which in the end had his entire sympathy, would have begun the war with that advantage in preparation which, as it was, was gained by the South. In this respect he did nothing. But, apart from this, if he had taken up a clear and comprehensible attitude towards South Carolina and had given a lead to Unionist sympathy, he would have consolidated public opinion in the North, and he would have greatly strengthened those in the South who remained averse to secession. There would have been a considerable further secession, but in all likelihood it would not have become so formidable as it did. As it was, the movement for secession proceeded with all the proud confidence that can be felt in a right which is not challenged, and the people of the South were not aware, though shrewd leaders like Jefferson Davis knew it well, of the risk they would encounter till they had committed themselves to defying it.

The problem before Buchanan was the same which, aggravated by his failure to deal with it, confronted Lincoln when he came into office, and it must be clearly understood. The secession of South Carolina was not a movement which could at once be quelled by prompt measures of repression. Even if sufficient military force and apt forms of law had existed for taking such measures they would have united the South in support of South Carolina, and alienated the North, which was anxious for conciliation. Yet it was possible for the Government of the Union, while patiently abstaining from violent or provocative action, to make plain that in the last resort it would maintain its rights in South Carolina with its full strength. The main dealings of the Union authorities with the people of a State came under a very few heads. There were local Federal Courts to try certain limited classes of issues; jurors, of course, could not be compelled to serve in these nor parties to appear. There was the postal service; the people of South Carolina did not at present interfere with this source of convenience to themselves and of revenue to the Union. There were customs duties to be collected at the ports, and there were forts at the entrance of the harbour in Charleston, South Carolina, as well as forts, dockyards and arsenals of the United States at a number of points in the Southern States; the Government should quietly but openly have taken steps to ensure that the collection should go on unmolested, and that the forts and the like should be made safe from attack, in South Carolina and everywhere else where they were likely to be threatened. Measures of this sort were early urged upon Buchanan by Scott, the Lieutenant-General (that is, Second in Command under the President) of the Army, who had been the officer that carried out Jackson's military dispositions when secession was threatened in South Carolina thirty years before, and by other officers concerned, particularly by Major Anderson, a keen Southerner, but a keen soldier, commanding the forts at Charleston, and by Cass and Black in his Cabinet. Public opinion in the North demanded such measures.

If further action than the proper manning and supply of certain forts had been in contemplation, an embarrassing legal question would have arisen. In the opinion of the Attorney-General, of leading Democrats like Cass and Douglas, and apparently of most legal authorities of every party, there was an important distinction, puzzling to an English lawyer even if he is versed in the American Constitution, between the steps which the Government might justly take in self-protection, and measures which could be regarded as coercion of the State of South Carolina as such. These latter would be unlawful. Buchanan, instead of acting on or declaring his intentions, entertained Congress, which met early in December, with a Message, laying down very clearly the illegality of secession, but discussing at large this abstract question of the precise powers of the Executive in resisting secession. The legal question will not further concern us because the distinction which it was really intended to draw between lawful and unlawful measures against secession quite coincided, in its practical application, with what common sense and just feeling would in these peculiar circumstances have dictated. But, as a natural consequence of such discussion, an impression was spread abroad of the illegality of something vaguely called coercion, and of the shadowy nature of any power which the Government claimed.

Up to Lincoln's inauguration the story of the Charleston forts, of which one, lying on an island in the mouth of the harbour, was the famous Fort Sumter, is briefly this. Buchanan was early informed that if the Union Government desired to hold them, troops and ships of war should instantly be sent. Congressmen from South Carolina remaining in Washington came to him and represented that their State regarded these forts upon its soil as their own; they gave assurances that there would be no attack on the forts if the existing military situation was not altered, and they tried to get a promise that the forts should not be reinforced. Buchanan would give them no promise, but he equally refused the entreaties of Scott and his own principal ministers that he should reinforce the forts, because he declared that this would precipitate a conflict. Towards the end of the year Major Anderson, not having men enough to hold all the forts if, as he expected, they were attacked, withdrew his whole force to Fort Sumter, which he thought the most defensible, dismantling the principal other fort. The Governor of South Carolina protested against this as a violation of a supposed understanding with the President, and seized upon the United States arsenal and the custom house, taking the revenue officers into State service. Commissioners had previously gone from South Carolina to Washington to request the surrender of the forts, upon terms of payment for property; they now declared that Anderson's withdrawal, as putting him in a better position for defence, was an act of war, and demanded that he should be ordered to retire to the mainland.

Buchanan wavered; decided to yield to them on this last point; ultimately, on the last day of 1860, yielded instead to severe pressure from Black, and decided to reinforce Anderson on Fort Sumter. The actual attempt to reinforce him was bungled; a transport sent for this purpose was fired upon by the South Carolina forces, and returned idle. This first act of war, for some curious reason, caused no excitement. The people of the North were intensely relieved that Buchanan had not yielded to whatever South Carolina might demand, and, being prone to forgive and to applaud, seem for a time to have experienced a thrill of glory in the thought that the national administration had a mind. Dix, the Secretary of the Treasury, elated them yet further by telegraphing to a Treasury official at New Orleans, "If any one attempts to haul down the American flag, shoot him on the spot." But Anderson remained without reinforcements or further provisions when Lincoln entered office; and troops in the service first of South Carolina and afterwards of the Southern Confederacy, which was formed in February, erected batteries and prepared to bombard Fort Sumter.

No possible plea for President Buchanan can make him rank among those who have held high office with any credit at all, but he must at once be acquitted of any intentional treachery to the Union. It is agreed that he was a truthful and sincere man, and there is something pleasant in the simple avowal he made to a Southern negotiator who was pressing him for some instant concession, that he always said his prayers before deciding any important matter of State. His previous dealings with Kansas would suggest to us robust unscrupulousness, but it seems that he had quite given his judgment over into the keeping of a little group of Southern Senators. Now that he was deprived of this help, he had only enough will left to be obstinate against other advice. It is suggested that he had now but one motive, the desire that the struggle should break out in his successor's time rather than his own. Even this is perhaps to judge Buchanan's notorious and calamitous laches unfairly. Any action that he took must to a certain extent have been provocative, and he knew it, and he may have clung to the hope that by sheer inaction he would give time for some possible forces of reason and conciliation to work. If so, he was wrong, but similar and about as foolish hopes paralysed Lincoln's Cabinet (and to a less but still very dangerous degree Lincoln himself) when they took up the problem which Buchanan's neglect had made more urgent. Buchanan had in this instance the advantage of far better advice, but this silly old man must not be gibbeted and Lincoln left free from criticism for his part in the same transaction. Both Presidents hesitated where to us who look back the case seems clear. The circumstances had altered in some respects when Lincoln came in, but it is only upon a somewhat broad survey of the governing tendencies of Lincoln's administration and of its mighty result in the mass that we discover what really distinguishes his slowness of action in such cases as this from the hesitation of a man like Buchanan. Buchanan waited in the hope of avoiding action,

the air. It seemed clear from the expressed opinions of his closest allies that Seward would support this compromise. Now Seward just at this time received Lincoln's offer of the office of Secretary of State, a great office and one in which Seward expected to rule Lincoln and the country, but in accepting which, as he did, he made it incumbent on himself not to part company at once with the man who would be nominally his chief. Then there occurred a visit paid on Seward's behalf by his friend Thurlow Weed, an astute political manager but also an able statesman, to Lincoln at Springfield. Weed brought back a written statement of Lincoln's views. Seward's support was not given to the compromise; nor naturally was that of the more radical Republicans, to use a term which now became common; and the Committee of Thirteen found itself unable to agree.

It is unnecessary to repeat what Lincoln's conviction on this, to him the one essential point of policy, was, or to quote from the numerous letters in which from the time of his nomination he tried to keep the minds of his friends firm on this single principle, and to show them that if there were the slightest further yielding as to this, save indeed as to the peculiar case of New Mexico, which did not matter, and which perhaps he regarded as conceded already, the Southern policy of extending slavery and of "filibustering" against neighbouring counties for that purpose would revive in full force, and the whole labour of the Republican movement would have to begin over again. Since his election he had been writing also to Southern politicians who were personally friendly, to Gilmer of North Carolina, to whom he offered Cabinet office, and to Stephens, making absolutely plain that his difference with them lay in this one point, but making it no less plain that on this point he was, with entire respect to them, immovable. Now, on December 22, the _New York Tribune_ was "enabled to state that Mr. Lincoln stands now as he stood in May last, square upon the Republican platform." The writing that Weed brought to Seward must have said, perhaps more elaborately, the same. If Lincoln had not stood square upon that platform there were others like Senator Wade of Ohio and Senator Grimes of Iowa who might have done so and might have been able to wreck the compromise. Lincoln, however, did wreck it, at a time when it seemed likely to succeed, and it is most probable that thereby he caused the Civil War. It cannot be said that he definitely expected the Civil War. Probably he avoided makin any definite forecast; but he expressed no alarm, and he privately told a friend about this time that "he could not in his heart believe that the South designed the overthrow of the Government." But, if he had in his heart believed it, nothing in his life gives reason to think that he would have been more anxious to conciliate the South; on the contrary, it is in line with all we know of his feelings to suppose that he would have thought firmness all the more imperative. We cannot recall the solemnity of his long-considered speech about "a house divided against itself," with which all his words and acts accorded, without seeing that, if perhaps he speculated little about the risks, he was prepared to face them whatever they were. Doubtless he took a heavy responsibility, but it is painful to find honourable historians, who heartily dislike the cause of slavery, capable to-day of wondering whether he was right to do so. "If he had not stood square" in December upon the same "platform" on which he had stoc : in May, if he had preferred to enroll himself among those statesmen of all countries whose strongest words are uttered for their own subsequent enjoyment in eating them, he might conceivably have saved much bloodshed, but he would not have left the United States a country of which any good man was proud to be a citizen.

Thus, by the end of 1860, the bottom was really out of the policy of compromise, and it is not worth while to examine the praiseworthy efforts that were still made for it while State after State in the South was deciding to secede. One interesting proposal, which was aired in January, 1861, deserves notice, namely, that the terms of compromise proposed by Crittenden should have been submitted to a vote of the whole people. It was not passed. Seward, whom many people now thought likely to catch at any and every proposal for a settlement, said afterwards with justice that it was "unconstitutional and ineffectual." Ineffectual it would have been in this sense: the compromise would in all probability have been carried by a majority consisting of men in the border States and of all those elsewhere who, though they feared war and desired good feeling, had no further definite opinion upon the chief questions at issue; but it would have left a local majority in many of the Southern

States and a local majority in many of the Northern States as irreconcilable with each other as ever. It was opposed also to the spirit of the Constitution. In a great country where the people with infinitely varied interests and opinions can slowly make their predominant wishes appear, but cannot really take counsel together and give a firm decision upon any emergency, there may be exceptional cases when a popular vote on a defined issue would be valuable, significant, desired by the people themselves; but the machinery of representative government, however faulty, is the only machinery by which the people can in some sense govern itself, instead of making itself ungovernable. Above all, in a serious crisis it is supremely repugnant to the spirit of popular government that the men chosen by a people to govern it should throw their responsibility back at the heads of the electors. It is well to be clear as to the kind of proceeding which the authors of this proposal were really advocating: a statesman has come before the ordinary citizen with a definite statement of the principle on which he would act, and an ordinary citizen has thereupon taken his part in entrusting him with power; then comes the moment for the statesman to carry out his principle, and the latent opposition becomes of necessity more alarming; the statesman is therefore to say to the ordinary citizen, "This is a more difficult matter than I thought; and if I am to act as I said I would, take on yourself the responsibility which I recently put myself forward to bear." The ordinary citizen will naturally as a rule decline a responsibility thus offered him, but he will not be grateful for the offer or glad to be a forced accomplice in this process of indecision.

If we could determine the prevailing sentiment in the North at some particular moment during the crisis, it would probably represent what very few individual men continued to think for six months together. Early in the crisis some strong opponents of slavery were for letting the South go, declaring, as did Horace Greeley of the 'New York Tribune', that "they would not be citizens of a Republic of which one part was pinned to the other part with bayonets"; but this sentiment seems soon to have given way when the same men began to consider, as Lincoln had considered, whether an agreement to sever the Union between the States, with the difficult adjustment of mutual interests which it would have involved, could be so effected as to secure a lasting peace. A blind rage on behalf of conciliation broke out later in prosperous business men in great towns—even in Boston it is related that "Beacon Street aristocrats" broke up a meeting to commemorate John Brown on the anniversary of his death, and grave persons thought the meeting an outrage. Waves of eager desire for compromise passed over the Northern community. Observers at the time and historians after are easily mistaken as to popular feeling; the acute fluctuations of opinion inevitable among journalists, and in any sort of circle where men are constantly meeting and talking politics, may leave the great mass of quiet folk almost unaffected. We may be sure that there was a considerable body of steady opinion very much in accord with Lincoln; this should not be forgotten, but it must not be supposed that it prevailed constantly. On the contrary, it was inherent in the nature of the crisis that opinion wavered and swayed. We should miss the whole significance of Lincoln's story if we did not think of the North now and to the end of the war as exposed to disunion, hesitation, and quick reaction. If at this time a sufficiently authoritative leader with sufficiently determined timidity had inaugurated a policy of stampede, he might have had a vast and tumultuous following. Only his following would quickly, if too late, have repented. What was wanted, if the people of the North were to have what most justly might be called their way, was a leader who would not seem to hurry them along, nor yet be ever looking round to see if they followed, but just go groping forward among the innumerable obstacles, guided by such principles of good sense and of right as would perhaps on the whole and in the long run be approved by the maturer thought of most men; and Lincoln was such a leader.

When we turn to the South, where, as has been said, the movement for secession was making steady though not unopposed progress, we have indeed to make exceptions to any sweeping statement, but we must recognise a far more clearly defined and far more prevailing general opinion. We may set aside for the moment the border slave States of Maryland, Virginia, Kentucky, and Missouri, each of which has a distinct and an important history. Delaware belonged in effect to the North. In Texas there were peculiar conditions, and Texas had an interesting history of its own in this matter, but may be treated as remote. There was also, as has been said, a highland region covering the west of Virginia and the east of Kentucky but reaching far south into the northern part of Alabama. Looking at the pathetic spectacle of enduring heroism in a mistaken cause which the South presented, many people have been ready to suppose that it was manoeuvred and tricked into its folly by its politicians and might have recovered itself from it if the North and the Government had exercised greater patience and given it time. In support of this view instances are cited of strong Unionist feeling in the South. Such instances probably belong to the peculiar people of this highland country, or else to the mixed and more or less neutral population that might be found at New Orleans or trading along the Mississippi. There remains a solid and far larger South in which indeed (except for South Carolina) dominant Southern policy was briskly debated, but as a question of time, degree, and expediency. Three mental forces worked for the same end: the alarmed vested interest of the people of substance, aristocratic and otherwise; the racial sentiment of the poor whites, a sentiment often strongest in those who have no subject of worldly pride but their colour; and the philosophy of the clergy and other professional men who constituted what in some countries is called the intellectual class. These influences resulted in a rare uniformity of opinion that slavery was right and all attacks on it were monstrous, that the Southern States were free to secede and form, if they chose, a new Confederacy, and that they ought to do this if the moment should arrive when they could not otherwise safeguard their interests. Doubtless there were leading men who had thought over the matter in advance of the rest and taken counsel together long before, but the fact seems to be that such leaders now found their followers in advance of them. Jefferson Davis, by far the most commanding man among them, now found himself—certainly it served him right—anxiously counselling delay, and spending nights in prayer before he made his farewell speech to the Senate in words of greater dignity and good feeling than seem to comport with the fanatical narrowness of his view and the progressive warping of his determined character to which it condemned him. Whatever fundamental loyalty to the Union existed in any man's heart there were months of debate in which it found no organised and hardly any audible expression. The most notable stand against actual secession was that which was made in Georgia by Stephens; he was determined and outspoken, but he proceeded wholly upon the ground that secession was premature. And this instance is significant of something further. It has been said that discussion and voting were not free, and it would be altogether unlikely that their freedom should in no cases be infringed, but there is no evidence that this charge was widely true. It is surely significant of the general temper of the South, and most honourable to it, that Stephens, who thus struggled against secession at that moment, was chosen Vice-President of the Southern Confederacy.

By February 4, 1861, the States of Mississippi, Florida, Alabama, Georgia, and Louisiana had followed South Carolina by passing Ordinances of Secession, and on that date representatives of these States met at Montgomery in Alabama to found a new Confederacy. Texas, where considerable resistance was offered by Governor Houston, the adventurous leader under whom that State had separated from Mexico, was in process of passing the like Ordinance. Virginia and North Carolina, which lie north of the region where cotton prevails, and with them their western neighbour Tennessee, and Arkansas, yet further west and separated from Tennessee by the Mississippi River, did not secede till after Lincoln's inauguration and the outbreak of war. But the position of Virginia (except for its western districts) admitted of very little doubt, and that of Tennessee and North Carolina was known to be much the same. Virginia took a historic pride in the Union, and its interest in slavery was not quite the same as that of the cotton States, yet its strongest social ties were to the South. This State was now engaged in a last idle attempt to keep itself and other border States in the Union, with some hope also that the departed States might return; and on this same February 6, a "Peace Convention," invited by Virginia and attended by delegates from twenty-one States, met at Washington with ex-President Tyler in the chair; but for Virginia it was all along a condition of any terms of agreement that the right of any State to secede should be fully acknowledged.

The Congress of the seceding States, which met at Montgomery, was described by Stephens as, "taken all in all, the noblest, soberest, most intelligent, and most conservative body I was ever in." It has been remarked that Southern politicians of the agitator type were not sent to it. It adopted a provisional Constitution modelled largely upon that of the United States. Jefferson Davis, who had retired to his farm, was sent for to become President; Stephens, as already said, became Vice-President. The delegates there were to continue in session for the present as the regular Congress. Whether sobered by the thought that they were acting in the eyes of the world, or in accordance with their own prevailing sentiment, these men, some of whom had before urged the revival of the slave trade, now placed in their Constitution a perpetual prohibition of it, and when, as a regular legislature, they afterwards passed a penal statute which carried out this intention inadequately, President Davis conscientiously vetoed it and demanded a more satisfactory measure. At his inauguration the Southern President delivered an address, typical of that curious blending of propriety and insincerity, of which the politics of that period in America had offered many examples. It may seem incredible, but it contained no word of slavery, but recited in dignified terms how the South had been driven to separation by "wanton aggression on the part of others," and after it had "vainly endeavoured to secure tranquillity." The new Southern Congress now resolved to take over the forts and other property in the seceded States that had belonged to the Union, and the first Confederate general, Beauregard, was sent to Charleston to hover over Fort Sumter.

3. The Inauguration of Lincoln.

The first necessary business of the President-elect, while he watched the gathering of what Emerson named "the hurricane in which he was called to the helm," was to construct a strong Cabinet, to which may be added the seemingly unnecessary business forced upon him of dealing with a horde of pilgrims who at once began visiting him to solicit some office or, in rarer cases, to press their disinterested opinions. His Cabinet, designed in principle, as has been said, while he was waiting in the telegraph office for election returns, was actually constructed with some delay and hesitation. Lincoln could not know personally all the men he invited to join him, but he proceeded with the view of conjoining in his administration representatives of the chief shades of opinion which in this critical time it would be his supreme duty to hold together. Not only different shades of opinion, but the local sentiment of different districts had to be considered; he once complained that if the twelve Apostles had to be chosen nowadays the principle of locality would have to be regarded; but at this time there was very solid reason why different States should be contented and why he should be advised as to their feelings. His own chief rivals for the Presidency offered a good choice from both these points of view. They were Seward of New York, Chase of Ohio, Bates of Missouri, Cameron of Pennsylvania. Seward and Chase were both able and outstanding men: the former was in a sense the old Republican leader, but was more and more coming to be regarded as the typical "Conservative," or cautious Republican; Chase on the other hand was a leader of the "Radicals," who were "stern and unbending" in their attitude towards slavery and towards the South. These two must be got and kept together if possible. Bates was a good and capable man who moreover came from Missouri, a border slave State, where his influence was much to be desired. He became Attorney-General. Cameron, an unfortunate choice as it turned out, was a very wealthy business man of Pennsylvania, representative of the weighty Protectionist influence there. After he had been offered office, which had been without Lincoln's authority promised him in the Republican Convention, Lincoln was dismayed by representations that he was "a bad, corrupted man"; he wrote a curious letter asking Cameron to refuse his offer; Cameron instead produced evidence of the desire of Pennsylvania for him; Lincoln stuck to his offer; the old Whig element among Republicans, the Protectionist element, and above all, the friends of the indispensable Seward, would otherwise have been outweighted in the Cabinet. Cameron eventually became for a time Secretary of War. To these Lincoln, upon somebody's strong representations, tried, without much hope, to add some distinctly Southern politician. The effort, of course, failed. Ultimately the Cabinet was completed by the addition of Caleb Smith of Indiana as Secretary of the Interior, Gideon Welles of Connecticut as Secretary of the Navy, and Montgomery Blair of Maryland as Postmaster-General. Welles, with the guidance of a brilliant subordinate, Fox, served usefully, was very loyal to Lincoln, had an antipathy to England which was dangerous, and kept very diligently a diary for which we may be grateful now. Blair was a vehement, irresponsible person with an influential connection, and, which was important, his influence and that of his family lay in Maryland and other border slave States. Of all these men, Seward, Secretary of State—that is, Foreign Minister and something more—and Chase, Secretary of the Treasury, most concern us. Lincoln's offer to Seward was made and accepted in terms that did credit to both men, and Seward, still smarting at his own defeat, was admirably loyal. But his friends, though they had secured the appointment of Cameron to support them, thought increasingly ill of the prospects of a Cabinet which included the Radical Chase. On the very night before his inauguration Lincoln received from Seward, who had just been helping to revise his Inaugural Address, a letter withdrawing his acceptance of office. By some not clearly recorded exercise of that great power over men, which, if with some failures, was generally at his command, he forced Seward to see that the unconditional withdrawal of this letter was his public duty. It must throughout what follows be remembered that Lincoln's first and most constant duty was to hold together the jarring elements in the North which these jarring elements in his own Cabinet represented; and it was one of his great achievements that he kept together, for as long as was needful, able but discordant public servants who could never have combined together without him.

On February 11, 1861, Lincoln, standing on the gallery at the end of a railway car, upon the instant of departure from the home to which he never returned, said to his old neighbours (according to the version of his speech which his private secretary got him to dictate immediately after): "My friends, no one, not in my situation, can appreciate my feeling of sadness at this parting. To this place, and the kindness of these people, I owe everything.

Here I have lived for a quarter of a century, and have passed from a young to an old man. Here my children have been born and one is buried. I now leave, not knowing when or whether ever I may return, with a task before me greater than that which rested upon Washington. Without the assistance of that Divine Being who ever attended him, I cannot succeed. With that assistance, I cannot fail. Trusting in Him who can go with me, and remain with you, and be everywhere for good, let us confidently hope that all will yet be well. To His care commending you, as I hope in your prayers you will commend me, I bid you an affectionate farewell."

He was, indeed, going to a task not less great than Washington's, but he was going to it with a preparation in many respects far inferior to his. For the last eight years he had laboured as a public speaker, and in a measure as a party leader, and had displayed and developed comprehension, perhaps unequalled, of some of the larger causes which mould public affairs. But, except in sheer moral discipline, those years had done nothing to supply the special training which he had previously lacked, for high executive office. In such office at such a time ready decision in an obscure and passing situation may often be a not less requisite than philosophic grasp either of the popular mind or of eternal laws. The powers which he had hitherto shown would still be needful to him, but so too would other powers which he had never practised in any comparable position, and which nature does not in a moment supply. Any attempt to judge of Lincoln's Presidency—and it can only be judged at all when it has gone on some way—must take account, not perhaps so much of his inexperience, as of his own reasonable consciousness of it and his great anxiety to use the advice of men who were in any way presumably more competent.

He deliberately delayed his arrival in Washington and availed himself of official invitations to stay at four great towns and five State capitals which he could conveniently pass on his way. The journey abounded in small incidents and speeches, some of which exposed him to a little ridicule in the press, though they probably created an undercurrent of sympathy for him. Near one station where the train stopped lived a little girl he knew, who had recently urged upon him to wear a beard or whiskers. To this dreadful young person, and to that persistent good nature of his which was now and then fatuous, was due the ill-designed hairy ornamentation which during his Presidency hid the really beautiful modelling of his jaw and chin. He enquired for her at the station, had her fetched from the crowd, claimed her praise for this supposed improvement, and kissed her in presence of the press. In New York he was guilty of a more sinister and tragic misfeasance. In that city, where, if it may be said with respect, there has existed from of old a fashionable circle not convinced of its own gentility and insisting the more rigorously on minor decorum, Lincoln went to the opera, and history still deplores that this misguided man went there and sat there with his large hands in black kid gloves. Here perhaps it is well to say that the educated world of the Eastern States, including those who privately deplored Lincoln's supposed unfitness, treated its untried chief magistrate with that engrained good breeding to which it was utterly indifferent how plain a man he might be. His lesser speeches as he went were unstudied appeals to loyalty, with very simple avowals of inadequacy to his task, and expressions of reliance on the people's support when he tried to do his duty. To a man who can sometimes speak from the heart and to the heart as Lincoln did it is perhaps not given to be uniformly felicitous. Among these speeches was that delivered at Philadelphia, which has already been quoted, but most of them were not considered felicitous at the time. They were too unpretentious. Moreover, they contained sentences which seemed to understate the gravity of the crisis in a way which threw doubt on his own serious statesmanship. Whether they were felicitous or not, the intention of these much-criticised utterances was the best proof of his statesmanship. He would appeal to the steady loyalty of the North, but he was not going to arouse its passion. He assumed to the last that calm reflection might prevail in the South, which was menaced by nothing but "an artificial crisis." He referred to war as a possibility, but left no doubt of his own wish by all means to avoid it. "There will," he said, "be no bloodshed unless it be forced on the Government. The Government will not use force unless force is used against it."

Before he passed through Baltimore he received earnest communications from Seward and from General Scott. Each had received trustworthy information of a plot, which existed, to murder him in that city. Owing to their warnings he went through Baltimore secretly at night, so that his arrival in Washington, on February 23, was unexpected. This was his obvious duty, and nobody who knew him was ever in doubt of his personal intrepidity; but of course it helped to damp the effect of what many people would have been glad to regard as a triumphal progress.

On March 4, 1861, old Buchanan came in his carriage to escort his successor to the inaugural ceremony, where it was the ironical fate of Chief Justice Taney to administer the oath to a President who had already gone far to undo his great work. Yet a third notable Democrat was there to do a pleasant little act. Douglas, Lincoln's defeated rival, placed himself with a fine ostentation by his side, and, observing that he was embarrassed as to where to put his new tall hat and preposterous gold-knobbed cane, took charge of these encumbrances before the moment arrived for the most eagerly awaited of all his speeches. Lincoln had submitted his draft of his "First Inaugural" to Seward, and this draft with Seward's abundant suggestions of amendment has been preserved. It has considerable literary interest, and, by the readiness with which most of Seward's suggestions were adopted, and the decision with which some, and those not the least important, were set aside by Lincoln, it illustrates well the working relation which, after one short struggle, was to be established between these two men. By Seward's advice Lincoln added to an otherwise dry speech some concluding paragraphs of emotional appeal. The last sentence of the speech, which alone is much remembered, is Seward's in the first conception of it, Seward's in the slightly hackneyed phrase with which it ends, Lincoln's alone in the touch of haunting beauty which is on it.

His "First Inaugural" was by general confession an able state paper, setting forth simply and well a situation with which we are now familiar. It sets out dispassionately the state of the controversy on slavery, lays down with brief argument the position that the Union is indissoluble, and proceeds to define

of the trained administrator, but just that rough perception and vigour which untaught genius might be supposed to possess. The passionate Jackson (who, by the way, was a far more educated man in the respects which count) would not have acted so. Lincoln, it is true, had declared that he would take no provocative step—"In your hands, my dissatisfied fellow-countrymen, and not in mine, is the momentous issue of civil war," and the risk which he would have taken by over-ruling that day the opinion of the bulk of his Cabinet based on that of his chief military adviser is obvious, but it seems to have been a lesser risk than he did take in delaying so long to overrule his Cabinet. It is precisely characteristic of his strength and of his weakness that he did not at once yield to his advisers; that he long continued weighing the matter undisturbed by the danger of delay; that he decided as soon as and no sooner than he felt sure as to the political results, which alone here mattered, for the military consequences amounted to nothing.

This story was entangled from the first with another difficult story. Commissioners from the Southern Confederacy came to Washington and sought interviews with Seward; they came to treat for the recognition of the Confederacy and the peaceful surrender of forts and the like within its borders. Meanwhile the action of Virginia was in the balance, and the "Peace Convention," summoned by Virginia, still "threshing again," as Lowell said, "the already twice-threshed straw of debate." The action of Virginia and of other border States, about which Lincoln was intensely solicitous, would certainly depend upon the action of the Government towards the States that had already seceded. Might it not be well that the Government should avoid immediate conflict with South Carolina about Fort Sumter, though conflict with the Confederacy about Fort Pickens and the rest would still impend? Was it not possible that conflict could be staved off till an agreement could be reached with Virginia and the border States, which would induce the seceded States to return? These questions were clearly absurd, but they were as clearly natural, and they greatly exercised Seward. Disappointed at not being President and equally disturbed at the prospect of civil war, but still inclined to large and sanguine hopes, he was rather anxious to take things out of Lincoln's hands and very anxious to serve his country as the great peacemaker. Indirect negotiations now took place between him and the Southern Commissioners, who of course could not be officially recognised, through the medium of two Supreme Court Judges, especially one Campbell, who was then in Washington. Seward was quite loyal to Lincoln and told him in a general way what he was doing; he was also candid with Campbell and his friends, and explained to them his lack of authority, but he talked freely and rashly of what he hoped to bring about. Lincoln gave Seward some proper cautions and left him all proper freedom; but it is possible that he once told Douglas that he intended, at that moment, to evacuate Fort Sumter. The upshot of the matter is that the decision of the Government was delayed by negotiations which, as it ought to have known, could come to nothing, and that the Southern Government and the Commissioners, after they had got home, thought they had been deceived in these negotiations.

Discussions were still proceeding as to Fort Sumter when a fresh difficulty arose for Lincoln, but one which enabled him to become henceforth master in his Cabinet. The strain of Seward's position upon a man inclined to be vain and weak can easily be imagined, but the sudden vagary in which it now resulted was surprising. Upon April 1 he sent to Lincoln "Some Thoughts for the President's Consideration." In this paper, after deploring what he described as the lack of any policy so far, and defining, in a way that does not matter, his attitude as to the forts in the South, he proceeded thus: "I would demand explanations from Great Britain and Russia, and send agents into Canada, Mexico, and Central America, to raise a vigorous spirit of independence on this continent against European intervention, and if satisfactory explanations are not received from Spain and France, would convene Congress and declare war against them." In other words, Seward would seek to end all domestic dissensions by suddenly creating out of nothing a dazzling foreign policy. But this was not the only point, even if it was the main point; he proceeded: "Either the President must do it" (that is the sole conduct of this policy) "himself, or devolve it on some member of his Cabinet. It is not my especial province. But I neither seek to evade nor assume responsibility." In other words, Seward put himself forward as the sole director of the Government. In his brief reply Lincoln made no reference whatever to Seward's amazing programme. He pointed out that the policy so far, as to which Seward had complained, was one in which Seward had entirely concurred. As to the concluding demand that some one man, and that man Seward, should control all policy, he wrote, "If this must be done, I must do it. When a general line of policy is adopted, I apprehend there is no danger of its being changed without good reason, or continuing to be a subject of unnecessary debate; still, upon points arising in its progress I wish, and suppose I am entitled to have, the advice of all the Cabinet." Seward was not a fool, far from it; he was one of the ablest men in America, only at that moment strained and excited beyond the limits of his good sense. Lincoln's quiet answer sobered him then and for ever after. He showed a generous mind; he wrote to his wife soon after: "Executive force and vigour are rare qualities; the President is the best of us." And Lincoln's generosity was no less; his private secretary, Nicolay, saw these papers; but no other man knew anything of Seward's abortive rebellion against Lincoln till after they both were dead. The story needs no explanation, but the more attentively all the circumstances are considered, the more Lincoln's handling of this emergency, which threatened the ruin of his Government, throws into shade the weakness he had hitherto shown.

Lincoln was thus in a stronger position when he finally decided as to Fort Sumter. It is unnecessary to follow the repeated consultations that took place. There were preparations for possible expeditions both to Fort Sumter and to Fort Pickens, and various blunders about them, and Seward made some trouble by officious interference about them. An announcement was sent to the Governor of South Carolina that provisions would be sent to Fort Sumter and he was assured that if this was unopposed no further steps would be taken. What chiefly concerns us is that the eventual decision to send provisions but not troops to Fort Sumter was Lincoln's decision; but that it was not taken till after Senators and Congressmen had made clear to him that Northern opinion would support him. It was the right decision, for it conspicuously avoided the appearance of provocation, while it upheld the right of the Union; but it was taken perilously late, and the delay exposed the Government to the risk of a great humiliation.

An Alabama gentleman had urged Jefferson Davis that the impending struggle must not be delayed. "Unless," he said, "you sprinkle blood in the face of the people of Alabama, they will be back in the old Union in ten days." There is every reason to suppose that the gentleman's statement as to the probable collapse of the South was mere rhetoric, but it seems that his advice led to orders being sent to Beauregard to reduce Fort Sumter. Beauregard sent a summons to Anderson; Anderson, now all but starved out, replied that unless he received supplies or instructions he would surrender on April 15. Whether by Beauregard's orders or through some misunderstanding, the Confederate batteries opened fire on Fort Sumter on April 12. Fort Sumter became untenable on the next day, when the relief ships, which Anderson had been led to expect sooner, but which could in no case really have helped him, were just appearing in the offing. Anderson very properly capitulated. On Sunday, April 14, 1861, he marched out with the honours of war. The Union flag had been fired upon in earnest by the Confederates, and, leaving Virginia and the States that went with it to join the Confederacy if they chose, the North sprang to arms.

In the events which had led up to the outbreak of war Abraham Lincoln had played a part more admirable and more decisive in its effect than his countrymen could have noted at the time or perhaps have appreciated since. He was confronted now with duties requiring mental gifts of a different kind from those which he had hitherto displayed, and with temptations to which he had not yet been exposed. In a general sense the greatness of mind and heart which he unfolded under fierce trial does not need to be demonstrated to-day. Yet in detail hardly an action of his Presidency is exempt from controversy; nor is his many-sided character one of those which men readily flatter themselves that they understand. There are always, moreover, those to whom it is a marvel how any great man came by his name. The particular tribute, which in the pages that follow it is desired to pay to him, consists in the careful examination of just those actions and just those qualities of his upon which candid detraction has in fact fastened, or on which candid admiration has pronounced with hesitancy.

CHAPTER VII

THE CONDITIONS OF THE WAR

In recounting the history of Lincoln's Presidency, it will be necessary to mark the course of the Civil War stage by stage as we proceed. There are, however, one or two general features of the contest with which it may be well to deal by way of preface.

It has seldom happened that a people entering upon a great war have understood at the outset what the character of that war would be. When the American Civil War broke out the North expected an easy victory, but, as disappointment came soon and was long maintained, many clever people adopted the opinion, which early prevailed in Europe, that there was no possibility of their success at all. At the first the difficulty of the task was unrecognised; under early and long-sustained disappointment the strength by which those difficulties could be overcome began to be despaired of without reason.

The North, after several slave States, which were at first doubtful, had adhered to it, had more than double the population of the South; of the Southern population a very large part were slaves, who, though industrially useful, could not be enlisted. In material resources the superiority of the North was no less marked, and its material wealth grew during the war to a greater extent than had perhaps ever happened to any other belligerent power. These advantages were likely to be decisive in the end, if the North could and would endure to the end. But at the very beginning these advantages simply did not tell at all, for the immediately available military force of the North was insignificant, and that of the South clearly superior to it; and even when they began to tell, it was bound to be very long before their full weight could be brought to bear. And the object which was to be obtained was supremely difficult of attainment. It was not a defeat of the South which might result in the alteration of a frontier, the cession of some Colonies, the payment of an indemnity, and such like matters; it was a conquest of the South so complete that the Union could be restored on a firmer basis than before. Any less result than this would be failure in the war. And the country, to be thus completely conquered by an unmilitary people of nineteen millions, was of enormous extent: leaving out of account the huge outlying State of Texas, which is larger than Germany, the remaining Southern States which joined in the Confederacy have an area somewhat larger than that of Germany, Austria-Hungary, Holland, and Belgium put together; and this great region had no industrial centres or other points of such great strategic importance that by the occupation of them the remaining area could be dominated. The feat which the Northern people eventually achieved has been said by the English historians of the war (perhaps with some exaggeration) to have been "a greater one than that which Napoleon attempted to his own undoing when he invaded Russia in 1812."

On the other hand, the South was in some respects very favourably placed for resisting invasion from the North. The Southern forces during most of the war were, in the language of military writers, operating on interior lines; that is, the different portions of them lay nearer to one another than did the different portions of the Northern forces, and could be more quickly brought to converge on the same point; the country abounded in strong positions for defence which could be held by a relatively small force, while in every invading movement the invaders had to advance long distances from the base, thus exposing their lines of communication to attack. The advantage of this situation, if competent use were made of it, was bound to go very far towards compensating for inferiority of numbers; the North could not make its superior numbers on land tell in any rapidly decisive fashion without exposing itself to dangerous counter-strokes. In naval strength its superiority was asserted almost from the first, and by cutting off foreign supplies caused the Southern armies to suffer severe privations before the war was half through; but its full effect could only be produced very slowly. Thus, if its people were brave and its leaders capable, the South was by no means in so hopeless a case as might at first have appeared; with good fortune it might hope to strike its powerful antagonist some deadly blow before that antagonist could bring its strength to bear; and even if this hope failed, a sufficiently tenacious defence might well wear down the patience of the North.

As soldiers the Southerners started with a superiority which the Northerners could only overtake slowly. If each people were taken in the mass, the proportion of Southerners bred to an outdoor life was higher. Generally speaking, if not exactly more frugal, they were far less used to living comfortably. Above all, all classes of people among them were still accustomed to think of fighting as a normal and suitable occupation for a man; while the prevailing temper of the North thought of man as meant for business, and its higher temper was apt to think of fighting as odious and war out of date. This, like the other advantages of the South, was transitory; before very long Northerners who became soldiers at a sacrifice of inclination, from the highest spirit of patriotism or in the methodic temper in which business has to be done, would become man for man as good soldiers as the Southerners; but the original superiority of the Southerners would continue to have a moral effect in their own ranks and on the mind of the enemy, more especially of the enemy's generals, even after its cause had ceased to exist; and herein the military advantage of the South was undoubtedly, through the first half of the war, considerable.

In the matter of leadership the South had certain very real and certain other apparent but probably delusive advantages. The United States had no large number of trained military officers, still capable of active service. The armies of the North and South alike had to be commanded and staffed to a great extent by men who first studied their profession in that war; and the lack of ripe military judgment was likely to be felt most in the higher commands where the forces to be employed and co-ordinated were largest. The South secured what may be called its fair proportion of the comparatively few officers, but it was of tremendous moment that, among the officers who, when the war began, were recognised as competent, two, who sadly but in simple loyalty to the State of Virginia took the Southern side, were men of genius. The advantages of the South would have been no advantages without skill and resolution to make use of them. The main conditions of the war—the vast space, the difficulty in all parts of it of moving troops, the generally low level of military knowledge—were all such as greatly enhance the opportunities of the most gifted commander. Lee and "Stonewall" Jackson thus became, the former throughout the war, the latter till he was killed in the summer of 1863, factors of primary importance in the struggle. Wolseley, who had, besides studying their record, conversed both with Lee and with Moltke, thought Lee even greater than Moltke, and the military writers of our day speak of him as one of the great commanders of history. As to Jackson, Lee's belief in him is sufficient testimony to his value. And the good fortune of the South was not confined to these two signal instances. Most of the Southern generals who appeared early in the war could be retained in important commands to the end.

The South might have seemed at first equally fortunate in the character of the Administration at the back of the generals. An ascendency was at once conceded to Jefferson Davis, a tried political leader, to which Lincoln had to win his way, and the past experiences of the two men had been very different. The operations of war in which Lincoln had taken part were confined, according to his own romantic account in a speech in Congress, to stealing ducks and onions from the civil population; his Ministers were as ignorant in the matter as he; their military adviser, Scott, was so infirm that he had soon to retire, and it proved most difficult to replace him. Jefferson Davis, on the other hand, started with knowledge of affairs, including military affairs; he had been Secretary of War in Pierce's Cabinet and Chairman of the Senate Committee on War since then; above all, he had been a soldier and had commanded a regiment with some distinction in the Mexican War. It is thought that he would have preferred a military command to the Presidency of the Confederacy, and as his own experience of actual war was as great as that of his generals, he can hardly be blamed for a disposition to interfere with them at the beginning. But military historians, while criticising (perhaps a little hastily) all Lincoln's interventions in the affairs of war up to the time when he found generals whom he trusted, insist that Davis' systematic interference was far more harmful to his cause; and Wolseley, who watched events closely from Canada and who visited the Southern Army in 1863, is most emphatic in this opinion. He interfered with Lee to an extent which nothing but Lee's devoted friendship and loyalty could have made tolerable. He put himself into relations of dire hostility with Joseph Johnston, and in 1864 suspended him in the most injudicious manner. Above all, when the military position of the South had begun to be acutely perilous, Jefferson Davis neither devised for himself, nor allowed his generals to devise, any bold policy by which the chance that still remained could be utilised. His energy of will showed itself in the end in nothing but a resolution to protract bloodshed after it had certainly become idle.

If we turn to the political conditions, on which, in any but a short war, so much depends, the South will appear to have had great advantages. Its people were more richly endowed than the mixed and crudely democratic multitude of the North, in the traditional aptitude for commanding or obeying which enables people to pull together in a crisis. And they were united in a cause such as would secure the sustained loyalty of any ordinary people under any ordinary leader. For, though it was nothing but slavery that led to their assertion of independence, from the moment that they found themselves involved in war, they were fighting for a freedom to which they felt themselves entitled, and for nothing else whatever. A few successful encounters at the start tempted the ordinary Southerner to think himself a better man than the ordinary Northerner, even as the Southern Congressmen felt themselves superior to the persons whom the mistaken democracy of the North too frequently elected. This claim of independence soon acquired something of the fierce pride that might have been felt by an ancient nation. But it would have been impossible that the Northern people as a whole should be similarly possessed by the cause in which they fought. They did not seem to be fighting for their own liberty, and they would have hated to think that they were fighting for conquest. They were fighting for the maintenance of a national unity which they held dear. The question how far it was worth fighting a formidable enemy for the sake of eventual unity with him, was bound to present itself. Thus, far from wondering that the cause of the Union aroused no fuller devotion than it did in the whole lump of the Northern people, we may wonder that it inspired with so lofty a patriotism men and women in every rank of life who were able to leaven that lump. But the political element in this war was of such importance as to lead to a startling result; the North came nearest to yielding at a time when in a military sense its success had become sure. To preserve a united North was the greatest and one of the hardest of the duties of President Lincoln.

To a civilian reader the history of the war, in spite of the picturesque incidents of many battles, may easily be made dreary. Till far on in the lengthy process of subjecting the South, we might easily become immersed in some futile story of how General X. was superseded by General Y. in a command, for which neither discovered any purpose but that of not co-operating with General Z. And this impression is not merely due to our failure to understand the difficulties which confronted these gallant officers. The dearth of trained military faculty, which was felt at the outset, could only be made good by the training which the war itself supplied. Such commanders as Grant and Sherman and Sheridan not only could not have been recognised at the beginning of the war; they were not then the soldiers that they afterwards became. And the want was necessarily very serious in the case of the higher commands which required the movement of large forces, the control of subordinates each of whom must have a wide discretion, and the energy of intellect and will necessary for resolving the more complex problems of strategy. We are called upon to admire upon both sides the devotion of forgotten thousands, and to admire upon the side of the South the brilliant and daring operations by which in so many battles Lee and Jackson defeated superior forces. On the Northern side, later on, great generals came to view, but it is in the main a different sort of achievement which we are called upon to appreciate. An Administration appointed to direct a stupendous operation of conquest was itself of necessity ill prepared for such a task; behind it were a Legislature and a public opinion equally ill prepared to support and to assist it. There were in its military service many intelligent and many enterprising men, but none, at first, so combining intelligence and enterprise that he could grapple with any great responsibility or that the civil power would have been warranted in reposing complete confidence in him. The history of the war has to be recounted in this volume chiefly with a view to these difficulties of the Administration.

One of the most interesting features of the war would, in any military study of it, be seen to be the character of the troops on both sides. On both sides their individual quality was high; on both, circumstances and the disposition of the people combined to make discipline weak. This character, common to the two armies, was conspicuous in many battles of the war, but a larger interest attaches to the policy of the two administrations in raising and organising their civilian armies. The Southern Government, if its proceedings were studied in detail, would probably seem to have been better advised at the start on matters of military organisation; for instance, it had early and long retained a superiority in cavalry which was not a mere result of good fortune. But here, too, there was an inherent advantage in the very fact that the South had started upon a desperate venture. There can hardly be a more difficult problem of detail for statesmen than the co-ordination of military and civil requirements in the raising of an army. But in the South all civil considerations merged themselves in the paramount necessity of a military success for which all knew the utmost effort was needed. The several States of the South, claiming as they did a far larger independence than the Northern States, knew that they could only make that claim good by being efficient members of the Confederacy. Thus it was comparatively easy for the Confederate Government to adopt and maintain a consecutive policy in this matter, and though, from the conditions of a widely spread agricultural population, voluntary enlistment produced poor results at the beginning of the war, it appears to have been easy to introduce quite early an entirely compulsory system of a stringent kind.

The introduction of compulsory service in the North has its place in our subsequent story. The system that preceded it need not be dwelt upon here, because, full of instruction as a technical study of it (such as has been made by Colonel Henderson) must be, no brief survey by an amateur could be useful. It is necessary, however, to understand the position in which Lincoln's Administration was placed, without much experience In America, or perhaps elsewhere in the world, to guide it. It must not be contended, for it cannot be known that the problem was fully and duly envisaged by Lincoln on his Cabinet, but it would probably in any case have been impossible for them to pursue from the first a consecutive and well-thought-out policy for raising an army and keeping up its strength. The position of the North differed fundamentally from that of the South; the North experienced neither the ardour nor the throes of a revolution; it was never in any fear of being conquered, only of not conquering. There was nothing, therefore, which at once bestowed on the Government a moral power over the country vastly in excess of that which it exercised in normal times. This, however, was really necessary to it if the problem of the Army was to be handled in the way which was desirable from a military point of view. Compulsory service could not at first be thought of. It was never supposed that the tiny regular Army of the United States Government could be raised to any very great size by voluntary enlistment, and the limited increase of it which was attempted was not altogether successful. The existing militia system of the several States was almost immediately found faulty and was discarded. A great Volunteer Force had to be raised which should be under the command of the President, who by the Constitution is Commander-in-Chief of the forces of the Union, but which must be raised in each State by the State Governor (or, if he was utterly wanting, by leading local citizens). Now State Governors are not—it must be recalled—officers under the President, but independent potentates acting usually in as much detachment from him as the Vice-Chancellor of Oxford or Cambridge from the Board of Education or a Presbyterian minister from a bishop. This group of men, for the most part able, patriotic, and determined, were there to be used and had to be consulted. It follows that the policy of the North in raising and organising its armies had at first to be a policy evolved between numerous independent authorities which never met and were held together by a somewhat ignorant public opinion, sometimes much depressed and sometimes, which was worse, oversanguine.

It is impossible to judge exactly how ill or how well Lincoln, under such circumstances, grappled with this particular problem, but many anomalies which seem to us preposterous – the raising of raw new regiments when fine seasoned regiments were short of half their strength, and so forth – were in these circumstances inevitable. The national system of recruiting, backed by compulsion, which was later set up, still required for its success the co-operation of State and local authorities of this wholly independent character.

Northern and Southern armies alike had necessarily to be commanded to a great extent by amateur officers; the number of officers, in the service or retired, who had been trained at West Point, was immeasurably too small for the needs of the armies. Amateurs had to be called in, and not only so, but they had in some cases to be given very important commands. The not altogether unwholesome tradition that a self-reliant man can turn his hand to anything was of course very strong in America, and the short military annals of the country had been thought to have added some illustrious instances to the roll of men of peace who have distinguished themselves in arms. So a political leader, no matter whether he was Democrat or Republican, who was a man of known general capacity, would sometimes at first seem suitable for an important command rather than the trained but unknown professional soldier who was the alternative. Moreover, it seemed foolish not to appoint him, when, as sometimes happened, he could bring thousands of recruits from his State. The Civil War turned out, however, to show the superiority of the duly trained military mind in a marked degree. Some West-Pointers of repute of course proved incapable, and a great many amateur colonels and generals, both North and South, attained a very fair level of competence in the service (the few conspicuous failures seem to have been quite exceptional); but, all the same, of the many clever and stirring men who then took up soldiering as novices and served for four years, not one achieved brilliant success; of the generals in the war whose names are remembered, some had indeed passed years in civil life, but every one had received a thorough military training in the years of his early manhood. It certainly does not appear that the Administration was really neglectful of professional merit; it hungered to find it; but many appointments must at first have been made in a haphazard fashion, for there was no machinery for sifting claims. A zealous but unknown West-Pointer put under an outsider would be apt to write as Sherman did in early days: "Mr. Lincoln meant to insult me and the Army"; and a considerable jealousy evidently arose between West-Pointers and amateurs. It was aggravated by the rivalry between officers of the Eastern army and those of the, more largely amateur, Western army. The amateurs, too, had something to say on their side; they were apt to accuse West-Pointers as a class of a cringing belief that the South was invincible. There was nothing unnatural or very serious in all this, but political influences which arose later caused complaints of this nature to be made the most of, and a general charge to be made against Lincoln's Administration of appointing generals and removing them under improper political influences. This general charge, however, rests upon a limited number of alleged instances, and all of these which are of any importance will necessarily be examined in later chapters.

It may be useful to a reader who wishes to follow the main course of the war carefully, if the chief ways in which geographical facts affected it are here summarised – necessarily somewhat dryly. Minor operations at outlying points on the coast or in the Far West will be left out of account, so also will a serious political consideration, which we shall later see caused doubt for a time as to the proper strategy of the North.

It must be noted first, startling as it may be to Englishmen who remember the war partly by the exploits of the _Alabama_, that the naval superiority of the North was overwhelming. In spite of many gallant efforts by the Southern sailors, the North could blockade their coasts and could capture most of the Southern ports long before its superiority on land was established. Turning then to land, we may treat the political frontier between the two powers, after a short preliminary stage of war, as being marked by the southern boundaries of Maryland, West Virginia, Kentucky, and Missouri, just as they are seen on the map to-day. In doing so, we must note that at the commencement of large operations parts of Kentucky and Missouri were occupied by Southern invading forces. This frontier is cut, not far from the Atlantic, by the parallel mountain chains which make up the Alleghanies or Appalachians. These in effect separated the field of operations into a narrow Eastern theatre of war, and an almost boundless Western theatre; and the operations in these two theatres were almost to the end independent of each other.

In the Eastern theatre of war lies Washington, the capital of the Union, a place of great importance to the North for obvious reasons, and especially because if it fell European powers would be likely to recognise the Confederacy. It lies, on the Potomac, right upon the frontier; and could be menaced also in the rear, for the broad and fertile trough between the mountain chains formed by the valley of the Shenandoah River, which flows northward to join the Potomac at a point north-west of Washington, was in Confederate hands and formed a sort of sally-port by which a force from Richmond could get almost behind Washington. A hundred miles south of Washington lay Richmond, which shortly became the capital of the Confederates, instead of Montgomery in Alabama. As a brand-new capital it mattered little to the Confederates, though at the very end of the war it became their last remaining stronghold. The intervening country, which was in Southern hands, was extraordinarily difficult. The reader may notice on the map the rivers with broad estuaries which are its most marked features, and with the names of which we shall become familiar. The rives themselves were obstacles to an invading Northern army; their estuaries, on the other hand, soon afforded it safe communication by sea.

In the Western theatre of war we must remember first the enormous length of frontier in proportion to the population on either side. This necessarily made the progress of Northern invasion slow, and its proper direction hard to determine, for diversions could be created by a counter-invasion elsewhere along the frontier or a stroke at the invaders' communications. The principal feature of the whole region is the great waterways, on which the same advantages which gave the sea to the North gave it also an immense superiority in the river warfare of flotillas of gunboats. When the North with its gunboats could get control of the Mississippi the South would be deprived of a considerable part of its territory and resources, and cut off from its last means of trading with Europe (save for the relief afforded by blockade-runners) by being cut off from Mexico and its ports. Further, when the North could control the tributaries of the Mississippi, especially the Cumberland and the Tennessee which flow into the great river through the Ohio, it would cut deep into the internal communications of the South. Against this menace the South could only contend by erecting powerful fortresses on the rivers, and the capture of some of them was the great object of the earlier Northern operations.

The railway system of the South must also be taken into account in connection with their waterways. This, of course, cannot be seen on a modern map. Perhaps the following may make the main points clear. The Southern railway system touched the Mississippi and the world beyond it at three points only: Memphis, Vicksburg, and New Orleans. A traveller wishing to go, say, from Richmond by rail towards the West could have, if distance were indifferent to him, a choice of three routes for part of the way. He could go through Knoxville in Tennessee to Chattanooga in that State, where he had a choice of routes further West, or he could take one of two alternative lines south into Georgia and thence go either to Atlanta or to Columbus in the west of that State. Arrived at Atlanta or Columbus, he could proceed further West either by making a detour northwards through Chattanooga or by making a detour southwards through the seaport town of Mobile, crossing the harbour by boat. Thus the capture of Chattanooga from the South would go far towards cutting the whole Southern railway system in two, and the capture of Mobile would complete it. Lastly, we may notice two lines running north and south through the State of Mississippi, one through Corinth and Meridian, and the other nearer the great river. From this and the course of the rivers the strategic importance of some of the towns mentioned may be partly appreciated.

The subjugation of the South in fact began by a process, necessarily slow and much interrupted, whereby having been blockaded by sea it was surrounded by land, cut off from its Western territory, and deprived of its main internal lines of communication. Richmond, against which the North began to move within the first three months of the war, did not fall till nearly four years later, when the process just described had been completed, and when a Northern army had triumphantly progressed, wasting the resources of the country as it went, from Chattanooga to Atlanta, thence to the Atlantic coast of Georgia, and thence northward through the two Carolinas till it was about to join hands with the army assailing Richmond. Throughout this time the attention of a large part of the Northern public and of all those who watched the war from Europe was naturally fastened to a great extent upon the desperate fighting which occurred in the region of Washington and of Richmond and upon the ill success of the North in endeavours of unforeseen difficulty against the latter city. We shall see, however, that the long and humiliating failure of the North in this quarter was neither so unaccountable nor nearly so important as it appeared.

CHAPTER VIII

THE OPENING OF THE WAR AND LINCOLN'S ADMINISTRATION

1. Preliminary Stages.

On the morning after the bombardment of Fort Sumter there appeared a Proclamation by the President calling upon the Militia of the several States to furnish 75,000 men for the service of the United States in the suppression of an "unlawful combination." Their service, however, would expire by law thirty days after the next meeting of Congress, and, in compliance with a further requirement of law upon this subject, the President also summoned Congress to meet in extraordinary session upon July 4. The Army already in the service of the United States consisted of but 16,000 officers and men, and, though the men of this force, being less affected by State ties than their officers, remained, as did the men of the Navy, true almost without exception to their allegiance, all but 3,000 of them were unavailable and scattered in small frontier forts in the West. A few days later, when it became plain that the struggle might long outlast the three months of the

Militia, the President called for Volunteers to enlist for three years' service, and perhaps (for the statements are conflicting) some 300,000 troops of one kind and another had been raised by June. The affair of Fort Sumter and the President's Proclamation at once aroused and concentrated the whole public opinion of the free States in the North and, in an opposite sense, of the States which had already seceded. The border slave States had now to declare for the one side or for the other. Virginia as a whole joined the Southern Confederacy forthwith, but several Counties in the mountainous region of the west of that State were strongly for the Union. These eventually succeeded with the support of Northern troops in separating from Virginia and forming the new State of West Virginia. Tennessee also joined the South, though in Eastern Tennessee the bulk of the people held out for the Union without such good fortune as their neighbours in West Virginia. Arkansas beyond the Mississippi followed the same example, though there were some doubt and division in all parts of that State. In Delaware, where the slaves were very few, the Governor did not formally comply with the President's Proclamation, but the people as a whole responded to it. The attitude of Maryland, which almost surrounds Washington, kept the Government at the capital in suspense and alarm for a while, for both the city of Baltimore and the existing State legislature were inclined to the South. In Kentucky and Missouri the State authorities were also for the South, and it was only after a struggle, and in Missouri much actual fighting, that the Unionist majority of the people in each State had its way. The secession of Virginia had consequences even more important than the loss to the Union of a powerful State. General Robert E. Lee, a Virginian, then in Washington, was esteemed by General Scott to be the ablest officer in the service. Lincoln and his Secretary of War desired to confer on him the command of the Army. Lee's decision was made with much reluctance and, it seems, hesitation. He was not only opposed to the policy of secession, but denied the right of a State to secede; yet he believed that his absolute allegiance was due to Virginia. He resigned his commission in the United States Army, went to Richmond, and, in accordance with what Wolseley describes as the prevailing principle that had influenced most of the soldiers he met in the South, placed his sword at the disposal of his own State. The same loyalty to Virginia governed another great soldier, Thomas J. Jackson, whose historic nickname, "Stonewall," fails to convey the dashing celerity of his movements. While they both lived these two men were to be linked together in the closest comradeship and mutual trust. They sprang from different social conditions and were of contrasting types. The epithet Cavalier has been fitly enough applied to Lee, and Jackson, after conversion from the wild courses of his youth, was an austere Puritan. To quote again from a soldier's memoirs, Wolseley calls Lee "one of the few men who ever seriously impressed and awed me with their natural, their inherent, greatness"; he speaks of his "majesty," and of the "beauty," of his character, and of the "sweetness of his smile and the impressive dignity of the old-fashioned style of his address"; "his greatness," he says, "made me humble." "There was nothing," he tells us, "of these refined characteristics in Stonewall Jackson," a man with "huge hands and feet." But he possessed "an assured self-confidence, the outcome of his sure trust in God. How simple, how humble-minded a man. As his impressive eyes met yours unflinchingly, you knew that his was an honest heart." To this he adds touches less to be expected concerning a Puritan warrior, whose Puritanism was in fact inclined to ferocity – how Jackson's "remarkable eyes lit up for the moment with a look of real enthusiasm as he recalled the architectural beauty of the seven lancet windows in York Minster," how "intense" was the "benignity" of his expression, and how in him it seemed that "great strength of character and obstinate determination were united with extreme gentleness of disposition and with absolute tenderness towards all about him." Men such as these brought to the Southern cause something besides their military capacity; but as to the greatness of that capacity, applied in a war in which the scope was so great for individual leaders of genius, there is no question. A civilian reader, looking in the history of war chiefly for the evidences of personal quality, can at least discern in these two famous soldiers the moral daring which in doubtful circumstances never flinches from the responsibility of a well-considered risk, and, in both their cases as in those of some other great commanders, can recognise in this rare and precious attribute the outcome of their personal piety. We shall henceforth have to do with the Southern Confederacy and its armies, not in their inner history but with sole regard to the task which they imposed upon Lincoln and the North. But at this parting of the ways a tribute is due to the two men, pre-eminent among many devoted people, who, in their soldier-like and unreflecting loyalty to their cause, gave to it a lustre in which, so far as they can be judged, neither its statesmen nor its spiritual guides had a share. There were Virginian officers who did not thus go with their State. Of these were Scott himself, and G. H. Thomas; and Farragut, the great sailor, was from Tennessee.

Throughout the free States of the North there took place a national uprising of which none who remember it have spoken without feeling anew its spontaneous ardour. Men flung off with delight the hesitancy of the preceding months, and recruiting went on with speed and enthusiasm. Party divisions for the moment disappeared. Old Buchanan made public his adhesion to the Government. Douglas called upon Lincoln to ask how best he could serve the public cause, and, at his request, went down to Illinois to guide opinion and advance recruiting there; so employed, the President's great rival, shortly after, fell ill and died, leaving the leadership of the Democrats to be filled thereafter by more scrupulous but less patriotic men. There was exultant confidence in the power of the nation to put down rebellion, and those who realised the peril in which for many days the capital and the administration were placed were only the more indignantly determined. Perhaps the most trustworthy record of popular emotions is to be found in popular humorists. Shortly after these days Artemus Ward, the author who almost vied with Shakespeare in Lincoln's affections, relates how the confiscation of his show in the South led him to have an interview with Jefferson Davis. "Even now," said Davis, in this pleasant fiction, "we have many frens in the North." "J. Davis," is the reply, "there's your grate mistaik. Many of us was your sincere frends, and thought certin parties amung us was fussin' about you and meddlin' with your consarns intirely too much. But, J. Davis, the minit you fire a gun at the piece of dry goods called the Star-Spangled Banner, the North gits up and rises en massy, in defence of that banner. Not agin you as individooals—not agin the South even—but to save the flag. We should indeed be weak in the knees, unsound in the heart, milk-white in the liver, and soft in the hed, if we stood quietly by and saw this glorus Govyment smashed to pieces, either by a furrin or a intestine foe. The gentle-harted mother hates to take her naughty child across her knee, but she knows it is her dooty to do it. So we shall hate to whip the naughty South, but we must do it if you don't make back tracks at onct, and we shall wallup you out of your boots!" In the days which followed, when this prompt chastisement could not be effected and it seemed indeed as if the South would do most of the whipping, the discordant elements which mingled in this unanimity soon showed themselves. The minority that opposed the war was for a time silent and insignificant, but among the supporters of the war there were those who loved the Union and the Constitution and who, partly for this very reason, had hitherto cultivated the sympathies of the South. These—adherents mainly of the Democratic party—would desire that civil war should be waged with the least possible breach of the Constitution, and be concluded with the least possible social change; many of them would wish to fight not to a finish but to a compromise. On the other hand, there were those who loved liberty and hated alike the slave system of the South and the arrogance which it had engendered. These—the people distinguished within the Republican party as Radicals—would pay little heed to constitutional restraints in repelling an attack on the Constitution, and they would wish from the first to make avowed war upon that which caused the war—slavery. In the border States there was of course more active sympathy with the South, and in conflict with this the Radicalism of some of these States became more stalwart and intractable. To such causes of dissension was added as time went on sheer fatigue of the war, and strangely enough this influence was as powerful with a few Radicals as it was with the ingrained Democratic partisans. They despaired of the result when success at last was imminent, and became sick of bloodshed when it passed what they presumably regarded as a reasonable amount.

It was the task of the Administration not only to conduct the war, but to preserve the unity of the North in spite of differences and its resolution in spite of disappointments. Lincoln was in more than one way well fitted for this task. Old experience in

Illinois and Kentucky enabled him to understand very different points of view in regard to the cause of the South. The new question that was now to arise about slavery was but a particular form of the larger question of principle to which he had long thought out an answer as firm and as definite as it was moderate and in a sense subtle. He had, moreover, a quality of heart which, as it seemed to those near him, the protraction of the conflict, with its necessary strain upon him, only strengthened. In him a tenacity, which scarcely could falter in the cause which he judged to be right, was not merely pure from bitterness towards his antagonists, it was actually bound up with a deep-seated kindliness towards them. Whatever rank may be assigned to his services and to his deserts, it is first and foremost in these directions, though not in these directions alone, that the reader of his story must look for them. Upon attentive study he will probably appear as the embodiment, in a degree and manner which are alike rare, of the more constant and the higher judgment of his people. It is plainer still that he embodied the resolute purpose which underlay the fluctuations upon the surface of their political life. The English military historians, Wood and Edmonds, in their retrospect over the course of the war, well sum up its dramatic aspect when they say: "Against the great military genius of certain of the Southern leaders fate opposed the unbroken resolution and passionate devotion to the Union, which he worshipped, of the great Northern President. As long as he lived, and ruled the people of the North, there could be no turning back."

There are plenty of indications in the literature of the time that Lincoln's determination soon began to be widely felt and to be appreciated by common people. Literally, crowds of people from all parts of the North saw him, exchanged a sentence or two, and carried home their impressions; and those who were near him record the constant fortitude of his bearing, noting as marked exceptions the unrestrained words of impatience and half-humorous despondency which did on rare occasions escape him. In a negative way, too, even the political world bore its testimony to this; his administration was charged with almost every other form of weakness, but there was never a suspicion that he would give in. Nor again, in the severest criticisms upon him by knowledgeable men that have been unearthed and collected, does the suggestion of petty personal aims or of anything but unselfish devotion ever find a place. The belief that he could be trusted spread itself among plain people, and, given this belief, plain people liked him the better because he was plain. But if at the distance at which we contemplate him, and at which from the moment of his death all America contemplated him, certain grand traits emerge, it is not for a moment to be supposed that in his life he stood out in front of the people as a great leader, or indeed as a leader at all, in the manner, say, of Chatham or even of Palmerston. Lincoln came to Washington doubtless with some deep thoughts which other men had not thought, doubtless also with some important knowledge, for instance of the border States, which many statesmen lacked, but he came there a man inexperienced in affairs. It was a part of his strength that he knew this very well, that he meant to learn, thought he could learn, did not mean to be hurried where he had not the knowledge to decide, entirely appreciated superior knowledge in others, and was entirely unawed by it. But Senators and Representatives in Congress and journalists of high standing, as a rule, perceived the inexperience and not the strength. The deliberation with which he acted, patiently watching events, saying little, listening to all sides, conversing with a naivete which was genuine but not quite artless, seemingly obdurate to the pressure of wise counsels on one side and on the other – all this struck many anxious observers as sheer incompetence, and when there was just and natural cause for their anxiety, there was no established presumption of his wisdom to set against it. And this effect was enhanced by what may be called his plainness, his awkwardness, and actual eccentricity in many minor matters. To many intelligent people who met him they were a grievous stumbling-block, and though some most cultivated men were not at all struck by them, and were pleased instead by his "seeming sincere, and honest, and steady," or the like, it is clear that no one in Washington was greatly impressed by him at first meeting. His oddities were real and incorrigible. Young John Hay, whom Nicolay, his private secretary, introduced as his assistant, a humorist like Lincoln himself, but with leanings to literary elegance and a keen eye for social distinctions, loved him all along and came to worship him, but irreverent amusement is to be traced in his recently published letters, and the glimpses which he gives us of "the Ancient" or "the Tycoon" when quite at home and quite at his ease fully justify him. Lincoln had great dignity and tact for use when he wanted them, but he did not always see the use of them. Senator Sherman was presented to the new President. "So you're John Sherman?" said Lincoln. "Let's see if you're as tall as I am. We'll measure." The grave politician, who was made to stand back to back with him before the company till this interesting question was settled, dimly perceived that the intention was friendly, but felt that there was a lack of ceremony. Lincoln's height was one of his subjects of harmless vanity; many tall men had to measure themselves against him in this manner, and probably felt like John Sherman. On all sorts of occasions and to all sorts of people he would "tell a little story," which was often enough, in Lord Lyons' phrase, an "extreme" story. This was the way in which he had grown accustomed to be friendly in company; it served a purpose when intrusive questions had to be evaded, or reproofs or refusals to be given without offence. As his laborious and sorrowful task came to weigh heavier upon him, his capacity for play of this sort became a great resource to him. As his fame became established people recognised him as a humorist; the inevitable "little story" became to many an endearing form of eccentricity; but we may be sure it was not so always or to everybody.

"Those," says Carl Schurz, a political exile from Prussia, who did good service, military and political, to the Northern cause—"those who visited the White House—and the White House appeared to be open to whosoever wished to enter—saw there a man of unconventional manners, who, without the slightest effort to put on dignity, treated all men alike, much like old neighbours; whose speech had not seldom a rustic flavour about it; who always seemed to have time for a homely talk and never to be in a hurry to press business; and who occasionally spoke about important affairs of State with the same nonchalance—I might almost say irreverence—with which he might have discussed an every-day law case in his office at Springfield, Illinois."

Thus Lincoln was very far from inspiring general confidence in anything beyond his good intentions. He is remembered as a personality with a "something" about him—the vague phrase is John Bright's—which widely endeared him, but his was by no means that "magnetic" personality which we might be led to believe was indispensable in America. Indeed, it is remarkable that to some really good judges he remained always unimpressive. Charles Francis Adams, who during the Civil War served his country as well as Minister in London as his grandfather had done after the War of Independence, lamented to the end that Seward, his immediate chief, had to serve under an inferior man; and a more sympathetic man, Lord Lyons, our representative at Washington, refers to Lincoln with nothing more than an amused kindliness. No detail of his policy has escaped fierce criticism, and the man himself while he lived was the subject of so much depreciation and condescending approval, that we are forced to ask who discovered his greatness till his death inclined them to idealise him. The answer is that precisely those Americans of trained intellect whose title to this description is clearest outside America were the first who began to see beneath his strange exterior. Lowell, watching the course of public events with ceaseless scrutiny; Walt Whitman, sauntering in Washington in the intervals of the labour among the wounded by which he broke down his robust strength, and seeing things as they passed with the sure observation of a poet; Motley, the historian of the Dutch Republic, studying affairs in the thick of them at the outset of the war, and not less closely by correspondence when he went as Minister to Vienna—such men when they praised Lincoln after his death expressed a judgment which they began to form from the first; a judgment which started with the recognition of his honesty, traced the evidence of his wisdom as it appeared, gradually and not by repentant impulse learned his greatness. And it is a judgment large enough to explain the lower estimate of Lincoln which certainly had wide currency. Not to multiply witnesses, Motley in June, 1861, having seen him for the second time, writes: "I went and had an hour's talk with Mr. Lincoln. I am very glad of it, for, had I not done so, I should have left Washington with a very inaccurate impression of the President. I am now satisfied that he is a man of very considerable native sagacity; and that he has an ingenuous, unsophisticated, frank, and noble character. I believe him to be as true as steel, and as courageous as true. At the same time there is doubtless an ignorance about State matters, and particularly about foreign affairs, which he does not attempt to conceal, but which we must of necessity regret in a man placed in such a position at such a crisis. Nevertheless his very modesty in this respect disarms criticism. We parted very affectionately, and perhaps I shall never set eyes on him again, but I feel that, so far as perfect integrity and directness of purpose go, the country will be safe in his hands." Three years had passed, and the political world of America was in that storm of general dissatisfaction in which not a member of Congress would be known as "a Lincoln man," when Motley writes again from Vienna to his mother, "I venerate Abraham Lincoln exactly because he is the true, honest type of American democracy. There is nothing of the shabby-genteel, the would-be-but-couldn't-be fine gentleman; he is the great American Demos, honest, shrewd, homely, wise, humorous, cheerful, brave, blundering occasionally, but through blunders struggling onwards towards what he believes the right." In a later letter he observes, "His mental abilities were large, and they became the more robust as the more weight was imposed upon them."

This last sentence, especially if in Lincoln's mental abilities the qualities of his character be included, probably indicates the chief point for remark in any estimate of his presidency. It is true that he was judged at first as a stranger among strangers. Walt Whitman has described vividly a scene, with "a dash of comedy, almost farce, such as Shakespeare puts in his blackest tragedies," outside the hotel in New York where Lincoln stayed on his journey to Washington; "his look and gait, his perfect composure and coolness," to cut it short, the usually noted marks of his eccentricity, "as he stood looking with curiosity on that immense sea of faces, and the sea of faces returned the look with similar curiosity, not a single one" among the crowd "his personal friend." He was not much otherwise situated when he came to Washington. It is true also that in the early days he was learning his business. "Why, Mr. President," said some one towards the end of his life, "you have changed your mind." "Yes, I have," said he, "and I don't think much of a man who isn't wiser to-day than he was yesterday." But it seems to be above all true that the exercise of power and the endurance of responsibility gave him new strength. This, of course, cannot be demonstrated, but Americans then living, who recall Abraham Lincoln, remark most frequently how the man grew to his task. And this perhaps is the main impression which the slight record here presented will convey, the impression of a man quite unlike the many statesmen whom power and the vexations attendant upon it have in some piteous way spoiled and marred, a man who started by being tough and shrewd and canny and became very strong and very wise, started with an inclination to honesty, courage, and kindness; and became, under a tremendous strain, honest, brave, and kind to an almost tremendous degree.

The North then started upon the struggle with an eagerness and unanimity from which the revulsion was to try all hearts, and the President's most of all; and not a man in the North guessed what the strain of that struggle was to be. At first indeed there was alarm in Washington for the immediate safety of the city. Confederate flags could be seen floating from the hotels in Alexandria across the river; Washington itself was full of rumours of plots and intended assassinations, and full of actual Southern spies; everything was disorganised; and Lincoln himself, walking round one night, found the arsenal with open doors, absolutely unguarded.

By April 20, first the Navy Yard at Gosport, in Virginia, had to be abandoned, then the Arsenal at Harper's Ferry, and on the day of this latter event Lee went over to the South. One regiment from Massachusetts, where the State authorities had prepared for war before the fall of Sumter, was already in Washington; but it had had to fight its way through a furious mob in Baltimore, with some loss of life on both sides. A deputation from many churches in that city came to the President, begging him to desist from his bloodthirsty preparations, but found him "constitutionally genial and jovial," and "wholly inaccessible to Christian appeals." It mattered more that a majority of the Maryland Legislature was for the South, and that the Governor temporised and requested that no more troops should pass through Baltimore. The Mayor of Baltimore and the railway authorities burned railway bridges and tore up railway lines, and the telegraph wires were cut. Thus for about five days the direct route to Washington from the North was barred. It seemed as if the boast of some Southern orator that the Confederate flag would float over the capital by May 1 might be fulfilled. Beauregard could have transported his now drilled troops by rail from South Carolina and would have found Washington isolated and hardly garrisoned. As a matter of fact, no such daring move was contemplated in the South, and the citizens of Richmond, Virginia, were themselves under a similar alarm; but the South had a real opportunity.

The fall of Washington at that moment would have had political consequences which no one realised better than Lincoln. It might well have led the Unionists in the border States to despair, and there is evidence that even then he so fully realised the task which lay before the North as to feel that the loss of Maryland, Kentucky, and Missouri would have made it impossible. He was at heart intensely anxious, and quaintly and injudiciously relieved his feelings by the remark to the "6th Massachusetts" that he felt as if all other help were a dream, and they were "the only real thing." Yet those who were with him testify to his composure and to the vigour with which he concerted with his Cabinet the various measures of naval, military, financial, postal, and police preparation which the occasion required, but which need not here be detailed. Many of the measures of course lay outside the powers which Congress had conferred on the public departments, but the President had no hesitation in "availing himself," as he put it, "of the broader powers conferred by the Constitution in cases of insurrection," and looking for the sanction of Congress afterwards, rather than "let the Government at once fall into ruin." The difficulties of government were greatly aggravated by the uncertainty as to which of its servants, civil, naval, or military, were loyal, and the need of rapidly filling the many posts left vacant by unexpected desertion. Meanwhile troops from New England, and also from New York, which had utterly disappointed some natural expectations in the South by the enthusiasm of its rally to the Union, quickly arrived near Baltimore. They repaired for themselves the interrupted railway tracks round the city, and by April 25 enough soldiers were in Washington to put an end to any present alarm. In case of need, the law of "habeas corpus" was suspended in Maryland. The President had no wish that unnecessary recourse should be had to martial law. Naturally, however, one of his generals summarily arrested a Southern recruiting agent in Baltimore. The ordinary law would probably have sufficed, and Lincoln is believed to have regretted this action, but it was obvious that he must support it when done. Hence arose an occasion for the old Chief Justice Taney to make a protest on behalf of legality, to which the President, who had armed force on his side, could not give way, and thus early began a controversy to which we must recur. It was gravely urged upon Lincoln that he should forcibly prevent the Legislature of Maryland from holding a formal sitting; he refused on the sensible ground that the legislators could assemble in some way and had better not assemble with a real grievance in constitutional law. Then a strange alteration came over Baltimore. Within three weeks all active demonstration in favour of the South had subsided; the disaffected Legislature resolved upon neutrality; the Governor, loyal at heart – if the brief epithet loyal may pass, as not begging any profound legal question – carried on affairs in the interest of the Union; postal communication and the passage of troops were free from interruption by the middle of May; and the pressing alarm about Maryland was over. These incidents of the first days of war have been recounted in some detail, because they may illustrate the gravity of the issue in the border States, in others of which the struggle, though further removed from observation, lasted longer; and because, too, it is well to realise the stress of agitation under which the Government had to make far-reaching preparation for a larger struggle, while Lincoln, whose will was decisive in all these measures, carried on all the while that seemingly unimportant routine of a President's life which is in the quietest times exacting.

The alarm in Washington was only transitory, and it was generally supposed in the North that insurrection would be easily put down. Some even specified the number of days necessary, agreeably fixing upon a smaller number than the ninety days for which the militia were called out. Secretary Seward has been credited with language of this kind, and even General Scott, whose political judgment was feeble, though his military judgment was sound,

Lincoln in 1860

Sketch of a young Abraham Lincoln

Abraham Lincoln

Symbolic log cabin at the Abraham Lincoln
Birthplace National Historical Park

It's Presidents Day, a combined bargain birthday celebration since for unexplained reasons neither No. 1 George Washington nor No. 16 Abraham Lincoln deserve their own holiday off anymore.

1864 Mathew Brady photo depicts President Lincoln reading a book with his youngest son, Tad

Tad and Abraham Lincoln taken by Alexander Gardner on February 5, 1865.

Abraham Lincoln

Mary Todd Lincoln, wife of
Abraham Lincoln, age 28

Daniel Chester French sculpture of Abraham Lincoln inside the Lincoln Memorial

Abraham Lincoln
Gettysburg Address, delivered 19 November 1863

PRESIDENT LINCOLN

Lincoln, in a top hat, with Allan Pinkerton
and Major General John Alexander McClernand
at Antietam

Lincoln met with his cabinet on July 22, 1862 for the first reading of a draft of the Emancipation Proclamation.

Lincoln's funeral train carried his remains, as well as 300 mourners and the casket of his son, William, 1,654 miles (2,662 km) to Illinois

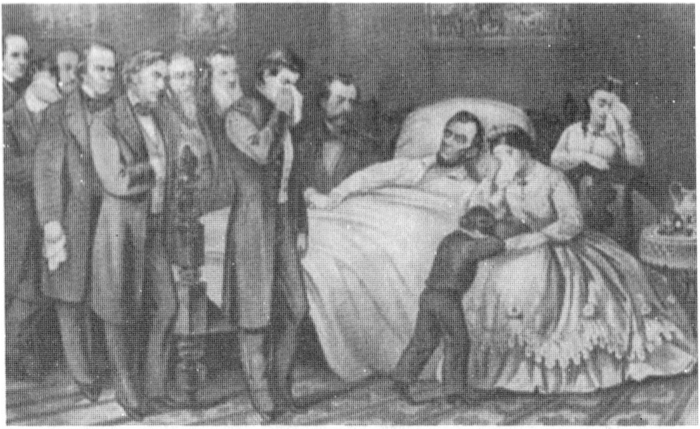

Death of President Lincoln/At Washington D.C.
April 15, 1865/The Nation's Martyr

A photograph of the March 4,
1861 inauguration of Abraham Lincoln
in front of United States Capitol

"The First Reading of the Emancipation Proclamation Before the Cabinet. From the original picture painted at the White House in 1864."

The Lincoln Family

US Postage, 1958 issue, commemorating the Lincoln and Douglas debates.

Abraham Lincoln is the only President whose portrait appears on U.S.Air Mail Postage

US Postage, 1959 issue,
depicting the young Lincoln

On April 14, 1866. one year to the day after Lincoln's assassination, the US Post Office issued its first postage stamp honoring the fallen President

seems at first to have rejected proposals, for example, for drilling irregular cavalry, made in the expectation of a war of some length. There is evidence that neither Lincoln nor Cameron, the Secretary of War, indulged in these pleasant fancies. Irresistible public opinion, in the East especially, demanded to see prompt activity. The North had arisen in its might; it was for the Administration to put forth that might, capture Richmond, to which the Confederate Government had moved, and therewith make an end of rebellion. The truth was that the North had to make its army before it could wisely advance into the assured territory of the South; the situation of the Southern Government in this respect was precisely the same. The North had enough to do meantime in making sure of the States which were still debatable ground. Such forces as were available must of necessity be used for this purpose, but for any larger operations of war military considerations, especially on the side which had the larger resources at its back, were in favour of waiting and perfecting the instrument which was to be used. But in the course of July the pressure of public opinion and of Congress, which had then assembled, overcame, not without some reason, the more cautious military view, and on the 21st of that month the North received its first great lesson in adversity at the battle of Bull Run.

Before recounting this disaster we may proceed with the story of the struggle in the border States. At an early date the rising armies of the North had been organised into three commands, called the Department of the Potomac, on the front between Washington and Richmond, the Department of the Ohio, on the upper watershed of the river of that name, and the Department of the West. Of necessity the generals commanding in these two more Western Departments exercised a larger discretion than the general at Washington. The Department of the Ohio was under General McClellan, before the war a captain of Engineers, who had retired from active service and had been engaged as a railway manager, in which capacity he has already been noticed, but who had earned a good name in the Mexican War, had been keen enough in his profession to visit the Crimea, and was esteemed by General Scott. The people of West Virginia, who, as has been said, were trying to organise themselves as a new State, adhering to the Union, were invaded by forces despatched by the Governor of their old State. They lay mainly west of the mountains, and help could reach them up tributary valleys of the Ohio. They appealed to McClellan, and the successes quickly won by forces despatched by him, and afterwards under his direct command, secured West Virginia, and incidentally the reputation of McClellan. In Kentucky, further west, the Governor endeavoured to hold the field for the South with a body known as the State Guard, while Unionist leaders among the people were raising volunteer regiments for the North. Nothing, however, was determined by fighting between these forces. The State Legislature at first took up an attitude of neutrality, but a new Legislature, elected in June, was overwhelmingly for the Union. Ultimately the Confederate armies invaded Kentucky, and the Legislature thereupon invited the Union armies into the State to expel them, and placed 40,000 Kentucky volunteers at the disposal of the President. Thenceforward, though Kentucky, stretching as it does for four hundred miles between the Mississippi and the Alleghanies, remained for long a battle-ground, the allegiance of its people to the Union was unshaken. But the uncertainty about their attitude continued till the autumn of 1861, and while it lasted was an important element in Lincoln's calculations. (It must be remembered that slavery existed in Kentucky, Maryland, and Missouri.) In Missouri the strife of factions was fierce. Already in January there had been reports of a conspiracy to seize the arsenal at St. Louis for the South when the time came, and General Scott had placed in command Captain Nathaniel Lyon, on whose loyalty he relied the more because he was an opponent of slavery. The Governor was in favour of the South—as was also the Legislature, and the Governor could count on some part of the State Militia; so Lincoln, when he called for volunteers, commissioned Lyon to raise them in Missouri. In this task a Union State Committee in St. Louis greatly helped him, and the large German population in that city was especially ready to enlist for the Union. Many of the German immigrants of those days had come to America partly for the sake of its free institutions. A State Convention was summoned by the Governor to pass an Ordinance of Secession, but its electors were minded otherwise, and the Convention voted against secession. In several encounters Lyon, who was an intrepid soldier, defeated the forces of the Governor; in June he took possession of the State capital, driving the Governor and Legislature away; the State Convention then again assembled and set up a Unionist Government for the State. This new State Government was not everywhere acknowledged; conspiracies in the Southern interest continued to exist in Missouri; and the State was repeatedly molested by invasions, of no great military consequence, from Arkansas. Indeed, in the autumn there was a serious recrudescence of trouble, in which Lyon lost his life. But substantially Missouri was secured for the Union. Naturally enough, a great many of the citizens of Missouri who had combined to save their State to the Union became among the strongest of the "Radicals" who will later engage our attention. Many, however, of the leading men who had done most in this cause, including the friends of Blair, Lincoln's Postmaster-General, adhered no less emphatically to the "Conservative" section of the Republicans.

2. Bull Run.

Thus, in the autumn of 1861, North and South had become solidified into something like two countries. In the month of July, which now concerns us, this process was well on its way, but it is to be marked that the whole long tract of Kentucky still formed a neutral zone, which the Northern Government did not wish to harass, and which perhaps the South would have done well to let alone, while further west in Missouri the forces of the North were not even as fully organised as in the East. So the only possible direction in which any great blow could be struck was the direction of Richmond, now the capital, and it might seem, therefore, the heart, of the Confederacy. The Confederate Congress was to meet there on July 20. The 'New York Tribune', which was edited by Mr. Horace Greeley, a vigorous writer whose omniscience was unabated by the variation of his own opinion, was the one journal of far-reaching influence in the North; and it only gave exaggerated point to a general feeling when it declared that the Confederate Congress must not meet. The Senators and Congressmen now in Washington were not quite so exacting, but they had come there unanimous in their readiness to vote taxes and support the war in every way, and they wanted to see something done; and they wanted it all the more because the three months' service of the militia was running out. General Scott, still the chief military adviser of Government, was quite distinct in his preference for waiting and for perfecting the discipline and organisation of the volunteers, who had not yet even been formed into brigades. On the militia he set no value at all. For long he refused to countenance any but minor movements preparatory to a later advance. It is not quite certain, however, that Congress and public opinion were wrong in clamouring for action. The Southern troops were not much, if at all, more ready for use than the Northerners; and Jefferson Davis and his military adviser, Lee, desired time for their defensive preparations. It was perhaps too much to expect that the country after its great uprising should be content to give supplies and men without end while nothing apparently happened; and the spirit of the troops themselves might suffer more from inaction than from defeat. A further thought, while it made defeat seem more dangerous, made battle more tempting. There was fear that European Powers might recognise the Southern Confederacy and enter into relations with it. Whether they did so depended on whether they were confirmed in their growing suspicion that the North could not conquer the South. Balancing the military advice which was given them as to the risk against this political importunity, Lincoln and his Cabinet chose the risk, and Scott at length withdrew his opposition. Lincoln was possibly more sensitive to pressure than he afterwards became, more prone to treat himself as a person under the orders of the people, but there is no reason to doubt that he acted on his own sober judgment as well as that of his Cabinet. Whatever degree of confidence he reposed in Scott, Scott was not very insistent; the risk was not overwhelming; the battle was very nearly won, would have been won if the orders of Scott had been carried out. No very great harm in fact followed the defeat of Bull Run; and the danger of inaction was real. He was probably then, as he certainly was afterwards, profoundly afraid that the excessive military caution which he often encountered would destroy the cause of the North by disheartening the people who supported the war. That is no doubt a kind of fear to which many statesmen are too prone, but Lincoln's sense of real popular feeling throughout the wide extent of the North is agreed to have been uncommonly sure. Definite judgment on such a question is impossible, but probably Lincoln and his Cabinet were wise.

However, they did not win their battle. The Southern army under Beauregard lay near the Bull Run river, some twenty miles from Washington, covering the railway junction of Manassas on the line to Richmond. The main Northern army, under General McDowell, a capable officer, lay south of the Potomac, where fortifications to guard Washington had already been erected on Virginian soil. In the Shenandoah Valley was another Southern force, under Joseph Johnston, watched by the Northern general Patterson at Harper's Ferry, which had been recovered by Scott's operations. Each of these Northern generals was in superior force to his opponent. McDowell was to attack the Confederate position at Manassas, while Patterson, whose numbers were nearly double Johnston's, was to keep him so seriously occupied that he could not join Beauregard. With whatever excuse of misunderstanding or the like, Patterson made hardly an attempt to carry out his part of Scott's orders, and Johnston, with the bulk of his force, succeeded in joining Beauregard the day before McDowell's attack, and without his gaining knowledge of this movement. The battle of Bull Run or Manassas (or rather the earlier and more famous of two battles so named) was an engagement of untrained troops in which up to a certain point the high individual quality of those troops supplied the place of discipline. McDowell handled with good judgment a very unhandy instrument. It was only since his advance had been contemplated that his army had been organised in brigades. The enemy, occupying high wooded banks on the south side of the Bull Run, a stream about as broad as the Thames at Oxford but fordable, was successfully pushed back to a high ridge beyond; but the stubborn attacks over difficult ground upon this further position failed from lack of co-ordination, and, when it already seemed doubtful whether the tired soldiers of the North could renew them with any hope, they were themselves attacked on their right flank. It seems that from that moment their success upon that day was really hopeless, but some declare that the

Northern soldiers with one accord became possessed of a belief that this flank attack by a comparatively small body was that of the whole force of Johnston, freshly arrived upon the scene. In any case they spontaneously retired in disorder; they were not effectively pursued, but McDowell was unable to rally them at Centreville, a mile or so behind the Bull Run. Among the camp followers the panic became extreme, and they pressed into Washington in wild alarm, accompanied by citizens and Congressmen who had come out to see a victory, and who left one or two of their number behind as prisoners of war. The result was a surprise to the Southern army. Johnston, who now took over the command, declared that it was as much disorganised by victory as the Northern army by defeat. With the full approval of his superiors in Richmond, he devoted himself to entrenching his position at Manassas. But in Washington, where rumours of victory had been arriving all through the day of battle, there prevailed for some time an impression that the city was exposed to immediate capture, and this impression was shared by McClellan, to whom universal opinion now turned as the appointed saviour, and who was forthwith summoned to Washington to take command of the army of the Potomac.

Within the circle of the Administration there was, of course, deep mortification. Old General Scott passionately declared himself to have been the greatest coward in America in having ever given way to the President's desire for action. Lincoln, who was often to prove his readiness to take blame on his own shoulders, evidently thought that the responsibility in this case was shared by Scott, and demanded to know whether Scott accused him of having overborne his judgment. The old general warmly, if a little ambiguously, replied that he had served under many Presidents, but never known a kinder master. Plainly he felt that his better judgment had somehow been overpowered, and yet that there was nothing in their relations for which in his heart he could blame the President; and this trivial dialogue is worth remembering during the dreary and controversial tale of Lincoln's relations with Scott's successor. Lincoln, however bitterly disappointed, showed no signs of discomposure or hesitancy. The business of making the army of the Potomac quietly began over again. To the four days after Bull Run belongs one of the few records of the visits to the troops which Lincoln constantly paid when they were not too far from Washington, cheering them with little talks which served a good purpose without being notable. He was reviewing the brigade commanded at Bull Run by William Sherman, later, but not yet, one of the great figures in the war. He was open to all complaints, and a colonel of militia came to him with a grievance; he claimed that his term of service had already expired, that he had intended to go home, but that Sherman unlawfully threatened to shoot him if he did so. Lincoln had a good look at Sherman, and then advised the colonel to keep out of Sherman's way, as he looked like a man of his word. This was said in the hearing of many men, and Sherman records his lively gratitude for a simple jest which helped him greatly in keeping his brigade in existence.

Not one of the much more serious defeats suffered later in the war produced by itself so lively a sense of discomfiture in the North as this; thus none will equally claim our attention. But, except for the first false alarms in Washington, there was no disposition to mistake its military significance. The "second uprising of the North," which followed upon this bracing shock, left as vivid a memory as the little disaster of Bull Run. But there was of necessity a long pause while McClellan remodelled the army in the East, and the situation in the West was becoming ripe for important movements. The eagerness of the Northern people to make some progress, again asserted itself before long, but to their surprise, and perhaps to that of a reader to-day, the last five months of 1861 passed without notable military events. Here then we may turn to the progress of other affairs, departmental affairs, foreign affairs, and domestic policy, which, it must not be forgotten, had pressed heavily upon the Administration from the moment that war began.

3. Lincoln's Administration Generally.

Long before the Eastern public was very keenly aware of Lincoln the members of his Cabinet had come to think of the

Administration as his Administration, some, like Seward, of whom it could have been little expected, with a loyal, and for America most fortunate, acceptance of real subordination, and one at least, Chase, with indignant surprise that his own really great abilities were not dominant. One Minister early told his friends that there was but one vote in the Cabinet, the President's. This must not be taken in the sense that Lincoln's personal guidance was present in every department. He had his own department, concerned with the maintenance of Northern unity and with that great underlying problem of internal policy which will before long appear again, and the business of the War Department was so immediately vital as to require his ceaseless attention; but in other matters the degree and manner of his control of course varied. Again, it is far from being the case that the Cabinet had little influence on his action. He not only consulted it much, but deferred to it much. His wisdom seems to have shown itself in nothing more strongly than in recognising when he wanted advice and when he did not, when he needed support and when he could stand alone. Sometimes he yielded to his Ministers because he valued their judgment, sometimes also because he gauged by them the public support without which his action must fail. Sometimes, when he was sure of the necessity, he took grave steps without advice from them or any one. More often he tried to arrive with them at a real community of decision. It is often impossible to guess what acts of an Administration are rightly credited to its chief. The hidden merit or demerit of many statesmen has constantly lain in the power, or the lack of it, of guiding their colleagues and being guided in turn. If we tried to be exact in saying Lincoln, or Lincoln's Cabinet, or the North did this or that, it would be necessary to thresh out many bushels of tittle-tattle. The broad impression, however, remains that in the many things in which Lincoln did not directly rule he ruled through a group of capable men of whom he made the best use, and whom no other chief could have induced to serve so long in concord. As we proceed some authentic examples of his precise relations with them will appear, in which, unimportant as they seem, one test of his quality as a statesman and of his character should be sought.

The naval operations of the war afford many tales of daring on both sides which cannot here be noticed. They afford incidents of strange interest now, such as the exploit of the first submarine. (It belonged to the South; its submersion invariably resulted in the death of the whole crew; and, with full knowledge of this, a devoted crew went down and destroyed a valuable Northern iron-clad.) The ravages on commerce of the _Alabama_ and some other Southern cruisers became only too famous in England, from whose ship-building yards they had escaped. The North failed too in some out of the fairly numerous combined naval and military expeditions, which were undertaken with a view to making the blockade more complete and less arduous by the occupation of Southern ports, and perhaps to more serious incursions into the South. Among those of them which will require no special notice, most succeeded. Thus by the spring of 1863 Florida was substantially in Northern hands, and by 1865 the South had but two ports left, Charleston and Wilmington; but the venture most attractive to Northern sentiment, an attack upon Charleston itself, proved a mere waste of military force. Moreover, till a strong military adviser was at last found in Grant there was some dissipation of military force in such expeditions. Nevertheless, the naval success of the North was so continuous and overwhelming that its history in detail need not be recounted in these pages. Almost from the first the ever-tightening grip of the blockade upon the Southern coasts made its power felt, and early in 1862 the inland waterways of the South were beginning to fall under the command of the Northern flotillas. Such a success needed, of course, the adoption of a decided policy from the outset; it needed great administrative ability to improvise a navy where hardly any existed, and where the conditions of its employment were in many respects novel; and it needed resourceful watching to meet the surprises of fresh naval invention by which the South, poor as were its possibilities for ship-building, might have rendered impotent, as once or twice it seemed likely to do, the Northern blockade. Gideon Welles, the responsible Cabinet Minister, was constant and would appear to have been capable at his task, but the inspiring mind of the Naval Department was found in Gustavus V. Fox, a retired naval officer, who at the beginning of Lincoln's administration was appointed Assistant Secretary of the Navy. The policy of blockade was begun by Lincoln's Proclamation on April 19, 1861. It was a hardy measure, certain to be a cause of friction with foreign Powers.

The United States Government had contended in 1812 that a blockade which is to confer any rights against neutral commerce must be an effective blockade, and has not lately been inclined to take lax views upon such questions; but when it declared its blockade of the South it possessed only three steamships of war with which to make it effective. But the policy was stoutly maintained. The Naval Department at the very first set about buying merchant ships in Northern ports and adapting them to warlike use, and building ships of its own, in the design of which it shortly obtained the help of a Commission of Congress on the subject of ironclads. The Naval Department had at least the fullest support and encouragement from Lincoln in the whole of its policy. Everything goes to show that he followed naval affairs carefully, but that, as he found them conducted on sound lines by men that he trusted, his intervention in them was of a modest kind. Welles continued throughout the member of his Cabinet with whom he had the least friction, and was probably one of those Ministers, common in England, who earn the confidence of their own departments without in any way impressing the imagination of the public; and a letter by Lincoln to Fox immediately after the affair of Fort Sumter shows the hearty esteem and confidence with which from the first he regarded Fox. Of the few slight records of his judgment in these matters one is significant. The unfortunate expedition against Charleston in the spring of 1863 was undertaken with high hopes by the Naval Department; but Lincoln, we happen to know, never believed it could succeed. He has, rightly or wrongly, been blamed for dealings with his military officers in which he may be said to have spurred them hard; he cannot reasonably be blamed for giving the rein to his expert subordinates, because his own judgment, which differed from theirs, turned out right. This is one of very many instances which suggest that at the time when his confidence in himself was full grown his disposition, if any, to interfere was well under control. It is also one of the indications that his attention was alert in many matters in which his hand was not seen.

He was no financier, and that important part of the history of the war, Northern finance, concerns us little. The real economic strength of the North was immense, for immigration and development were going on so fast, that, for all the strain of the war, production and exports increased. But the superficial disturbance caused by borrowing and the issue of paper money was great, and, though the North never bore the pinching that was endured in the South, it is an honourable thing that, for all the rise in the cost of living and for all the trouble that occurred in business when the premium on gold often fluctuated between 40 and 60 and on one occasion rose to 185, neither the solid working class of the country generally nor the solid business class of New York were deeply affected by the grumbling at the duration of the war. The American verdict upon the financial policy of Chase, a man of intellect but new to such affairs, is one of high praise. Lincoln left him free in that policy. He had watched the acts and utterances of his chief contemporaries closely and early acquired a firm belief in Chase's ability. How much praise is due to the President, who for this reason kept Chase in his Cabinet, a later part of this story may show.

One function of Government was that of the President alone. An English statesman is alleged to have said upon becoming Prime Minister, "I had important and interesting business in my old office, but now my chief duty will be to create undeserving Peers." Lincoln, in the anxious days that followed his first inauguration, once looked especially harassed; a Senator said to him: "What is the matter, Mr. President? Is there bad news from Fort Sumter?" "Oh, no," he answered, "it's the Post Office at Baldinsville." The patronage of the President was enormous, including the most trifling offices under Government, such as village postmasterships. In the appointment to local offices, he was expected to consult the local Senators and Representatives of his own party, and of course to choose men who had worked for the party. In the vast majority of cases decent competence for the office in the people so recommended might be presumed. The established practice further required that a Republican President on coming in should replace with good Republicans most of the nominees of the late Democratic administration, which had done the like in its day. Lincoln's experience after a while led him to prophesy that the prevalence of office-seeking would be the ruin of American politics, but it certainly never occurred to him to try and break down then the accepted rule, of which no party yet complained. It would have been unmeasured folly, even if he had thought of it, to have taken during such a crisis a new departure which would have vexed the Republicans far more than it would have pleased the Democrats. And at that time it was really of great consequence that public officials should be men of known loyalty to the Union, for obviously a postmaster of doubtful loyalty might do mischief. Lincoln, then, except in dealing with posts of special consequence, for which men with really special qualifications were to be found, frankly and without a question took as the great principle of his patronage the fairest possible distribution of favours among different classes and individuals among the supporters of the Government, whom it was his primary duty to keep together. His attitude in the whole business was perfectly understood and respected by scrupulous men who watched politics critically. It was the cause in one way of great worry to him, for, except when his indignation was kindled, he was abnormally reluctant to say "no,"—he once shuddered to think what would have happened to him if he had been a woman, but was consoled by the thought that his ugliness would have been a shield; and his private secretaries accuse him of carrying out his principle with needless and even ridiculous care. In appointments to which the party principle did not apply, but in which an ordinary man would have felt party prejudice, Lincoln's old opponents were often startled by his freedom from it. If jobbery be the right name for his persistent endeavour to keep the partisans of the Union pleased and united, his jobbery proved to have one shining attribute of virtue; later on, when, apart from the Democratic opposition which revived, there arose in the Republican party sections hostile to himself, the claims of personal adherence to him and the wavering prospects of his own reelection seem, from recorded instances, to have affected his choice remarkably little.

4. Foreign Policy and England.

The question, what was his influence upon foreign policy, is more difficult than the general praise bestowed upon it might lead us to expect; because, though he is known to have exercised a constant supervision over Seward, that influence was concealed from the diplomatic world.

For at least the first eighteen months of the war, apart from lesser points of quarrel, a real danger of foreign intervention hung over the North. The danger was increased by the ambitions of Napoleon III. in regard to Mexico, and by the loss and suffering caused to England, above all, not merely from the interruption of trade but from the suspension of cotton supplies by the blockade. From the first there was the fear that foreign powers would recognise the Southern Confederacy as an independent country; that they were then likely to offer mediation which it would at the best have been embarrassing for the President to reject; that they might ultimately, when their mediation had been rejected, be tempted to active intervention. It is curious that the one European Government which was recognised all along as friendly to the Republic was that of the Czar, Alexander II. of Russia, who in this same year, 1861, was accomplishing the project, bequeathed to him by his father, of emancipating the serfs. Mercier, the French Minister in Washington, advised his Government to recognise the South Confederacy as early as March, 1861. The Emperor of the French, though not the French people, inclined throughout to this policy; but he would not act apart from England, and the English Government, though Americans did not know it, had determined, and for the present was quite resolute, against any hasty action. Nevertheless an almost accidental cause very soon brought England and the North within sight of a war from which neither people was in appearance averse.

Neither the foreign policy of Lincoln's Government nor, indeed, the relations of England and America from his day to our own can be understood without some study of the attitude of the two countries to each other during the war. If we could put aside any previous judgment on the cause as between North and South, there are still some marked features in the attitude of England during the war which every Englishman must now regret. It should emphatically be added that there were some upon which every Englishman should look back with satisfaction. Many of the expressions of English opinion at that time betray a powerlessness to comprehend another country and a self-sufficiency in judging it, which, it may humbly be claimed, were not always and are not now so characteristic of Englishmen as they were in that period of our history, in many ways so noble, which we associate with the rival influences of Palmerston and of Cobden. It is not at all surprising that ordinary English gentlemen started with a leaning towards the South; they liked Southerners and there was much in the manners of the North, and in the experiences of Englishmen trading with or investing in the North, which did not impress them favourably. Many Northerners discovered something snobbish and unsound in this preference, but they were not quite right. With this leaning, Englishmen readily accepted the plea of the South that it was threatened with intolerable interference; indeed to this day it is hardly credible to Englishmen that the grievance against which the South arose in such passionate revolt was so unsubstantial as it really was. On the other hand, the case of the North was not apprehended. How it came to pass, in the intricate and usually uninteresting play of American politics, that a business community, which had seemed pretty tolerant of slavery, was now at war on some point which was said to be and said not to be slavery, was a little hard to understand. Those of us who remember our parents' talk of the American Civil War did not hear from them the true and fairly simple explanation of the war, that the North fought because it refused to connive further in the extension of slavery, and would not—could not decently—accept the disruption of a great country as the alternative. It is strictly true that the chivalrous South rose in blind passion for a cause at the bottom of which lay the narrowest of pecuniary interests, while the over-sharp Yankees, guided by a sort of comic backwoodsman, fought, whether wisely or not, for a cause as untainted as ever animated a nation in arms. But it seems a paradox even now, and there is no reproach in the fact, that our fathers, who had not followed the vacillating course of Northern politics hitherto, did not generally take it in. We shall see in a later chapter how Northern statesmanship added to their perplexity. But it is impossible not to be ashamed of some of the forms in which English feeling showed itself and was well known in the North to show itself. Not only the articles of some English newspapers, but the private letters of Americans who then found themselves in the politest circles in London, are unpleasant to read now. It is painful, too, that a leader of political thought like Cobden should even for a little while—and it was only a little while—have been swayed in such a matter by a sympathy relatively so petty as agreement with the Southern doctrine of Free Trade. We might now call it worthier of Prussia than of England that a great Englishman like Lord Salisbury (then Lord Robert Cecil) should have expressed friendship for the South as a good customer of ours, and antagonism for the North as a rival in our business. When such men as these said such things they were, of course, not brutally indifferent to right, they were merely blind to the fact that a very great and plain issue of right and wrong was really involved in the war. Gladstone, to take another instance, was not blind to that, but with irritating misapprehension he protested against the madness of plunging into war to propagate the cause of emancipation. Then came in his love of small states, and from his mouth, while he was a Cabinet Minister, came the impulsive pronouncement, bitterly regretted by him and bitterly resented in the North: "Jefferson Davis and other leaders of the South have made an army; they are making, it appears, a navy; and they have made—what is more than either—they have made a nation." Many other Englishmen simply sympathised with the weaker side; many too, it should be confessed, with the apparently weaker side which they were really persuaded would win. ("Win the battles," said Lord Robert Cecil to a Northern lady, "and we Tories shall come round at once.") These things are recalled because their natural effect in America has to be understood. What is really lamentable is not that in this distant and debatable affair the sympathy of so many inclined to the South, but that, when at least there was a Northern side, there seemed at first to be hardly any capable of understanding or being stirred by it. Apart from politicians there were only two Englishmen of the first rank, Tennyson and Darwin, who, whether or not they understood the matter in detail, are known to have cared from their hearts for the Northern cause. It is pleasant to associate with these greater names that of the author of "Tom Brown." The names of those hostile to the North or apparently quite uninterested are numerous and surprising. Even Dickens, who had hated slavery, and who in "Martin Chuzzlewit" had appealed however bitterly to the higher national spirit which he thought latent in America, now, when that spirit had at last and in deed asserted itself, gave way in his letters to nothing but hatred of the whole country. And a disposition like this—explicable but odious—did no doubt exist in the England of those days.

There is, however, quite another aspect of this question besides that which has so painfully impressed many American memories. When the largest manufacturing industry of England was brought near to famine by the blockade, the voice of the stricken working population was loudly and persistently uttered on the side of the North. There has been no other demonstration so splendid of the spirit which remains widely diffused among individual English working men and which at one time animated labour as a concentrated political force. John Bright, who completely grasped the situation in America, took a stand, in which J. S. Mill, W. E. Forster, and the Duke of Argyll share his credit, but which did peculiar and great honour to him as a Quaker who hated war. But there is something more that must be said. The conduct of the English Government, supported by the responsible leaders of the Opposition, was at that time, no less than now, the surest indication of the more deep-seated feelings of the real bulk of Englishmen on any great question affecting our international relations; and the attitude of the Government, in which Lord Palmerston was Prime Minister and Lord John Russell Foreign Secretary, and with which in this matter Conservative leaders like Disraeli and Sir Stafford Northcote entirely concurred, was at the very least free from grave reproach. Lord John Russell, and, there can be little doubt, his colleagues generally, regarded slavery as an "accursed institution," but they felt no anger with the people of the South for it, because, as he said, "we gave them that curse and ours were the hands from which they received that fatal gift"; in Lord John at least the one overmastering sentiment upon the outbreak of the war was that of sheer pain that "a great Republic, which has enjoyed institutions under which the people have been free and happy, is placed in jeopardy." Their insight into American affairs did not go deep; but the more seriously we rate "the strong antipathy to the North, the strong sympathy with the South, and the passionate wish to have cotton," of which a Minister, Lord Granville, wrote at the time, the greater is the credit due both to the Government as a whole and to Disraeli for having been conspicuously unmoved by these considerations; and "the general approval from Parliament, the press, and the public," which, as Lord Granville added, their policy received, is creditable too. It is perfectly true, as will be seen later, that at one dark moment in the fortunes of the North, the Government very cautiously considered the possibility of intervention, but Disraeli, to whom a less patriotic course would have offered a party advantage, recalled to them their own better judgment; and it is impossible to read their correspondence on this question without perceiving that in this they were actuated by no hostility to the North, but by a sincere belief that the cause of the North was hopeless and that intervention, with a view to stopping bloodshed, might prove the course of honest friendship to all America. Englishmen of a later time have become deeply interested in America, and may wish that their fathers had better understood the great issue of the Civil War, but it is matter for pride, which in honesty should be here asserted, that with many selfish interests in this contest, of which they were most keenly aware, Englishmen, in their capacity as a nation, acted with complete integrity.

But for our immediate purpose the object of thus reviewing a subject on which American historians have lavished much research is to explain the effect produced in America by demonstrations of strong antipathy and sympathy in England. The effect in some ways has been long lasting.

The South caught at every mark of sympathy with avidity, was led by its politicians to expect help, received none, and became resentful. It is surprising to be told, but may be true, that the embers of this resentment became dangerous to England in the autumn of 1914. In the North the memory of an antipathy which was almost instantly perceived has burnt deep—as many memoirs, for instance those recently published by Senator Lodge, show—into the minds of precisely those Americans to whom Englishmen have ever since been the readiest to accord their esteem. There were many men in the North with a ready-made dislike of England, but there were many also whose sensitiveness to English opinion, if in some ways difficult for us to appreciate, was intense. Republicans such as James Russell Lowell had writhed under the reproaches cast by Englishmen upon the acquiescence of all America in slavery; they felt that the North had suddenly cut off this reproach and staked everything on the refusal to give way to slavery any further; they looked now for expressions of sympathy from many quarters in England; but in the English newspapers which they read and the reports of Americans in England they found evidence of nothing but dislike. There soon came evidence, as it seemed to the whole North, of actually hostile action on the part of the British Government. It issued a Proclamation enjoining neutrality upon British subjects. This was a matter of course on the outbreak of what was nothing less than war; but Northerners thought that at least some courteous explanation should first have been made to their Government, and there were other matters which they misinterpreted as signs of an agreement of England with France to go further and open diplomatic relations with the Confederate Government. Thus alike in the most prejudiced and in the most enlightened quarters in the North there arose an irritation which an Englishman must see to have been natural but can hardly think to have been warranted by the real facts.

Here came in the one clearly known and most certainly happy intervention of Lincoln's in foreign affairs. Early in May Seward brought to him the draft of a vehement despatch, telling the British Government peremptorily what the United States would not stand, and framed in a manner which must have frustrated any attempt by Adams in London to establish good relations with Lord John Russell. That draft now exists with the alterations made in Lincoln's own hand. With a few touches, some of them very minute, made with the skill of a master of language and of a life-long peacemaker, he changed the draft into a firm but entirely courteous despatch. In particular, instead of requiring Adams, as Seward would have done, to read the hole despatch to Russell and leave him with a copy of it, he left it to the man on the spot to convey its sense in what manner he judged best. Probably, as has been claimed for him, his few penstrokes made peaceful relations easy when Seward's despatch would have made them almost impossible; certainly a study of this document will prove both his strange, untutored diplomatic skill and the general soundness of his view of foreign affairs.

Now, however, followed a graver crisis in which his action requires some discussion. Messrs. Mason and Slidell were sent by the Confederate Government as their emissaries to England and France. They got to Havana and there took ship again on the British steamer _Trent_. A watchful Northern sea captain overhauled the _Trent_, took Mason and Slidell off her, and let her go. If he had taken the course, far more inconvenient to the _Trent_, of bringing her into a Northern harbour, where a Northern Prize Court might have adjudged these gentlemen to be bearers of enemy despatches, he would have been within the law. As it was he violated well-established usage, and no one has questioned the right and even the duty of the British Government to demand the release of the prisoners. This they did in a note of which the expression was made milder by the wish of the Queen (conveyed in almost the last letter of the Prince Consort), but which required compliance within a fortnight. Meanwhile Secretary Welles had approved the sea captain's action. The North was jubilant at the capture, the more so because Mason and Slidell were Southern statesmen of the lower type and held to be specially obnoxious; and the House of Representatives, to make matters worse, voted its approval of what had been done. Lincoln, on the very day when the news of the capture came, had seen and said privately that on the principles which America had itself upheld in the past the prisoners would have to be given up with an apology. But there is evidence that he now wavered, and that, bent as he was on maintaining a united North, he was still too distrustful of his own better judgment as against that of the public. At this very time he was already on other points in painful conflict with many friends. In any case he submitted to Seward a draft despatch making the ill-judged proposal of arbitration. He gave way to Seward, but at the Cabinet meeting on Christmas Eve, at which Seward submitted a despatch yielding to the British demand, it is reported that Lincoln, as well as Chase and others, was at first reluctant to agree, and that it was Bates and Seward that persuaded the Cabinet to a just and necessary surrender.

This was the last time that there was serious friction in the actual intercourse of the two Governments. The lapse of Great Britain in allowing the famous 'Alabama' to sail was due to delay and misadventure ("week-ends" or the like) in the proceedings of subordinate officials, and was never defended, and the numerous minor controversies that arose, as well as the standing disagreement as to the law of blockade never reached the point of danger. For all this great credit was due to Lord Lyons and to C. F. Adams, and to Seward also, when he had a little sobered down, but it might seem as if the credit commonly given to Lincoln by Americans rested on little but the single happy performance with the earlier despatch which has been mentioned. Adams and Lyons were not aware of his beneficent influence – the papers of the latter contain little reference to him beyond a kindly record of a trivial conversation, at the end of which, as the Ambassador was going for a holiday to England, the President said, "Tell the English people I mean them no harm." Yet it is evident that Lincoln's supporters in America, the writer of the Biglow Papers, for instance, ascribed to him a wise, restraining power in the Trent_ dispute. What is more, Lincoln later claimed this for himself. Two or three years later, in one of the confidences with which he often startled men who were but slight acquaintances, but who generally turned out worthy of confidence, he exclaimed with emphatic self-satisfaction, "Seward knows that I am his master," and recalled with satisfaction how he had forced Seward to yield to England in the _Trent_ affair. It would have been entirely unlike him to claim praise when it was wholly undue to him; we find him, for example, writing to Fox, of the Navy Department, about "a blunder which was probably in part mine, and certainly was not yours"; so that a puzzling question arises here. It is quite possible that Lincoln, who did not press his proposal of arbitration, really manoeuvred Seward and the Cabinet into full acceptance of the British demands by making them see the consequences of any other action. It is also, however, likely enough that, being, as he was, interested in arbitration generally, he was too inexperienced to see the inappropriateness of the proposal in this case. If so, we may none the less credit him with having forced Seward to work for peace and friendly relations with Great Britain, and made that minister the agent, more skilful than himself, of a peaceful resolution which in its origin was his own.

5. The Great Questions of Domestic Policy.

The larger questions of civil policy which arose out of the fact of the war, and which weighed heavily on Lincoln before the end of 1861, can be related with less intricate detail if the fundamental point of difficulty is made clear.

Upon July 4 Congress met. In an able Message which was a skilful but simple appeal not only to Congress, but to the "plain people," the President set forth the nature of the struggle as he conceived it, putting perhaps in its most powerful form the contention that the Union was indissoluble, and declaring that the "experiment" of "our popular government" would have failed once for all if it did not prove that "when ballots have fairly and constitutionally decided, there can be no successful appeal back to bullets." He recounted the steps which he had taken since the bombardment of Fort Sumter, some of which might be held to exceed his constitutional authority as indeed they did, saying he would have been false to his trust if for fear of such illegality he had let the whole Constitution perish, and asking that, if necessary, Congress should ratify them. He appealed to Congress now to do its part, and especially he appealed for such prompt and adequate provision of money and men as would enable the war to be speedily brought to a close. Congress, with but a few dissentient voices, chiefly from the border States, approved all that he had done, and voted the supplies that he had asked. Then, by a resolution of both Houses, it defined the object of the war; the war was not for any purpose of conquest or subjugation, or of "overthrowing or interfering with the rights or established institutions" of the Southern States; it was solely "to preserve the Union with all the dignity, equality, and rights of the several States unimpaired."

In this resolution may be found the clue to the supreme political problem with which, side by side with the conduct of the war, Lincoln was called upon to grapple unceasingly for the rest of his life. That problem lay in the inevitable change, as the war dragged on, of the political object involved in it. The North as yet was not making war upon the institutions of Southern States, in other words upon slavery, and it would have been wrong to do so. It was simply asserting the supremacy of law by putting down what every man in the North regarded as rebellion. That rebellion, it seemed likely, would completely subside after a decisive defeat or two of the Southern forces. The law and the Union would then have been restored as before. A great victory would in fact have been won over slavery, for the policy of restricting its further spread would have prevailed, but the constitutional right of each Southern State to retain slavery within its borders was not to be denied by those who were fighting, as they claimed, for the Constitution. Such at first was the position taken up by an unanimous Congress. It was obviously in accord with those political principles of Lincoln which have been examined in a former chapter. More than that, it was the position which, as he thought, his official duty as President imposed on him. It is exceedingly difficult for any Englishman to follow his course as the political situation developed. He was neither a dictator, nor an English Prime Minister. He was first and foremost an elected officer with powers and duties prescribed by a fixed Constitution which he had sworn to obey. His oath was continually present to his mind.

He was there to uphold the Union and the laws, with just so much infraction of the letter of the law, and no more, as might be obviously necessary if the Union and the whole fabric of law were not to perish.

The mere duration of the war altered of necessity the policy of the North and of the President. Their task had presented itself as in theory the "suppression of an unlawful combination" within their country; it became in manifest fact the reabsorption of a country now hostile, with which reunion was possible only if slavery, the fundamental cause of difference, was uprooted.

As the hope of a speedy victory and an easy settlement vanished, wide differences of opinion appeared again in the North, and the lines on which this cleavage proceeded very soon showed themselves. There were those who gladly welcomed the idea of a crusade against slavery, and among them was an unreasonable section of so-called Radicals. These resented that delay in a policy of wholesale liberation which was enforced by legal and constitutional scruples, and by such practical considerations as the situation in the slave States which adhered to the North. There was, on the other hand, a Democratic party Opposition which before long began to revive. It combined many shades of opinion. There were supporters or actual agents of the South, few at first and very quiet, but ultimately developing a treasonable activity. There were those who constituted themselves the guardians of legality and jealously criticised all the measures of emergency which became more or less necessary. Of the bulk of the Democrats it would probably be fair to say that their conscious intention throughout was to be true to the Union, but that throughout they were beset by a respect for Southern rights which would have gone far to paralyse the arm of the Government. Lastly, there were Republicans, by no means in sympathy with the Democratic view, who became suspect to their Radical fellows and were vaguely classed together as Conservatives. This term may be taken to cover men simply of moderate and cautious, or in some cases, of variable disposition, but it included, too, some men who, while rigorous against the South, were half-hearted in their detestation of slavery.

So far as Lincoln's private opinions were concerned, it would have been impossible to rank him in any of these sections. He had as strong a sympathy with the Southern people as any Democrat, but he was for the restoration of the Union absolutely and without compromise. He was the most cautious of men, but his caution veiled a detestation of slavery of which he once said that he could not remember the time when he had not felt it. It was his business, so far as might be, to retain the support of all sections in the North to the Union. In the course, full of painful deliberation, which we shall see him pursuing, he tried to be guided by a two-fold principle which he constantly avowed. The Union was to be restored with as few departures from the ways of the Constitution as was possible; but such departures became his duty whenever he was thoroughly convinced that they were needful for the restoration of the Union.

Before the war was four months old, the inevitable subject of dispute between Northern parties had begun to trouble Lincoln. As soon as a Northern force set foot on Southern soil slaves were apt to escape to it, and the question arose, what should the Northern general do with them, for he was not there to make war on the private property of Southern citizens. General Butler – a newspaper character of some fame or notoriety throughout the war – commanded at Fort Monroe, a point on the coast of Virginia which was always held by the North. He learnt that the slaves who fled to him had been employed on making entrenchments for the Southern troops, so he adopted a view, which took the fancy of the North, that they were "contraband of war," and should be kept from their owners. The circumstances in which slaves could thus escape varied so much that great discretion must be left to the general on the spot, and the practice of generals varied. Lincoln was well content to leave the matter so. Congress, however, passed an Act by which private property could be confiscated, if used in aid of the "insurrection" but not otherwise, and slaves were similarly dealt with. This moderate provision as to slaves met with a certain amount of opposition; it raised an alarming question in slave States like Missouri that had not seceded. Lincoln himself seems to have been averse to any legislation on the subject. He had deliberately concentrated his mind, or, as his critics would have said, narrowed it down to the sole question of maintaining the Union, and was resolved to treat all other questions as subordinate to this.

Shortly after, there reappeared upon the political scene a leader with what might seem a more sympathetic outlook. This was Fremont, Lincoln's predecessor as the Republican candidate for the Presidency. Fremont was one of those men who make brilliant and romantic figures in their earlier career, and later appear to have lost all solid qualities. It must be recalled that, though scarcely a professional soldier (for he had held a commission, but served only in the Ordnance Survey) he had conducted a great exploring expedition, had seen fighting as a free-lance in California, and, it is claimed, had with his handful of men done much to win that great State from Mexico. Add to this that he, a Southerner by birth, was known among the leaders who had made California a free State, and it is plain how appropriate it must have seemed when he was set to command the Western Department, which for the moment meant Missouri. Here by want of competence, and, which was more surprising, lethargy he had made a present of some successes to a Southern invading force, and had sacrificed the promising life of General Lyon. Lincoln, loath to remove him, had made a good effort at helping him out by tactfully persuading a more experienced general to serve as a subordinate on his staff. At the end of August Fremont suddenly issued a proclamation establishing martial law throughout Missouri. This contained other dangerous provisions, but above all it liberated the slaves and confiscated the whole property of all persons proved (before Court Martial) to have taken active part with the enemy in the field. It is obvious that such a measure was liable to shocking abuse, that it was certain to infuriate many friends of the Union, and that it was in conflict with the law which Congress had just passed on the subject. To Lincoln's mind it presented the alarming prospect that it might turn the scale against the Union cause in the still pending deliberations in Kentucky.

Lincoln's overpowering solicitude on such a point is among the proofs that his understanding of the military situation, however elementary, was sound. He wished, characteristically, that Fremont himself should withdraw his Proclamation. He invited him to withdraw it in private letters from which one sentence may be taken: "You speak of it as being the only means of saving the Government. On the contrary, it is itself the surrender of the Government. Can it be pretended that it is any longer the Government of the United States – any government of constitution and laws – wherein a general or a president may make permanent rules of property by proclamation?" Fremont preferred to make Lincoln publicly overrule him, which he did; and the inevitable consequence followed. When some months later, the utter military disorganisation, which Fremont let arise while he busied himself with politics, and the scandalous waste, out of which his flatterers enriched themselves, compelled the President to remove him from his command, Fremont became, for a time at least, to patriotic crowds and to many intelligent, upright and earnest men from St. Louis to Boston, the chivalrous and pure-hearted soldier of freedom, and Lincoln, the soulless politician, dead to the cause of liberty, who, to gratify a few wire-pulling friends, had struck this hero down on the eve of victory to his army—an army which, by the way, he had reduced almost to nonentity.

This salient instance explains well enough the nature of one half of the trial which Lincoln throughout the war had to undergo. Pursuing the restoration of the Union with a thoroughness which must estrange from him the Democrats of the North, he was fated from the first to estrange also Radicals who were generally as devoted to the Union as himself and with whose over-mastering hatred of slavery he really sympathised. In the following chapter we are more concerned with the other half of his trial, the war itself. Of his minor political difficulties few instances need be given—only it must be remembered that they were many and involved, besides delicate questions of principle, the careful sifting of much confident hearsay; and, though the critics of public men are wont to forget it, that there are only twenty-four hours in the day.

But the year 1861 was to close with a further vexation that must be related. Secretary Cameron proved incapable on the business side of war administration. Waste and alleged corruption called down upon him a searching investigation by a committee of the House of Representatives. He had not added to his own considerable riches, but his political henchmen had grown fat. The displeasure with the whole Administration was the greater because the war was not progressing favourably, or at all. There were complaints of the Naval Department also, but politicians testified their belief in the honesty of Welles without saying a word for Cameron. There is every reason to think he was not personally dishonourable. Lincoln believed in his complete integrity, and so also did sterner critics, Chase, an apostle of economy and uprightness, and Senator Sumner. But he had to go. He opened the door for his removal by a circular to generals on the subject of slaves, which was comparable to Fremont's Proclamation and of which Lincoln had to forbid the issue. He accepted the appointment of Minister to Russia, and when, before long, he returned, he justified himself and Lincoln's judgment by his disinterested friendship and support. He was removed from the War Office at the end of December and a remarkable incident followed. While Lincoln's heart was still set on his law practice, the prospect of appearing as something more than a backwoods attorney smiled for a single moment on him. He was briefed to appear in an important case outside Illinois with an eminent lawyer from the East, Edwin M. Stanton; but he was not allowed to open his mouth, for Stanton snuffed him out with supreme contempt, and he returned home crestfallen. Stanton before the war was a strong Democrat, but hated slavery. In the last days of Buchanan's Presidency he was made Attorney-General and helped much to restore the lost credit of that Administration. He was now in Washington, criticising the slow conduct of the war with that explosive fury and scorn which led him to commit frequent injustice (at the very end of the war he publicly and monstrously accused Sherman of being bribed into terms of peace by Southern gold), which concealed from most eyes his real kindness and a lurking tenderness of heart, but which made him a vigorous administrator intolerant of dishonesty and inefficiency. He was more contemptuous of Lincoln than ever, he would constantly be denouncing his imbecility, and it is incredible that kind friends were wanting to convey his opinion to Lincoln. Lincoln made him Secretary of War.

Since the summer, to the impatient bewilderment of the Northern people, of Congress, now again in session, and of the President himself, their armies in the field were accomplishing just nothing at all, and, as this agitating year, 1861, closed, a deep gloom settled on the North, to be broken after a while by the glare of recurrent disaster.

CHAPTER IX

THE DISASTERS OF THE NORTH

1. Military Policy of the North.

The story of the war has here to be told from the point of view of the civilian administrator, the President; stirring incidents of combat and much else of interest must be neglected; episodes in the war which peculiarly concerned him, or have given rise to controversy about him, must be related lengthily. The President was an inexperienced man. It should be said, too – for respect requires perfect frankness – that he was one of an inexperienced people. The Americans had conquered their independence from Great Britain at the time when the ruling factions of our country had reached their utmost degree of inefficiency. They had fought an indecisive war with us in 1812-14, while our main business was to win at Salamanca and Vittoria. These experiences in some ways warped American ideas of war and politics, and their influence perhaps survives to this day. The extent of the President's authority and his position in regard to the advice he could obtain have been explained. An examination of the tangle in which military policy was first involved may make the chief incidents of the war throughout easier to follow.

Immediately after Bull Run McClellan had been summoned to Washington to command the army of the Potomac. In November, Scott, worn out by infirmity, and finding his authority slighted by "my ambitious junior," retired, and thereupon McClellan, while retaining his immediate command upon the Potomac, was made for the time General-in-Chief over all the armies of the North. There were, it should be repeated, two other principal armies besides that of the Potomac: the army of the Ohio, of which General Buell was given command in July; and that of the West, to which General Halleck was appointed, though Fremont seems to have retained independent command in Missouri. All these armies were in an early stage of formation and training, and from a purely military point of view there could be no haste to undertake a movement of invasion with any of them.

Three distinct views of military policy were presented to Lincoln in the early days. Scott, as soon as it was clear that the South meant real fighting, saw how serious its resistance would be. His military judgment was in favour of a strictly defensive attitude before Washington; of training the volunteers for at least four months in healthy camps; and of then pushing a large army right down the Mississippi valley to New Orleans, making the whole line of that river secure, and establishing a pressure on the South between this Western army and the naval blockade which must slowly have strangled the Confederacy. He was aware that public impatience might not allow a rigid adherence to his policy, and in fact, when his view was made public before Bull Run, "Scott's Anaconda," coiling itself round the Confederacy, was the subject of general derision. The view of the Northern public and of the influential men in Congress was in favour of speedy and, as it was hoped, decisive action, and this was understood as involving, whatever else was done, an attempt soon to capture Richmond. In McClellan's view, as in Scott's, the first object was the full preparation of the Army, but he would have wished to wait till he had a fully trained force of 273,000 men on the Potomac, and a powerful fleet with many transports to support his movements; and, when he had all this, to move southwards in irresistible force, both advancing direct into Virginia and landing at points on the coast, subduing each of the Atlantic States of the Confederacy in turn. If the indefinite delay and the overwhelming force which his fancy pictured could have been granted him, it is plain, the military critics have said, that "he could not have destroyed the Southern armies—they would have withdrawn inland, and the heart of the Confederacy would have remained untouched." But neither the time nor the force for which he wished could be allowed him. So he had to put aside his plan, but in some ways perhaps it still influenced him.

It would have been impossible to disregard the wishes of those, who in the last resort were masters, for a vigorous attempt on Richmond, and the continually unsuccessful attempts that were made did serve a military purpose, for they kept up a constant drain upon the resources of the South. In any well-thought-out policy the objects both of Scott's plan and of the popular plan would have been borne in mind. That no such policy was consistently followed from the first was partly a result of the long-continued difficulty in finding any younger man who could adequately take the place of Scott; it was not for a want of clear ideas, right or wrong, on Lincoln's part.

Only two days after the battle of Bull Run, he put on paper his own view as to the future employment of the three armies. He thought that one should "threaten" Richmond; that one should move from Cincinnati, in Ohio, by a pass called Cumberland Gap in Kentucky, upon Knoxville in Eastern Tennessee; and that the third, using Cairo on the Mississippi as its base, should advance upon Memphis, some 120 miles further south on that river. Apparently he did not at first wish to commit the army of the Potomac very deeply in its advance on Richmond, and he certainly wished throughout that it should cover Washington against any possible attack. Memphis was one of the three points at which the Southern railway system touched the great river and communicated with the States beyond—Vicksburg and New Orleans, much further south, were the others.

Knoxville again is a point, by occupying which, the Northern forces would have cut the direct railway communication between Virginia and the West, but for this move into Eastern Tennessee

Lincoln had other reasons nearer his heart. The people of that region were strongly for the Union; they were invaded by the Confederates and held down by severe coercion, and distressing appeals from them for help kept arriving through the autumn; could they have been succoured and their mountainous country occupied by the North, a great stronghold of the Union would, it seemed to Lincoln, have been planted securely far into the midst of the Confederacy. Therefore he persistently urged this part of his scheme on the attention of his generals. The chief military objection raised by Buell was that his army would have to advance 150 miles from the nearest base of supply upon a railway; (for 200 miles to the west of the Alleghanies there were no railways running from north to south). To meet this Lincoln, in September, urged upon a meeting of important Senators and Representatives the construction of a railway line from Lexington in Kentucky southwards, but his hearers, with their minds narrowed down to an advance on Richmond, seem to have thought the relatively small cost in time and money of this work too great. Lincoln still thought an expedition to Eastern Tennessee practicable at once, and it has been argued from the circumstances in which one was made nearly two years later that he was right. It would, one may suppose, have been unwise to separate the armies of the Ohio and of the West so widely; for the main army of the Confederates in the West, under their most trusted general, Albert Sidney Johnston, was from September onwards in South-western Kentucky, and could have struck at either of these two Northern armies; and this was in Buell's mind. On the other hand, Lincoln's object was a wise one in itself and would have been worth some postponement of the advance along the Mississippi if thereby the army in the West could have been used in support of it. However this may be, the fact is that Lincoln's plan, as it stood, was backed up by McClellan; McClellan was perhaps unduly anxious for Buell to move on Eastern Tennessee, because this would have supported the invasion of Virginia which he himself was now contemplating, and he was probably forgetful of the West; but he was Lincoln's highest military adviser and his capacity was still trusted. Buell's own view was that, when he moved, it should be towards Western Tennessee. He would have had a railway connection behind him all his way, and Albert

Johnston's army would have lain before him. He wished that Halleck meanwhile should advance up the courses of the Tennessee and Cumberland Rivers; Eastern Tennessee (he may have thought) would be in the end more effectively succoured; their two armies would thus have converged on Johnston's. Halleck agreed with Buell to the extent of disagreeing with Lincoln and McClellan, but no further. He declined to move in concert with Buell. Fremont had disorganised the army of the West, and Halleck, till he had repaired the mischief, permitted only certain minor enterprises under his command.

Each of the three generals, including the General-in-Chief, who was the Government's chief adviser, was set upon his own immediate purpose, and indisposed to understanding the situation of the others – Buell perhaps the least so. Each of them had at first a very sound reason, the unreadiness of his army, for being in no hurry to move, but then each of them soon appeared to be a slow or unenterprising commander. Buell was perhaps unlucky in this, for his whole conduct is the subject of some controversy; but he did appear slow, and the two others, it is universally agreed, really were so. As 1861 drew to a close, it became urgent that something should be done somewhere, even if it were not done in the best possible direction. The political pressure upon the Administration became as great as before Bull Run. The army of the Potomac had rapidly become a fine army, and its enemy, in no way superior, lay entrenching at Manassas, twenty miles in front of it. When Lincoln grew despondent and declared that "if something was not done soon, the bottom would drop out of the whole concern," soldiers remark that the military situation was really sound; but he was right, for a people can hardly be kept up to the pitch of a high enterprise if it is forced to think that nothing will happen. Before the end of the year 1861 military reasons for waiting were no longer being urged; McClellan had long been promising immediate action, Buell and Halleck seemed merely unable to agree.

In later days when Lincoln had learnt much by experience it is hard to trace the signs of his influence in military matters, because, though he followed them closely, he was commonly in full agreement with his chief general and he invariably and rightly left him free. At this stage, when his position was more difficult, and his guidance came from common sense and the military books, of which, ever since Bull Run, he had been trying, amidst all his work, to tear out the heart, there is evidence on which to judge the intelligence which he applied to the war. Certainly he now and ever after looked at the matter as a whole and formed a clear view of it, which, for a civilian at any rate, was a reasonable view. Certainly also at this time and for long after no military adviser attempted, in correcting any error of his, to supply him with a better opinion equally clear and comprehensive. This is probably why some Northern military critics, when they came to read his correspondence with his generals, called him, as his chief biographers were tempted to think him, "the ablest strategist of the war." Grant and Sherman did not say this; they said, what is another thing, that his was the greatest intellectual force that they had met with.

Strictly speaking, he could not be a strategist. If he were so judged, he would certainly be found guilty of having, till Grant came to Washington, unduly scattered his forces. He could pick out the main objects; but as to how to economise effort, what force and how composed and equipped was necessary for a particular enterprise, whether in given conditions of roads, weather, supplies, and previous fatigue, a movement was practicable, and how long it would take any clever subaltern with actual experience of campaigning ought to have been a better judge than he. The test, which the reader must be asked to apply to his conduct of the war, is whether he followed, duly or unduly his own imperfect judgment, whether, on the whole, he gave in whenever it was wise to the generals under him, and whether he did so without losing his broad view or surrendering his ultimate purpose. It is really no small proof of strength that, with the definite judgments which he constantly formed, he very rarely indeed gave imperative orders as Commander-in-Chief, which he was, to any general. The circumstances, all of which will soon appear, in which he was tempted or obliged to do so, are only the few marked exceptions to his habitual conduct. There are significant contrary instances in which he abstained even from seeking to know his general's precise intentions. At the time which has just been reviewed, when the scheme of the war was in the making, his correspondence with Buell and Halleck shows his fundamental intention. He emphatically abstains from forcing them; he lucidly, though not so tactfully as later, urges his own view upon the consideration of his general, begging him, not necessarily to act upon it, but at least to see the point, and if he will not do what is wished, to form and explain as clearly a plan for doing something better.

2. The War in the West Up to May, 1862.

The pressure upon McClellan to move grew stronger and indeed more justifiable month after month, and when at last, in March, 1862, McClellan did move, the story of the severest adversity to the North, of Lincoln's sorest trials, and, some still say, his gravest failures, began. Its details will concern us more than those of any other part of the war. But events in the West began earlier, proceeded faster, and should be told first. Buell could not obtain from McClellan permission to carry out his own scheme. He did, however, obtain permission for Halleck, if he consented, to send flotillas up the Tennessee and Cumberland Rivers to make a diversion while Buell, as Lincoln had proposed and as McClellan had now ordered, marched upon Eastern Tennessee. Halleck would not move. Buell prepared to move alone, and in January, 1862, sent forward a small force under Thomas to meet an equally small Confederate force that had advanced through Cumberland Gap into Eastern Kentucky. Thomas won a complete victory, most welcome as the first success since the defeat of Bull Run, at a place called Mill Springs, far up the Cumberland River towards the mountains. But at the end of January, while Buell was following up with his forces rather widely dispersed because he expected no support from Halleck, he was brought to a stop, for Halleck, without warning, did make an important movement of his own, in which he would need Buell's support.

The Cumberland and the Tennessee are navigable rivers which in their lower course flow parallel in a northerly or north-westerly direction to join the Ohio not far above its junction with the

Mississippi at Cairo. Fort Henry was a Confederate fort guarding the navigation of the Tennessee near the northern boundary of the State of that name, Fort Donelson was another on the Cumberland not far off. Ulysses Simpson Grant, who had served with real distinction in the Mexican War, had retired from the Army and had been more or less employed about his father's leather store in Illinois and in the gloomy pursuit of intoxication and of raising small sums from reluctant friends when he met them. On the outbreak of the Civil War he suddenly pulled himself together, and with some difficulty got employment from the Governor of Illinois as a Major-General in the State Militia (obtaining Army rank later). Since then, while serving under Halleck, he had shown sense and promptitude in seizing an important point on the Ohio, upon which the Confederates had designs. He had a quick eye for seeing important points. Grant was now ordered or obtained permission from Halleck to capture Fort Henry and Fort Donelson. By the sudden movements of Grant and of the flotilla acting with him, the Confederates were forced to abandon Fort Henry on February 6, 1862. Ten days later Fort Donelson surrendered with nearly 10,000 prisoners, after a brilliant and nearly successful sortie by the garrison, in which Grant showed, further, tenacity and a collected mind under the pressure of imminent calamity.

Halleck had given Grant little help. Buell was reluctant to detach any, of his volunteer troops from their comrades to act with a strange army, and Halleck had not warned him of his intentions. Halleck soon applied to Lincoln for the supreme command over the two Western armies with Buell under him. This was given to him. Experience showed that one or the other must command now that concerted action was necessary. Nothing was known at Washington to set against Halleck's own claim of the credit for the late successes. So Lincoln gave him the command, though present knowledge shows clearly that Buell was the better man. Grant had been left before Fort Donelson in a position of some danger from the army under Albert Johnston; and, from needless fear of Beauregard with a Confederate force under him yet further West, Halleck let slip the chance of sending Grant in pursuit of Johnston, who was falling back up the Cumberland valley. As it was, Johnston for a time evacuated Nashville, further up the Cumberland, the chief town of Tennessee and a great railway centre, which Buell promptly occupied; Beauregard withdrew the Confederate troops from Columbus, a fortress of great reputed strength on the Mississippi not far below Cairo, to positions forty or fifty miles (as the crow flies) further down the stream. Thus, as it was, some important steps had been gained in securing that control of the navigation of the river which was one of the great military objects of the North. Furthermore, successful work was being done still further West by General Curtis in Missouri, who drove an invading force back into Arkansas and inflicted a crushing defeat upon them there in March. But a great stroke should now have been struck. Buell, it is said, saw plainly that his forces and Halleck's should have been concentrated as far up the Tennessee as possible in an endeavour to seize upon the main railway system of the Confederacy in the West. Halleck preferred, it would seem, to concentrate upon nothing and to scatter his forces upon minor enterprises, provided he did not risk any important engagement. An important engagement with the hope of destroying an army of the enemy was the very thing which, as Johnston's forces now stood, he should have sought, but he appears to have been contented by the temporary retirement of an unscathed enemy who would return again reinforced.

Buell was an unlucky man, and Halleck got quite all he deserved, so it is possible that events have been described to us without enough regard to Halleck's case as against Buell. But at any rate, while much should have been happening, nothing very definite did happen till April 6, when Albert Johnston, now strongly reinforced from the extreme South, came upon Grant, who (it is not clear why) had lain encamped, without entrenching, and not expecting immediate attack, near Shiloh, far up the Tennessee River in the extreme south of Tennessee State. Buell at the time, though without clear information as to Grant's danger, was on his way to join him. There seems to have been negligence both on Halleck's part and on Grant's. The battle of Shiloh is said to have been highly characteristic of the combats of partly disciplined armies, in which the individual qualities, good or bad, of the troops play a conspicuous part. Direction on the part of Johnston or Grant was not conspicuously seen, but the latter, whose troops were surprised and driven back some distance, was intensely determined. In the course of that afternoon Albert Johnston was killed. Rightly or wrongly Jefferson Davis and his other friends regarded his death as the greatest of calamities to the South. After the manner of many battles, more especially in this war, the battle of Shiloh was the subject of long subsequent dispute between friends of Grant and of Buell, and far more bitter dispute between friends of Albert Johnston and Beauregard. But it seems that the South was on the point of winning, till late on the 6th the approach of the first reinforcements from Buell made it useless to attempt more. By the following morning further large reinforcements had come up; Grant in his turn attacked, and Beauregard had difficulty in turning a precipitate retirement into an orderly retreat upon Corinth, forty miles away, a junction upon the principal railway line to be defended. The next day General Pope, who had some time before been detached by Halleck for this purpose, after arduous work in canal cutting, captured, with 7,000 prisoners, the northernmost forts held by the Confederacy on the Mississippi. But Halleck's plans required that his further advance should be stopped. Halleck himself, in his own time, arrived at the front. In his own time, after being joined by Pope, he advanced, carefully entrenching himself every night. He covered in something over a month the forty miles route to Corinth, which, to his surprise, was bloodlessly evacuated before him. He was an engineer, and like some other engineers in the Civil War, was overmuch set upon a methodical and cautious procedure. But his mere advance to Corinth caused the Confederates to abandon yet another fort on the Mississippi, and on June 6 the Northern troops were able to occupy Memphis, for which Lincoln had long wished, while the flotilla accompanying them destroyed a Confederate flotilla. Meanwhile, on May 1, Admiral Farragut, daringly running up the Mississippi, had captured New Orleans, and a Northern force under Butler was able to establish itself in Louisiana. The North had now gained the command of most of the Mississippi, for only the hundred miles or so between Vicksburg far south and Port Hudson, between that and New Orleans, was still held by the South; and command by Northern gunboats of the chief tributaries of the great river was also established. The Confederate armies in the

West were left intact, though with some severe losses, and would be able before long to strike northward in a well-chosen direction; for all that these were great and permanent gains. Yet the North was not cheered. The great loss of life at Shiloh, the greatest battle in the war so far, created a horrible impression. Halleck, under whom all this progress had been made, properly enough received a credit, which critics later have found to be excessive, though it is plain that he had reorganised his army well; but Grant was felt to have been caught napping at Shiloh; there were other rumours about him, too, and he fell deep into general disfavour. The events of the Western war did not pause for long, but, till the end of this year 1862, the North made no further definite progress, and the South, though it was able to invade the North, achieved no Important result. It will be well then here to take up the story of events in the East and to follow them continuously till May, 1863, when the dazzling fortune of the South in that theatre if the war reached its highest point.

3. The War in the East Up to May, 1863.

The interest of this part of the Civil War lies chiefly in the achievements of Lee and "Stonewall" Jackson. From the point of view of the North, it was not only disastrous but forms a dreary and controversial chapter. George McClellan came to Washington amid overwhelming demonstrations of public confidence. His comparative youth added to the interest taken in him; and he was spoken of as "the young Napoleon." This ridiculous name for a man already thirty-four was a sign that the people expected impossible things from him. Letters to his wife, which have been injudiciously published, show him to us delighting at first in the consideration paid to him by Lincoln and Scott, proudly confident in his own powers, rather elated than otherwise by a sense that the safety of the country rested on him alone. "I shall carry the thing _en grande_, and crush the rebels in one campaign." He soon had a magnificent army; he may be said to have made it himself. Before, as he thought, the time had come to use it, he had fallen from favour, and a dead set was being made against him in Washington. A little later, at the crisis of his great venture, when, as he claimed, the Confederate capital could have been taken, his expedition was recalled. Then at a moment of deadly peril to the country his services were again called in. He warded off the danger. Yet a little while and his services were discarded for ever. This summary, which is the truth, but not the whole truth, must enlist a certain sympathy for him. The chief fact of his later life should at once be added. In 1864, when a Presidential election was approaching and despondency prevailed widely in the North, he was selected as the champion of a great party. The Democrats adopted a "platform" which expressed neither more nor less than a desire to end the war on any terms. In accordance with the invariable tradition of party opposition in war time, they chose a war hero as their candidate for the Presidency. McClellan publicly repudiated their principles, and no doubt he meant it, but he became their candidate—their master or their servant as it might prove. That he was Lincoln's opponent in the election of that year ensured that his merits and his misfortunes would be long remembered, but his action then may suggest to any one the doubtful point in his career all along.

Some estimate of his curious yet by no means uncommon type of character is necessary, if Lincoln's relations with him are to be understood at all. The devotion to him shown by his troops proves that he had great titles to confidence, besides, what he also had, a certain faculty of parade, with his handsome charger, his imposing staff and the rest. He was a great trainer of soldiers, and with some strange lapses, a good organiser. He was careful for the welfare of his men; and his almost tender carefulness of their lives contrasted afterwards with what appeared the ruthless carelessness of Grant. Unlike some of his successors, he could never be called an incapable commander. His great opponent, Lee, who had known him of old, was wont to calculate on his extraordinary want of enterprise, but he spoke of him on the whole in terms of ample respect—also, by the way, he sympathised with him like a soldier when, as he naturally assumed, he became a victim to scheming politicians; and Lee confided this feeling to the ready ears of another great soldier, Wolseley. As he showed himself in civil life, McClellan was an attractive gentleman of genial address; it was voted that he was "magnetic," and his private life was so entirely irreproachable as to afford lively satisfaction. More than this, it may be conjectured that to a certain standard of honour, loyalty, and patriotism, which he set consciously before himself, he would always have been devotedly true. But if it be asked further whether McClellan was the desired instrument for Lincoln's and the country's needs, and whether, as the saying is, he was a man to go tiger-hunting with, something very much against him, though hard to define, appears in every part of his record (except indeed, one performance in his Peninsular Campaign). Did he ever do his best to beat the enemy? Did he ever, except for a moment, concentrate himself singly upon any great object? Were even his preparations thorough? Was his information ever accurate? Was his purpose in the war ever definite, and, if so, made plain to his Government? Was he often betrayed into marked frankness, or into marked generosity? No one would be ready to answer yes to any of these questions. McClellan fills so memorable a place in American history that he demands such a label as can be given to him. In the most moving and the most authentic of all Visions of Judgment, men were not set on the right hand or the left according as they were of irreproachable or reproachable character; they were divided into those who did and those who did not. In the provisional judgment which men, if they make it modestly, should at times make with decision, McClellan's place is clear. The quality, "spiacente a Dio ed ai nemici suoi," of the men who did not, ran through and through him.

Lincoln required first a general who would make no fatal blunder, but he required too, when he could find him, a general of undaunted enterprise; he did not wish to expose the North to disaster, but he did mean to conquer the South. There was some security in employing McClellan, though employing him did at one time throw on Lincoln's unfit shoulders the task of defending Washington. It proved very hard to find another general equally trustworthy. But, in the light of facts which Lincoln came to perceive, it proved impossible to consider McClellan as the man to finish the war.

We need only notice the doings of the main armies in this theatre of the war and take no account of various minor affairs at outlying posts. From the battle of Bull Run, which was on July 21, 1861, to March 5, 1862, the Southern army under Joseph Johnston lay quietly drilling at Manassas. It, of course, entrenched its position, but to add to the appearance of its strength, it constructed embrasures for more than its number of guns and had dummy guns to show in them. At one moment there was a prospect that it might move. Johnston and the general with him had no idea of attacking the army of the Potomac where it lay, but they did think that with a further 50,000 or 60,000 they might successfully invade Maryland, crossing higher up the Potomac, and by drawing McClellan away from his present position, get a chance of defeating him. The Southern President came to Manassas, at their invitation, on October 1, but he did not think well to withdraw the trained men whom he could have sent to Johnston from the various points in the South at which they were stationed; he may have had good reasons but it is likely that he sacrificed one of the best chances of the South. McClellan's army was soon in as good a state of preparation as Johnston's. Early in October McClellan had, on his own statement, over 147,000 men at his disposal; Joseph Johnston, on his own statement, under 47,000. Johnston was well informed as to McClellan's numbers—very likely he could get information from Maryland more easily than McClellan from Virginia. The two armies lay not twenty-five miles apart. The weather and the roads were good to the end of December; the roads were practicable by March and they seem to have been so all the time. As spring approached, it appeared to the Southern generals that McClellan must soon advance. Johnston thought that his right flank was liable to be turned and the railway communications south of Manassas liable to be cut. In the course of February it was realised that his position was too dangerous; the large stores accumulated there were removed; and when, early in March, there were reports of unusual activity in the Northern camp, Johnston, still expecting attack from the same direction, began his retreat. On March 9 it was learned in Washington that Manassas had been completely evacuated. McClellan marched his whole army there, and marched it back. Johnston withdrew quietly behind the Rapidan River, some 30 miles further south, and to his surprise was left free from any pursuit.

For months past the incessant report in the papers, "all quiet upon the Potomac," had been getting upon the nerves of the North. The gradual conversion of their pride in an imposing army into puzzled rage at its inactivity has left a deeper impression on Northern memories than the shock of disappointment at Bull Run. Public men of weight had been pressing for an advance in November, and when the Joint Committee of Congress, an arbitrary and meddlesome, but able and perhaps on the whole useful body, was set up in December, it brought its full influence to bear on the President. Lincoln was already anxious enough; he wished to rouse McClellan himself to activity, while he screened him against excessive impatience or interference with his plans. It is impossible to say what was McClellan's real mind. Quite early he seems to have held out hopes to Lincoln that he would soon attack, but he was writing to his wife that he expected to be attacked by superior numbers. It is certain, however, that he was possessed now and always by a delusion as to the enemy's strength. For instance Lincoln at last felt bound to work out for himself definite prospects for a forward movement; it is sufficient to say of this layman's effort that he proposed substantially the line of advance which Johnston a little later began to dread most; Lincoln's plan was submitted for McClellan's consideration; McClellan rejected it, and his reasons were based on his assertion that he would have to meet nearly equal numbers. He, in fact, out-numbered the enemy by more than three to one. If we find the President later setting aside the general's judgment on grounds that are not fully explained, we must recall McClellan's vast and persistent miscalculations of an enemy resident in his neighbourhood. And the distrust which he thus created was aggravated by another propensity of his vague mind. His illusory fear was the companion of an extravagant hope; the Confederate army was invincible when all the world expected him to attack it then and there, but the blow which he would deal it in his own place and his own time was to have decisive results, which were indeed impossible; the enemy was to "pass beneath the Caudine Forks." The demands which he made on the Administration for men and supplies seemed to have no finality about them; his tone in regard to them seemed to degenerate into a chronic grumble. The War

Department certainly did not intend to stint him in any way; but he was an unsatisfactory man to deal with in these matters. There was a great mystery as to what became of the men sent to him. In the idyllic phrase, which Lincoln once used of him or of some other general, sending troops to him was "like shifting fleas across a barn floor with a shovel—not half of them ever get there." But his fault was graver than this; utterly ignoring the needs of the West, he tried, as General-in-Chief, to divert to his own army the recruits and the stores required for the other armies.

The difficulty with him went yet further; McClellan himself deliberately set to work to destroy personal harmony between himself and his Government. It counts for little that in private he soon set down all the civil authorities as the "greatest set of incapables," and so forth, but it counts for more that he was personally insolent to the President. Lincoln had been in the habit, mistaken in this case but natural in a chief who desires to be friendly, of calling at McClellan's house rather than summoning him to his own. McClellan acquired a habit of avoiding him, he treated his enquiries as idle curiosity, and he probably thought, not without a grain of reason, that Lincoln's way of discussing matters with many people led him into indiscretion. So one evening when Lincoln and Seward were waiting at the general's house for his return, McClellan came in and went upstairs; a message was sent that the President would be glad to see him; he said he was tired and would rather be excused that night. Lincoln damped down his friends' indignation at this; he would, he once said, "hold General McClellan's stirrup for him if he will only win us victories." But he called no more at McClellan's, and a curious abruptness in some of his orders later marks his unsuccessful effort to deal with McClellan in another way. The slightly ridiculous light in which the story shows Lincoln would not obscure to any soldier the full gravity of such an incident. It was not merely foolish to treat a kind superior rudely; a general who thus drew down a curtain between his own mind and that of the Government evidently went a very long way to ensure failure in war.

Lincoln had failed to move McClellan early in December. For part of that month and January McClellan was very ill.

Consultations were held with other generals, including McDowell, who could not be given the chief command because the troops did not trust him. McDowell and the rest were in agreement with Lincoln. Then McClellan suddenly recovered and was present at a renewed consultation. He snubbed McDowell; the inadequacy of his force to meet, in fact, less than a third of its number was "so plain that a blind man could see it"; he was severely and abruptly tackled as to his own plans by Secretary Chase; Lincoln intervened to shield him, got from him a distinct statement that he had in his mind a definite time for moving, and adjourned the meeting. Stanton, one of the friends to whom McClellan had confided his grievances, was now at the War Department and was at one with the Joint Committee of Congress in his impatience that McClellan should move. At last, on January 27, Lincoln published a "General War Order" that a forward movement was to be made by the army of the Potomac and the Western armies on February 22. It seems a blundering step, but it roused McClellan. For a time he even thought of acting as Lincoln wished; he would move straight against Johnston, and "in ten days," he told Chase on February 13, "I shall be in Richmond." But he quickly returned to the plan which he seems to have been forming before but which he only now revealed to the Government, and it was a plan which involved further delay. When February 22 passed and nothing was done, the Joint Committee were indignant that Lincoln still stood by McClellan. But McClellan now was proposing definite action; apart from the difficulty of finding a better man, there was the fact that McClellan had made his army and was beloved by it; above all, Lincoln had not lost all the belief he had formed at first in McClellan's capacity; he believed that "if he could once get McClellan started" he would do well. Professional criticism, alive to McClellan's military faults, has justified Lincoln in this, and it was for something other than professional failure that Lincoln at last removed him.

McClellan had determined to move his army by sea to some point further down the coast of the Chesapeake Bay. The questions which Lincoln wrote to him requesting a written answer have never been adequately answered. Did McClellan's plan, he asked, require less time or money than Lincoln's? Did it make victory more certain? Did it make it more valuable? In case of disaster, did it make retreat more easy? The one point for consideration in McClellan's reply to him is that the enemy did not expect such a movement. This was quite true; but the enemy was able to meet it, and McClellan was far too deliberate to reap any advantage from a surprise. His original plan was to land near a place called Urbana on the estuary of the Rappahannock, not fifty miles east of Richmond. When he heard that Johnston had retreated further south, he assumed, and ever after declared, that this was to anticipate his design upon Urbana, which, he said, must have reached the enemy's ears through the loose chattering of the Administration. As has been seen, this was quite untrue. His project of going to Urbana was now changed, by himself or the Government, upon the unanimous advice of his chief subordinate generals, into a movement to Fort Monroe, which he had even before regarded as preferable to a direct advance southwards. A few days after Johnston's retreat, the War Department began the embarkation of his troops for this point. Fort Monroe is at the end of the peninsula which lies between the estuaries of the York River on the north and the James on the south. Near the base of this projection of land, seventy-five miles from Fort Monroe, stands Richmond. On April 2, 1862, McClellan himself landed to begin the celebrated Peninsula Campaign which was to close in disappointment at the end of July.

Before the troops were sent to the Peninsula several things were to be done. An expedition to restore communication westward by the Baltimore and Ohio Rail way involved bridging the Potomac with boats which were to be brought by canal. It collapsed because McClellan's boats were six inches too wide for the canal locks. Then Lincoln had insisted that the navigation of the lower Potomac should be made free from the menace of Confederate batteries which, if McClellan would have co-operated with the Navy Department, would have been cleared away long before. This was now done, and though a new peril to the transportation of McClellan's army suddenly and dramatically disclosed itself, it was as suddenly and dramatically removed. In the hasty abandonment of Norfolk harbour on the south of the James estuary by the North, a screw steamer called the _Merrimac_ had been partly burnt and scuttled by the North. On March 1 she steamed out of the harbour in sight of the North. The Confederates had raised her and converted her into an ironclad. Three wooden ships of the North gave gallant but useless fight to her and were destroyed that day; and the news spread consternation in every Northern port. On the very next morning there came into the mouth of the James the rival product of the Northern Navy Department and of the Swedish engineer Ericsson's invention. She was compared to a "cheesebox on a raft"; she was named the _Monitor_, and was the parent of a type of vessel so called which has been heard of much more recently. The _Merrimac_ and the _Monitor_ forthwith fought a three hours' duel; then each retired into harbour without fatal damage. But the _Merrimac_ never came out again; she was destroyed by the Confederates when McClellan had advanced some way up the Peninsula; and it will be unnecessary to speak of the several similar efforts of the South, which nearly but not quite achieved very important successes later.

Before and after his arrival at the Peninsula, McClellan received several mortifications. Immediately after the humiliation of the enemy's escape from Manassas, he was without warning relieved of his command as General-in-Chief. This would in any case have followed naturally upon his expedition away from Washington; it was in public put on that ground alone; and he took it well. He had been urged to appoint corps commanders, for so large a force as his could not remain organised only in divisions; he preferred to wait till he had made trial of the generals under him; Lincoln would not have this delay, and appointed corps commanders chosen by himself because he believed them to be fighting men. The manner in which these and some other preparatory steps were taken were, without a doubt, intended to make McClellan feel the whip. They mark a departure, not quite happy at first, from Lincoln's formerly too gentle manner. A worse shock to McClellan followed. The President had been emphatic in his orders that a sufficient force should be left to make Washington safe, and supposed that he had come to a precise understanding on this point. He suddenly discovered that McClellan, who had now left for Fort Monroe, had ordered McDowell to follow him with a force so large that it would not leave the required number behind. Lincoln immediately ordered McDowell and his whole corps to remain, though he subsequently sent a part of it to McClellan. McClellan's story later gives reason for thinking that he had intended no deception; but if so, he had expressed himself with unpardonable vagueness, and he had not in fact left Washington secure. Now and throughout this campaign Lincoln took the line that Washington must be kept safe—safe in the judgment of all the best military authorities available.

McClellan's progress up the Peninsula was slow. He had not informed himself correctly as to the geography; he found the enemy not so unprepared as he had supposed; he wasted, it is agreed, a month in regular approaches to their thinly-manned fortifications at Yorktown, when he might have carried them by assault. He was soon confronted by Joseph Johnston, and he seems both to have exaggerated Johnston's numbers again and to have been unprepared for his movements. The Administration does not seem to have spared any effort to support him.

In addition to the 100,000 troops he took with him, 40,000 altogether were before long despatched to him. He was operating in a very difficult country, but he was opposed at first by not half his own number. Lincoln, in friendly letters, urged upon him that delay enabled the enemy to strengthen himself both in numbers and in fortifications. The War Department did its best for him. The whole of his incessant complaints on this score are rendered unconvincing by the language of his private letters about that "sink of iniquity, Washington," "those treacherous hounds," the civil authorities, who were at least honest and intelligent men, and the "Abolitionists and other scoundrels," who, he supposed, wished the destruction of his army. The criticism in Congress of himself and his generals was no doubt free, but so, as Lincoln reminded him, was the criticism of Lincoln himself. Justly or not, there were complaints of his relations with corps commanders. Lincoln gave no weight to them, but wrote him a manly and a kindly warning. The points of controversy which McClellan bequeathed to writers on the Civil War are innumerable, but no one can read his correspondence at this stage without concluding that he was almost impossible to deal with, and that the whole of his evidence in his own case was vitiated by a sheer hallucination that people wished him to fail. He had been nearly two months in the Peninsula when he was attacked at a disadvantage by Johnston, but defeated him on May 31 and June 1 in a battle which gave confidence and prestige to the Northern side, but which he did not follow up. A part of his army pursued the enemy to within four miles of Richmond, and it has been contended that if he had acted with energy he could at this time have taken that city. His delay, to whatever it was due, gave the enemy time to strengthen himself greatly both in men and in fortifications. The capable Johnston was severely wounded in the battle, and was replaced by the inspired Lee. According to McClellan's own account, which English writers have followed, his movements had been greatly embarrassed by the false hope given him that McDowell was now to march overland and join him. His statement that he was influenced by this is refuted by his own letters at the time. McClellan, however, suffered a great disappointment. The front of Washington was now clear of the enemy and Lincoln had determined to send McDowell when he was induced to keep him back by a diversion in the war which he had not expected, and which indeed McClellan had advised him not to expect.

"Stonewall" Jackson's most famous campaign happened at this juncture, and to save Washington, Lincoln and Stanton placed themselves, or were placed, in the trying position of actually directing movements of troops. There were to the south and south-west of Washington, besides the troops under McDowell's command, two Northern forces respectively commanded by Generals Banks and Fremont. These two men were among the chief examples of those "political generals," the use of whom in this early and necessarily blundering stage of the war has been the subject of much comment. Banks was certainly a politician, a self-made man, who had worked in a factory and who had risen to be at one time Speaker of the House. He was now a general because as a powerful man in the patriotic State of Massachusetts he brought with him many men, and these were ready to obey him. On the other hand, he on several occasions showed good judgment both in military matters and in the questions of civil administration which came under him; his heart was in his duty; and, though he held high commands almost to the end of the

as the Seven Days' Battles. The fortunes of the fighting varied greatly, but the upshot is that, though the corps on McClellan's left won a strong position not far from Richmond, the sudden approach of Jackson's forces upon McClellan's right flank, which began on the 26th, placed him in what appears to have been, as he himself thought it, a situation of great danger. Lee is said to have "read McClellan like an open book," playing upon his caution, which made him, while his subordinates fought, more anxious to secure their retreat than to seize upon any advantage they gained. But Lee's reading deceived him in one respect. He had counted upon McClellan's retreating, but thought he would retreat under difficulties right down the Peninsula to his original base and be thoroughly cut up on the way. But on July 2 McClellan with great skill withdrew his whole army to Harrison's Landing far up the James estuary, having effected with the Navy a complete transference of his base. Here his army lay in a position of security; they might yet threaten Richmond, and McClellan's soldiers still believed in him. But the South was led by a great commander and had now learned to give him unbounded confidence; there was some excuse for a panic in Wall Street, and every reason for dejection in the North.

On the third of the Seven Days, McClellan, much moved by the sight of dead and wounded comrades, sent a gloomy telegram to the Secretary of War, appealing with excessive eloquence for more men. "I only wish to say to the President," he remarked in it, "that I think he is wrong in regarding me as ungenerous when I said that my force was too weak." He concluded: "If I save the army now, I tell you plainly that I owe no thanks to you nor to any other persons in Washington. You have done your best to sacrifice this army." Stanton still expressed the extraordinary hope that Richmond would fall in a day or two. He had lately committed the folly of suspending enlistment, an act which, though of course there is an explanation of it, must rank as the one first-rate blunder of Lincoln's Administration. He was now negotiating through the astute Seward for offers from the State Governors of a levy of 300,000 men to follow up McClellan's success. Lincoln, as was his way, feared the worst. He seems at one moment to have had fears for McClellan's sanity. But he telegraphed, himself, an answer to him, which affords as fair an example as can be given of his characteristic manner. "Save your army at all events. Will send reinforcements as fast as we can. Of course they cannot reach you to-day or to-morrow, or next day. I have not said you were ungenerous for saying you needed reinforcements. I thought you were ungenerous in assuming that I did not send them as fast as I could. I feel any misfortune to you and your army quite as keenly as you feel it yourself. If you have had a drawn battle or repulse, it is the price we pay for the enemy not being in Washington. We protected Washington and the enemy concentrated on you. Had we stripped Washington, he would have been upon us before the troops could have gotten to you. Less than a week ago you notified us reinforcements were leaving Richmond to come in front of us. It is the nature of the case, and neither you nor the Government are to blame. Please tell me at once the present condition and aspect of things."

Demands for an impossible number of reinforcements continued. Lincoln explained to McClellan a few days later that they were impossible, and added: "If in your frequent mention of responsibility you have the impression that I blame you for not doing more than you can, please be relieved of such an impression. I only beg that, in like manner, you will not ask impossibilities of me." Much argument upon Lincoln's next important act may be saved by the simple observations that the problem in regard to the defence of Washington was real, that McClellan's propensity to ask for the impossible was also real, and that Lincoln's patient and loyal attitude to him was real too.

Five days after his arrival at Harrison's Landing, McClellan wrote Lincoln a long letter. It was a treatise upon Lincoln's political duties. It was written as "on the brink of eternity." He was not then in fact in any danger, and possibly he had composed it seven days before as his political testament; and apprehensions, free from personal fear, excuse, without quite redeeming, its inappropriateness.

The President is before all things not to abandon the cause. But the cause should be fought for upon Christian principles. Christian principles exclude warfare on private property. More especially do they exclude measures for emancipating slaves. And if the President gives way to radical views on slavery, he will get no soldiers. Then follows a mandate to the President to appoint a Commander-in-Chief, not necessarily the writer. Such a summary does injustice to a certain elevation of tone in the letter, but that elevation is itself slightly strained. McClellan, whatever his private opinions, had not meddled with politics before he left Washington. The question why in this military crisis he should have written what a Democratic politician might have composed as a party manifesto must later have caused Lincoln some thought, but it apparently did not enter into the decision he next took. He arrived himself at Harrison's Landing next day. McClellan handed him the letter. Lincoln read it, and said that he was obliged to him. McClellan sent a copy to his wife as "a very important record."

Lincoln had come in order to learn the views of McClellan and all his corps commanders. They differed a good deal on important points, but a majority of them were naturally anxious to stay and fight there. Lincoln was left in some anxiety as to how the health of the troops would stand the climate of the coming months if they had to wait long where they were. He was also disturbed by McClellan's vagueness about the number of his men, for he now returned as present for duty a number which far exceeded that which some of his recent telegrams had given and yet fell short of the number sent him by an amount which no reasonable estimate of killed, wounded, and sick could explain. This added to Lincoln's doubt on the main question presented to him. McClellan believed that he could take Richmond, but he demanded for this very large reinforcements. Some part of them were already being collected, but the rest could by no means be given him without leaving Washington with far fewer troops to defend it than McClellan or anybody else had hitherto thought necessary.

On July 24, the day after his arrival at Washington, Halleck was sent to consult with McClellan and his generals. The record of their consultations sufficiently shows the intricacy of the problem to be decided. The question of the health of the climate in August weighed much with Halleck, but the most striking feature of their conversation was the fluctuation of McClellan's own opinion upon each important point—at one moment he even gave Halleck the impression that he wished under all the circumstances to withdraw and to join Pope. When Halleck returned to Washington McClellan telegraphed in passionate anxiety to be left in the Peninsula and reinforced. On the other hand, some of the officers of highest rank with him wrote strongly urging withdrawal. This latter was the course on which Lincoln and Halleck decided. In the circumstances it was certainly the simplest course to concentrate all available forces in an attack upon the enemy from the direction of Washington which would keep that capital covered all the while. It was in any case no hasty and no indefensible decision, nor is there any justification for the frequent assertion that some malignant influence brought it about. It is one of the steps taken by Lincoln which have been the most often lamented. But if McClellan had had all he demanded to take Richmond and had made good his promise, what would Lee have done? Lee's own answer to a similar question later was, "We would swap queens"; that is, he would have taken Washington. If so the Confederacy would not have fallen, but in all probability the North would have collapsed, and European Powers would at the least have recognised the Confederacy.

Lincoln indeed had acted as any prudent civilian Minister would then have acted. But disaster followed, or rather there followed, with brief interruption, a succession of disasters which, after this long tale of hesitation, can be quickly told. It would be easy to represent them as a judgment upon the Administration which had rejected the guidance of McClellan. But in the true perspective of the war, the point which has now been reached marks the final election by the North of the policy by which it won the war. McClellan, even if he had taken Richmond while Washington remained safe, would have concentrated the efforts of the North upon a line of advance which gave little promise of finally reducing the Confederacy. It is evident to-day that the right course for the North was to keep the threatening of Richmond and the recurrent hammering at the Southern forces on that front duly related to that continual process by which the vitals of the Southern country were being eaten into from the west. This policy, it has been seen, was present to Lincoln's mind from an early day; the temptation to depart from it was now once for all

solicitude as to how he would rise to his opportunity.

Lee, in his advance, expected his opponent to be slow. He actually again divided his small army, leaving Jackson with a part of it behind for a while to capture, as he did, the Northern fort at Harper's Ferry. A Northern private picked up a packet of cigars dropped by some Southern officer with a piece of paper round it. The paper was a copy of an order of Lee's which revealed to McClellan the opportunity now given him of crushing Lee in detail. But he did not rouse himself. He was somewhat hampered by lack of cavalry, and his greatest quality in the field was his care not to give chances to the enemy. His want of energy allowed Lee time to discover what, had happened and fall back a little towards Harper's Ferry. Yet Lee dared, without having yet reunited his forces, to stop at a point where McClellan must be tempted to give him battle, and where, if he could only stand against McClellan, Jackson would be in a position to deliver a deadly counter-stroke. Lee knew that for the South the chance of rapid success was worth any risk. McClellan, however, moved so slowly that Jackson was able to join Lee before the battle. The Northern army came up with them near the north bank of the Potomac on the Antietam Creek, a small tributary of that river, about sixty miles north-east of Washington. There, on September 17, 1862, McClellan ordered an attack, to which he did not attempt to give his personal direction. His corps commanders led assaults on Lee's position at different times and in so disconnected a manner that each was repulsed singly. But on the following morning Lee found himself in a situation which determined him to retreat.

As a military success the battle of Antietam demanded to be followed up. Reinforcements had now come to McClellan, and Lincoln telegraphed, "Please do not let him get off without being hurt." Lee was between the broad Potomac and a Northern army fully twice as large as his own, with other large forces near. McClellan's subordinates urged him to renew the attack and drive Lee into the river. But Lee was allowed to cross the river, and McClellan lay camped on the Antietam battlefield for a fortnight. He may have been dissatisfied with the condition of his army and its supplies. Some of his men wanted new boots; many of

Lee's were limping barefoot. He certainly, as often before, exaggerated the strength of his enemy. Lee recrossed the Potomac little damaged. Lincoln, occupied in those days over the most momentous act of his political life, watched McClellan eagerly, and came to the Antietam to see things for himself. He came back in the full belief that McClellan would move at once. Once more undeceived, he pressed him with letters and telegrams from himself and Halleck. He was convinced that McClellan, if he tried, could cut off Lee from Richmond. Hearing of the fatigue of McClellan's horses, he telegraphed about the middle of October, "Will you pardon me for asking what your horses have done since the battle of Antietam that tires anything."

This was unkind; McClellan indeed should have seen about cavalry in the days when he was organising in Washington, but at this moment the Southern horse had just raided right round his lines and got safe back, and his own much inferior cavalry was probably worn out with vain pursuit of them. On the same day Lincoln wrote more kindly, "My dear Sir, you remember my speaking to you of what I called your over-cautiousness. Are you not over-cautious when you assume that you cannot do what the enemy is constantly doing? Change positions with the enemy, and think you not, he would break your communications with Richmond within the next twenty-four hours." And after a brief analysis of the situation, which seems conclusive, he ends: "I say 'try'; if we never try we shall never succeed. . . . If we cannot beat him now when he bears the wastage of coming to us, we never can when we bear the wastage of going to him." His patience was nearing a limit which he had already fixed in his own mind. On October 28, more than five weeks after the battle, McClellan began to cross the Potomac, and took a week in the process. On November 5, McClellan was removed from his command, and General Burnside appointed in his place.

Lincoln had longed for the clear victory that he thought McClellan would win; he gloomily foreboded that he might not find a better man to put in his place; he felt sadly how he would be accused, as he has been ever since, of displacing McClellan because he was a Democrat. "In considering military merit," he wrote privately, "the world has abundant evidence that I disregard politics." A friend, a Republican general, wrote to him a week or so after McClellan had been removed to urge that all the generals ought to be men in thorough sympathy with the Administration. He received a crushing reply (to be followed in a day or two by a friendly invitation) indignantly proving that Democrats served as well in the field as Republicans. But in regard to McClellan himself we now know that a grave suspicion had entered Lincoln's mind.

He might, perhaps, in the fear of finding no one better, have tolerated his "over-cautiousness"; he did not care what line an officer who did his duty might in civil life take politically; but he would not take the risk of entrusting the war further to a general who let his politics govern his strategy, and who, as he put it simply, "did not want to hurt the enemy." This, he had begun to believe, was the cause of McClellan's lack of energy. He resolved to treat McClellan's conduct now, in fighting Lee or in letting him escape South, as the test of whether his own suspicion about him was justified or not. Lee did get clear away, and Lincoln dismissed McClellan in the full belief, right or wrong, that he was not sorry for Lee's escape.

It is not known exactly what further evidence Lincoln then had for his belief, but information which seems to have come later made him think afterwards that he had been right. The following story was told him by the Governor of Vermont, whose brother, a certain General Smith, served under McClellan and was long his intimate friend. Lincoln believed the story; so may we. The Mayor of New York, a shifty demagogue named Fernando Wood, had visited McClellan in the Peninsula with a proposal that he should become the Democratic candidate for the Presidency, and with a view to this should pledge himself to certain Democratic politicians to conduct the war in a way that should conciliate the South, which to Lincoln's mind meant an "inefficient" way. McClellan, after some days of unusual reserve, told Smith of this and showed him a letter which he had drafted giving the desired pledge. On Smith's earnest remonstrance that this "looked like treason," he did not send the letter then. But Wood came again after the battle of Antietam, and this time McClellan sent a letter in the same sense. This he afterwards confessed to Smith, showing him a copy of the letter. Smith and other generals asked, after this, to be relieved from service under him. If, as can hardly be doubted, McClellan did this, there can be no serious excuse for him, and no serious question that Lincoln was right when he concluded it was unsafe to employ him. McClellan, according to all evidence except his own letters, was a nice man, and was not likely to harbour a thought of what to him seemed treason; it is honourable to him that he wished later to serve under Grant but was refused by him. But, to one of his views, the political situation before and after Antietam was alarming, and it is certain that to his inconclusive mind and character an attitude of half loyalty would be easy. He may not have wished that Lee should escape, but he had no ardent desire that he should not. Right or wrong, such was the ground of Lincoln's independent and conscientiously deliberate decision.

The result again did not reward him. His choice of Burnside was a mistake. There were corps commanders under McClellan who had earned special confidence, but they were all rather old. General Burnside, who was the senior among the rest, had lately succeeded in operations in connection with the Navy on the North Carolina coast, whereby certain harbours were permanently closed to the South. He had since served under McClellan at the Antietam, but had not earned much credit. He was a loyal friend to McClellan and very modest about his own capacity. Perhaps both these things prejudiced Lincoln in his favour. He continued in active service till nearly the end of the war, when a failure led to his retirement; and he was always popular and respected. At this juncture he failed disastrously. On December 11 and 12, 1862, Lee's army lay strongly posted on the south of the Rappahannock. Burnside, in spite, as it appears, of express warnings from Lincoln, attacked Lee at precisely the point, near the town of Fredericksburg, where his position was really impregnable. The defeat of the Northern army was bloody and overwhelming. Burnside's army became all but mutinous; his corps commanders, especially General Hooker, were loud in complaint. He was tempted to persist, in spite of all protests, in some further effort of rashness. Lincoln endeavoured to restrain him. Halleck, whom Lincoln begged to give a definite military opinion, upholding or overriding Burnside's, had nothing more useful to offer than his own resignation. After discussions and recriminations among all officers concerned, Burnside offered his resignation. Lincoln was by no means disposed to remove a general upon a first failure or to side with his subordinates against him, and refused to accept it. Burnside then offered the impossible alternative of the dismissal of all his corps commanders for disaffection to him, and on January 25, 1863, his resignation was accepted.

There was much discussion in the Cabinet as to the choice of his successor. It was thought unwise to give the Eastern army a commander from the West again. At Chase's instance [Transcriber's note: insistance?] the senior corps commander who was not too old, General Hooker, sometimes called "Fighting Joe Hooker," was appointed. He received a letter, often quoted as the letter of a man much altered from the Lincoln who had been groping a year earlier after the right way of treating McClellan: "I have placed you," wrote Lincoln, "at the head of the Army of the Potomac. Of course I have done this upon what appear to me to be sufficient reasons, and yet I think it best for you to know that there are some things in regard to which I am not quite satisfied with you. I believe you to be a brave and skilful soldier, which of course I like. I also believe that you do not mix politics with your profession, in which you are right. You have confidence in yourself, which is a valuable, if not indispensable, quality. You are ambitious, which, within reasonable bounds, does good rather than harm; but I think that during General Burnside's command of the army you have taken counsel of your ambition and thwarted him as much as you could, in which you did a great wrong to the country, and to a most meritorious and honourable brother officer. I have heard, in such a way as to believe it, of your recently saying that both the Army and the Government needed a dictator. Of course it was not for this, but in spite of it, that I gave you the command. Only those generals who gain successes can set up dictators. What I now ask of you is military success, and I will risk the dictatorship. The Government will support you to the utmost of its ability, which is neither more nor less than it has done and will do for all commanders. I much fear that the spirit which you have aided to infuse into the army, of criticising their commander and withholding confidence from him, will now turn upon you. Neither you nor Napoleon, if he were alive again, could get any good out of an army while such a spirit prevails in it; and now beware of rashness. Beware of rashness, but with energy and sleepless vigilance go forward and give us victories."

"He talks to me like a father," exclaimed Hooker, enchanted with a rebuke such as this. He was a fine, frank, soldierly fellow, with a noble figure, with "a grand fighting head," fresh complexion and bright blue eyes. He was a good organiser; he put a stop to the constant desertions; he felt the need of improving the Northern cavalry; and he groaned at the spirit with which McClellan had infected his army, a curious collective inertness among men who individually were daring. He seems to have been highly strung; the very little wine that he drank perceptibly affected him; he gave it up altogether in his campaigns.

And he cannot have been very clever, for the handsomest beating that Lee could give him left him unaware that Lee was a general. In the end of April he crossed the Rappahannock and the Rapidan, which still divided the two armies, and in the first week of May, 1863, a brief campaign, full of stirring incident, came to a close with the three days' battle of Chancellorsville, in which Hooker, hurt and dazed with pain, lost control and presence of mind, and, with heavy loss, drew back across the Rappahannock. The South had won another amazing victory; but "Stonewall" Jackson, at the age of thirty-nine, had fallen in the battle.

Abroad, this crowning disaster to the North seemed to presage the full triumph of the Confederacy; and it was a gloomy time enough for Lincoln and his Ministers. A second and more serious invasion by Lee was impending, and the lingering progress of events in the West, of which the story must soon be resumed, caused protracted and deepening anxiety. But the tide turned soon. Moreover, Lincoln's military perplexities, which have demanded our detailed attention during these particular campaigns, were very nearly at an end. We have here to turn back to the political problem of his Presidency, for the bloody and inconclusive battle upon the Antietam, more than seven months before, had led strangely to political consequences which were great and memorable.

CHAPTER X

EMANCIPATION

When the news of a second battle of Bull Run reached England it seemed at first to Lord John Russell that the failure of the North was certain, and he asked Palmerston and his colleagues to consider whether they must not soon recognise the Confederacy, and whether mediation in the interest of peace and humanity might not perhaps follow. But within two months all thoughts of recognising the Confederacy had been so completely put aside that even Fredericksburg and Chancellorsville caused no renewal of the suggestion, and an invitation from Louis Napoleon to joint action of this kind between England and France had once for all been rejected. The battle of Antietam had been fought in the meantime. This made men think that the South could no more win a speedy and decisive success than the North, and that victory must rest in the end with the side that could last. But that was not all; the battle of Antietam was followed within five days by an event which made it impossible for any Government of this country to take action unfriendly to the North.

On September 22, 1862, Abraham Lincoln set his hand to a Proclamation of which the principal words were these: "That, on the first day of January in the year of our Lord one thousand eight hundred and sixty-three, all persons held as slaves within any State, or designated part of a State, the people whereof shall then be in rebellion against the United States, shall be then, thenceforward and forever free."

The policy and the true effect of this act cannot be understood without some examination. Still less so can the course of the man who will always be remembered as its author. First, in regard to the legal effect of the Proclamation; in normal times the President would of course not have had the power, which even the Legislature did not possess, to set free a single slave; the Proclamation was an act of war on his part, as Commander-in-Chief of the forces, by which slaves were to be taken from people at war with the United States, just as horses or carts might be taken, to subtract from their resources and add to those of the United States. In a curiously prophetic manner, ex-President John Quincy Adams had argued in Congress many years before that, if rebellion ever arose, this very thing might be done. Adams would probably have claimed that the command of the President became law in the States which took part in the rebellion. Lincoln only claimed legal force for his Proclamation in so far as it was an act of war based on sufficient necessity and plainly tending to help the Northern arms. If the legal question had ever been tried out, the Courts would no doubt have had to hold that at least those slaves who obtained actual freedom under the Proclamation became free in law; for it was certainly in good faith an act of war, and the military result justified it. A large amount of labour was withdrawn from the industry necessary to the South, and by the end of the war 180,000 coloured troops were in arms for the North, rendering services, especially in occupying conquered territory that was unhealthy for white troops, without which, in Lincoln's opinion, the war could never have been finished. The Proclamation had indeed an indirect effect more far-reaching than this; it committed the North to a course from which there could be no turning back, except by surrender; it made it a political certainty that by one means or another slavery would be ended if the North won. But in Lincoln's view of his duty as President, this ulterior consequence was not to determine his action. The fateful step by which the end of slavery was precipitated would not have taken the form it did take if it had not come to commend itself to him as a military measure conducing to the suppression of rebellion.

On the broader grounds on which we naturally look at this measure, many people in the North had, as we have seen, been anxious from the beginning that he should adopt an active policy of freeing Southern slaves. It was intolerable to think that the war might end and leave slavery where it was. To convert the war into a crusade against slavery seemed to many the best way of arousing and uniting the North. This argument was reinforced by some of the American Ministers abroad. They were aware that people in Europe misunderstood and disliked the Constitutional propriety with which the Union government insisted that it was not attacking the domestic institutions of Southern States.

English people did not know the American Constitution, and when told that the North did not threaten to abolish slavery would answer "Why not?" Many Englishmen, who might dislike the North and might have their doubts as to whether slavery was as bad as it was said to be, would none the less have respected men who would fight against it. They had no interest in the attempt of some of their own seceded Colonists to coerce, upon some metaphysical ground of law, others who in their turn wished to secede from them. Seward, with wonderful misjudgment, had instructed Ministers abroad to explain that no attack was threatened on slavery, for he was afraid that the purchasers of cotton in Europe would feel threatened in their selfish interests; the agents of the South were astute enough to take the same line and insist like him that the North was no more hostile to slavery than the South. If this misunderstanding were removed English hostility to the North would never again take a dangerous form. Lincoln, who knew less of affairs but more of men than Seward, was easily made to see this. Yet, with full knowledge of the reasons for adopting a decided policy against slavery, Lincoln waited through seventeen months of the war till the moment had come for him to strike his blow.

Some of his reasons for waiting were very plain. He was not going to take action on the alleged ground of military necessity till he was sure that the necessity existed. Nor was he going to take it till it would actually lead to the emancipation of a great number of slaves. Above all, he would not act till he felt that the North generally would sustain his action, for he knew, better than Congressmen who judged from their own friends in their own constituencies, how doubtful a large part of Northern opinion really was. We have seen how in the summer of 1861 he felt bound to disappoint the advanced opinion which supported Fremont. He continued for more than a year after in a course which alienated from himself the confidence of the men with whom he had most sympathy. He did this deliberately rather than imperil the unanimity with which the North supported the war. There was indeed grave danger of splitting the North in two if he appeared unnecessarily to change the issue from Union to Liberation. We have to remember that in all the Northern States the right of the Southern States to choose for themselves about slavery had been fully admitted, and that four of the Northern States were themselves slave States all this while.

But this is not the whole explanation of his delay. It is certain that apart from this danger he would at first rather not have played the historic part which he did play as the liberator of the slaves, if he could have succeeded in the more modest part of encouraging a process of gradual emancipation. In his Annual Message to Congress in December, 1861, he laid down the general principles of his policy in this matter. He gave warning in advance to the Democrats of the North, who were against all interference with Southern institutions, that "radical and extreme measures" might become indispensable to military success, and if indispensable would be taken; but he declared his anxiety that if possible the conflict with the South should not "degenerate into a violent and remorseless revolutionary struggle," for he looked forward with fear to a complete overturning of the social system of the South. He feared it not only for the white people but also for the black. "Gradual and not sudden emancipation," he said, in a later Message, "is better for all." It is now probable that he was right, and yet it is difficult not to sympathise with the earnest Republicans who were impatient at his delay, who were puzzled and pained by the free and easy way in which in grave conversation he would allude to "the nigger question," and who concluded that "the President is not with us; has no sound Anti-slavery sentiment." Indeed, his sentiment did differ from theirs. Certainly, he hated slavery, for he had contended more stubbornly than any other man against any concession which seemed to him to perpetuate slavery by stamping it with approval; but his hatred of it left him quite without the passion of moral indignation against the slave owners, in whose guilt the whole country, North and South, seemed to him an accomplice. He would have classed that very natural indignation under the head of "malice" — "I shall do nothing in malice," he wrote to a citizen of Louisiana; "what I deal with is too vast for malicious dealing." But it was not, as we shall see before long, too vast for an interest, as sympathetic as it wasmatter of fact, in the welfare of the negroes. They were actual human beings to him, and he knew that the mere abrogation of the law of slavery was not the only thing necessary to their advancement. Looking back, with knowledge of what happened later, we cannot fail to be glad that they were emancipated somehow, but we are forced to regret that they could not have been emancipated by some more considerate process. Lincoln, perhaps alone among the Americans who were in earnest in this matter, looked at it very much in the light in which all men look at it to-day.

In the early part of 1862 the United States Government concluded a treaty with Great Britain for the more effectual suppression of the African slave trade, and it happened about the same time that the first white man ever executed as a pirate under the American law against the slave trade was hanged in New York. In those months Lincoln was privately trying to bring about the passing by the Legislature of Delaware of an Act for emancipating, with fit provisions for their welfare, the few slaves in that State, conditionally upon compensation to be paid to the owners by the United States. He hoped that if this example were set by Delaware, it would be followed in Maryland, and would spread later. The Delaware House were favourable to the scheme, but the Senate of the State rejected it. Lincoln now made a more public appeal in favour of his policy. In March, 1862, he sent a Message to Congress, which has already been quoted, and in which he urged the two Houses to pass Resolutions pledging the United States to give pecuniary help to any State which adopted gradual emancipation. It must be obvious that if the slave States of the North could have been led to adopt this policy it would have been a fitting preliminary to any action which might be taken against slavery in the South; and the policy might have been extended to those Southern States which were first recovered for the Union. The point, however, upon which Lincoln dwelt in his Message was that, if slavery were once given up by the border States, the South would abandon all hope that they would ever join the Confederacy. In private letters to an editor of a newspaper and others he pressed the consideration that the cost of compensated abolition was small in proportion to what might be gained by a quicker ending of the war. During the discussion of his proposal in Congress and again after the end of the Session he invited the Senators and Representatives of the border States to private conference with him in which he besought of them "a calm and enlarged consideration, ranging, if it may be, far above, personal and partisan politics," of the opportunity of good now open to them. The hope of the Confederacy was, as he then conceived, fixed upon the sympathy which it might arouse in the border States, two of which, Kentucky and Maryland, were in fact invaded that year with some hope of a rising among the inhabitants. The "lever" which the Confederates hoped to use in these States was the interest of the slave owners there; "Break that lever before their eyes," he urged. But the hundred and one reasons which can always be found against action presented themselves at once to the Representatives of the border States. Congress itself so far accepted the President's view that both Houses passed the Resolution which he had suggested. Indeed it gladly did something more; a Bill, such as Lincoln himself had prepared as a Congressman fourteen years before, was passed for abolishing slavery in the District of Columbia; compensation was paid to the owners; a sum was set apart to help the settlement in Liberia of any of the slaves who were willing to go; and at Lincoln's suggestion provision was added for the education of the negro children. Nothing more was done at this time.

Throughout this matter Lincoln took counsel chiefly with himself. He could not speak his full thought to the public, and apparently he did not do so to any of his Cabinet. Supposing that the border States had yielded to his persuasion, it may still strike us as a very sanguine calculation that their action would have had much effect upon the resolution of the Confederates. But it must be noted that when Lincoln first approached the Representatives of the border States, the highest expectations were entertained of the victory that McClellan would win in Virginia, and when he made his last, rather despairing, appeal to them, the decision to withdraw the army from the Peninsula had not yet been taken. If a really heavy blow had been struck at the Confederates in Virginia, their chief hope of retrieving their military fortunes would certainly have lain in that invasion of Kentucky, which did shortly afterwards occur and which was greatly encouraged by the hope of a rising of Kentucky men who wished to join the Confederacy. This part of Lincoln's calculations was therefore quite reasonable. And it was further reasonable to suppose that, if the South had then given in and Congress had acted in the spirit of the Resolution which it had passed, the policy, of gradual emancipation, starting in the border States, would have spread steadily. The States which were disposed to hold out against the inducement that the cost of compensated emancipation, if they adopted it, would be borne by the whole Union, would have done so at a great risk; for each new free State would have been disposed before long to support a Constitutional Amendment to impose enfranchisement, possibly with no compensation, upon the States that still delayed. The force of example and the presence of this fear could not have been resisted long. Lincoln was not a man who could be accused of taking any course without a reason well thought out; we can safely conclude that in the summer of 1862 he nursed a hope, by no means visionary, of initiating a process of liberation free from certain evils in that upon which he was driven back.

Before, however, he had quite abandoned this hope he had already begun to see his way in case it failed. His last appeal to the border States was made on July 12, 1862, while McClellan's army still lay at Harrison's Landing. On the following day he privately told Seward and Bates that he had "about come to the conclusion that it was a military necessity, absolutely essential to the salvation of the nation, that we must free the slaves or be ourselves subdued." On July 22 he read to his Cabinet the first draft of his Proclamation of Emancipation; telling them before he consulted them that substantially his mind was made up. Various members of the Cabinet raised points on which he had already thought and had come to a conclusion, but, as he afterwards told a friend, Seward raised a point which had never struck him before. He said that, if issued at that time of depression, just after the failure in the Peninsula, the Proclamation would seem like "a cry of distress"; and that it would have a much better effect if it were issued after some military success.

Seward was certainly right. The danger of division in the North would have been increased and the prospect of a good effect abroad would have been diminished if the Proclamation had been issued at a time of depression and manifest failure. Lincoln, who had been set on issuing it, instantly felt the force of this objection. He put aside his draft, and resolved not to issue the Proclamation till the right moment, and apparently resolved to keep the whole question open in his own mind till the time for action came.

Accordingly the two months which followed were not only full of anxiety about the war; they were full for him of a suspense painfully maintained. It troubled him perhaps comparatively little that he was driven into a position of greater aloofness from the support and sympathy of any party or school. He must now expect an opposition from the Democrats of the North, for they had declared themselves strongly against the Resolution which he had induced Congress to pass. And the strong Republicans for their part had acquiesced in it coldly, some of them contemptuously. In May of this year he had been forced for a second time publicly to repress a keen Republican general who tried to take this question of great policy into his own hands. General Hunter, commanding a small expedition which had seized Port Royal in South Carolina and some adjacent islands rich in cotton, had in a grand manner assumed to declare free all the slaves in South Carolina, Georgia and Florida. This, of course, could not be let pass. Congress, too, had been occupied in the summer with a new measure for confiscating rebel property; some Republicans in the West set great store on such confiscation; other Republicans saw in it the incidental advantage that more slaves might be liberated under it. It was learnt that the President might put his veto upon it. It seemed to purport, contrary to the Constitution, to attaint the property of rebels after their death, and Lincoln was unwilling that the Constitution should be stretched in the direction of revengeful harshness. The objectionable feature in the Bill was removed, and Lincoln accepted it. But the suspicion with which many Republicans were beginning to regard him was now reinforced by a certain jealousy of Congressmen against the Executive power; they grumbled and sneered about having to "ascertain the Royal pleasure" before they could legislate. This was an able, energetic, and truly patriotic Congress, and must not be despised for its reluctance to be guided by Lincoln. But it was reluctant.

Throughout August and September he had to deal in the country with dread on the one side of any revolutionary action, and belief on the other side that he was timid and half-hearted. The precise state of his intentions could not with advantage be made public. To up-holders of slavery he wrote plainly, "It may as well be understood once for all that I shall not surrender this game leaving any available card unplayed"; to its most zealous opponents he had to speak in an entirely different strain. While the second battle of Bull Run was impending, Horace Greeley published in the _New York Tribune_ an "open letter" of angry complaint about Lincoln's supposed bias for slavery. Lincoln at once published a reply to his letter. "If there be in it," he said, "any statements or assumptions of fact which I may know to be erroneous, I do not now and here controvert them. If there be perceptible in it an impatient and dictatorial tone, I waive it in deference to an old friend whose heart I have always supposed to be right. My paramount object in this struggle is to save the Union. If I could save the Union without freeing any slaves I would do it; and if I could save it by freeing all the slaves I would do it; and if I could save it by freeing some and leaving others alone, I would also do that. I shall do less whenever I shall believe what I am doing hurts the cause, and I shall do more whenever I shall believe doing more will help the cause. I shall adopt new views so fast as they shall appear to be true views."

It was probably easy to him now to write these masterful generalities, but a week or two later, after Pope's defeat, he had to engage in a controversy which tried his feelings much more sorely. It had really grieved him that clergymen in Illinois had opposed him as unorthodox, when he was fighting against the extension of slavery. Now, a week or two after his correspondence with Greeley, a deputation from a number of

Churches in Chicago waited upon him, and some of their members spoke to him with assumed authority from on high, commanding him in God's name to emancipate the slaves. He said, "I am approached with the most opposite opinions and advice, and that by religious men who are equally certain that they represent the divine will. I am sure that either the one or the other class is mistaken in that belief, and perhaps in some respects both. I hope it will not be irreverent for me to say that, if it is probable that God would reveal His will to others, on a point so connected with my duty, it might be supposed He would reveal it directly to me. What good would a proclamation of emancipation from me do especially as we are now situated? I do not want to issue a document that the whole world will see must necessarily be inoperative like the Pope's Bull against the comet. Do not misunderstand me, because I have mentioned these objections. They indicate the difficulties that have thus far prevented my acting in some such way as you desire. I have not decided against a proclamation of liberty to the slaves, but hold the matter under advisement. And I can assure you that the subject is on my mind, by day and night, more than any other. Whatever shall appear to be God's will, I will do." The language of this speech, especially when the touch is humorous, seems that of a strained and slightly irritated man, but the solemnity blended in it showed Lincoln's true mind.

In this month, September, 1862, he composed for his own reading alone a sad and inconclusive fragment of meditation which was found after his death. "The will of God prevails," he wrote. "In great contests each party claims to act in accordance with the will of God. Both may be and one must be wrong. God cannot be for and against the same thing at the same time. In the present civil war it is quite possible that God's purpose is something different from the purpose of either party, and yet the human instrumentalities, working just as they do, are of the best adaptation to effect His purpose. I am almost ready to say that this is probably true, that God wills this contest, and wills that it shall not end yet. By His mere great power on the minds of the contestants, He could have either saved or destroyed the Union without a human contest. Yet the contest began, and, having begun, He could give the final victory to either side any day.

Yet the contest proceeds." For Lincoln's own part it seemed his plain duty to do what in the circumstances he thought safest for the Union, and yet he was almost of a mind with the deputation which had preached to him, that he must be doing God's will in taking a great step towards emancipation. The solution, that the great step must be taken at the first opportune moment, was doubtless clear enough in principle, but it must always remain arguable whether any particular moment was opportune. He told soon afterwards how his mind was finally made up.

On the day that he received the news of the battle of Antietam, the draft Proclamation was taken from its drawer and studied afresh; his visit to McClellan on the battlefield intervened; but on the fifth day after the battle the Cabinet was suddenly called together. When the Ministers had assembled Lincoln first entertained them by reading the short chapter of Artemus Ward entitled "High-handed Outrage at Utica."

It is less amusing than most of Artemus Ward; but it had just appeared; it pleased all the Ministers except Stanton, to whom the frivolous reading he sometimes had to hear from Lincoln was a standing vexation; and it was precisely that sort of relief to which Lincoln's mind when overwrought could always turn. Having thus composed himself for business, he reminded his Cabinet that he had, as they were aware, thought a great deal about the relation of the war to slavery, and had a few weeks before read them a draft Proclamation on this subject. Ever since then, he said, his mind had been occupied on the matter, and, though he wished it were a better time, he thought the time had come now. "When the rebel army was at Frederick," he is related to have continued, "I determined, as soon as it should be driven out of Maryland, to issue a Proclamation of Emancipation such as I thought likely to be most useful. I said nothing to any one, but I made the promise to myself and"—here he hesitated a little—"to my Maker. The rebel army is now driven out, and I am going to fulfil that promise. I have got you together to hear what I have written down. I do not wish your advice about the main matter, for that I have determined for myself. This I say without intending anything but respect for any one of you." He then invited their suggestions upon the expressions used in his draft and other minor matters, and concluded: "One other observation I will make. I know very well that many others might in this matter, as in others, do better than I can; and if I was satisfied that the public confidence was more fully possessed by any one of them than by me, and knew of any constitutional way in which he could be put in my place, he should have it. I would gladly yield it to him. But though I believe I have not so much of the confidence of the people as I had some time since, I do not know that, all things considered, any other person has more; and, however this may be, there is no way in which I can have any other man put where I am. I am here; I must do the best I can, and bear the responsibility of taking the course which I feel I ought to take." Then he read his draft, and in the long discussion which followed, and owing to which a few slight changes were made in it, he told them further, without any false reserve, just how he came to his decision. In his great perplexity he had gone on his knees, before the battle of Antietam, and, like a child, he had promised that if a victory was given which drove the enemy out of Maryland he would consider it as an indication that it was his duty to move forward. "It might be thought strange," he said, "that he had in this way submitted the disposal of matters, when the way was not clear to his mind what he should do. God had decided this question in favour of the slaves."

Such is the story of what we may now remember as one of the signal events in the chequered progress of Christianity. We have to follow its consequences a little further. These were not at first all that its author would have hoped. "Commendation in newspapers and by distinguished individuals is," he said in a private letter, "all that a vain man could wish," but recruits for the Army did not seem to come in faster. In October and November there were elections for Congress, and in a number of States the Democrats gained considerably, though it was noteworthy that the Republicans held their ground not only in New England and in the furthest Western States, but also in the border slave States. The Democrats, who from this time on became very formidable to Lincoln, had other matters of complaint, as will be seen later, but they chiefly denounced the President for trying to turn the war into one against slavery. "The Constitution as it is and the Union as it was" had been their election cry. The good hearing that they got, now as at a later time, was due to the fact that people were depressed about the war; and it is plain enough that Lincoln had been well advised in delaying his action till after a military success. As it was, there was much that seemed to show that public confidence in him was not strong, but public confidence in any man is hard to estimate, and the forces that in the end move opinion most are not quickly apparent. There are little indications that his power and character were slowly establishing their hold; it seems, for instance, to have been about this time that "old Abe" or "Uncle Abe" began to be widely known among common people by the significant name of "Father Abraham," and his secretaries say that he was becoming conscious that his official utterances had a deeper effect on public opinion than any immediate response to them in Congress showed.

In his Annual Message of December, 1862, Lincoln put before Congress, probably with little hope of result, a comprehensive policy for dealing with slavery justly and finally. He proposed that a Constitutional Amendment should be submitted to the people providing: first, that compensation should be given in United States bonds to any State, whether now in rebellion or not, which should abolish slavery before the year 1900; secondly, that the slaves who had once enjoyed actual freedom through the chances of the war should be permanently free and that their owners should be compensated; thirdly, that Congress should have authority to spend money on colonisation for negroes. Even if the greater part of these objects could have been accomplished without a Constitutional Amendment, it is evident that such a procedure would have been more satisfactory in the eventual resettlement of the Union. He urged in his Message how desirable it was, as a part of the effort to restore the Union, that the whole North should be agreed in a concerted policy as to slavery, and that parties should for this purpose reconsider their positions. "The dogmas of the quiet past," he said, "are inadequate to the stormy present. The occasion is piled high with difficulty, and we must rise with the occasion. As our case is new, so we must think anew and act anew. We must disenthrall ourselves, and then we shall save our country. Fellow citizens, we cannot escape history. We of this Congress and this Administration will be remembered in spite of ourselves. No personal significance or insignificance can spare one or another of us. We say we are for the Union. The world will not forget that we say this. We know how to save the Union. The world knows we do know how to save it. In giving freedom to the slave we assure freedom to the free. We shall nobly save or meanly lose the last, best hope of earth. Other means may succeed, this could not fail." The last four words expressed too confident a hope as to what Northern policy apart from Northern arms could do towards ending the war, but it was impossible to exaggerate the value which a policy, concerted between parties in a spirit of moderation, would have had in the settlement after victory. Every honest Democrat who then refused any action against slavery must have regretted it before three years were out, and many sensible Republicans who saw no use in such moderation may have lived to regret their part too. Nothing was done. It is thought that Lincoln expected this; but the Proclamation of Emancipation would begin to operate within a month; it would produce by the end of the war a situation in which the country would be compelled to decide on the principle of slavery, and Lincoln had at least done his part in preparing men to face the issue.

Before this, the nervous and irritable feeling of many Northern politicians, who found in emancipation a good subject for quarrel among themselves and in the slow progress of the war a good subject of quarrel with the Administration, led to a crisis in Lincoln's Cabinet. Radicals were inclined to think Seward's influence in the Administration the cause of all public evils; some of them had now got hold of a foolish private letter, which he had written to Adams in England a few months before, denouncing the advocates of emancipation. Desiring his downfall, they induced a small "caucus" of Republican Senators to speak in the name of the party and the nation and send the President a resolution demanding such changes in his Cabinet as would produce better results in the war. Discontented men of opposite opinions could unite in demanding success in the war; and Conservative Senators joined in this resolution hoping that it would get rid not only of Seward, but also of Chase and Stanton, the objects of their particular antipathy. Seward, on hearing of this, gave Lincoln his resignation, which was kept private.

Though egotistic, he was a clever man, and evidently a pleasant man to work with; he was a useful Minister under a wise chief, though he later proved a harmful one under a foolish chief. Stanton was most loyal, and invaluable as head of the War Department. Chase, as Lincoln said in private afterwards, was "a pretty good fellow and a very able man"; Lincoln had complete confidence in him as a Finance Minister, and could not easily have replaced him. But this handsome, dignified, and righteous person was unhappily a sneak. Lincoln found as time went on that, if he ever had to do what was disagreeable to some important man, Chase would pay court to that important man and hint how differently he himself would have done as President. On this occasion he was evidently aware that Chase had encouraged the Senators who attacked Seward. Much as he wished to retain each of the two for his own worth, he was above all determined that one should not gain a victory over the other.

Accordingly, when a deputation of nine important Senators came to Lincoln to present their grievances against Seward, they found themselves, to their great annoyance, confronted with all the Cabinet except Seward, who had resigned, and they were invited by Lincoln to discuss the matter in his presence with these Ministers. Chase, to his still greater annoyance, found himself, as the principal Minister there, compelled for decency's sake to defend Seward from the very attack which he had helped to instigate. The deputation withdrew, not sure that, after all, it wanted Seward removed. Chase next day tendered, as was natural, his resignation. Lincoln was able, now that he had the resignations of both men, to persuade both of their joint duty to continue in the public service. By this remarkable piece of riding he saved the Union from a great danger. The Democratic opposition, not actually to the prosecution of the war, but to any and every measure essential for it, was now developing, and a serious division, such as at this stage any important resignation would have produced in the ranks of the Republicans, or, as they now called themselves, the "Union men," would have been perilous.

On the first day of January, 1863, the President signed the further Proclamation needed to give effect to emancipation. The small portions of the South which were not in rebellion were duly excepted; the naval and military authorities were ordered to maintain the freedom of the slaves seeking their protection; the slaves were enjoined to abstain from violence and to "labour faithfully for reasonable wages" if opportunity were given them; all suitable slaves were to be taken into armed service, especially for garrison duties. Before the end of 1863, a hundred thousand coloured men were already serving, as combatants or as labourers, on military work in about equal number. They were needed, for volunteering was getting slack, and the work of guarding and repairing railway lines was specially repellent to Northern volunteers. The coloured regiments fought well; they behaved well in every way. Atrocious threats of vengeance on them and their white officers were officially uttered by Jefferson Davis, but, except for one hideous massacre wrought in the hottest of hot blood, only a few crimes by individuals were committed in execution of these threats. To Lincoln himself it was a stirring thought that when democratic government was finally vindicated and restored by the victory of the Union, "then there will be some black men who can remember that with silent tongue and clenched teeth and steady eye and well-poised bayonet they have helped mankind on to this great consummation." There was, however, prejudice at first among many Northern officers against negro enlistment. The greatest of the few great American artists, St. Gaudens, commemorated in sculpture (as the donor of the new playing fields at Harvard commemorated by his gift) the action of a brilliant and popular Massachusetts officer, Robert Gould Shaw, who set the example of leaving his own beloved regiment to take command of a coloured regiment, at the head of which he died, gallantly leading them and gallantly followed by them in a desperate fight.

It was easier to raise and train these negro soldiers than to arrange for the control, shelter, and employment of the other refugees who crowded especially to the protection of Grant's army in the West. The efforts made for their benefit cannot be related here, but the recollections of Army Chaplain John Eaton, whom Grant selected to take charge of them in the West, throw a little more light on Lincoln and on the spirit of his dealing with "the nigger question." When Eaton after some time had to come to

Washington, upon the business of his charge and to visit the President, he received that impression, of versatile power and of easy mastery over many details as well as over broad issues, which many who worked under Lincoln have described, but he was above all struck with the fact that from a very slight experience in early life Lincoln had gained a knowledge of negro character such as very few indeed in the North possessed. He was subjected to many seemingly trivial questions, of which he was quick enough to see the grave purpose, about all sorts of persons and things in the West, but he was also examined closely, in a way which commanded his fullest respect as an expert, about the ideas, understanding, and expectations of the ordinary negroes under his care, and more particularly as to the past history and the attainments of the few negroes who had become prominent men, and who therefore best illustrated the real capacities of their race. Later visits to the capital and to Lincoln deepened this impression, and convinced Eaton, though by trifling signs, of the rare quality of Lincoln's sympathy. Once, after Eaton's difficult business had been disposed of, the President turned to relating his own recent worries about a colony of negroes which he was trying to establish on a small island off Hayti. There flourishes in Southern latitudes a minute creature called 'Dermatophilus penetrans', or the jigger, which can inflict great pain on barefooted people by housing itself under their toe-nails. This Colony had a plague of jiggers, and every expedient for defeating them had failed. Lincoln was not merely giving the practical attention to this difficulty that might perhaps be expected; the Chaplain was amazed to find that at that moment, at the turning point of the war, a few days only after Vicksburg and Gettysburg, with his enormous pre-occupations, the President's mind had room for real and keen distress about the toes of the blacks in the Cow Island. At the end of yet another interview Eaton was startled by the question, put by the President with an air of shyness, whether Frederick Douglass, a well-known negro preacher, could be induced to visit him. Of course he could. Frederick Douglass was then reputed to be the ablest man ever born as a negro slave; he must have met many of the best and kindest Northern friends of the negro; and he went to Lincoln distressed at some points in his policy, particularly at his failure to make reprisals for murders of negro prisoners by Southern troops. When he came away he was in a state little short of ecstasy. It was not because he now understood, as he did, Lincoln's policy. Lincoln had indeed won his warm approval when he told him "with a quiver in his voice" of his horror of killing men in cold blood for what had been done by others, and his dread of what might follow such a policy; but he had a deeper gratification, the strangeness of which it is sad to realise. "He treated me as a man," exclaimed Douglass. "He did not let me feel for a moment that there was any difference in the colour of our skins."

Perhaps the hardest effort of speech that Lincoln ever essayed was an address to negroes which had to do with this very subject of colour. His audience were men who had been free from birth or for some time and were believed to be leaders among their community. It was Lincoln's object to induce some of them to be pioneers in an attempt at colonisation in some suitable climate, an attempt which he felt must fail if it started with negroes whose "intellects were clouded by slavery." He clung to these projects of colonisation, as probably the best among the various means by which the improvement of the negro must be attempted, because their race, "suffering the greatest wrong ever inflicted on any people," would "yet be far removed from being on an equality with the white race" when they ceased to be slaves; a "physical difference broader than exists between almost any other two races" and constituting "a greater disadvantage to us both," would always set a "ban" upon the negroes even where they were best treated in America. This unpalatable fact he put before them with that total absence of pretence which was probably the only possible form of tact in such a discussion, with no affectation of a hope that progress would remove it or of a desire that the ordinary white man should lose the instinct that kept him apart from the black. But this only makes more apparent his simple recognition of an equality and fellowship which did exist between him and his hearers in a larger matter than that of social intercourse or political combination. His appeal to their capacity for taking large and unselfish views was as direct and as confident as in his addresses to his own people; it was made in the language of a man to whom the public spirit which might exist among black people was of the same quality as that which existed among white, in whose belief he and his hearers could equally find happiness in "being worthy of themselves" and in realising the "claim of kindred to the great God who made them."

It may be well here, without waiting to trace further the course of the war, in which at the point where we left it the slow but irresistible progress of conquest was about to set in, to recount briefly the later stages of the abolition of slavery in America. In 1863 it became apparent that popular feeling in Missouri and in Maryland was getting ripe for abolition. Bills were introduced into Congress to compensate their States if they did away with slavery; the compensation was to be larger if the abolition was immediate and not gradual. There was a majority in each House for these Bills, but the Democratic minority was able to kill them in the House of Representatives by the methods of "filibustering," or, as we call it, obstruction, to which the procedure of that body seems well adapted. The Republican majority had not been very zealous for the Bills; its members asked "why compensate for a wrong" which they had begun to feel would soon be abolished without compensation; but their leaders at least did their best for the Bills.

It would have been idle after the failure of these proposals to introduce the Bills that had been contemplated for buying out the loyal slave owners in West Virginia, Kentucky, and Tennessee, which was now fast being regained for the Union. Lincoln after his Message of December, 1862, recognised it as useless for him to press again the principles of gradual emancipation or of compensation, as to which it is worth remembrance that the compensation which he proposed was for loyal and disloyal owners alike. His Administration, however, bought every suitable slave in Delaware for service (service as a free man) in the Army. In the course of 1864 a remarkable development of public opinion began to be manifest in the States chiefly concerned. In the autumn of that year Maryland, whose representatives had paid so little attention to Lincoln two years before, passed an Amendment to the State Constitution abolishing slavery without compensation. A movement in the same direction was felt to be making progress in Kentucky and Tennessee; and Missouri followed Maryland's example in January, 1865. Meanwhile, Louisiana had been reconquered, and the Unionists in these States, constantly encouraged and protected by Lincoln when Congress looked upon them somewhat coldly or his generals showed jealousy of their action, had banded themselves together to form State Governments with Constitutions that forbade slavery. Lincoln, it may be noted, had suggested to Louisiana that it would be well to frame some plan by which the best educated of the negroes should be admitted to the franchise. Four years after his death a Constitutional Amendment was passed by which any distinction as to franchise on the ground of race or colour is forbidden in America. The policy of giving the vote to negroes indiscriminately had commended itself to the cold pedantry of some persons, including Chase, on the ground of some natural right of all men to the suffrage; but it was adopted as the most effective protection for the negroes against laws, as to vagrancy and the like, by which it was feared they might practically be enslaved again.

Whatever the excuse for it, it would seem to have proved in fact a great obstacle to healthy relations between the two races. The true policy in such a matter is doubtless that which Rhodes and other statesmen adopted in the Cape Colony and which Lincoln had advocated in the case of Louisiana. It would be absurd to imagine that the spirit which could champion the rights of the negro and yet face fairly the abiding difficulty of his case died in America with Lincoln, but it lost for many a year to come its only great exponent.

But the question of overwhelming importance, between the principles of slavery and of freedom, was ready for final decision when local opinion in six slave States was already moving as we have seen. The Republican Convention of 1864, which again chose Lincoln as its candidate for the Presidency, declared itself in favour of a Constitutional Amendment to abolish slavery once for all throughout America. Whether the first suggestion came from him or not, it is known that Lincoln's private influence was energetically used to procure this resolution of the Convention. In his Message to Congress in 1864 he urged the initiation of this Amendment. Observation of elections made it all but certain that the next Congress would be ready to take this action, but

Lincoln pleaded with the present doubtful Congress for the advantage which would be gained by ready, and if possible, unanimous concurrence in the North in the course which would soon prevail. The necessary Resolution was passed in the Senate, but in the House of Representatives till within a few hours of the vote it was said to be "the toss of a copper" whether the majority of two-thirds, required for such a purpose, would be obtained. In the efforts made on either side to win over the few doubtful voters Lincoln had taken his part. Right or wrong, he was not the man to see a great and beneficent Act in danger of postponement without being tempted to secure it if he could do so by terrifying some unprincipled and white-livered opponents. With the knowledge that he was always acquiring of the persons in politics, he had been able to pick out two Democratic Congressmen who were fit for his purpose – presumably they lay under suspicion of one of those treasonable practices which martial law under Lincoln treated very unceremoniously. He sent for them. He told them that the gaining of a certain number of doubtful votes would secure the Resolution. He told them that he was President of the United States. He told them that the President of the United States in war time exercised great and dreadful powers. And he told them that he looked to them personally to get him those votes. Whether this wrong manoeuvre affected the result or not, on January 31, 1865, the Resolution was passed in the House by a two-thirds majority with a few votes to spare, and the great crowd in the galleries, defying all precedent, broke out in a demonstration of enthusiasm which some still recall as the most memorable scene in their lives. On December 18 of that year, when Lincoln had been eight months dead, William Seward, as Secretary of State, was able to certify that the requisite majority of States had passed the Thirteenth Amendment to the Constitution, and the cause of that "irrepressible conflict" which he had foretold, and in which he had played a weak but valuable part, was for ever extinguished.

At the present day, alike in the British Empire and in America, the unending difficulty of wholesome human relations between races of different and unequal development exercises many minds; but this difficulty cannot obscure the great service done by those who, first in England and later and more hardly in

America, stamped out that cardinal principle of error that any race is without its human claim. Among these men William Lloyd Garrison lived to see the fruit of his labours, and to know and have friendly intercourse with Lincoln. There have been some comparable instances in which men with such different characters and methods have unconsciously conspired for a common end, as these two did when Garrison was projecting the "Liberator" and Lincoln began shaping himself for honourable public work in the vague. The part that Lincoln played in these events did not seem to him a personal achievement of his own. He appeared to himself rather as an instrument. "I claim not," he once said in this connection, "to have controlled events, but confess plainly that events have controlled me." In 1864, when a petition was sent to him from some children that there should be no more child slaves, he wrote, "Please tell these little people that I am very glad their young hearts are so full of just and generous sympathy, and that, while I have not the power to grant all they ask, I trust they will remember that God has, and that, as it seems, He wills to do it." Yet, at least, he redeemed the boyish pledge that has been, fancifully perhaps, ascribed to him; each opportunity that to his judgment ever presented itself of striking some blow for human freedom was taken; the blows were timed and directed by the full force of his sagacity, and they were never restrained by private ambition or fear. It is probable that upon that cool review, which in the case of this singular figure is difficult, the sense of his potent accomplishment would not diminish, but increase.

CHAPTER XI

THE APPROACH OF VICTORY

1. The War to the End of 1863.

The events of the Eastern theatre of war have been followed into the early summer of 1863, when Lee was for the second time about to invade the North. The Western theatre of war has been left unnoticed since the end of May, 1862. From that time to the end of the year no definite progress was made here by either side, but here also the perplexities of the military administration were considerable; and in Lincoln's life it must be noted that in these months the strain of anxiety about the Eastern army and about the policy of emancipation was accompanied by acute doubt in regard to the conduct of war in the West.

When Halleck had been summoned from the West, Lincoln had again a general by his side in Washington to exercise command under him of all the armies. Halleck was a man of some intellectual distinction who might be expected to take a broad view of the war as a whole; this and his freedom from petty feelings, as to which Lincoln's known opinion of him can be corroborated, doubtless made him useful as an adviser; nor for a considerable time was there any man with apparently better qualifications for his position. But Lincoln soon found, as has been seen, that Halleck lacked energy of will, and cannot have been long in discovering that his judgment was not very good. The President had thus to make the best use he could of expert advice upon which he would not have been justified in relying very fully.

When Halleck arrived at Corinth at the end of May, 1862, the whole of Western and Middle Tennessee was for the time clear of the enemy, and he turned his attention at once to the long delayed project of rescuing the Unionists in Eastern Tennessee, which was occupied by a Confederate army under General Kirby Smith. His object was to seize Chattanooga, which lay about 150 miles to the east of him, and invade Eastern Tennessee by way of the valley of the Tennessee River, which cuts through the mountains behind Chattanooga. With this in view he would doubtless have been wise if he had first continued his advance with his whole force against the Confederate army under Beauregard, which after evacuating Corinth had fallen back to rest and recruit in a far healthier situation 50 miles further south. Beauregard would have been obliged either to fight him with inferior numbers or to shut himself up in the fortress of Vicksburg. As it was, Halleck spent the month of June merely in repairing the railway line which runs from Corinth in the direction of Chattanooga. When he was called to Washington he left Grant, who for several months past had been kept idle as his second in command, in independent command of a force which was to remain near the Mississippi confronting Beauregard, but he restricted him to a merely defensive part by ordering him to keep a part of his army ready to send to Buell whenever that general needed it, as he soon did. Buell, who again took over his former independent command, was ordered by Halleck to advance on Chattanooga, using Corinth as his base of supply. Buell had wished that the base for the advance upon Chattanooga should be transferred to Nashville, in the centre of Tennessee, in which case the line of railway communication would have been shorter and also less exposed to raids by the Southern cavalry. After Halleck had gone, Buell obtained permission to effect this change of base. The whole month of June had been wasted in repairing the railway with a view to Halleck's faulty plan. When Buell himself was allowed to proceed on his own lines and was approaching Chattanooga, his communications with Nashville were twice, in the middle of July and in the middle of August, cut by Confederate cavalry raids, which did such serious damage as to impose great delay upon him. In the end of August and beginning of September Kirby Smith, whose army had been strengthened by troops transferred from Beauregard, crossed the mountains from East Tennessee by passes some distance northeast of Chattanooga, and invaded Kentucky, sending detachments to threaten Louisville on the Indiana border of Kentucky and Cincinnati in Ohio. It was necessary for Buell to retreat, when, after a week or more of uncertainty, it became clear that Kirby Smith's main force was committed to this invasion. Meanwhile General Bragg, who, owing to the illness of Beauregard, had succeeded to his command, left part of his force to hold Grant in check, marched with the remainder to support Kirby Smith, and succeeded in placing himself between Buell's army and Louisville, to protect which from Kirby Smith had become Buell's first object. It seems that Bragg, who could easily have been reinforced by Kirby Smith, had now an opportunity of fighting Buell with great advantage. But the Confederate generals, who mistakenly believed that Kentucky was at heart with them, saw an imaginary political gain in occupying Frankfort, the State capital, and formally setting up a new State Government there. Bragg therefore marched on to join Kirby Smith at Frankfort, which was well to the east of Buell's line of retreat, and Buell was able to reach Louisville unopposed by September 25. These events were watched in the North with all the more anxiety because the Confederate invasion of Kentucky began just about the time of the second battle of Bull Run, and Buell arrived at Louisville within a week after the battle of Antietam while people were wondering how that victory would be followed up. Men of intelligence and influence, especially in the Western States, were loud in their complaints of Buell's want of vigour. It is remarkable that the Unionists of Kentucky, who suffered the most through his supposed faults, expressed their confidence in him; but his own soldiers did not like him, for he was a strict disciplinarian without either tact or any quality which much impressed them. Their reports to their homes in Ohio, Indiana, and Illinois, from which they mostly came, increased the feeling against him which was arising in those States, and his relations with the Governors of Ohio and Indiana, who were busy in sending him recruits and whose States were threatened with invasion, seem, wherever the fault may have lain, to have been unfortunate. Buell's most powerful friend had been McClellan, and by an irrational but unavoidable process of thought the real dilatoriness of McClellan became an argument for blaming Buell as well. Halleck defended him loyally, but this by now probably seemed to Lincoln the apology of one irresolute man for another. Stanton, whose efficiency in the business of the War Department gave him great weight, had become eager for the removal of Buell. Lincoln expected that as soon as Buell could cover Louisville he would take the offensive promptly. His army appears to have exceeded in numbers, though not very much, the combined forces of Bragg and Kirby Smith, and except as to cavalry it was probably as good in quality. If energetically used by Halleck some months before, the Western armies should have been strong enough to accomplish great results; and if the attempt had been made at first to raise much larger armies, it seems likely that the difficulties of training and organisation and command would have increased out of proportion to any gain. Buell remained some days at Louisville itself, receiving reinforcements which were considerable, but consisted mainly of raw recruits. While he was there orders arrived from Lincoln removing him and appointing his second in command, the Virginian Thomas, in his place. This was a wise choice; Thomas was one of the four Northern generals who won abiding distinction in the Civil War. But Thomas felt the injustice which was done to Buell, and he refused the command in a letter magnanimously defending him. The fact was that Lincoln had rescinded his orders before they were received, for he had issued them under the belief that Buell was remaining on the defensive, but learnt immediately that an offensive movement was in progress, and had no intention of changing commanders under those circumstances.

On October 8 a battle, which began in an accidental minor conflict, took place between Buell with 58,000 men and Bragg with considerably less than half that number of tried veterans. Buell made little use of his superior numbers, for which the fault may have lain with the corps commander who first became engaged and who did not report at once to him; the part of Buell's army which bore the brunt of the fighting suffered heavy losses, which made a painful impression in the North, and the public outcry against him, which had begun as soon as Kentucky was invaded by the Confederates, now increased. After the battle Bragg fell back and effected a junction with Kirby Smith. Their joint forces were not very far inferior to Buell's in numbers, but after a few more days Bragg determined to evacuate Kentucky, in which his hope of raising many recruits had been disappointed. Buell, on perceiving his intention, pursued him some distance, but, finding the roads bad for the movement of large bodies of troops, finally took up a position at Bowling Green, on the railway to the north of Nashville, intending later in the autumn to move a little south of Nashville and there to wait for the spring before again moving on Chattanooga. He was urged from Washington to press forward towards Chattanooga at once, but replied decidedly that he was unable to do so, and added that if a change of command was desired the present was a suitable time for it. At the end of October he was removed from command. In the meantime the Confederate forces that had been left to oppose Grant had attacked him and been signally defeated in two engagements, in each of which General Rosecrans, who was serving under Grant, was in immediate command on the Northern side. Rosecrans, who therefore began to be looked upon as a promising general, and indeed was one of those who, in the chatter of the time, were occasionally spoken of as suitable for a "military dictatorship," was now put in Buell's place, which Thomas had once refused. He advanced to Nashville, but was as firm as Buell in refusing to go further till he had accumulated rations enough to make him for a time independent of the railway. Ultimately he moved on Murfreesborough, some thirty miles further in the direction of Chattanooga. Here on December 31, 1862, Bragg, with somewhat inferior numbers, attacked him and gained an initial success, which Rosecrans and his subordinates, Thomas and Sheridan, were able to prevent him from making good. Bragg's losses were heavy, and, after waiting a few days in the hope that Rosecrans might retreat first, he fell back to a point near the Cumberland mountains a little in advance of Chattanooga. Thus the battle of Murfreesborough counted as a victory to the North, a slight set-off to the disaster at Fredericksburg a little while before. But it had no very striking consequences. For over six months Rosecrans proceeded no further. The Northern armies remained in more secure possession of all Tennessee west of the mountains than they had obtained in the first half of 1862; but the length of their communications and the great superiority of the South in cavalry, which could threaten those communications, suspended their further advance. Lincoln urged that their army could subsist on the country which it invaded, but Buell and Rosecrans treated the idea as impracticable; in fact, till a little later all Northern generals so regarded it.

Thus Chattanooga, which it was hoped would be occupied soon after Halleck had occupied Corinth, remained in Southern hands for more than a year after that, notwithstanding the removal of Buell, to whom this disappointment and the mortifying invasion of Kentucky were at first attributed. This was rightly felt to be unsatisfactory, but the chief blame that can now be imputed falls upon the mistakes of Halleck while he was still commanding in the West. There is no reason to suppose that Buell had any exceptional amount of intuition or of energy and it was right to demand that a general with both these qualities should be appointed if he could be found. But he was at least a prudent officer, of fair capacity, doing his best. The criticisms upon him, of which the well informed were lavish, were uttered without appreciation of practical difficulties or of the standard by which he was really to be judged. So, with far more justice than McClellan, he has been numbered among the misused generals. Lincoln, there is no doubt, had watched his proceedings, as he watched those of Rosecrans after him, with a feeling of impatience, and set him down as unenterprising and obstinate. In one point his Administration was much to blame in its treatment of the Western commanders. It became common political talk that the way to get victories was to treat unsuccessful generals almost as harshly as the French in the Revolution were understood to have treated them. Lincoln did not go thus far, but it was probably with his authority that before Buell was removed Halleck, with reluctance on his own part, wrote a letter referring to this prevalent idea and calculated to put about among the Western commanders an expectation that whichever of them first did something notable would be put over his less successful colleagues. Later on, and, as we can hardly doubt, with Lincoln's consent, Grant and Rosecrans were each informed that the first of them to win a victory would get the vacant major-generalship in the United States Army in place of his present volunteer rank. This was not the way to handle men with proper professional pride, and it is one of those cases, which are strangely few, where Lincoln made the sort of mistake that might have been expected from his want of training and not from his native generosity. But in the main his treatment of this difficult question was sound. Sharing as he did the prevailing impatience with Buell, he had no intention of yielding to it till there was a real prospect that a change of generals would be a change for the better. When the appointment of Thomas was proposed there really was such a prospect. When Rosecrans was eventually put in Buell's place the result was disappointing to Lincoln, but it was evidently not a bad appointment, and a situation had then arisen in which it would have been folly to retain Buell if any capable successor to him could be found; for the Governors of Indiana, Ohio and Illinois, of whom the first named was reputed the ablest of the "war Governors" in the West, and on whom his army depended for recruits, now combined in representations against him which could not be ignored. Lincoln, who could not have personal acquaintance with the generals of the Western armies as he had with those in the East, was, it should be observed, throughout unceasing in his efforts to get the fullest and clearest impression of them that he could; he was always, as it has been put, "taking measurements" of men, and a good deal of what seemed idle and gossipy talk with chance visitors, who could tell him little incidents or give him new impressions, seems to have had this serious purpose. For the first half of the war the choice of men for high commands was the most harassing of all the difficulties of his administration. There is no doubt of his constant watchfulness to discern and promote merit. He was certainly beset by the feeling that generals were apt to be wanting in the vigour and boldness which the conduct of the war demanded, but, though this in some cases probably misled him, upon the whole there was good reason for it. On the other hand, it must be considered that all this while he knew himself to be losing influence through his supposed want of energy in the war, and that he was under strong and unceasing pressure from every influential quarter to dismiss every general who caused disappointment. Newspapers and private letters of the time demonstrate that there was intense impatience against him for not producing victorious generals. This being so, his own patience in this matter and his resolution to give those under him a fair chance appear very remarkable and were certainly very wise. We have come, however, to the end, not of all the clamour against Lincoln, but of his own worst perplexities. In passing to the operations further west we are passing to an instance in which Lincoln felt it right to stand to the end by a decried commander, and that decried commander proved to possess the very qualities for which he had vainly looked in others. The reverse side of General Grant's fame is well enough known to the world. Before the war he had been living under a cloud. In the autumn of 1862, while his army lay between Corinth and Memphis, the cloud still rested on his reputation. In spite of the glory he had won for a moment at Fort Donelson, large circles were ready to speak of him simply as an "incompetent and disagreeable man." The crowning work of his life was accomplished with terrible bloodshed which was often attributed to callousness and incapacity on his part. The eight years of his Presidency afterwards, which cannot properly be discussed here, added at the best no lustre to his memory. Later still, when he visited Europe as a celebrity the general impression which he created seems to be contained in the words "a rude man." Thus the Grant that we discover in the recollections of a few loyal and loving friends, and in the memoirs which he himself began when late in life he lost his money and which he finished with the pains of death upon him, is a surprising, in some ways pathetic, figure. He had been a shy country boy, ready enough at all the work of a farm and good with horses, but with none of the business aptitude that make a successful farmer, when his father made him go to West Point. Here he showed no great promise and made few friends; his health became delicate, and he wanted to leave the army and become a teacher of mathematics. But the Mexican War, one of the most unjust in all history, as he afterwards said, broke out, and—so he later thought—saved his life from consumption by keeping him in the open air. After that he did retire, failed at farming and other ventures, and at thirty-nine, when the Civil War began, was as has been seen, a shabby-looking, shiftless fellow, pretty far gone in the habit of drink, and more or less occupied about a leather business of his father's. Rough in appearance and in manner he remained—the very opposite of smart, the very opposite of versatile, the very opposite of expansive in speech or social intercourse. Unlike many rough people, he had a really simple character—truthful, modest, and kind; without varied interests, or complicated emotions, or much sense of fun, but thinking intensely on the problems that he did see before him, and in his silent way keenly sensitive on most of the points on which it is well to be sensitive. His friends reckoned up the very few occasions on which he was ever seen to be angry; only one could be recalled on which he was angry on his own account; the cruelty of a driver to animals in his supply train, heartless neglect in carrying out the arrangements he had made for the comfort of the sick and wounded, these were the sort of occasions which broke down Grant's habitual self-possession and good temper. "He was never too anxious," wrote Chaplain Eaton, who, having been set by him in charge of the negro refugees with his army, had excellent means of judging, "never too preoccupied with the great problems that beset him, to take a sincere and humane interest in the welfare of the most subordinate labourer dependent upon him." And he had delicacy of feeling in other ways. Once in the crowd at some hotel, in which he mingled an undistinguished figure, an old officer under him tried on a lecherous story for the entertainment of the General, who did not look the sort of man to resent it; Grant, who did not wish to set down an older man roughly, and had no ready phrases, but had, as it happens, a sensitive skin, was observed to blush to the roots of his hair in exquisite discomfort. It would be easy to multiply little recorded traits of this somewhat unexpected kind, which give grace to the memory of his determination in a duty which became very grim.

The simplicity of character as well as manner which endeared him to a few close associates was probably a very poor equipment for the Presidency, which, from that very simplicity, he afterwards treated as his due; and Grant presented in some ways as great a contrast as can be imagined to the large and complex mind of Lincoln. But he was the man that Lincoln had yearned for. Whatever degree of military skill may be ascribed to him, he had in the fullest measure the moral attributes of a commander. The sense that the war could be put through and must be put through possessed his soul. He was insusceptible to personal danger—at least, so observers said, though he himself told a different story—and he taught himself to keep a quiet mind in the presence of losses, rout in battle, or failure in a campaign. It was said that he never troubled himself with fancies as to what the enemy might be doing, and he confessed to having constantly told himself that the enemy was as much afraid of him as he of the enemy. His military talent was doubled in efficacy by his indomitable constancy. In one sense, moreover, and that a wholly good sense, he was a political general; for he had constantly before his mind the aims of the Government which employed him, perceiving early that there were only two possible ends to the war, the complete subjugation of the South or the complete failure of the Union; perceiving also that there was no danger of exhausting the resources of the North and great danger of discouraging its spirit, while the position of the South was in this respect the precise contrary. He was therefore the better able to serve the State as a soldier, because throughout he measured by a just standard the ulterior good or harm of success or failure in his enterprises.

The affectionate confidence which existed between Lee and "Stonewall" Jackson till the latter was killed at Chancellorsville had a parallel in the endearing friendship which sprung up between Grant and his principal subordinate, William T. Sherman, who was to bear a hardly less momentous part than his own in the conclusion of the war. Sherman was a man of quick wits and fancy, bright and mercurial disposition, capable of being a delightful companion to children, and capable of being sharp and inconsiderate to duller subordinates. It is a high tribute both to this brilliant soldier and to Grant himself that he always regarded Grant ashaving made him, not only by his confidence but by his example. As has been said, Grant was required to remain on the defensive between Memphis and Corinth, which mark the line of the Northern frontier at this period, while Buell was advancing on Chattanooga. Later, while the Confederates were invading Kentucky further east, attacks were also directed against Grant to keep him quiet. These were defeated, though Grant was unable to follow up his success at the time. When the invasion of Kentucky had collapsed and the Confederates under Bragg were retreating before Buell and his successor out of Middle Tennessee, it became possible for Grant and for Halleck and the Government at Washington to look to completing the conquest of the Mississippi River. The importance to the Confederates of a hold upon the Mississippi has been pointed out; if it were lost the whole of far South-West would manifestly be lost with it; in the North, on the other hand, public sentiment was strongly set upon freeing the navigation of the great river. The Confederacy now held the river from the fortress of Vicksburg, which after taking New Orleans Admiral Farragut had attacked in vain, down to Port Hudson, 120 miles further south, where the Confederate forces had since then seized and fortified another point of vantage. Vicksburg, it will be observed, lies 175 to 180 miles south of Memphis, or from Grand Junction, between Memphis and Corinth, the points in the occupation of the North which must serve Grant as a base. At Vicksburg itself, and for some distance south of it, a line of bluffs or steep-sided hills lying east of the Mississippi comes right up to the edge of the river. The river as it approaches these bluffs makes a sudden bend to the north-east and then again to the south-west, so that two successive reaches of the stream, each from three to four miles long, were commanded by the Vicksburg guns, 200 feet above the valley; the eastward or landward side of the fortress was also well situated for defence. To the north of Vicksburg the country on the east side of the Mississippi is cut up by innumerable streams and "bayous" or marshy creeks, winding and intersecting amid a dense growth of cedars. The North, with a flotilla under Admiral Porter, commanded the Mississippi itself, and the Northern forces could freely move along its western shore to the impregnable river face of Vicksburg beyond. But the question of how to get safely to the assailable side of Vicksburg presented formidable difficulty to Grant and to the Government. Grant's operations began in November, 1862. Advancing directly southward along the railway from Memphis with the bulk of his forces, he after a while detached Sherman with a force which proceeded down the Mississippi to the mouth of the Yazoo, a little north-west of Vicksburg. Here Sherman was to land, and, it was hoped, surprise the enemy at Vicksburg itself while the bulk of the enemy's forces were fully occupied by Grant's advance from the north. But Grant's lengthening communications were cut up by a cavalry raid, and he had to retreat, while Sherman came upon an enemy fully prepared and sustained a defeat a fortnight after Burnside's defeat at Fredericksburg. This was the first of a long series of failures during which Grant, who for his part was conspicuously frank and loyal in his relations with the Government, received upon the whole the fullest confidence and support from them. There occurred, however, about this time an incident which was trying to Grant, and of which the very simple facts must be stated, since it was the last of the occasions upon which severe criticism of Lincoln's military administration has been founded. General McClernand was an ambitious Illinois lawyer-politician of energy and courage; he was an old acquaintance of Lincoln's, and an old opponent; since the death of Douglas he and another lawyer-politician, Logan, had been the most powerful of the Democrats in Illinois; both were zealous in the war and had joined the Army upon its outbreak. Logan served as a general under Grant with confessed ability. It must be repeated that, North and South, former civilians had to be placed in command for lack of enough soldiers of known capacity to go round, and that many of them, like Logan and like the Southern general, Polk, who was a bishop in the American Episcopal Church, did very good service. McClernand had early obtained high rank and had shown no sign as yet of having less aptitude for his new career than other men of similar antecedents. Grant, however, distrusted him, and proved to be right. In October, 1862, McClernand came to Lincoln with an offer of his personal services in raising troops from Illinois, Indiana, and Iowa, with a special view to clearing the Mississippi. He of course expected to be himself employed in this operation. Recruiting was at a low ebb, and it would have been folly to slight this offer. McClernand did in fact raise volunteers to the number of a whole army corps. He was placed under Grant in command of the expedition down the Mississippi which had already started under Sherman. Sherman's great promise had not yet been proved to any one but Grant; he appears at this time to have come under the disapproval of the Joint Committee of Congress on the War, and the newspaper Press had not long before announced, with affected regret, the news that he had become insane. McClernand, arriving just after Sherman's defeat near Vicksburg, fell in at once with a suggestion of his to attack the Post of Arkansas, a Confederate stronghold in the State of Arkansas and upon the river of that name, from the shelter of which Confederate gunboats had some chance of raiding the Mississippi above Vicksburg. The expedition succeeded in this early in January, 1863, and was then recalled to join Grant. This was a mortification to McClernand, who had hoped for a command independent of Grant. In his subsequent conduct he seems to have shown incapacity; he was certainly insubordinate to Grant, and he busied himself in intrigues against him, with such result as will soon be seen. As soon as Grant told the Administration that he was dissatisfied with McClernand, he was assured that he was at liberty to remove him from command. This he eventually did after some months of trial. In the first three months of 1863, while the army of the Potomac, shattered at Fredericksburg, was being prepared for the fresh attack upon Lee which ended at Chancellorsville, and while Bragg and Rosecrans lay confronting each other in Middle Tennessee, each content that the other was afraid to weaken himself by sending troops to the Mississippi, Grant was occupied in a series of enterprises apparently more cautious than that in which he eventually succeeded, but each in its turn futile. An attempt was made to render Vicksburg useless by a canal cutting across the bend of the Mississippi to the west of that fortress. Then Grant endeavoured with the able co-operation of Admiral Porter and his flotilla to secure a safe landing on the Yazoo, which enters the Mississippi a little above Vicksburg, so that he could move his army to the rear of Vicksburg by this route. Next Grant and Porter tried to establish a sure line of water communication from a point far up the Mississippi through an old canal, then somehow obstructed, into the upper waters of the Yazoo and so to a point on that river 30 or 40 miles to the north-east of Vicksburg, by which they would have turned the right of the main Confederate force; but this was frustrated by the Confederates, who succeeded in establishing a strong fort further up the Yazoo. Yet a further effort was made to establish a waterway by a canal quitting the Mississippi about 40 miles north of Vicksburg and communicating, through lakes, bayous, and smaller rivers, with its great tributary the Red River far to the south. This, like the first canal attempted, would have rendered Vicksburg useless.

Each of these projects failed in turn. The tedious engineering work which two of them involved was rendered more depressing by adverse conditions of weather and by ill-health among Grant's men. Natural grumbling among the troops was repeated and exaggerated in the North. McClernand employed the gift for intrigue, which perhaps had helped him to secure his command, in an effort to get Grant removed. It is melancholy to add that a good many newspapers at this time began to print statements that Grant had again taken to drink. It is certain that he was at this time a total abstainer. It is said that he had offended the authors of this villainy by the restrictions which he had long before found necessary to put upon information to the Press. Some of the men freely confessed afterwards that they had been convinced of his sobriety, and added the marvellous apology that their business was to give the public "the news." Able and more honest journalists urged that Grant had proved his incompetence. Secretary Chase took up their complaints and pressed that Grant should be removed. Lincoln, before the outcry against Grant had risen to its height, had felt the need of closer information than he possessed about the situation on the Mississippi; and had hit upon the happy expedient of sending an able official of the War Department, who deserved and obtained the confidence of Grant and his officers, to accompany the Western army and report to him. Apart, however, from the reports he thus received, he had always treated the attacks on Grant with contempt. "I cannot spare this general; he fights," he said. In reply to complaints that Grant drank, he enquired (adapting, as he knew, George II.'s famous saying about Wolfe) what whisky he drank, explaining that he wished to send barrels of it to some of his other generals. His attitude is remarkable, because in his own mind he had not thought well of any of Grant's plans after his first failure in December; he had himself wished from an early day that Grant would take the very course by which he ultimately succeeded. He let him go his own way, as he afterwards told him, from "a general hope that you know better than I."

At the end of March Grant took a memorable determination to transfer his whole force to the south of Vicksburg and approach it from that direction. He was urged by Sherman to give up any further attempt to use the river, and, instead, to bring his whole army back to Memphis and begin a necessarily slow approach on Vicksburg by the railway. He declared himself that on ordinary grounds of military prudence this would have been the proper course, but he decided for himself that the depressing effect of the retreat to Memphis would be politically disastrous. At Grand Gulf, 30 miles south of Vicksburg, the South possessed another fortified post on the river; to reach this Grant required the help of the Navy, not only in crossing from the western bank of the river, but in transporting the supplies for which the roads west of the river were inadequate. Admiral Porter, with his gunboats and laden barges, successfully ran the gauntlet of the Vicksburg batteries by night without serious damage. Grand Gulf was taken on May 3, and Grant's army established at this new base. A further doubt now arose. General Banks in Louisiana was at this time preparing to besiege Port Hudson. It might be well for Grant to go south and join him, and, after reducing Port Hudson, return with Banks' forces against Vicksburg. This was what now commended itself to Lincoln. In the letter of congratulation which some time later he was able to send to Grant, after referring to his former opinion which had been right, he confessed that he had now been wrong. Banks was not yet ready to move, and Vicksburg, now seriously threatened, might soon be reinforced. Orders to join Banks, though they were probably meant to be discretionary, were actually sent to Grant, but too late. He had cut himself loose from his base at Grand Gulf and marched his troops north, to live with great hardship to themselves on the country and the supplies they could take with them. He had with him 35,000 men. General Pemberton, to whom he had so far been opposed, lay covering Vicksburg with 20,000 and a further force in the city; Joseph Johnston, whom he afterwards described as the Southern general who in all the war gave him most trouble, had been sent by Jefferson Davis to take supreme command in the West, and had collected 11,000 men at Jackson, the capital of Mississippi, 45 miles east of Vicksburg. Grant was able to take his enemy in detail. Having broken up Johnston's force he defeated Pemberton in a series of battles. His victory at Champion's Hill on May 16, not a fortnight after Chancellorsville, conveyed to his mind the assurance that the North would win the war. An assault on Vicksburg failed with heavy loss. Pemberton was at last closely invested in Vicksburg and Grant could establish safe communications with the North by way of the lower Yazoo and up the Mississippi above its mouth. There had been dissension between Pemberton and Johnston, who, seeing that gunboats proved able to pass Vicksburg in any case, thought that Pemberton, whom he could not at the moment hope to relieve, should abandon Vicksburg and try to save his army. Long before Johnston could be sufficiently reinforced to attack Grant, Grant's force had been raised to 71,000. On July 4, 1863, the day of the annual commemoration of national Independence, Vicksburg was surrendered. Its garrison, who had suffered severely, were well victualled by Grant and allowed to go free on parole. Pemberton in his vexation treated Grant with peculiar insolence, which provoked a singular exhibition of the conqueror's good temper to him; and in his despatches to the President, Grant mentioned nothing with greater pride than the absence of a word or a sign on the part of his men which could hurt the feelings of the fallen. Johnston was forced to abandon the town of Jackson with its large stores to Sherman, but could not be pursued in his retreat. On July 9, five days later, the defender of Port Hudson, invested shortly before by Banks, who had not force enough for an assault, heard the news of Vicksburg and surrendered. Lincoln could now boast to the North that "the Father of Waters again goes unvexed to the sea."

At the very hour when Vicksburg was surrendered Lincoln had been issuing the news of another victory won in the preceding three days, which, along with the capture of Vicksburg, marked the turning point of the war. For more than a month after the battle of Chancellorsville the two opposing armies in the East had lain inactive. The Conscription Law, with which we must deal later, had recently been passed, and various elements of discontent and disloyalty in the North showed a great deal of activity.

It seems that Jefferson Davis at first saw no political advantage in the military risk of invading the North. Lee thought otherwise, and was eager to follow up his success. At last, early in June, 1863, he started northward. This time he aimed at the great industrial regions of Pennsylvania, hoping also while assailing them to draw Hooker further from Washington. Hooker, on first learning that Lee had crossed the Rappahannock, entertained the thought of himself going south of it and attacking Richmond. Lincoln dissuaded him, since he might be "entangled upon the river, like an ox jumped half over a fence"; he could not take Richmond for weeks, and his communications might be cut; besides, Lincoln added, his true objective point throughout was Lee's army and not Richmond. Hooker's later movements, in conformity with what he could gather of Lee's movements, were prudent and skilful. He rejected a later suggestion of Lincoln's that he should strike quickly at the most assailable point in Lee's lengthening line of communications, and he was wise, for Lee could live on the country he was traversing, and Hooker now aimed at covering Philadelphia or Baltimore and Washington, according to the direction which Lee might take, watching all the while for the moment to strike. He found himself hampered in some details by probably injudicious orders of his superior, Halleck, and became irritable and querulous; Lincoln had to exercise his simple arts to keep him to his duty and to soothe him, and was for the moment successful. Suddenly on June 27, with a battle in near prospect, Hooker sent in his resignation; probably he meant it, but there was no time to debate the matter. Probably he had lost confidence in himself, as he did before at Chancellorsville. Lincoln evidently judged that his state of mind made it wise to accept this resignation. He promptly appointed in Hooker's place one of his subordinates, General George Meade, a lean, tall, studious, somewhat sharp-tongued man, not brilliant or popular or the choice that the army would have expected, but with a record in previous campaigns which made him seem to Lincoln trustworthy, as he was. A subordinate command in which he could really distinguish himself was later found for Hooker, who now took leave of his army in words of marked generosity towards Meade. All this while there was great excitement in the North. Urgent demands had been raised for the recall of McClellan, a course of which, Lincoln justly observed, no one could measure the inconvenience so well as he.

Lee was now feeling his way, somewhat in the dark as to his enemy's movements, because he had despatched most of his cavalry upon raiding expeditions towards the important industrial centre of Harrisburg. Meade continued on a parallel course to him, with his army spread out to guard against any movements of Lee's to the eastward. Each commander would have preferred to fight the other upon the defensive. Suddenly on July 1, three days after Meade had taken command, a chance collision took place north of the town of Gettysburg between the advance guards of the two armies. It developed into a general engagement, of which the result must partly depend on the speed with which each commander could bring up the remainder of his army. On the first day Lee achieved a decided success. The Northern troops were driven back upon steep heights just south of Gettysburg, of which the contour made it difficult for the enemy to co-ordinate his movements in any attack on them. Here Meade, who when the battle began was ten miles away and did not expect it, was able by the morning of the 2nd or during that day to bring up his full force; and here, contrary to his original choice of a position for bringing on a battle, he made his stand. The attack planned by Lee on the following day must, in his opinion, afterwards have been successful if "Stonewall" Jackson had been alive and with him. As it was, his most brilliant remaining subordinate, Longstreet, disapproved of any assault, and on this and the following day obeyed his orders reluctantly and too slowly. On July 3, 1863, Lee renewed his attack. In previous battles the Northern troops had been contending with invisible enemies in woods; now, after a heavy cannonade, the whole Southern line could be seen advancing in the open to a desperate assault. This attack was crushed by the Northern fire. First and last in the fighting round Gettysburg the North lost 23,000 out of about 93,000 men, and the South about an equal number out of 78,000. The net result was that, after a day's delay,

Lee felt compelled to retreat. Nothing but an actual victory would have made it wise for him to persist in his adventurous invasion.

The importance of this, which has been remembered as the chief battle of the war, must be estimated rather by the peril from which the North was delivered than by the results it immediately reaped. Neither on July 3 nor during Lee's subsequent retreat did Meade follow up his advantage with the boldness to which Lincoln, in the midst of his congratulations, exhorted him. On July 12 Lee recrossed the Potomac. Meade on the day before had thought of attacking him, but desisted on the advice of the majority in a council of war. That council of war, as Lincoln said, should never have been held. Its decision was demonstrably wrong, since it rested on the hope that Lee would himself attack. Lincoln writhed at a phrase in Meade's general orders about "driving the invader from our soil." "Will our generals," he exclaimed in private, "never get that idea out of their heads? The whole country is our soil." Meade, however, unlike McClellan, was only cautious, not lukewarm, nor without a mind of his own. The army opposed to him was much larger than that which McClellan failed to overwhelm after Antietam. He had offered to resign when he inferred Lincoln's dissatisfaction from a telegram. Lincoln refused this, and made it clear through another officer that his strong opinion as to what might have been done did not imply ingratitude or want of confidence towards "a brave and skilful officer, and a true man." Characteristically he relieved his sense of Meade's omissions in a letter of most lucid criticism, and characteristically he never sent it. Step by step Meade moved on Lee's track into the enemy's country. Indecisive manoeuvres on both sides continued over four months. Lee was forced over the Rappahannock, then over the Rapidan; Meade followed him, found his army in peril, and prudently and promptly withdrew. In December the two armies went into winter quarters on the two sides of the Rappahannock to await the opening of a very different campaign when the next spring was far advanced.

The autumn months of 1863 witnessed in the Middle West a varying conflict ending in a Northern victory hardly less memorable than those of Gettysburg and Vicksburg. At last, after the fall of Vicksburg, Rosecrans in Middle Tennessee found himself ready to advance. By skilful manoeuvres, in the difficult country where the Tennessee River cuts the Cumberland mountains and the parallel ranges which run from north-east to south-west behind, he turned the flank of Bragg's position at Chattanooga and compelled him to evacuate that town in the beginning of September. Bragg, as he retreated, succeeded in getting false reports as to his movements and the condition of his army conveyed to Rosecrans, who accordingly followed him up in an incautious manner. By this time the bulk of the forces that had been used against Vicksburg should have been brought to support Rosecrans. Halleck, however, at first scattered them for purposes which he thought important in the West. After a while, however, one part of the army at Vicksburg was brought back to General Burnside in Ohio, from whom it had been borrowed. Burnside accomplished the very advance by Lexington, in Kentucky, over the mountains into Eastern Tennessee, which Lincoln had so long desired for the relief of the Unionists there, and he was able to hold his ground, defeating at Knoxville a little later an expedition under Longstreet which was sent to dislodge him. Other portions of the Western army were at last ordered to join Rosecrans, but did not reach him before he had met with disaster. For the Confederate authorities, eager to retrieve their losses, sent every available reinforcement to Bragg, and he was shortly able to turn back towards Chattanooga with over 71,000 men against the 57,000 with which Rosecrans, scattering his troops in false security, was pursuing him. The two armies came upon one another, without clear expectation, upon the Chicamauga Creek beyond the ridge which lies south-east of Chattanooga. The battle fought among the woods and hills by Chicamauga on September 19 and 20 surpassed any other in the war in the heaviness of the loss on each side. On the second day Bragg's manoeuvres broke Rosecrans' line, and only an extraordinarily gallant stand by Thomas with a part of the line, in successive positions of retreat, prevented Bragg from turning the hasty retirement of the remainder into a disastrous rout. As it was, Rosecrans made good his retreat to Chattanooga, but there he was in danger of being completely cut off. A corps was promptly detached from Meade in Virginia, placed under Hooker, and sent to relieve him. Rosecrans, who in a situation of real difficulty seems to have had no resourcefulness, was replaced in his command by Thomas. Grant was appointed to supreme command of all the forces in the West and ordered to Chattanooga. There, after many intricate operations on either side, a great battle was eventually fought on November 24 and 25, 1863. Grant had about 60,000 men; Bragg, who had detached Longstreet for his vain attack on Burnside, had only 33,000, but he had one steep and entrenched ridge behind another on which to stand. The fight was marked by notable incidents—Hooker's "battle above the clouds"; and the impulse by which apparently with no word of command, Thomas' corps, tired of waiting while Sherman advanced upon the one flank and Hooker upon the other, arose and carried a ridge which the enemy and Grant himself had regarded as impregnable. It ended in a rout of the Confederates, which was energetically followed up. Bragg's army was broken and driven right back into Georgia. To sum up the events of the year, the one serious invasion of the North by the South had failed, and the dominion on which the Confederacy had any real hold was now restricted to the Atlantic States, Alabama, and a part of the State of Mississippi.

At this point, at which the issue of the war, if it were only pursued, could not be doubted, and at which, as it happens, the need of Lincoln's personal intervention in military matters became greatly diminished, we may try to obtain a general impression of his wisdom, or want of it, in such affairs. The closeness and keen intelligence with which he followed the war is undoubted, but could only be demonstrated by a lengthy accumulation of evidence. The larger strategy of the North, sound in the main, was of course the product of more than one co-operating mind, but as his was undoubtedly the dominant will of his Administration, so too it seems likely that, with his early and sustained grasp of the general problem, he contributed not a little to the clearness and consistency of the strategical plans. The amount of the forces raised was for long, as we shall see later, beyond his control, and, in the distribution of what he had to the best effect, his own want of knowledge and the poor judgment of his earlier advisers seem to have caused some errors. He started with the evident desire to put himself almost unreservedly in the hands of the competent military counsellors, and he was able in the end to do so; but for a long intermediate period, as we have seen, he was compelled as a responsible statesman to forego this wish. It was all that time his function first to pick out, with very little to go by, the best officers he could find, replacing them with better when he could; and secondly to give them just so much direction, and no more, as his wisdom at a distance and their more expert skill upon the spot made proper. In each of these respects his occasional mistakes are plain enough, but the evidence, upon which he has often been thought capable of setting aside sound military considerations causelessly or in obedience to interested pressure, breaks down when the facts of any imputed instance are known. It is manifest that he gained rapidly both in knowledge of the men he dealt with and in the firm kindness with which he treated them. It is remarkable that, with his ever-burning desire to see vigour and ability displayed, he could watch so constantly as he did for the precise opportunity or the urgent necessity before he made changes in command. It is equally remarkable that, with his decided and often right views as to what should be done, his advice was always offered with equal deference and plainness. "Quite possibly I was wrong both then and now," he once wrote to Hooker, "but in the great responsibility resting upon me, I cannot be entirely silent. Now, all I ask is that you will be in such mood that we can get into action the best cordial judgment of yourself and General Halleck, with my poor mite added, if indeed he and you shall think it entitled to any consideration at all." The man whose habitual attitude was this, and who yet could upon the instant take his own decision, may be presumed to have been wise in many cases where we do not know his reasons. Few statesmen, perhaps, have so often stood waiting and refrained themselves from a firm will and not from the want of it, and for the sake of the rare moment of action.

The passing of the crisis in the war was fittingly commemorated by a number of State Governors who combined to institute a National Cemetery upon the field of Gettysburg. It was dedicated on November 19, 1863. The speech of the occasion was delivered by Edward Everett, the accomplished man once already mentioned as the orator of highest repute in his day. The President was bidden then to say a few words at the close. The oration with which for two hours Everett delighted his vast audience charms no longer, though it is full of graceful sentiment and contains a very reasonable survey of the rights and wrongs involved in the war, and of its progress till then. The few words of Abraham Lincoln were such as perhaps sank deep, but left his audience unaware that a classic had been spoken which would endure with the English language. The most literary man present was also Lincoln's greatest admirer, young John Hay. To him it seemed that Mr. Everett spoke perfectly, and "the old man" gracefully for him. These were the few words: "Four score and seven years ago our fathers brought forth on this continent a new nation, conceived in liberty and dedicated to the proposition that all men are created equal. Now we are engaged in a great civil war, testing whether that nation, or any nation so conceived and so dedicated, can long endure. We are met on a great battlefield of that war. We have come to dedicate a portion of that field as a final resting place for those who here gave their lives that that nation might live. It is altogether fitting and proper that we should do this. But, in a larger sense, we cannot dedicate—we cannot consecrate—we cannot hallow—this ground. The brave men, living and dead, who struggled here have consecrated it far above our poor power to add or to detract. The world will little note nor long remember what we say here, but it can never forget what they did here. It is for us, the living, rather to be dedicated here to the unfinished work which they who fought here have thus far so nobly advanced. It is rather for us to be here dedicated to the great task remaining before us—that from these honoured dead we take increased devotion to that cause for which they gave the last full measure of devotion; that we here highly resolve that these dead shall not have died in vain; that this nation, under God, shall have a new birth of freedom; and that government of the people, by the people, for the people, shall not perish from the earth."

2. Conscription and the Politics of 1863.

The events of our day may tempt us to underestimate the magnitude of the American Civil War, not only in respect of its issues, but in respect of the efforts that were put forth. Impartial historians declare that "no previous war had ever in the same time entailed upon the combatants such enormous sacrifices of life and wealth." Even such battles as Malplaquet had not rivalled in carnage the battles of this war, and in the space of these four years there took place a number of engagements—far more than can be recounted here—in many of which, as at Gettysburg, the casualties amounted to a quarter of the whole forces engaged. The Southern armies, especially towards the end of the war, were continually being pitted against vastly superior numbers; the Northern armies, whether we look at the whole war as one vast enterprise of conquest or at almost any important battle save that of Gettysburg, were as continually confronted with great obstacles in the matter of locality and position. In this case, of a new and not much organised country unprepared for war, exact or intelligible figures as to losses or as to the forces raised must not be expected, but, according to what seems to be a fair estimate, the total deaths on the Northern and the Southern side directly due to the war stood to the population of the whole country at its beginning as at least 1 to 32. Of these deaths about half occurred on the Northern and half on the Southern side; this, however, implies that in proportion to its population the South lost twice as heavily as the North.

Neither side obtained the levies of men that it needed without resort to compulsion. The South, in which this necessity either arose more quickly or was seen more readily, had called up before the end of the war its whole available manhood. In the North the proportion of effort and sacrifice required was obviously less, and, at least at one critical moment, it was disastrously underestimated. A system of compulsion, to be used in default of volunteering, was brought into effect half-way through the war. Under this system there were in arms at the end of the war 980,000 white Northern soldiers, who probably stood to the population at that time in as high a proportion as 1 to 25, and everything was in readiness for calling up a vastly greater number if necessary. After twenty months of war, when the purely voluntary system still existed but was proving itself inadequate to make good the wastage of the armies, the number in arms for the North was 860,717, perhaps as much as 1 in 27 of the population then. It would be useless to evade the question which at once suggests itself, whether the results of voluntary enlistment in this country during the present war have surpassed to the extent to which they undoubtedly ought to have surpassed the standard set by the North in the Civil War. For these two cases furnish the only instances in which the institution of voluntary enlistment has been submitted to a severe test by Governments reluctant to abandon it. The two cases are of course not strictly comparable. Our own country in this matter had the advantages of riper organisation, political and social, and of the preparatory education given it by the Territorials and by Lord Roberts. The extremity of the need was in our case immediately apparent; and the cause at issue appealed with the utmost simplicity and intensity to every brave and to every gentle nature. In the Northern States, on the other hand, apart from all other considerations, there were certain to be sections, local, racial, and political, upon which the national cause could take no very firm hold. That this was so proves no unusual prevalence of selfishness or of stupidity; and the apathy of such sections of the people, like that of smaller sections in our own case, sets in a brighter light the devotion which made so many eager to give their all. Moreover, the general patriotism of the Northern people is not to be judged by the failure of the purely voluntary system, but rather, as will be seen later, by the success of the system which succeeded it. There is in our case no official statement of the exact number serving on any particular day, but the facts which are published make it safe to conclude that, at the end of fifteen months of war, when no compulsion was in force, the soldiers then in service and drawn from the United Kingdom alone amounted to 1 in 17 of the population. The population in this case is one of which a smaller proportion are of military age than was the case in the Northern States, with their great number of immigrants. The apparent effect of these figures would be a good deal heightened if it were possible to make a correct addition in the case of each country for the numbers killed or disabled in war up to the dates in question and for the numbers serving afloat. Moreover, the North, when it was driven to abandon the purely voluntary system, had not reached the point at which the withdrawal of men from civil occupations could have been regarded among the people as itself a national danger, or at which the Government was compelled to deter some classes from enlisting; new industries unconnected with the war were all the while springing up, and the production and export of foodstuffs were increasing rapidly. For the reasons which have been stated, there is nothing invidious in thus answering an unavoidable question. Judged by any previous standard of voluntary national effort, the North answered the test well. Each of our related peoples must look upon the rally of its fathers and grandfathers in the one case, its brothers and sons in the other, with mingled feelings in which pride predominates, the most legitimate source of pride in our case being the unity of the Empire. To each the question must present itself whether the nations, democratic and otherwise, which have followed from the first, or, like the South, have rapidly adopted a different principle, have not, in this respect, a juster cause of pride. In some of these countries, by common and almost unquestioning consent, generation after generation of youths and men in their prime have held themselves at the instant disposal of their country if need should arise; and, in the absence of need and the absence of excitement, have contentedly borne the appreciable sacrifice of training. With this it is surely necessary to join a further question, whether the compulsion which, under conscription, the public imposes on individuals is comparable in its harshness to the sacrifice and the conflict of duties imposed by the voluntary system upon the best people in all classes as such. From the manner in which the war arose it will easily be understood that the South was quicker than the North in shaping its policy for raising armies. Before a shot had been fired at Fort Sumter, and when only seven of the ten Southern States had yet seceded, President Jefferson Davis had at his command more than double the number of the United States Army as it then was. He had already lawful authority to raise that number to nearly three times as many. And, though there was protest in some States, and some friction between the Confederate War Department and the State militias, on the whole the seceding States, in theory jealous of their rights, submitted very readily in questions of defence to the Confederacy.

It is not clear how far the Southern people displayed their warlike temper by a sustained flow of voluntary enlistment; but their Congress showed the utmost promptitude in granting every necessary power to their President, and on April 16, 1862, a sweeping measure of compulsory service was passed. The President of the Confederacy could call into the service any white resident in the South between the ages of eighteen and thirty-five, with certain statutory exemptions. There was, of course, trouble about the difficult question of exemptions, and under conflicting pressure the Confederate Congress made and unmade various laws about them. After a time all statutory exemptions were done away, and it was left entirely in the discretion of the Southern President to say what men were required in various departments of civil life. The liability to serve was extended in September, 1862, to all between eighteen and forty-five, and finally in February, 1864, to all between seventeen and fifty. The rigorous conscription which necessity required could not be worked without much complaint. There was a party disposed to regard the law as unconstitutional. The existence of sovereign States within the Confederacy was very likely an obstacle to the local and largely voluntary organisation for deciding claims which can exist in a unified country. A Government so hard driven must, even if liberally minded, have enforced the law with much actual hardship. A belief in the ruthlessness of the Southern conscription penetrated to the North. If was probably exaggerated from the temptation to suppose that secession was the work of a tyranny and not of the Southern people. Desertion and failure of the Conscription Law became common in the course of 1864, but this would seem to have been due not so much to resentment at the system as to the actual loss of a large part of the South, and the spread of a perception that the war was now hopelessly lost. In the last extremities of the Confederate Government the power of compulsion of course completely broke down. But, upon the surface at least, it seems plain that what has been called the military despotism of Jefferson Davis rested upon the determination rather than upon the submissiveness of the people.

In the North, where there was double the population to draw upon, the need for compulsion was not likely to be felt as soon. The various influences which would later depress enlistment had hardly begun to assert themselves, when the Government, as if to aggravate them in advance, committed a blunder which has never been surpassed in its own line. On April 3, 1862, recruiting was stopped dead; the central recruiting office at Washington was closed and its staff dispersed. Many writers agree in charging this error against Stanton. He must have been the prime author of it, but this does not exonerate Lincoln. It was no departmental matter, but a matter of supreme policy. Lincoln's knowledge of human nature and his appreciation of the larger bearings of every question might have been expected to set Stanton right, unless, indeed, the thing was done suddenly behind his back. In any case, this must be added to the indications seen in an earlier chapter, that Lincoln's calm strength and sure judgment had at that time not yet reached their full development. As for Stanton, a man of much narrower mind, but acute, devoted, and morally fearless, kept in the War Department as a sort of tame tiger to prey on abuses, negligences, pretensions, and political influences, this was one among a hundred smaller erratic doings, which his critics have never thought of as outweighing his peculiar usefulness. His departmental point of view can easily be understood. Recruits, embarrassingly, presented themselves much faster than they could be organised or equipped, and an overdriven office did not pause to think out some scheme of enlistment for deferred service. Waste had been terrific, and Stanton did not dislike a petty economy which might shock people in Washington. McClellan clamoured for more men – let him do something with what he had got; Stanton, indeed, very readily became sanguine that McClellan, once in motion, would crush the Confederacy. Events conspired to make the mistake disastrous. In these very days the Confederacy was about to pass its own Conscription Act. McClellan, instead of pressing on to Richmond, sat down before Yorktown and let the Confederate conscripts come up. Halleck was crawling southward, when a rapid advance might have robbed the South of a large recruiting area. The reopening of enlistment came on the top of the huge disappointment at McClellan's failure in the peninsula. There was a creditable response to the call which was then made for volunteers. But the disappointment of the war continued throughout 1862; the second Bull Run; the inconclusive sequel to Antietam; Fredericksburg; and, side by side with these events, the long-drawn failure of Buell's and Rosecrans' operations. The spirit of voluntary service seems to have revived vigorously enough wherever and whenever the danger of Southern invasion became pressing, but under this protracted depressing influence it no longer rose to the task of subduing the South. It must be added that wages in civil employment were very high. Lincoln, it is evident, felt this apparent failure of patriotism sadly, but in calm retrospect it cannot seem surprising.

In the latter part of 1862 attempts were made to use the powers of compulsion which the several States possessed, under the antiquated laws as to militia which existed in all of them, in order to supplement recruiting. The number of men raised for short periods in this way is so small that the description of the Northern armies at this time as purely volunteer armies hardly needs qualification. It would probably be worth no one's while to investigate the makeshift system with which the Government, very properly, then tried to help itself out; for it speedily and completely failed. The Conscription Act, which became law on March 3, 1863, set up for the first time an organisation for recruiting which covered the whole country but was under the complete control of the Federal Government. It was placed under an officer of great ability, General J. B. Fry, formerly chief of staff to Buell, and now entitled Provost-Marshal-General. It was his business, through provost-marshals in a number of districts, each divisible into sub-districts as convenience might require, to enroll all male citizens between twenty and forty-five. He was to assign a quota, in other words a stated proportion of the number of troops for which the Government might at any time call, to each district, having regard to the number of previous enlistments from each district. The management of voluntary enlistment was placed in his hands, in order that the two methods of recruiting might be worked in harmony. The system as a whole was quite distinct from any such system of universal service as might have been set up beforehand in time of peace. Compulsion only came into force in default of sufficient volunteers from any district to provide its required number of the troops wanted. When it came into force the "drafts" of conscripts were chosen by lot from among those enrolled as liable for service. But there was a way of escape from actual service. It seems, from what Lincoln wrote, to have been looked upon as a time-honoured principle, established by precedent in all countries, that the man on whom the lot fell might provide a substitute if he could. The market price of a substitute (a commodity for the provision of which a class of "substitute brokers" came into being) proved to be about 1,000 dollars. Business or professional men, who felt they could not be spared from home but wished to act patriotically, did buy substitutes; but they need not have done so, for the law contained a provision intended, as Lincoln recorded, to safeguard poorer men against such a rise in prices. They could escape by paying 300 dollars, or 60 pounds, not, in the then state of wages, an extravagant penalty upon an able-bodied man. The sums paid under this provision covered the cost of the recruiting business. Most emphatically the Conscription Law operated mainly as a stimulus to voluntary enlistment. The volunteer received, as the conscript did not, a bounty from the Government; States, counties, and smaller localities, when once a quota was assigned to them, vied with one another in filling their quota with volunteers, and for that purpose added to the Government bounty. It goes without saying that in a new country, with its scattered country population and its disorganised great new towns, there were plenty of abuses. Substitute brokers provided the wrong article; ingenious rascals invented the trade of "bounty-jumping," and would enlist for a bounty, desert, enlist for another bounty, and so on indefinitely; and the number of men enrolled who were afterwards unaccounted for was large. There was of course also grumbling of localities at the quotas assigned to them, though no pains were spared to assign them fairly. There was some opposition to the working of the law after it was passed, but it was, not general, but partly the opposition of rowdies in degraded neighbourhoods, partly factitious political opposition, and partly seditious and openly friendly to the South. In general the country accepted the law as a manifest military necessity. The spirit and manner of its acceptance may be judged from the results of any of the calls for troops under this law. For example, in December, 1864, towards the end of the war, 211,752 men were brought up to the colours; of these it seems that 194,715 were ordinary volunteers, 10,192 were substitutes provided by conscripts, and only 6,845 were actually compelled men. It is perhaps more significant still that among those who did not serve there were only 460 who paid the 300-dollar penalty, as against the 10,192 who must have paid at least three times that sum for substitutes. Behind the men who had been called up by the end of the war the North had, enrolled and ready to be called, over two million men. The North had not to suffer as the South suffered, but unquestionably in this matter it rose to the occasion.

The constitutional validity of the law was much questioned by politicians, but never finally tried out on appeal to the Supreme Court. There seems to be no room for doubt that Lincoln's own reasoning on this matter was sound. The Constitution simply gave to Congress "power to raise and support armies," without a word as to the particular means to be used for the purpose; the new and extremely well-considered Constitution of the Confederacy was in this respect the same. The Constitution, argued Lincoln, would not have given the power of raising armies without one word as to the mode in which it was to be exercised, if it had not meant Congress to be the sole judge as to the mode. "The principle," he wrote, "of the draft, which simply is involuntary or enforced service, is not new. It has been practised in all ages of the world. It was well known to the framers of our Constitution as one of the modes of raising armies. . . . It had been used just before, in establishing our independence, and it was also used under the Constitution in 1812." In fact, as we have seen, a certain power of compelling military service existed in each of the States and had existed in them from the first. Their ancestors had brought the principle with them from the old country, in which the system of the "militia ballot" had not fallen into desuetude when they became independent. The traditional English jealousy, which the American Colonies had imbibed, against the military power of the Crown had never manifested itself in any objection to the means which might be taken to raise soldiers, but in establishing a strict control of the number which the Crown could at any moment maintain; and this control had long been in England and had always been in America completely effective. We may therefore treat the protest which was raised against the law as unconstitutional, and the companion argument that it tended towards military despotism, as having belonged to the realm of political verbiage, and as neither founded in reason nor addressed to living popular emotions.

This is the way in which the Northern people, of whom a large part were, it must be remembered, Democrats, seem to have regarded these contentions, and a real sense, apart from these contentions, that conscription was unnecessary or produced avoidable hardship seems scarcely to have existed. It was probably for this reason that Lincoln never published the address to the people, or perhaps more particularly to the Democratic opposition, to which several references have already been made. In the course of it he said: "At the beginning of the war, and ever since, a variety of motives, pressing, some in one direction and some in the other, would be presented to the mind of each man physically fit to be a soldier, upon the combined effect of which motives he would, or would not, voluntarily enter the service. Among these motives would be patriotism, political bias, ambition, personal courage, love of adventure, want of employment, and convenience, or the opposite of some of these. We already have and have had in the service, as it appears, substantially all that can be obtained upon this voluntary weighing of motives. And yet we must somehow obtain more or relinquish the original object of the contest, together with all the blood and treasure already expended in the effort to secure it. To meet this necessity the law for the draft has been enacted. You who do not wish to be soldiers do not like this law. This is natural; nor does it imply want of patriotism. Nothing can be so just and necessary as to make us like it if it is disagreeable to us. We are prone, too, to find false arguments with which to excuse ourselves for opposing such disagreeable things." He proceeded to meet some of these arguments upon the lines which have already been indicated. After speaking of the precedents for conscription in America, he continued: "Wherein is the peculiar hardship now? Shall we shrink from the necessary means to maintain our free government, which our grandfathers employed to establish it and our fathers have already once employed to maintain it? Are we degenerate? Has the manhood of our race run out?" Unfair administration was apprehended. "This law," he said, "belongs to a class, which class is composed of those laws whose object is to distribute burthens or benefits on the principle of equality. No one of these laws can ever be practically administered with that exactness which can be conceived of in the mind. A tax law . . . will be a dead letter if no one will be compelled to pay until it can be shown that every other one will be compelled to pay in precisely the same proportion according to value; nay, even it will be a dead letter if no one can be compelled to pay until it is certain that every other one will pay at all. . . . This sort of difficulty applies in full force to the practical administration of the draft law. In fact, the difficulty is greater in the case of the draft law"; and he proceeded to state the difficulties. "In all these points," he continued, "errors will occur in spite of the utmost fidelity. The Government is bound to administer the law with such an approach to exactness as is usual in analogous cases, and as entire good faith and fidelity will reach." Errors, capable of correction, should, he promised, be corrected when pointed out; but he concluded: "With these views and on these principles, I feel bound to tell you it is my purpose to see the draft law faithfully executed." It was his way, as has been seen, sometimes to set his thoughts very plainly on paper and to consider afterwards the wisdom of publishing them. This paper never saw the light till after his death. It is said that some scruple as to the custom in his office restrained him from sending it out, but this scruple probably weighed with him the more because he saw that the sincere people whom he had thought of addressing needed no such appeal. It was surely a wise man who, writing so wisely, could see the greater wisdom of silence.

The opposition to the Conscription Law may be treated simply as one element in the propaganda of the official Opposition to the Administration. The opposition to such a measure which we might possibly have expected to arise from churches, or from schools of thought independent of the ordinary parties, does not seem, as a matter of fact, to have arisen. The Democratic party had, as we have seen, revived in force in the latter part of 1862. Persons, ambitious, from whatever mixture of motives, of figuring as leaders of opposition during a war which they did not condemn, found a public to which to appeal, mainly because the war was not going well. They found a principle of opposition satisfactory to themselves in condemning the Proclamation of Emancipation. (It was significant that McClellan shortly after the Proclamation issued a General Order enjoining obedience to the Government and adding the hint that "the remedy for political errors, if any are committed, is to be found only in the action of the people at the polls.") In the curious creed which respectable men, with whom allegiance to an ancient party could be a powerful motive at such a time, were driven to construct for themselves, enforcement of the duty to defend the country and liberation of the enemy's slaves appeared as twin offences against the sacred principles of constitutional freedom. It would have been monstrous to say that most of the Democrats were opposed to the war. Though a considerable number had always disliked it and now found courage to speak loudly, the bulk were as loyal to the Union as those very strong Republicans like Greeley, who later on despaired of maintaining it. But there were naturally Democrats for whom a chance now appeared in politics, and who possessed that common type of political mind that meditates deeply on minor issues and is inflamed by zeal against minor evils. Such men began to debate with their consciences whether the wicked Government might not become more odious than the enemy. There arose, too, as there often arises in war time, a fraternal feeling between men who hated the war and men who reflected how much better they could have if waged it themselves.

There was, of course, much in the conduct of the Government which called for criticism, and on that account it was a grievous pity that independence should have stultified itself by reviving in any form the root principle of party government, and recognising as the best critics of the Administration men who desired to take its place. More useful censure of the Government at that time might have come from men who, if they had axes to grind, would have publicly thrown them away. There were two points which especially called for criticism, apart from military administration, upon which, as it happened, Lincoln knew more than his critics knew and more than he could say. One of these points was extravagance and corruption in the matter of army contracts and the like; these evils were dangerously prevalent, but members of the Cabinet were as anxious to prevent them as any outside critic could be, and it was friendly help, not censure, that was required. The other point was the exercise of martial law, a difficult question, upon which a word must here be said, but upon which only those could usefully have spoken out whose general support of the Government was pronounced and sincere.

In almost every rebellion or civil war statesmen and the military officers under them are confronted with the need, for the sake of the public safety or even of ordinary justice, of rules and procedure which the law in peace time would abhor. In great conflicts, such as our own wars after the French Revolution and the American Civil War, statesmen such as Pitt and Lincoln, capable of handling such a problem well, have had their hands full of yet more urgent matters. The puzzling part of the problem does not lie in the neighbourhood of the actual fighting, where for the moment there can be no law but the will of the commander, but in the districts more distantly affected, or in the period when the war is smouldering out. Lincoln's Government had at first to guard itself against dangerous plots which could be scented but not proved in Washington; later on it had to answer such questions as this: What should be done when a suspected agent of the enemy is vaguely seen to be working against enlistment, when an attack by the civil mob upon the recruits is likely to result, and when the local magistrate and police are not much to be trusted? There is no doubt that Seward at the beginning, and Stanton persistently, and zealous local commanders now and then solved such problems in a very hasty fashion, or that Lincoln throughout was far more anxious to stand by vigorous agents of the Government than to correct them.

Lincoln claimed that as Commander-in-Chief he had during the continuance of civil war a lawful authority over the lives and liberties of all citizens, whether loyal or otherwise, such as any military commander exercises in hostile country occupied by his troops. He held that there was no proper legal remedy for persons injured under this authority except by impeachment of himself. He held, further, that this authority extended to every place to which the action of the enemy in any form extended—that is, to the whole country. This he took to be the doctrine of English Common Law, and he contended that the Constitution left this doctrine in full force. Whatever may be said as to his view of the Common Law doctrine, his construction of the Constitution would now be held by every one to have been wrong. Plainly read, the Constitution swept away the whole of that somewhat undefined doctrine of martial law which may be found in some decisions of our Courts, and it did much more. Every Legislature in the British Empire can, subject to the veto of the Crown, enact whatever exceptional measures of public safety it thinks necessary in an emergency. The Constitution restricted this legislative power within the very narrowest limits. There is, moreover, a recognised British practice, initiated by Wellington and Castlereagh, by which all question as to the authority of martial law is avoided; a governor or commander during great public peril is encouraged to consider what is right and necessary, not what is lawful, knowing that if necessary there will be enquiry into his conduct afterwards, but knowing also that, unless he acts quite unconscionably, he and his agents will be protected by an Act of Indemnity from the legal consequences of whatever they have done in good faith. The American Constitution would seem to render any such Act of Indemnity impossible. In a strictly legal sense, therefore, the power which Lincoln exercised must be said to have been usurped. The arguments by which he defended his own legality read now as good arguments on what the law should have been, but bad arguments on what the law was. He did not, perhaps, attach extreme importance to this legal contention, for he declared plainly that he was ready to break the law in minor matters rather than let the whole fabric of law go to ruin. This, however, does not prove that he was insincere when he pleaded legal as well as moral justification; he probably regarded the Constitution in a manner which modern lawyers find it difficult to realise; he probably applied in construing it a principle such as Hamilton laid down for the construction of statutes, that it was "qualified and controlled" by the Common Law and by considerations of "convenience" and of "reason" and of the policy which its framers, as wise and honest men, would have followed in present circumstances; he probably would have adapted to the occasion Hamilton's position that "construction may be made against the letter of the statute to render it agreeable to natural justice."

In the exercise of his supposed prerogative Lincoln sanctioned from beginning to end of the war the arrest of many suspected dangerous persons under what may be called "letters de cachet" from Seward and afterwards from Stanton. He publicly professed in 1863 his regret that he had not caused this to be done in cases, such as those of Lee and Joseph Johnston, where it had not been done. When agitation arose on the matter in the end of 1862 many political prisoners were, no doubt wisely, released. Congress then proceeded, in 1863, to exercise such powers in the matter as the Constitution gave it by an Act suspending, where the President thought fit, the privilege of the writ of _habeas corpus_. A decision of the Supreme Court, delivered curiously enough by Lincoln's old friend David Davis, showed that the real effect of this Act, so far as valid under the Constitution, was ridiculously small. In any case the Act was hedged about with many precautions. These were entirely disregarded by the Government, which proceeded avowedly upon Lincoln's theory of martial law. The whole country was eventually proclaimed to be under martial law, and many persons were at the orders of the local military commander tried and punished by court-martial for offences, such as the discouragement of enlistment or the encouragement of desertion, which might not have been punishable by the ordinary law, or of which the ordinary Courts might not have convicted them. This fresh outbreak of martial law must in large part be ascribed to Lincoln's determination that the Conscription Act should not be frustrated; but apart from offences relating to enlistment there was from 1863 onwards no lack of seditious plots fomented by the agents of the Confederacy in Canada, and there were several secret societies, "knights" of this, that, or the other. Lincoln, it is true, scoffed at these, but very often the general on the spot thought seriously of them, and the extreme Democratic leader, Vallandigham, boasted that there were half a million men in the North enrolled in such seditious organisations. Drastic as the Government proceedings were, the opposition to them died down before the popular conviction that strong measures were necessary, and the popular appreciation that the blood-thirsty despot "King Abraham I.," as some Democrats were pleased to call him, was not of the stuff of which despots were made and was among the least blood-thirsty men living. The civil Courts made no attempt to interfere; they said that, whatever the law, they could not in fact resist generals commanding armies. British Courts would in many cases have declined to interfere, not on the ground that the general had the might, but on the ground that he had the right; yet, it seems, they would not quite have relinquished their hold on the matter, but would have held themselves free to consider whether the district in which martial law was exercised was materially affected by the state of war or not. The legal controversy ended in a manner hardly edifying to the layman; in the course of 1865 the Supreme Court solemnly tried out the question of the right of one Milligan to a writ of _habeas corpus_. At that time the war, the only ground on which the right could have been refused him, had for some months been ended; and nobody in court knew or cared whether Milligan was then living to enjoy his right or had been shot long before.

Save in a few cases of special public interest, Lincoln took no personal part in the actual administration of these coercive measures. So great a tax was put upon his time, and indeed his strength, by the personal consideration of cases of discipline in the army, that he could not possibly have undertaken a further labour of the sort. Moreover, he thought it more necessary for the public good to give steady support to his ministers and generals than to check their action in detail. He contended that no great injustice was likely to arise. Very likely he was wrong; not only Democrats, but men like Senator John Sherman, a strong and sensible Republican, thought him wrong. There are evil stories about the secret police under Stanton, and some records of the proceedings of the courts-martial, composed sometimes of the officers least useful at the front, are not creditable. Very likely, as John Sherman thought, the ordinary law would have met the needs of the case in many districts. The mere number of the political prisoners, who counted by thousands, proves nothing, for the least consideration of the circumstances will show that the active supporters of the Confederacy in the North must have been very numerous. Nor does it matter much that, to the horror of some people, there were persons of station, culture, and respectability among the sufferers; persons of this kind were not likely to be exposed to charges of disloyal conduct if they were actively loyal. Obscure and ignorant men are much more likely to have become the innocent victims of spiteful accusers or vile agents of police. Doubtless this might happen; but that does not of itself condemn Lincoln for having maintained an extreme form of martial law. The particular kind of oppression that is likely to have occurred is one against which the normal procedure of justice and police in America is said to-day to provide no sufficient safeguard. It is almost certain that the regular course of law would have exposed the public weal to formidable dangers; but it by no means follows that it would have saved individuals from wrong. The risk that many individuals would be grievously wronged was at least not very great. The Government was not pursuing men for erroneous opinions, but for certain very definite kinds of action dangerous to the State. These were indeed kinds of action with which Lincoln thought ordinary Courts of justice "utterly incompetent" to deal, and he avowed that he aimed rather at preventing intended actions than at punishing them when done. To some minds this will seem to be an attitude dangerous to liberty, but he was surely justified when he said, "In such cases the purposes of men are much more easily understood than in cases of ordinary crime. The man who stands by and says nothing when the peril of his Government is discussed cannot be misunderstood. If not hindered, he is sure to help the enemy, much more if he talks ambiguously – talks for his country with 'buts' and 'ifs' and 'ands.'" In any case, Lincoln stood clearly and boldly for repressing speech or act, that could help the enemy, with extreme vigour and total disregard for the legalities of peace time. A little later on we shall see fully whether this imported on his part any touch whatever of the ferocity which it may seem to suggest. The Democratic opposition which made some headway in the first half of 1863 comprised a more extreme opposition prevailing in the West and led by Clement Vallandigham, a Congressman from Ohio, and a milder opposition led by Horatio Seymour, who from the end of 1862 to the end of 1864, when he failed of re-election, was Governor of New York State. The extreme section were often called "Copperheads," after a venomous snake of that name. Strictly, perhaps, this political term should be limited to the few who went so far as to desire the victory of the South; more loosely it was applied to a far larger number who went no further than to say that the war should be stopped. This demand, it must be observed, was based upon the change of policy shown in the Proclamation of Emancipation. "The war for the Union," said

Vallandigham in Congress in January, 1863, "is in your hands a most bloody and costly failure. War for the Union was abandoned; war for the negro openly begun. With what success? Let the dead at Fredericksburg answer.—Ought this war to continue? I answer no—not a day, not an hour. What then? Shall we separate? Again I answer, no, no, no.—Stop fighting. Make an armistice. Accept at once friendly foreign mediation." And further: "The secret but real purpose of the war was to abolish slavery in the States, and with it the change of our present democratical form of government into an imperial despotism." This was in no sense treason; it was merely humbug. The alleged design to establish despotism, chiefly revealed at that moment by the liberation of slaves, had of course no existence. Equally false, as will be seen later, was the whole suggestion that any peace could have been had with the South except on the terms of separation. Vallandigham, a demagogue of real vigour, had perhaps so much honesty as is compatible with self-deception; at any rate, upon his subsequent visit to the South his intercourse with Southern leaders was conducted on the footing that the Union should be restored. But his character inspired no respect. Burnside, now commanding the troops in Ohio, held that violent denunciation of the Government in a tone that tended to demoralise the troops was treason, since it certainly was not patriotism, and when in May, 1863, Vallandigham made a very violent and offensive speech in Ohio he had him arrested in his house at night, and sent him before a court-martial which imprisoned him. Loud protest was raised by every Democrat. This worry came upon Lincoln just after Chancellorsville. He regretted Burnside's action—later on he had to reverse the rash suppression of a newspaper by which Burnside provoked violent indignation—but on this occasion he would only say in public that he "regretted the necessity" of such action. Evidently he thought it his duty to support a well-intentioned general against a dangerous agitator. The course which after some consideration he took was of the nature of a practical joke, perhaps justified by its success. Vallandigham was indeed released; he was taken to the front and handed over to the Confederates as if he had been an exchanged prisoner of war. In reply to demands from the Democratic organisation in Ohio that Vallandigham might be allowed to return home, Lincoln offered to consent if their leaders would sign a pledge to support the war and promote the efficiency of the army. This they called an evasion. Vallandigham made his way to Canada and conducted intrigues from thence. In his absence he was put up for the governorship of Ohio in November, but defeated by a huge majority, doubtless the larger because of Gettysburg and Vicksburg. The next year he suddenly returned home, braving the chance of arrest, and, probably to his disappointment, Lincoln let him be. In reply to protests against Vallandigham's arrest which had been sent by meetings in Ohio and New York, Lincoln had written clear defences of his action, from which the foregoing account of his views on martial law has been taken. In one of them was a sentence which probably went further with the people of the North than any other: "Must I shoot a simple-minded soldier boy who deserts, while I must not touch a hair of a wily agitator who induces him to desert?" There may or may not be some fallacy lurking here, but it must not be supposed that this sentence came from a pleader's ingenuity. It was the expression of a man really agonised by his weekly task of confirming sentences on deserters from the army.

Governor Seymour was a more presentable antagonist than Vallandigham. He did not propose to stop the war. On the contrary, his case was that the war could only be effectively carried on by a law-abiding Government, which would unite the people by maintaining the Constitution, not, as the Radicals argued, by the flagitious policy of freeing the slaves. It should be added that he was really concerned at the corruption which was becoming rife, for which war contracts gave some scope, and which, with a critic's obliviousness to the limitations of a human force, he thought the most heavily-burdened Administration of its time could easily have put down. With a little imagination it is easy to understand the difficult position of the orthodox Democrats, who two years before had voted against restricting the extension of slavery, and were now asked for the sake of the Union to support a Government which was actually abolishing slavery by martial law. Also the attitude of the thoroughly self-righteous partisan is perfectly usual. Many of Governor Seymour's utterances were fair enough, and much of his conduct was patriotic enough. His main proceedings can be briefly summarised. His election as Governor in the end of 1862 was regarded as an important event, the appearance of a new leader holding an office of the greatest influence. Lincoln, assuming, as he had a right to do, the full willingness of Seymour to co-operate in prosecuting the war, did the simplest and best thing. He wrote and invited Seymour after his inauguration in March, 1863, to a personal conference with himself as to the ways in which, with their divergent views, they could best co-operate. The Governor waited three weeks before he acknowledged this letter. He then wrote and promised a full reply later. He never sent this reply. He protested energetically and firmly against the arrest of Vallandigham. In July, 1863, the Conscription Act began to be put in force in New York city; then occurred the only serious trouble that ever did occur under the Act; and it was very serious. A mob of foreign immigrants, mainly Irish, put a forcible stop to the proceeding of the draft. It set fire to the houses of prominent Republicans, and prevented the fire brigade from saving them. It gave chase to all negroes that it met, beating some to death, stringing up others to trees and lamp-posts and burning them as they hung. It burned down an orphanage for coloured children after the police had with difficulty saved its helpless inmates. Four days of rioting prevailed throughout the city before the arrival of fresh troops restored order. After an interval of prudent length the draft was successfully carried out. Governor Seymour arrived in the city during the riots. He harangued this defiled mob in gentle terms, promising them, if they would be good, to help them in securing redress of the grievance to which he attributed their conduct. Thenceforward to the end of his term of office he persecuted Lincoln with complaints as to the unfairness of the quota imposed on certain districts under the Conscription Act. It is true that he also protested on presumably sincere constitutional grounds against the Act itself, begging Lincoln to suspend its enforcement till its validity had been determined by the Courts. As to this Lincoln most properly agreed to facilitate, if he could, an appeal to the Supreme Court, but declined, on the ground of urgent military necessity, to delay the drafts in the meantime. Seymour's obstructive conduct, however, was not confined to the intelligible ground of objection to the Act itself; it showed itself in the perpetual assertion that the quotas were unfair. No complaint as to this had been raised before the riots. It seems that a quite unintended error may in fact at first have been made. Lincoln, however, immediately reduced the quotas in question to the full extent which the alleged error would have required. Fresh complaints from Seymour followed, and so on to the end. Ultimately Seymour was invited to come to Washington and have out the whole matter of his complaints in conference with Stanton. Like a prudent man, he again refused to face personal conference. It seems that Governor Seymour, who was a great person in his day, was very decidedly, in the common acceptance of the term, a gentleman. This has been counted unto him for righteousness. It should rather be treated as an aggravation of his very unmeritable conduct.

Thus, since the Proclamation of Emancipation the North had again become possessed of what is sometimes considered a necessity of good government, an organised Opposition ready and anxious to take the place of the existing Administration. It can well be understood that honourable men entered into this combination, but it is difficult to conceive on what common principle they could hold together which would not have been disastrous in its working. The more extreme leaders, who were likely to prove the driving force among them, were not unfitly satirised in a novel of the time called the "Man Without a Country." Their chance of success in fact depended upon the ill-fortune of their country in the war and on the irritation against the Government, which could be aroused by that cause alone and not by such abuses as they fairly criticised. In the latter part of 1863 the war was going well. A great meeting of "Union men" was summoned in August in Illinois. Lincoln was tempted to go and speak to them, but he contented himself with a letter. Phrases in it might suggest the stump orator, more than in fact his actual stump speeches usually did. In it, however, he made plain in the simplest language the total fallacy of such talk of peace as had lately become common; the Confederacy meant the Confederate army and the men who controlled it; as a fact no suggestion of peace or compromise came from them; if it ever came, the people should know it. In equally simple terms he sought to justify, even to supporters of the Union who did not share his "wish that all men could be free," his policy in regard to emancipation. In any case, freedom had for the sake of the Union been promised to negroes who were now fighting or working for the North, "and the promise being made must be kept." As that most critical year of the war drew to a close there was a prevailing recognition that the rough but straight path along which the President groped his way was the right path, and upon the whole he enjoyed a degree of general favour which was not often his portion.

3. The War in 1864.

It is the general military opinion that before the war entered on its final stage Jefferson Davis should have concentrated all his forces for a larger invasion of the North than was ever in fact undertaken. In the Gettysburg campaign he might have strengthened Lee's army by 20,000 men if he could have withdrawn them from the forts at Charleston. Charleston, however, was threatened during 1863 by the sea and land forces of the North, in an expedition which was probably itself unwise, as Lincoln himself seems to have suspected, but which helped to divert a Confederate army. In the beginning of 1864 Davis still kept this force at Charleston; he persisted also in keeping a hold on his own State, Mississippi, with a further small army; while Longstreet still remained in the south-east corner of Tennessee, where a useful employment of his force was contemplated but none was made. The chief Southern armies with which we have to deal are that of Lee, lying south of the Rapidan, and that of Bragg, now superseded by Joseph Johnston, at Dalton, south of Chattanooga. The Confederacy, it is thought, was now in a position in which it might take long to reduce it, but the only military chance for it was concentration on one great counter-stroke. This seems to have been the opinion of Lee and Longstreet. Jefferson Davis clung, even late in the year 1864, to the belief that disaster must somehow overtake any invading Northern army which pushed far. Possibly he reckoned also that the North would weary of the repeated checks in the process of conquest. Indeed, as will be seen later, the North came near to doing so, while a serious invasion of the North, unless overwhelmingly successful, might really have revived its spirit. In any case Jefferson Davis, unlike Lincoln, had no desire to be guided by his best officers. He was for ever quarrelling with Joseph Johnston and often with Beauregard; the less capable Bragg, though removed from the West, was now installed as his chief adviser in Richmond; and the genius of Lee was not encouraged to apply itself to the larger strategy of the war.

At the beginning of 1864 an advance from Chattanooga southward into the heart of the Confederate country was in contemplation. Grant and Farragut wished that it should be supported by a joint military and naval attack upon Mobile, in Alabama, on the Gulf of Mexico. Other considerations on the part of the Government prevented this. In 1863 Marshal Bazaine had invaded Mexico to set up Louis Napoleon's ill-fated client the Archduke Maximilian as Emperor. As the so-called "Monroe Doctrine" (really attributable to the teaching of Hamilton and the action of John Quincy Adams, who was Secretary of State under President Monroe) declared, such an extension of European influence, more especially dynastic influence, on the American continent was highly unacceptable to the United States. Many in the North were much excited, so much so that during 1864 a preposterous resolution, which meant, if anything, war with France, was passed on the motion of one Henry Winter Davis. It was of course the business of Lincoln and of Seward, now moulded to his views, to avoid this disaster, and yet, with such dignity as the situation allowed, keep the French Government aware of the enmity which they might one day incur. They did this. But they apprehended that the French, with a footing for the moment in Mexico, had designs on Texas; and thus, though the Southern forces in Texas were cut off from the rest of the Confederacy and there was no haste for subduing them, it was thought expedient, with an eye on France, to assert the interest of the Union in Texas. General Banks, in Louisiana, was sent to Texas with the forces which would otherwise have been sent to Mobile. His various endeavours ended in May, 1864, with the serious defeat of an expedition up the Red River. This defeat gave great annoyance to the North and made an end of Banks' reputation. It might conceivably have had a calamitous sequel in the capture by the South of Admiral Porter's river flotilla, which accompanied Banks, and the consequent undoing of the conquest of the Mississippi. As it was it wasted much force.

Before Grant could safely launch his forces southward from Chattanooga against Johnston, it was necessary to deal in some way with the Confederate force still at large in Mississippi. Grant determined to do this by the destruction of the railway system by which alone it could move eastward. For this purpose he left Thomas to hold Chattanooga, while Sherman was sent to Meridian, the chief railway centre in the Southern part of Mississippi. In February Sherman arrived there, and, though a subsidiary force, sent from Memphis on a similar but less important errand somewhat further north, met with a severe repulse, he was able unmolested to do such damage to the lines around Meridian as to secure Grant's purpose.

There was yet a further preliminary to the great final struggle. On March 1, 1864, pursuant to an Act of Congress which was necessary for this object, Lincoln conferred upon Grant the rank of Lieutenant-General, never held by any one else since Washington, for it was only brevet rank that was conferred on Scott. Therewith Grant took the command, under the President, of all the Northern armies. Grant came to Washington to receive his new honour. He had taken leave of Sherman in an interchange of letters which it is good to read; but he had intended to return to the West. Sherman, who might have desired the command in the West for himself, had unselfishly pressed him to return. He feared that the dreaded politicians would in some way hurt Grant, and that he would be thwarted by them, become disgusted, and retire; they did hurt him, but not then, nor in the way that Sherman had expected. Grant, however, could trust Sherman to carry out the work he wanted done in the West, and he now saw that, as Lincoln might have told him and possibly did, the work he wanted done in the East must be done by him. He went West again for a few days only, to settle his plans with Sherman. Sherman with his army of 100,000 was to follow Johnston's army of about 60,000, wherever it went, till he destroyed it. Grant with his 120,000 was to keep up an equally unfaltering fight with Lee's army, also of 60,000. There was, of course, nothing original about this conception except the idea, fully present to both men's minds, of the risk and sacrifice with which it was worth while to carry it out. Lincoln and Grant had never met till this month. Grant at the first encounter was evidently somewhat on his guard. He was prepared to like Lincoln, but he was afraid of mistaken dictation from him, and determined to discourage it. Also Stanton had advised him that Lincoln, out of mere good nature, would talk unwisely of any plans discussed with him. This was probably quite unjust. Stanton, in order to keep politicians and officers in their places, was accustomed to bite off the noses of all comers. Lincoln, on the contrary, would talk to all sorts of people with a readiness which was sometimes astonishing, but there was a good deal of method in this—he learnt something from these people all the time—and he certainly had a very great power of keeping his own counsel when he chose. In any case, when Grant at the end of April left Washington for the front, he parted with Lincoln on terms of mutual trust which never afterwards varied. Lincoln in fact, satisfied as to his general purpose, had been happy to leave him to make his plans for himself. He wrote to Grant: "Not expecting to see you again before the spring campaign begins, I wish to express in this way my entire satisfaction with what you have done up to this time so far as I understand it. The particulars of your plan I neither know nor seek to know. You are vigilant and self-reliant, and, pleased with this, I wish not to obtrude any constraints or restraints upon you. While I am very anxious that any great disaster or capture of our men in great numbers shall be avoided, I know these points are less likely to escape your attention than they would be mine. If there is anything wanting which is within my power to give, do not fail to let me know it. And now, with a brave army and a just cause, may God sustain you." Grant replied: "From my first entrance into the volunteer service of the country to the present day I have never had cause of complaint—have never expressed or implied a complaint against the Administration, or the Secretary of War, for throwing any embarrassment in the way of my vigorously prosecuting what appeared to me my duty. Indeed, since the promotion which placed me in command of all the armies, and in view of the great responsibility and importance of success, I have been astonished at the readiness with which everything asked for has been yielded, without even an explanation being asked. Should my success be less than I desire or expect, the least I can say is, the fault is not with you." At this point the real responsibility of Lincoln in regard to military events became comparatively small, and to the end of the war those events may be traced with even less detail than has hitherto been necessary.

Upon joining the Army of the Potomac Grant retained Meade, with whom he was pleased, in a somewhat anomalous position under him as commander of that army. "Wherever Lee goes," he told him, "there you will go too." His object of attack was, in agreement with the opinion which Lincoln had from an early date formed, Lee's army. If Lee could be compelled, or should choose, to shut himself up in Richmond, as did happen, then Richmond would become an object of attack, but not otherwise. Grant, however, hoped that he might force Lee to give him battle in the open. In the open or behind entrenchments, he meant to fight him, reckoning that if he lost double the number that Lee did, his own loss could easily be made up, but Lee's would be irreparable. His hope was to a large extent disappointed. He had to do with a greater general than himself, who, with his men, knew every inch of a tangled country. In the engagements which now followed, Grant's men were constantly being hurled against chosen positions, entrenched and with the new device of wire entanglements in front of them. "I mean," he wrote, "to fight it out on this line if it takes all summer." It took summer, autumn, winter, and the early spring. Once across the Rapidan he was in the tract of scrubby jungle called the Wilderness. He had hoped to escape out of this unopposed and at the same time to turn Lee's right by a rapid march to his own left. But he found Lee in his way. On May 5 and 6 there was stubborn and indecisive fighting, with a loss to Grant of 17,660 and to Lee of perhaps over 10,000—from Grant's point of view something gained. Then followed a further movement to the left to outflank Lee. Again Lee was to be found in the way in a chosen position of his own near Spottsylvania Court House. Here on the five days from May 8 to May 12 the heavy fighting was continued, with a total loss to Grant of over 18,000 and probably a proportionate loss to Lee. Another move by Grant to the left now caused Lee to fall back to a position beyond the North Anna River, on which an attack was made but speedily given up. Further movements in the same general direction, but without any such serious fighting – Grant still endeavouring to turn Lee's right, Lee still moving so as to cover Richmond – brought Grant by the end of the month to Cold Harbour, some ten miles east by north of Richmond, close upon the scene of McClellan's misadventures. Meanwhile Grant had caused an expedition under General Butler to go by sea up the James, and to land a little south of Richmond, which, with the connected fortress of Petersburg, twenty-two miles to the south of it, had only a weak garrison left. Butler was a man with remarkable powers of self-advertisement; he had now a very good chance of taking Petersburg, but his expedition failed totally. From June 1 to June 3 Grant was occupied on the most disastrous enterprise of his career, a hopeless attack upon a strong entrenched position, which, with the lesser encounters that took place within the next few days, cost the North 14,000 men, against a loss to the South which has been put as low as 1,700. It was the one battle which Grant regretted having fought. He gave up the hope of a fight with Lee on advantageous conditions outside Richmond. On June 12 he suddenly moved his army across the James to the neighbourhood of City Point, east of Petersburg. Lee must now stand siege in Richmond and Petersburg. Had he now marched north against Washington, Grant would have been after him and would have secured for his vastly larger force the battle in the open which he had so far vainly sought. Yet another disappointment followed. On July 30 an attempt was made to carry Petersburg by assault immediately after the explosion of an enormous mine. It failed with heavy loss, through the fault of the amiable but injudicious Burnside, who now passed into civil life, and of the officers under him. The siege was to be a long affair. In reality, for all the disappointment, and in spite of Grant's confessed mistake at Cold Harbour, his grim plan was progressing. The force which the South could ill spare was being worn down, and Grant was in a position in which, though he might have got there at less cost, and though the end would not be yet, the end was sure. His army was for the time a good deal shaken, and the estimation in which the West Point officers held him sank low. His own determination was quite unshaken, and, though Lincoln hinted somewhat mildly that these enormous losses ought not to recur, his confidence in Grant was unabated, too.

People in Washington who had watched all this with alternations of feeling that ended in dejection had had another trial to their nerves early in July. The Northern General Sigel, who commanded in the lower part of the Shenandoah Valley, protecting the Baltimore and Ohio Railway, had marched southward in June in pursuance of a subsidiary part of Grant's scheme, but in a careless and rather purposeless manner. General Early, detached by Lee to deal with him, defeated him; outmanoeuvred and defeated General Hunter, who was sent to supersede him; overwhelmed with superior force General Lew Wallace, who stood in his way further on; and upon July 11 appeared before Washington itself. The threat to Washington had been meant as no more than a threat, but the garrison was largely made up of recruits; reinforcements to it sent back by Grant arrived only on the same day as Early, and if that enterprising general had not wasted some previous days there might have been a chance that he could get into Washington, though not that he could hold it. As it was he attacked one of the Washington forts. Lincoln was present, exhibiting, till the officers there insisted on his retiring, the indifference to personal danger which he showed on other occasions too. The attack was soon given up, and in a few days Early had escaped back across the Potomac, leaving in Grant's mind a determination that the Shenandoah Valley should cease to be so useful to the South.

Sherman set out from Chattanooga on the day when Grant crossed the Rapidan. Joseph Johnston barred his way in one entrenched position after another. Sherman, with greater caution than Grant, or perhaps with greater facilities of ground, manoeuvred him out of each position in turn, pushing him slowly back along the line of the railway towards Atlanta, the great manufacturing centre of Georgia, one hundred and twenty miles south by east from Chattanooga. Only once, towards the end of June at Kenesaw Mountain, some twenty miles north of Atlanta, did he attack Johnston's entrenchments, causing himself some unnecessary loss and failing in his direct attack on them, but probably thinking it necessary to show that he would attack whenever needed. Johnston has left a name as a master of defensive warfare, and doubtless delayed and hampered Sherman as much as he could. Jefferson Davis angrily and unwisely sent General Hood to supersede him. This less prudent officer gave battle several times, bringing up the Confederate loss before Atlanta fell to 34,000 against 30,000 on the other side, and being, by great skill on Sherman's part, compelled to evacuate Atlanta on September 2.

By this time there had occurred the last and most brilliant exploit of old Admiral Farragut, who on August 5 in a naval engagement of extraordinarily varied incident, had possessed himself of the harbour of Mobile, with its forts, though the town remained as a stronghold in Confederate hands and prevented a junction with Sherman which would have quite cut the Confederacy in two.

Nearer Washington, too, a memorable campaign was in process. For three weeks after Early's unwelcome visit, military mismanagement prevailed near Washington. Early was able to turn on his pursuers, and a further raid, this time into Pennsylvania, took place. Grant was too far off to exercise control except through a sufficiently able subordinate, which Hunter was not. Halleck, as in a former crisis, did not help matters. Lincoln, though at this time he issued a large new call for recruits, was unwilling any longer to give military orders. Just now his political anxieties had reached their height. His judgment was never firmer, but friends thought his strength was breaking under the strain. On this and on all grounds he was certainly wise to decline direct interference in military affairs. On August 1 Grant ordered General Philip H. Sheridan to the Shenandoah on temporary duty, expressing a wish that he should be put "in command of all the troops in the field, with instructions to put himself south of the enemy or follow him to the death." Lincoln telegraphed to Grant, quoting this despatch and adding, "This I think is exactly right; but please look over the despatches you may have received from here even since you made that order and see if there is any idea in the head of any one here of putting our army south of the enemy or following him to the death in any direction. I repeat to you it will neither be done nor attempted unless you watch it every day and hour and force it." Grant now came to Hunter's army and gently placed Sheridan in that general's place. The operations of that autumn, which established Sheridan's fame and culminated in his final defeat of Early at Cedar Creek on October 19, made him master of all the lower part of the valley. Before he retired into winter quarters he had so laid waste the resources of that unfortunate district that Richmond could no longer draw supplies from it, nor could it again support a Southern army in a sally against the North.

In the month of November Sherman began a new and extraordinary movement, of which the conception was all his own, sanctioned with reluctance by Grant, and viewed with anxiety by Lincoln, though he maintained his absolute resolve not to interfere. He had fortified himself in Atlanta, removing its civil inhabitants, in an entirely humane fashion, to places of safety, and he had secured a little rest for his army. But he lay far south in the heart of what he called "Jeff Davis' Empire," and Hood could continually harass him by attacks on his communications. Hood, now supervised by Beauregard, was gathering reinforcements, and Sherman learnt that he contemplated a diversion by invading Tennessee. Sherman determined to divide his forces, to send Thomas far back into Tennessee with sufficient men, as he calculated, to defend it, and himself with the rest of his army to set out for the eastern sea-coast, wasting no men on the maintenance of his communications, but living on the country and "making the people of Georgia feel the weight of the war." He set out for the East on November 15. Hood, at Beauregard's orders, shortly marched off for the North, where the cautious Thomas awaited events within the fortifications of Nashville. At Franklin, in the heart of Tennessee, about twenty miles south of Nashville, Hood's army suffered badly in an attack upon General Schofield, whom Thomas had left to check his advance while further reinforcements came to Nashville. Schofield fell back slowly on Thomas, Hood rashly pressing after him with a small but veteran army now numbering 44,000. Grant and the Washington authorities viewed with much concern an invasion which Thomas had suffered to proceed so far. Grant had not shared Sherman's faith in Thomas. He now repeatedly urged him to act, but Thomas had his own views and obstinately bided his time. Days followed when frozen sleet made an advance impossible. Grant had already sent Logan to supersede Thomas, and, growing still more anxious, had started to come west himself, when the news reached him of a battle on December 15 and 16 in which Thomas had fallen on Hood, completely routing him, taking on these days and in the pursuit that followed no less than 13,000 prisoners.

There was a song, "As we go marching through Georgia," which was afterwards famous, and which Sherman could not endure. What his men most often sang, while they actually were marching through Georgia, was another, and of its kind a great song:—

"John Brown's body lies amouldering in the grave,

But his soul goes marching on.

Glory, glory, Hallelujah."

Their progress was of the nature of a frolic, though in one way a very stern frolic. They had little trouble from the small and scattered Confederate forces that lay near their route. They industriously and ingeniously destroyed the railway track of the South, heating the rails and twisting them into knots; and the rich country of Georgia, which had become the chief granary of the Confederates, was devastated as they passed, for a space fifty or sixty miles broad, by the destruction of all the produce they could not consume. This was done under control by organised forage parties. Reasonable measures were taken to prevent private pillage of houses. No doubt it happened. Sherman's able cavalry commander earned a bad name, and "Uncle Billy," as they called him to his face, clearly had a soft corner in his heart for the light-hearted and light-fingered gentlemen called "bummers" (a "bummer," says the Oxford Dictionary, "is one who quits the ranks and goes on an independent foraging expedition on his own account"). They were, incidentally, Sherman found, good scouts. But the serious crimes committed were very few, judged by the standard of the ordinary civil population. The authentic complaints recorded relate to such matters as the smashing of a grand piano or the disappearance of some fine old Madeira. Thus the suffering caused to individuals was probably not extreme, and a long continuance of the war was rendered almost impossible. A little before Christmas Day, 1864, Sherman had captured, with slight opposition, the city of Savannah, on the Atlantic, with many guns and other spoils, and was soon ready to turn northwards on the last lap of his triumphant course. Lincoln's letter of thanks characteristically confessed his earlier unexpressed and unfulfilled fears.

Grant was proceeding all the time with his pressure on the single large fortress which Richmond and Petersburg together constituted. Its circuit was far too great for complete investment. His efforts were for a time directed to seizing the three railway lines which converged from the south on Petersburg and to that extent cutting off the supplies of the enemy. But he failed to get hold of the most important of these railways. He settled down to the slow process of entrenching his own lines securely and extending the entrenchment further and further round the south side of Petersburg. Lee was thus being forced to extend the position held by his own small army further and further. In time the lines would crack and the end come.

It need hardly be said that despair was invading the remnant of the Confederacy; supplies began to run short in Richmond, recruiting had ceased, desertion was increasing. Before the story of its long resistance closes it is better to face the gravest charge against the South. That charge relates to the misery inflicted upon many thousands of Northern prisoners in certain prisons or detention camps of the South. The alleged horrors were real and were great. The details should not be commemorated, but it is right to observe that the pitiable condition in which the stricken survivors of this captivity returned, and the tale they had to tell, caused the bitterness which might be noted afterwards in some Northerners. The guilt lay mainly with a few subordinate but uncontrolled officials. In some degree it must have been shared by Jefferson Davis and his Administration, though a large allowance should be made for men so sorely driven. But it affords no ground whatever, as more fortunate prisoners taken by the Confederates have sometimes testified, for any general imputation of cruelty against the Southern officers, soldiers, or people. There is nothing in the record of the war which dishonours the South, nothing to restrain the tribute to its heroism which is due from a foreign writer, and which is irrepressible in the case of a writer who rejoices that the Confederacy failed.

4. The Second Election of Lincoln: 1864.

Having the general for whom he had long sought, Lincoln could now be in military matters little more than the most intelligent onlooker; he could maintain the attitude, congenial to him where he dealt with skilled men, that when he differed from them they probably knew better than he. This was well, for in 1864 his political anxieties became greater than they had been since war declared itself at Fort Sumter. Whole States which had belonged to the Confederacy were now securely held by the Union armies, and the difficult problem of their government was approaching its final settlement. It seemed that the war should soon end; so the question of peace was pressed urgently. Moreover, the election of a President was due in the autumn, and, strange as it is, the issue was to be whether, with victory in their grasp, the victors should themselves surrender.

It was not given to Lincoln after all to play a great part in the reconstruction of the South; that was reserved for much rougher and much weaker hands. But the lines on which he had moved from the first are of interest. West Virginia, with its solid Unionist population, was simply allowed to form itself into an ordinary new State. But matters were not so simple where the Northern occupation was insecure, or where a tiny fraction of a State was held, or where a large part of the people leaned to the Confederacy. Military governors were of course appointed; in Tennessee this position was given to a strong Unionist, Andrew Johnson, who was already Senator for that State. In Louisiana and elsewhere Lincoln encouraged the citizens who would unreservedly accept the Union to organise State Governments for themselves. Where they did so there was friction between them and the Northern military governor who was still indispensable. There was also to the end triangular trouble between the factions in Missouri and the general commanding there. To these little difficulties, which were of course unceasing, Lincoln applied the firmness and tact which were no longer surprising in him, with a pleasing mixture of good temper and healthy irritation. But further difficulties lay in the attitude of Congress, which was concerned in the matter because each House could admit or reject the Senators or Representatives claiming to sit for a Southern State. There were questions about slavery in such States. Lincoln, as we have seen, had desired, if he could, to bring about the abolition of slavery through gradual and through local action, and he had wished to see the franchise given only to the few educated negroes. Nothing came of this, but it kept up the suspicion of Radicals in Congress that he was not sound on slavery; and, apart from slavery, the whole question of the terms on which people lately in arms against the country could be admitted as participators in the government of the country was one on which statesmen in Congress had their own very important point of view. Lincoln's main wish was that, with the greatest speed and the least heat spent on avoidable controversy, State government of spontaneous local growth should spring up in the reconquered South. "In all available ways," he had written to one of his military governors, "give the people a chance to express their wishes at these elections. Follow forms of law as far as convenient, but at all events get the expression of the largest number of people possible." Above all he was afraid lest in the Southern elections to Congress that very thing should happen which after his death did happen. "To send a parcel of Northern men here as representatives, elected, as would be understood (and perhaps really so), at the point of the bayonet, would be disgraceful and outrageous." For a time he and Congress worked together well enough, but sharp disagreement arose in 1864. He had propounded a particular plan for the reconstruction of Southern States. Senator Wade, the formidable Chairman of the Joint Committee on the War, and Henry Winter Davis, a keen, acrid, and fluent man who was powerful with the House, carried a Bill under which a State could only be reconstructed on their own plan, which differed from Lincoln's. The Bill came to Lincoln for signature in the last hours of the session, and, amidst frightened protests from friendly legislators then in his room, he let it lie there unsigned, till it expired with the session, and went on with his work. This was in July, 1864; his re-election was at stake. The Democrats were gaining ground; he might be giving extreme offence to the strongest Republican. "If they choose," he said, "to make a point of this I do not doubt that they can do harm" (indeed, those powerful men Wade and Davis now declared against his re-election with ability and extraordinary bitterness); but he continued: "At all events I must keep some consciousness of being somewhere near right. I must keep some standard or principle fixed within myself." The Bill would have repressed loyal efforts already made to establish State Governments in the South. It contained also a provision imposing the abolition of slavery on every such reconstructed State. This was an attempt to remedy any flaw in the constitutional effect of the Proclamation of Emancipation. But it was certainly in itself flagrantly unconstitutional; and the only conclusive way of abolishing slavery was the Constitutional Amendment, for which Lincoln was now anxious. This was not a pedantic point, for there might have been great trouble if the courts had later found a constitutional flaw in some negro's title to freedom. But the correctness of Lincoln's view hardly matters. In lots of little things, like a tired man who was careless by nature, Lincoln may perhaps have yielded to influence or acted for his political convenience in ways which may justly be censured, but it would be merely immoral to care whether he did so or did not, since at the crisis of his fate he could risk all for one scruple. In an earlier stage of his controversies with the parties he had written: "From time to time I have done and said what appeared to me proper to do and say. The public knows it all. It obliges nobody to follow me, and I trust it obliges me to follow nobody. The Radicals and Conservatives each agree with me in some things and disagree in others. I could wish both to agree with me in all things; for then they would agree with each other, and be too strong for any foe from any quarter. They, however, choose to do otherwise, and I do not question their right. I, too, shall do what seems to be my duty. I hold whoever commands in Missouri or elsewhere responsible to me and not to either Radicals or Conservatives. It is my duty to hear all; but at last I must, within my sphere, judge what to do and what to forbear."

In this same month of July, after the Confederate General Early's appearance before Washington had given Lincoln a pause from political cares, another trouble reached a point at which it is known to have tried his patience more than any other trouble of his Presidency. Peace after war is not always a matter of substituting the diplomatist for the soldier. When two sides were fighting, one for Union and the other for Independence, one or the other had to surrender the whole point at issue.

In this case there might appear to have been a third possibility. The Southern States might have been invited to return to the Union on terms which admitted their right to secede again if they felt aggrieved. The invitation would in fact have been refused. But, if it had been made and accepted, this would have been a worse surrender for the North than any mere acknowledgment that the South could not be reconquered; for national unity from that day to this would have existed on the sufferance of a factious or a foreign majority in any single State. Lincoln had faced this. He was there to restore the Union on a firm foundation. He meant to insist to the point of pedantry that, by not so much as a word or line from the President or any one seeming to act for him, should the lawful right of secession even appear to be acknowledged. Some men would have been glad to hang Jefferson Davis as a traitor, yet would have been ready to negotiate with him as with a foreign king. Lincoln, who would not have hurt one hair of his head, and would have talked things over with Mr. Davis quite pleasantly, would have died rather than treat with him on the footing that he was head of an independent Confederacy. The blood shed might have been shed for nothing if he had done so. But to many men, in the long agony of the war and its disappointments, the plain position became much obscured. The idea in various forms that by some sort of negotiation the issue could be evaded began to assert itself again and again. The delusion was freely propagated that the South was ready to give in if only Lincoln would encourage its approaches. It was sheer delusion. Jefferson Davis said frankly to the last that the Confederacy would have "independence or extermination," and though Stephens and many others spoke of peace to the electors in their own States, Jefferson Davis had his army with him, and the only result which agitation against him ever produced was that two months before the irreparable collapse the chief command under him was given to his most faithful servant Lee. But it was useless for Lincoln to expose the delusion in the plainest terms; it survived exposure and became a danger to Northern unity.

Lincoln therefore took a strange course, which generally succeeded. When honest men came to him and said that the South could be induced to yield, he proposed to them that they should go to Jefferson Davis and see for themselves. The Chairman of the Republican organisation ultimately approached Lincoln on this matter at the request of a strong committee; but he was a sensible man whom Lincoln at once converted by drafting the precise message that would have to be sent to the Confederate President. On two earlier occasions such labourers for peace were allowed to go across the lines and talk with Davis; it could be trusted to their honour to pretend to no authority; they had interesting talks with the great enemy, and made religious appeals to him or entertained him with wild proposals for a joint war on France over Mexico. They returned, converted also. But in July Horace Greeley, the great editor, who was too opinionated to be quite honest, was somehow convinced that Southern agents at Niagara, who had really come to hold intercourse with the disloyal group among the Democrats, were "two ambassadors" from the Confederacy seeking an audience of Lincoln. He wrote to Lincoln, begging him to receive them. Lincoln caused Greeley to go to Niagara and see the supposed ambassadors himself. He gave him written authority to bring to him any person with proper credentials, provided, as he made plain in terms that perhaps were blunt, that the basis of any negotiation should include the recognition of the Union and the abolition of slavery. The persons whom Greeley saw had no authority to treat about anything. Greeley in his irritation now urged Lincoln to convey to Jefferson Davis through these mysterious men his readiness to receive them if they were accredited. In other words, the North was to begin suing for peace—a thing clearly unwise, which Lincoln refused. Greeley now involved Lincoln in a tangled controversy to which he gave such a turn that, unless Lincoln would publish the most passionately pacific of Greeley's letters, to the great discouragement of the public with whom Greeley counted, he must himself keep silent on what had passed. He elected to keep silent while Greeley in his paper criticised him as the person responsible for the continuance of senseless bloodshed. This was publicly harmful; and, as for its private bearing, the reputation of obstinate blood-thirstiness was certain to be painful to Lincoln.

The history of Lincoln's Cabinet has a bearing upon what is to follow. He ruled his Ministers with undisputed authority, talked with them collectively upon the easiest terms, spoke to them as a headmaster to his school when they caballed against one another, kept them in some sort of unison in a manner which astonished all who knew them. Cameron had had to retire early; so did the little-known Caleb Smith, who was succeeded in his unimportant office as Secretary of the Interior by a Mr. Usher, who seems to have been well chosen. Bates, the Attorney-General, retired, weary of his work, towards the end of 1864, and Lincoln had the keen pleasure of appointing James Speed, the brother of that unforgotten and greatly honoured friend whom he honoured the more for his contentedness with private station. James Speed himself was in Lincoln's opinion "an honest man and a gentleman, and one of those well-poised men, not too common here, who are not spoiled by a big office."

Blair might be regarded as a delightful, or equally as an intolerable man. He attacked all manner of people causelessly and violently, and earned implacable dislike from the Radicals In his party. Then he frankly asked Lincoln to dismiss him whenever it was convenient. There came a time when Lincoln's re-election was in great peril, and he might, it was urged, have made it sure by dismissing Blair. It is significant that Lincoln then refused to promote his own cause by seeming to sacrifice Blair, but later on, when his own election was fairly certain, but a greater degree of unity in the Republican party was to be gained, did ask Blair to go; (Blair's quarrels, it should be added, had become more and more outrageous). So he went and immediately flung himself with enthusiasm into the advocacy of Lincoln's cause. All the men who left Lincoln remained his friends, except one who will shortly concern us. Of Lincoln's more important ministers Welles did his work for the Navy industriously but unnoted. Stanton, on the other hand, and Lincoln's relations with Stanton are the subjects of many pages of literature. These two curious and seemingly incompatible men hit upon extraordinary methods of working together. It can be seen that Lincoln's chief care in dealing with his subordinates was to give support and to give free play to any man whose heart was in his work. In countless small matters he would let Stanton disobey him and flout him openly. ("Did Stanton tell you I was a damned fool? Then I expect I must be one, for he is almost always right and generally says what he means.") But every now and then, when he cared much about his own wish, he would step in and crush Stanton flat. Crowds of applicants to Lincoln with requests of a kind that must be granted sparingly were passed on to Stanton, pleased with the President, or mystified by his sadly observing that he had not much influence with this Administration but hoped to have more with the next.

Stanton always refused them. He enjoyed doing it. Yet it seems a low trick to have thus indulged his taste for unpopularity, till one discovers that, when Stanton might have been blamed seriously and unfairly, Lincoln was very careful to shoulder the blame himself. The gist of their mutual dealings was that the hated Stanton received a thinly disguised, but quite unfailing support, and that hated or applauded, ill or well, wrong in this detail and right in that, he abode in his department and drove, and drove, and drove, and worshipped Lincoln. To Seward, who played first and last a notable part in history, and who all this time conducted foreign affairs under Lincoln without any mishap in the end, one tribute is due. When he had not a master it is said that his abilities were made useless by his egotism; yet it can be seen that, with his especial cause to be jealous of Lincoln, he could not even conceive how men let private jealousy divide them in the performance of duty.

It was otherwise with the ablest man in the Cabinet. Salmon P. Chase must really have been a good man in the days before he fell in love with his own goodness. Lincoln and the country had confidence in his management of the Treasury, and Lincoln thought more highly of his general ability than of that of any other man about him. He, for his part, distrusted and despised Lincoln. Those who read Lincoln's important letters and speeches see in him at once a great gentleman; there were but few among the really well-educated men of America who made much of his lacking some of the minor points of gentility to which most of them were born; but of these few Chase betrayed himself as one. At the beginning of 1864 Chase was putting it about that he had himself no wish to be President, but—; that of course he was loyal to Mr. Lincoln, but—; and so forth. He had, as indeed he deserved, admirers who wished he should be President, and early in the year some of them expressed this wish in a manifesto. Chase wrote to Lincoln that this was not his own doing; Lincoln replied that he himself knew as little of these things "as my friends will allow me to know." To those who spoke to him of Chase's intrigues he only said that Chase would in some ways make a very good President, and he hoped they would never have a worse President than he. The movement in favour of Chase collapsed very soon, and it evidently had no effect on Lincoln. Chase, however, was beginning to foster grievances of his own against Lincoln. These related always to appointments in the service of the Treasury. He professed a horror of party influences in appointments, and imputed corrupt motives to Lincoln in such matters. He shared the sound ideas of the later civil service reformers, though he was far too easily managed by a low class of flatterers to have been of the least use in carrying them out. Lincoln would certainly not at that crisis have permitted strife over civil service reform, but some of his admirers have probably gone too far in claiming him as a sturdy supporter of the old school who would despise the reforming idea. Letters of his much earlier betray his doubts as to the old system, and he was exactly the man who in quieter times could have improved matters with the least possible fuss. However that may be, all the tiresome circumstances of Chase's differences with him are well known, and in these instances Lincoln was clearly in the right, and Chase quarrelled only because he could not force upon him appointments that would have created fury. Once Chase was overruled and wrote his resignation. Lincoln went to him with the resignation in his hand, treated him with simple affection

light-headed section of the so-called Radicals who favoured Fremont organised for themselves a "national meeting" of some few people at which they nominated him for the Presidency. They had no chance of success, but they might have helped the Democrats by carrying off some Republican votes. Besides, there are of course men who, having started as extremists in one direction and failed, will go over to the opposite extreme rather than moderate their aims. Months later, when a Republican victory of some sort became certain, unanimity among Republicans was secured; for some passions were appeased by the resignation of Blair, and Fremont was prevailed upon to withdraw. But in the meantime the Republican party had sent its delegates to a Convention at Baltimore early in June. This Convention met in a comparatively fortunate hour. In spite of the open disaffection of small sections, the Northern people had been in good spirits about the war when Grant set out to overcome Lee. At first he was felt to be progressing pretty well, and, though the reverse at Cold Harbour had happened a few days before, the size of that mishap was not yet appreciated. Ordinary citizens, called upon now and then to decide a broad and grave issue, often judge with greater calm than is possible to any but the best of the politicians and the journalists. Indeed, some serious politicians had been anxious to postpone the Convention, justly fearing that these ignorant delegates were not yet imbued with that contempt for Lincoln which they had worked up among themselves. At the Baltimore Convention the delegates of one State wanted Grant, but the nomination of Lincoln was immediate and almost unanimous. This same Convention declared for a Constitutional Amendment to abolish slavery. Lincoln would say nothing as to the choice of a candidate for the Vice-Presidency. He was right, but the result was most unhappy in the end. The Convention chose Andrew Johnson. Johnson, whom Lincoln could hardly endure, began life as a journeyman tailor. He had raised himself like Lincoln, and had performed a great part in rallying the Unionists of Tennessee. But—not to dwell upon the fact that he was drunk when he was sworn in as Vice-President—his political creed was that of bitter class-hatred, and his character degenerated into a weak and brutal obstinacy. This man was to succeed Lincoln. Lincoln, in his letter to accept the nomination, wrote modestly, refusing to take the decision of the Convention as a tribute to his peculiar fitness for his post, but was "reminded in this connection of a story of an old Dutch farmer, who remarked to a companion that it was not best to swap horses when crossing a stream."

It remained possible that the dissatisfied Republicans would revolt later and put another champion in the field. But now attention turned to the Democrats. Their Convention was to meet at Chicago at the end of August, and in the interval the North entered upon the period of deepest mental depression that came to it during the war. It is startling to learn now that in the course of that year, when the Confederacy lay like a nut in the nutcrackers, when the crushing of its resistance might indeed require a little stronger pressure than was expected, and the first splitting in its hard substance might not come on the side on which it was looked for, but when no wise man could have a doubt as to the end, the victorious people were inclined to think that the moment had come for giving in. "In this purpose to save the country and its liberties," said Lincoln, "no class of people seem so nearly unanimous as the soldiers in the field and the sailors afloat. Do they not have the hardest of it? Who should quail while they do not?" Yet there is conclusive authority for saying that there was now more quailing in the North than there had ever been before. When the war had gone on long, checks to the course of victory shook the nerves of people at home more than crushing defeats had shaken them in the first two years of the struggle, and men who would have wrapped the word "surrender" in periphrasis went about with surrender in their hearts. Thus the two months that went before the great rally of the Democrats at Chicago were months of good omen for a party which, however little the many honourable men in its ranks were willing to face the fact, must base its only hope upon the weakening of the national will. For public attention was turned away from other fields of war and fixed upon the Army of the Potomac. Sherman drove back Johnston, and routed Hood; Farragut at Mobile enriched the annals of the sea; but what told upon the imagination of the North was that Grant's earlier progress was followed by the definite failure of his original enterprise against Lee's army, by Northern defeats on the

Shenandoah and an actual dash by the South against Washington, by the further failure of Grant's first assault upon Petersburg, and by hideous losses and some demoralisation in his army. The candidate that the Democrats would put forward and the general principle of their political strategy were well known many weeks before their Convention met; and the Republicans already despaired of defeating them. In the Chicago Convention there were men, apparently less reputable in character than their frank attitude suggests, who were outspoken against the war; their leader was Vallandigham. There were men who spoke boldly for the war, but more boldly against emancipation and the faults of the Government; their leader was Seymour, talking with the accent of dignity and of patriotism. Seymour, for the war, presided over the Convention; Vallandigham, against the war, was the master spirit in its debates. It was hard for such men, with any saving of conscience, to combine. The mode of combination which they discovered is memorable in the history of faction. First they adopted a platform which meant peace; then they adopted a candidate intended to symbolise successful war. They resolved "that this Convention does explicitly declare, as the sense of the American people, that after four years of failure to restore the Union by the experiment of war . . . justice, humanity, liberty, and the public welfare demand that immediate efforts be made for a cessation of hostilities, with a view to an ultimate convention of the States or other peaceable means, to the end that at the earliest practicable moment peace may be restored on the basis of the Federal Union of the States." The fallacy which named the Union as the end while demanding as a means the immediate cessation of hostilities needs no demonstration. The resolution was thus translated: "Resolved that the war is a failure"; and the translation had that trenchant accuracy which is often found in American popular epigram. The candidate chosen was McClellan; McClellan in set terms repudiated the resolution that the war was a failure, and then accepted the candidature. He meant no harm to the cause of the Union, but he meant no definite and clearly conceived good. Electors might now vote Democratic because the party was peaceful or because the candidate was a warrior. The turn of fortune was about to arrest this combination in the really formidable progress of its crawling approach to power. Perhaps it was not only, as contemporary observers thought, events in the field that began within a few days to make havoc with the schemes of McClellan and his managers. Perhaps if the patience of the North had been tried a little longer the sense of the people would still have recoiled from the policy of the Democrats, which had now been defined in hard outline. As a matter of fact it was only in the months while the Chicago Convention was still impending and for a few days or weeks after it had actually taken place that the panic of the Republicans lasted. But during that time the alarm among them was very great, whether it was wholly due to the discouragement of the people about the war or originated among the leaders and was communicated to their flock. Sagacious party men reported from their own neighbourhoods that there was no chance of winning the election. In one quarter or another there was talk of setting aside Lincoln and compelling Grant to be a candidate. About August 12 Lincoln was told by Thurlow Weed, the greatest of party managers, that his election was hopeless. Ten days later he received the same assurance from the central Republican Committee through their chairman, Raymond, together with the advice that he should make overtures for peace.

Supposing that in the following November McClellan should have been elected, and that in the following March he should have come into office with the war unfinished, it seems now hardly credible that he would have returned to slavery, or at least disbanded without protection the 150,000 negroes who were now serving the North. Lincoln, however, seriously believed that this was the course to which McClellan's principles and those of his party committed him, and that (policy and honour apart) this would have been for military reasons fatal. McClellan had repudiated the Peace Resolution, but his followers and his character were to be reckoned with rather than his words, and indeed his honest principles committed him deeply to some attempt to reverse Lincoln's policy as to slavery, and he clearly must have been driven into negotiations with the South. The confusion which must inevitably be created by attempts to satisfy the South, when it was in no humour of moderation, and by the fury which yielding would have provoked in half the people of the North, was well and tersely described by Grant in a letter to a friend, which that friend published in support of Lincoln. At a fair at Philadelphia for the help of the wounded Lincoln said: "We accepted this war; we did not begin it. We accepted it for an object, and when that object is accomplished the war will end, and I hope to God that it will never end until that object is accomplished." Whatever the real mind of McClellan and of the average Democrat may have been, it was not this; and the posterity of Mr. Facing-both-ways may succeed in an election, but never in war or the making of lasting peace.

Lincoln looked forward with happiness, after he was actually re-elected, to the quieter pursuits of private life which might await him in four years' time. He looked forward not less happily to a period of peace administration first, and there can be no doubt that he would have prized as much as any man the highest honour that his countrymen could bestow, a second election to the Presidency. But, even in a smaller man who had passed through such an experience as he had and was not warped by power, these personal wishes might well have been merged in concern for the cause in hand. There is everything to indicate that they were completely so in his case. A President cannot wisely do much directly to promote his own re-election, but he appears to have done singularly little. At the beginning of 1864, when the end of the war seemed near, and the election of a Republican probable, he may well have thought that he would be the Republican candidate, but he had faced the possible choice of Chase very placidly, and of Grant he said, "If he takes Richmond let him have the Presidency." It was another matter when the war again seemed likely to drag on and a Democratic President might come in before the end of it. An editor who visited the over-burdened President in August told him that he needed some weeks of rest and seclusion. But he said, "I cannot fly from my thoughts. I do not think it is personal vanity or ambition, though I am not free from those infirmities, but I cannot but feel that the weal or woe of the nation will be decided in November. There is no proposal offered by any wing of the Democratic party but that must result in the permanent destruction of the Union." He would have been well content to make place for Grant if Grant had finished his work. But that work was delayed, and then

Lincoln became greatly troubled by the movement to force Grant, the general whom he had at last found, into politics with his work undone; for all would have been lost if McClellan had come in with the war still progressing badly. Lincoln had been invited in June to a gathering in honour of Grant, got up with the thinly disguised object of putting the general forward as his rival. He wrote, with true diplomacy: "It is impossible for me to attend. I approve nevertheless of whatever may tend to strengthen and sustain General Grant and the noble armies now under his command. He and his brave soldiers are now in the midst of their great trial, and I trust that at your meeting you will so shape your good words that they may turn to men and guns, moving to his and their support." In August he told his mind plainly to Grant's friend Eaton. He never dreamed for a moment that Grant would willingly go off into politics with the military situation still insecure, and he believed that no possible pressure could force Grant to do so; but on this latter question he wished to make himself sure; with a view to future military measures he really needed to be sure of it. Eaton saw Grant, and in the course of conversation very tactfully brought to Grant's notice the designs of his would-be friends. "We had," writes Eaton, "been talking very quietly, but Grant's reply came in an instant and with a violence for which I was not prepared. He brought his clenched fists down hard on the strap arms of his camp chair, 'They can't do it. They can't compel me to do it.' Emphatic gesture was not a strong point with Grant. 'Have you said this to the President?' I asked. 'No,' said Grant. 'I have not thought it worth while to assure the President of my opinion. I consider it as important for the cause that he should be elected as that the army should be successful in the field.'" "I told you," said Lincoln afterwards, "they could not get him to run till he had closed out the rebellion." Since the great danger was now only that McClellan would become President in March, there was but one thing to do – to try and finish the war before then. Raymond's advice in favour of negotiations with the South now came, and Lincoln's mode of replying to this has been noticed. Rumours were afloat that if McClellan won in November there would be an attempt to bring him irregularly into power at once. Lincoln let it be known that he should stay at his post at all costs till the last lawful day. On August 23, in that curious way in which deep emotion showed itself with him, he wrote a resolution upon a paper, which he folded and asked his ministers to endorse with their signatures without reading it. They all wrote their names on the back of it, ready, if that were possible, to commit themselves blindly to support of him in whatever he had resolved; a great tribute to him and to themselves. He sealed it up and put it away.

How far in this dark time the confidence of the people had departed from Lincoln no one can tell. It might be too sanguine a view of the world to suppose that they would have been proof against what may be called a conspiracy to run him down. There were certainly quarters in which the perception of his worth came soon and remained. Not all those who are poor or roughly brought up were among those plain men whose approval Lincoln desired and often expected; but at least the plain man does exist and the plain people did read Lincoln's words. The soldiers of the armies in the East by this time knew Lincoln well, and there were by now, as we shall see, in every part of the North, honest parents who had gone to Washington, and entered the White House very sad, and came out very happy, and taken their report of him home. No less could there be found, among those to whom America had given the greatest advantages that birth and upbringing can offer, families in which, when Lincoln died, a daughter could write to her father as Lady Harcourt (then Miss Lily Motley) wrote: "I echo your 'thank God' that we always appreciated him before he was taken from us." But if we look at the political world, we find indeed noble exceptions such as that of Charles Sumner among those who had been honestly perplexed by Lincoln's attitude on slavery; we have to allow for the feelings of some good State Governor who had come to him with a tiresome but serious proposition and been adroitly parried with an untactful and coarse apologue; yet it remains to be said that a thick veil, woven of self-conceit and half-education, blinded most politicians to any rare quality in Lincoln, and blinded them to what was due in decency to any man discharging his task. The evidence collected by Mr. Rhodes as to the tone prevailing in 1864 at Washington and among those in touch with Washington suggests that strictly political society was on the average as poor in brain and heart as the court of the most decadent European monarchy. It presents a stern picture of the isolation, on one side at least, in which Lincoln had to live and work.

A little before this crowning period of Lincoln's career Walt Whitman described him as a man in the streets of Washington could see him, if he chose. He has been speaking of the cavalry escort which the President's advisers insisted should go clanking about with him. "The party," he continues, "makes no great show in uniform or horses. Mr. Lincoln on the saddle generally rides a good-sized, easy-going grey horse, is dressed in plain black, somewhat rusty and dusty, and looks about as ordinary in attire, etc., as the commonest man. The entirely unornamental _cortege_ arouses no sensation; only some curious stranger stops and gazes. I see very plainly Abraham Lincoln's dark brown face, with the deep-cut lines, the eyes always to me with a deep latent sadness in the expression. We have got so that we exchange bows, and very cordial ones. Sometimes the President goes and comes in an open barouche" (not, the poet intimates, a very smart turn-out). "Sometimes one of his sons, a boy of ten or twelve, accompanies him, riding at his right on a pony. They passed me once very close, and I saw the President in the face fully as they were moving slowly, and his look, though abstracted, happened to be directed steadily in my eye. He bowed and smiled, but far beneath his smile I noticed well the expression I have alluded to. None of the artists or pictures has caught the deep though subtle and indirect expression of this man's face. There is something else there. One of the great portrait painters of two or three centuries ago is needed."

The little boy on the pony was Thomas, called "Tad," a constant companion of his father's little leisure, now dead. An elder boy, Robert, has lived to be welcomed as Ambassador in this country, and was at this time a student at Harvard. Willie, a clever and lovably mischievous child, "the chartered libertine of the White House" for a little while, had died at the age of twelve in the early days of 1862, when his father was getting so impatient to stir McClellan into action. These and a son who had long before died in infancy were the only children of Mr. and Mrs. Lincoln. Little has been made public concerning them, but enough to convey the impression of a wise and tender father, trusted by his children and delighting in them. John Nicolay, his loyal and capable secretary, and the delightful John Hay must be reckoned on the cheerful side—for there was one—of Lincoln's daily life. The life of the home at the White House, and sometimes in summer at the "Soldiers' Home" near Washington, was simple, and in his own case (not in that of his guests) regardless of the time, sufficiency, or quality of meals. He cannot have given people much trouble, but he gave some to the guard who watched him, themselves keenly watched by Stanton; for he loved, if he could, to walk alone from his midnight conferences at the War Department to the White House or the Soldiers' Home. The barest history of the events with which he dealt is proof enough of long and hard and anxious working days, which continued with hardly a break through four years. In that history many a complication has here been barely glanced at or clean left out; in this year, for example, the difficulty about France and Mexico and the failure of the very estimable Banks in Texas have been but briefly noted. And there must be remembered, in addition, the duty of a President to be accessible to all people, a duty which Lincoln especially strove to fulfil.

Apart from formal receptions, the stream of callers on him must have given Lincoln many compensations for its huge monotony. Very odd, and sometimes attractive, samples of human nature would come under his keen eye. Now and then a visitor came neither with a troublesome request, nor for form's sake or for curiosity, but in simple honesty to pay a tribute of loyalty or speak a word of good cheer which Lincoln received with unfeigned gratitude. Farmers and back-country folk, of the type he could best talk with, came and had more time than he ought to have spared bestowed on them. At long intervals there came a friend of very different days. Some ingenious men, for instance, fitted out Dennis Hanks in a new suit of clothes and sent him as their ambassador to plead for certain political offenders. It is much to be feared that they were more successful than they deserved, though Stanton intervened and Dennis, when he had seen him, favoured his old companion, the President, with advice to dismiss that minister. But the immense variety of puzzling requests to be dealt with in such interviews must have made heavy demands upon a conscientious and a kind man, especially if his conscience and his kindness were, in small matters, sometimes at variance. Lincoln sent a multitude away with that feeling, so grateful to poor people, that at least they had received such hearing as it was possible to give them; and in dealing with the applications which imposed the greatest strain on himself he made an ineffaceable impression upon the memory of his countrymen.

The American soldier did not take naturally to discipline. Death sentences, chiefly for desertion or for sleeping or other negligence on the part of sentries, were continually being passed by courts-martial. In some cases or at some period these used to come before the President on a stated day of the week, of which Lincoln would often speak with horror. He was continually being appealed to in relation to such sentences by the father or mother of the culprit, or some friend. At one time, it may be, he was too ready with pardon; "You do not know," he said, "how hard it is to let a human being die, when you feel that a stroke of your pen will save him." Butler used to write to him that he was destroying the discipline of the army. A letter of his to Meade shows clearly that, later at least, he did not wish to exercise a merely cheap and inconsiderate mercy. The import of the numberless pardon stories really is that he would spare himself no trouble to enquire, and to intervene wherever he could rightly give scope to his longing for clemency. A Congressman might force his way into his bedroom in the middle of the night, rouse him from his sleep to bring to his notice extenuating facts that had been overlooked, and receive the decision, "Well, I don't see that it will do him any good to be shot." It is related that William Scott, a lad from a farm in Vermont, after a tremendous march in the Peninsula campaign, volunteered to do double guard duty to spare a sick comrade, slept at his post, was caught, and was under sentence of death, when the President came to the army and heard of him. The President visited him, chatted about his home, looked at his mother's photograph, and so forth. Then he laid his hands on the boy's shoulders and said with a trembling voice, "My boy, you are not going to be shot. I believe you when you tell me that you could not keep awake. I am going to trust you and send you back to the regiment. But I have been put to a great deal of trouble on your account. . . . Now what

I want to know is, how are you going to pay my bill?" Scott told afterwards how difficult it was to think, when his fixed expectation of death was suddenly changed; but how he managed to master himself, thank Mr. Lincoln and reckon up how, with his pay and what his parents could raise by mortgage on their farm and some help from his comrades, he might pay the bill if it were not more than five or six hundred dollars. "But it is a great deal more than that," said the President. "My bill is a very large one. Your friends cannot pay it, nor your bounty, nor the farm, nor all your comrades. There is only one man in the world who can pay it, and his name is William Scott. If from this day William Scott does his duty, so that, when he comes to die, he can look me in the face as he does now and say, 'I have kept my promise and I have done my duty as a soldier,' then my debt will be paid. Will you make the promise and try to keep it?" And William Scott did promise; and, not very long after, he was desperately wounded, and he died, but not before he could send a message to the President that he had tried to be a good soldier, and would have paid his debt in full if he had lived, and that he died thinking of Lincoln's kind face and thanking him for the chance he gave him to fall like a soldier in battle. If the story is not true—and there is no reason whatever to doubt it—still it is a remarkable man of whom people spin yarns of that kind.

When Lincoln's strength became visibly tried friends often sought to persuade him to spare himself the needless, and to him very often harrowing, labour of incessant interviews. They never succeeded. Lincoln told them he could not forget what he himself would feel in the place of the many poor souls who came to him desiring so little and with so little to get. But he owned to the severity of the strain. He was not too sensitive to the ridicule and reproach that surrounded him. "Give yourself no uneasiness," he had once said to some one who had sympathised with him over some such annoyance, "I have endured a great deal of ridicule without much malice, and have received a great deal of kindness not quite free from ridicule. I am used to it." But the gentle nature that such words express, and that made itself deeply felt by those that were nearest him, cannot but have suffered from want of appreciation. With all this added to the larger cares, which before the closing phases of the war opened had become so intense, Lincoln must have been taxed near to the limit of what men have endured without loss of judgment, or loss of courage or loss of ordinary human feeling. There is no sign that any of these things happened to him; the study of his record rather shows a steady ripening of mind and character to the end. It has been seen how throughout his previous life the melancholy of his temperament impressed those who had the opportunity of observing it. A colleague of his at the Illinois bar has told how on circuit he sometimes came down in the morning and found Lincoln sitting alone over the embers of the fire, where he had sat all night in sad meditation, after an evening of jest apparently none the less hilarious for his total abstinence. There was no scope for this brooding now, and in a sense the time of his severest trial cannot have been the saddest time of Lincoln's life. It must have been a cause not of added depression but of added strength that he had long been accustomed to face the sternest aspect of the world. He had within his own mind two resources, often, perhaps normally, associated together, but seldom so fully combined as with him. In his most intimate circle he would draw upon his stores of poetry, particularly of tragedy; often, for instance, he would recite such speeches as Richard II.'s:

"For God's sake let us sit upon the ground

And tell sad stories of the death of kings.

. . . . . All murdered."

Slighter acquaintances saw, day by day, another element in his thoughts, the companion to this; for the hardly interrupted play of humour in which he found relief continued to help him to the end. Whatever there was in it either of mannerism or of coarseness, no one can grudge it him; it is an oddity which endears. The humour of real life fades in reproduction, but Lincoln's, there is no doubt was a vein of genuine comedy, deep, rich, and unsoured, of a larger human quality than marks the brilliant works of literary American humorists. It was, like the comedy of Shakespeare, plainly if unaccountably akin with the graver and grander strain of thought and feeling that inspired the greatest of his speeches. Physically his splendid health does not seem to have been impaired beyond recovery. But it was manifestly near to breaking; and the "deep-cut lines" were cut still deeper, and the long legs were always cold.

The cloud over the North passed very suddenly. The North indeed paid the penalty of a nation which is spared the full strain of a war at the first, and begins to discover its seriousness when the hope of easy victory has been many times dashed down. It has been necessary to dwell upon the despondency which at one time prevailed; but it would be hard to rate too highly the military difficulty of the conquest undertaken by the North, or the trial involved to human nature by perseverance in such a task. If the depression during the summer was excessive, as it clearly was, at least the recovery which followed was fully adequate to the occasion which produced it. On September 2 Sherman telegraphed, "Atlanta is ours and fairly won." The strategic importance of earlier successes may have been greater, but the most ignorant man who looked at a map could see what it signified that the North could occupy an important city in the heart of Georgia. Then they recalled Farragut's victory of a month before. Then there followed, close to Washington, putting an end to a continual menace, stirring and picturesquely brilliant beyond other incidents of the war, Sheridan's repeated victories in the Shenandoah Valley. The war which had been "voted a failure" was evidently not a failure. At the same time men of high character conducted a vigorous campaign of speeches for Lincoln. General Schurz, the German revolutionary Liberal, who lived to tell Bismarck at his table that he still preferred democracy to his amused host's method of government, sacrificed his command in the Army—for Lincoln told him it could not be restored—to speak for Lincoln. Even Chase was carried away, and after months of insidious detraction, went for Lincoln on the stump. In the elections in November Lincoln was elected by an enormous popular majority, giving him 212 out of the 233 votes in the electoral college, where in form the election is made. Three Northern States only, one of them his native State, had gone against him. He made some little speeches to parties which came to "serenade" him; some were not very formal speeches, for, as he said, he was now too old to "care much about the mode of doing things." But one was this: "It has long been a grave question whether any Government not too strong for the liberties of its people can be strong enough to maintain its existence in great emergencies. On this point the present rebellion brought our Government to a severe test, and a Presidential election occurring in regular course during the rebellion added not a little to the strain. But we cannot have a free Government without elections; and if the rebellion could force us to forego or postpone a national election it might fairly claim to have already conquered and ruined us. But the election along with its incidental and undesirable strife has done good too. It has demonstrated that a people's Government can sustain a national election in the midst of a great civil war. Until now it has not been known to the world that this was a possibility. But the rebellion continues, and now that the election is over may not all have a common interest to reunite in a common effort to save our common country? For my own part I have striven and shall strive to avoid placing any obstacle in the way. So long as I have been here I have not willingly planted a thorn in any man's bosom. While I am duly sensible to the high compliment of a re-election, and duly grateful as I trust to Almighty God for having directed my countrymen to a right conclusion, as I think, for their good, it adds nothing to my satisfaction that any man may be disappointed by the result. May I ask those who have not differed from me to join with me in this same spirit towards those who have? And now let me close by asking three hearty cheers for our brave soldiers and seamen, and their gallant and skilful commanders."

In the Cabinet he brought out the paper that he had sealed up in the dark days of August; he reminded his ministers of how they had endorsed it unread, and he read it them. Its contents ran thus: "This morning, as for some days past, it seems exceedingly probable that this Administration will not be re-elected. Then it will be my duty to so co-operate with the President-elect as to save the Union between the election and the inauguration, as he will have secured his election on such ground that he cannot possibly save it afterwards." Lincoln explained what he had intended to do if McClellan had won. He would have gone to him and said, "General, this election shows that you are stronger, have more influence with the people of this country than I"; and he would have invited him to co-operate in saving the Union now, by using that great influence to secure from the people the willing enlistment of enough recruits. "And the general," said Seward, "would have said, 'Yes, yes'; and again the next day, when you spoke to him about it, 'Yes, yes'; and so on indefinitely, and he would have done nothing."

"Seldom in history," wrote Emerson in a letter after the election, "was so much staked upon a popular vote. I suppose never in history."

And to those Americans of all classes and in all districts of the North, who had set their hearts and were giving all they had to give to preserve the life of the nation, the political crisis of 1864 would seem to have been the most anxious moment of the war. It is impossible—it must be repeated—to guess how great the danger really was that their popular government might in the result betray the true and underlying will of the people; for in any country (and in America perhaps more than most) the average of politicians, whose voices are most loudly heard, can only in a rough and approximate fashion be representative. But there is in any case no cause for surprise that the North should at one time have trembled. Historic imagination is easily, though not one whit too deeply, moved by the heroic stand of the South. It is only after the effort to understand the light in which the task of the North has presented itself to capable soldiers, that a civilian can perceive what sustained resolution was required if, though far the stronger, it was to make its strength tell. Notwithstanding the somewhat painful impression which the political chronicle of this time at some points gives, it is the fact that the wisest Englishmen who were in those days in America and had means of observing what passed have retained a lasting sense of the constancy, under trial, of the North.

CHAPTER XII

THE END

On December 6, 1864, Lincoln sent the last of his Annual Messages to Congress. He treated as matter for oblivion the "impugning of motives and heated controversy as to the proper means of advancing the Union cause," which had played so large a part in the Presidential election and the other elections of the autumn. For, as he said, "on the distinct issue of Union or no Union the politicians have shown their instinctive knowledge that there is no diversity among the people." This was accurate as well as generous, for though many Democrats had opposed the war, none had avowed that for the sake of peace he would give up the Union. Passing then to the means by which the Union could be made to prevail he wrote: "On careful consideration of all the evidence accessible it seems to me that no attempt at negotiation with the insurgent leader could result in any good. He would accept nothing short of severance of the Union—precisely what we will not and cannot give. Between him and us the issue is distinct, simple, and inflexible. It is an issue which can only be tried by war and decided by victory. The abandonment of armed resistance to the national authority on the part of the insurgents is the only indispensable condition to ending the war on the part of the Government." To avoid a possible misunderstanding he added that not a single person who was free by the terms of the

Emancipation Proclamation or of any Act of Congress would be returned to slavery while he held the executive authority. "If the people should by whatever mode or means make it an executive duty to re-enslave such persons, another, and not I, must be their instrument to perform it." This last sentence was no meaningless flourish; the Constitutional Amendment prohibiting slavery could not be passed for some time, and might conceivably be defeated; in the meantime the Courts might possibly have declared any negro in the Southern States a slave; Lincoln's words let it be seen that they would have found themselves without an arm to enforce their decision. But in fact there was no longer an issue with the South as to abolition. Jefferson Davis had himself declared that slavery was gone, for most slaves had now freed themselves, and that he for his part troubled very little over that. There remained, then, no issue between North and South except that between Independence and Union.

On the same day that he sent his annual message Lincoln gave himself a characteristic pleasure by another communication which he sent to the Senate. Old Roger Taney of the Dred Scott case had died in October; the Senate was now requested to confirm the President's nomination of a new Chief Justice to succeed him; and the President had nominated Chase. Chase's reputation as a lawyer had seemed to fit him for the position, but the well informed declared that, in spite of some appearances on the platform for Lincoln he still kept "going around peddling his griefs in private ears and sowing dissatisfaction against Lincoln." So in spite of Lincoln's pregnant remark on this subject that he "did not believe in keeping any man under," nobody supposed that Lincoln would appoint him. Sumner and Congressman Alley of Massachusetts had indeed gone to Lincoln to urge the appointment. "We found, to our dismay," Alley relates, "that the President had heard of the bitter criticisms of Mr. Chase upon himself and his Administration. Mr. Lincoln urged many of Chase's defects, to discover, as we afterwards learned, how his objection could be answered. We were both discouraged and made up our minds that the President did not mean to appoint Mr. Chase. It really seemed too much to expect of poor human nature." One morning Alley again saw the President. "I have something to tell you that will make you happy," said Lincoln. "I have just sent Mr. Chase word that he is to be appointed Chief Justice, and you are the first man I have told of it." Alley said something natural about Lincoln's magnanimity, but was told in reply what the only real difficulty had been. Lincoln from his "convictions of duty to the Republican party and the country" had always meant to appoint Chase, subject to one doubt which he had revolved in his mind till he had settled it. This doubt was simply whether Chase, beset as he was by a craving for the Presidency which he could never obtain, would ever really turn his attention with a will to becoming the great Chief Justice that Lincoln thought he could be. Lincoln's occasional failures of tact had sometimes a noble side to them; he even thought now of writing to Chase and telling him with simple seriousness where he felt his temptation lay, and he with difficulty came to see that this attempt at brotherly frankness would be misconstrued by a suspicious and jealous man. Charles Sumner, Chase's advocate on this occasion, was all this time the most weighty and the most pronounced of those Radicals who were beginning to press for unrestricted negro suffrage in the South and in general for a hard and inelastic scheme of "reconstruction," which they would have imposed on the conquered South without an attempt to conciliate the feeling of the vanquished or to invite their co-operation in building up the new order. He was thus the chief opponent of that more tentative, but as is now seen, more liberal and more practical policy which lay very close to Lincoln's heart; enough has been said of him to suggest too that this grave person, bereft of any glimmering of fun, was in one sense no congenial companion for Lincoln. But he was stainlessly unselfish and sincere, and he was the politician above all others in Washington with whom Lincoln most gladly and most successfully maintained easy social intercourse. And, to please him in little ways, Lincoln would disentangle his long frame from the "grotesque position of comfort" into which he had twisted it in talk with some other friend, and would assume in an instant a courtly demeanour when Sumner was about to enter his room.

On January 31, 1865, the resolution earlier passed by the Senate for a Constitutional Amendment to prohibit slavery was passed by the House of Representatives, as Lincoln had eagerly desired, so that the requisite voting of three quarters of the States in its favour could now begin. Before that time the Confederate Congress had, on March 13, 1865, closed its last, most anxious and distracted session by passing an Act for the enlistment of negro volunteers, who were to become free on enlistment. As a military measure it was belated and inoperative, but nothing could more eloquently have marked the practical extinction of slavery which the war had wrought than the consent of Southern legislators to convert the remaining slaves into soldiers.

The military operations of 1865 had proceeded but a very little way when the sense of what they portended was felt among the Southern leaders in Richmond. The fall of that capital itself might be hastened or be delayed; Lee's army if it escaped from Richmond might prolong resistance for a shorter or for a longer time, but Sherman's march to the sea, and the far harder achievements of the same kind which he was now beginning, made the South feel, as he knew it would feel, that not a port, not an arsenal, not a railway, not a corn district of the South lay any longer beyond the striking range of the North. Congressmen and public officials in Richmond knew that the people of the South now longed for peace and that the authority of the Confederacy was gone.

They beset Jefferson Davis with demands that he should start negotiations. But none of them had determined what price they would pay for peace; and there was not among them any will that could really withstand their President. In one point indeed Jefferson Davis did wisely yield. On February 9, 1865, he consented to make Lee General-in-Chief of all the Southern armies. This belated delegation of larger authority to Lee had certain military results, but no political result whatever. Lee could have been the dictator of the Confederacy if he had chosen, and no one then or since would have blamed him; but it was not in his mind to do anything but his duty as a soldier. The best beloved and most memorable by far of all the men who served that lost cause, he had done nothing to bring about secession at the beginning, nor now did he do anything but conform to the wishes of his political chief. As for that chief, Lincoln had interpreted Davis' simple position quite rightly. Having once embraced the cause of Southern independence and taken the oath as chief magistrate of an independent Confederacy, he would not yield up that cause while there was a man to obey his orders. Whether this attitude should be set down, as it usually has been set down, to a diseased pride or to a very real heroism on his part, he never faced the truth that the situation was desperate and the spirit of his people daunted at last. But it is probable that just like Lincoln he was ready that those who were in haste to make peace should see what peace involved; and it is probable too that, in his terrible position, he deluded himself with some vague and vain hopes as to the attitude of the North. Lincoln on the other hand would not enter into any proceedings in which the secession of the South was treated otherwise than as a rebellion which must cease; but this did not absolutely compel him to refuse every sort of informal communication with influential men in the South, which might help them to see where they stood and from which he too might learn something.

Old Mr. Francis Blair, the father of Lincoln's late Postmaster-General, was the last of the honest peace-makers whom Lincoln had allowed to see things for themselves by meeting Jefferson Davis. His visit took place in January, 1865, and from his determination to be a go-between and the curious and difficult position in which Lincoln and Davis both stood in this respect an odd result arose. The Confederate Vice-President Stephens, who had preached peace in the autumn without a quarrel with Davis, and two other Southern leaders presented themselves at Grant's headquarters with the pathetic misrepresentation that they were sent by Davis on a mission which Lincoln had undertaken to receive. What they could show was authority from Davis to negotiate with Lincoln on the footing of the independence of the Confederacy, and a politely turned intimation from Lincoln that he would at any time receive persons informally sent to talk with a view to the surrender of the rebel armies. Grant, however, was deeply impressed with the sincerity of their desire for peace, and he entreated Lincoln to receive them.

Lincoln therefore decided to overlook the false pretence under which they came. He gave Grant strict orders not to delay his operations on this account, but he came himself with Seward and met Davis' three commissioners on a ship at Hampton Roads on February 3. He and Stephens had in old days been Whig Congressmen together, and Lincoln had once been moved to tears by a speech of Stephens. They met now as friends. Lincoln lost no time in making his position clear. The unhappy commissioners made every effort to lead him away from the plain ground he had chosen. It is evident that they and possible that Jefferson Davis had hoped that when face to face with them he would change his mind, and possibly Blair's talk had served to encourage this hope. They failed, but the conversation continued in a frank and friendly manner. Lincoln told them very freely his personal opinions as to how the North ought to treat the South when it did surrender, but was careful to point out that he could make no promise or bargain, except indeed this promise that so far as penalties for rebellion were concerned the executive power, which lay in his sole hands, would be liberally used. Slavery was discussed, and Seward told them of the Constitutional Amendment which Congress had now submitted to the people. One of the commissioners returning again to Lincoln's refusal to negotiate with armed rebels, as he considered them, cited the precedent of Charles I.'s conduct in this respect. "I do not profess," said Lincoln, "to be posted in history. On all such matters I turn you over to Seward. All I distinctly recollect about Charles I. is that he lost his head in the end." Then he broke out into simple advice to Stephens as to the action he could now pursue. He had to report to Congress afterwards that the conference had had no result. He brought home, however, a personal compliment which he valued. "I understand, then," Stephens had said, "that you regard us as rebels, who are liable to be hanged for treason." "That is so," said Lincoln. "Well," said Stephens, "we supposed that would have to be your view. But, to tell you the truth, we have none of us been much afraid of being hanged with you as President." He brought home, besides the compliment, an idea of a kind which, if he could have had his way with his friends, might have been rich in good. He had discovered how hopeless the people of the South were, and he considered whether a friendly pronouncement might not lead them more readily to surrender. He deplored the suffering in which the South might now lie plunged, and it was a fixed part of his creed that slavery was the sin not of the South but of the nation. So he spent the day after his return in drafting a joint resolution which he hoped the two Houses of Congress might pass, and a Proclamation which he would in that case issue. In these he proposed to offer to the Southern States four hundred million dollars in United States bonds, being, as he calculated the cost to the North of two hundred days of war, to be allotted among those States in proportion to the property in slaves which each had lost. One half of this sum was to be paid at once if the war ended by April 1, and the other half upon the final adoption of the Constitutional Amendment. It would have been a happy thing if the work of restoring peace could have lain with a statesman whose rare aberrations from the path of practical politics were of this kind. Yet, considering the natural passions which even in this least revengeful of civil wars could not quite be repressed, we should be judging the Congress of that day by a higher standard than we should apply in other countries if we regarded this proposal as one that could have been hopefully submitted to them. Lincoln's illusions were dispelled on the following day when he read what he had written to his Cabinet, and found that even among his own ministers not one man supported him. It would have been worse than useless to put forward his proposals and to fail. "You are all opposed to me," he said sadly; and he put his papers away. But the war had now so far progressed that it is necessary to turn back to the point at which we left it at the end of 1864.

Winter weather brought a brief pause to the operations of the armies. Sherman at Savannah was preparing to begin his northward march, a harder matter, owing to the rivers and marshes that lay in his way, than his triumphal progress from Atlanta. Efforts were made to concentrate all available forces against him at Augusta to his north-west. Making feints against Augusta on the one side, and against the city and port of Charleston on the other, he displayed the marvellous engineering capacity of his army by an advance of unlooked-for speed across the marshes to Columbia, due north of him, which is the State capital of South Carolina. He reached it on February 17, 1865. The intended concentration of the South at Augusta was broken up. The retreating Confederates set fire to great stores of cotton and the unfortunate city was burnt, a calamity for which the South, by a natural but most unjust mistake, blamed Sherman. The railway communications of Charleston were now certain to be severed; so the Confederates were forced to evacuate it, and on February 18, 1865, the North occupied the chief home of the misbegotten political ideals of the South and of its real culture and chivalry.

Admiral Porter (for age and ill-health had come upon Farragut) was ready at sea to co-operate with Sherman. Thomas' army in Tennessee had not been allowed by Grant to go into winter quarters. A part of it under Schofield was brought to Washington and there shipped for North Carolina, where, ever since Burnside's successful expedition in 1862, the Union Government had held the ports north of Wilmington. Wilmington itself was the only port left to the South, and Richmond had now come to depend largely on the precarious and costly supplies which could still, notwithstanding the blockade, be run into that harbour. At the end of December, Butler, acting in flagrant disobedience to Grant, had achieved his crowning failure in a joint expedition with Porter against Wilmington. But Porter was not discouraged, nor was Grant, who from beginning to end of his career had worked well together with the Navy. On February 8, Porter, this time supported by an energetic general, Terry, effected a brilliant capture of Fort Fisher at the mouth of Wilmington harbour. The port was closed to the South. On the 22nd, the city itself fell to Schofield, and Sherman had now this sea base at hand if he needed it.

Meanwhile Grant's entrenchments on the east of Richmond and Petersburg were still extending southward, and Lee's defences had been stretched till they covered nearly forty miles. Grant's lines now cut the principal railway southward from the huge fortress, and he was able effectually to interrupt communication by road to the southwest. There could be little doubt that Richmond would fall soon, and the real question was coming to be whether Lee and his army could escape from Richmond and still carry on the war.

The appointment of Lee as General-in-Chief was not too late to bear one consequence which may have prolonged the war a little. Joseph Johnston, whose ability in a campaign of constant retirement before overwhelming force had been respected and redoubted by Sherman, had been discarded by Davis in the previous July. He was now put in command of the forces which it was hoped to concentrate against Sherman, with a view to holding up his northward advance and preventing him from joining hands with Grant before Richmond. There were altogether about 89,000 Confederate troops scattered in the Carolinas, Georgia, and Florida, and there would be about the same number under Sherman when Schofield in North Carolina could join him, but the number which Johnston could now collect together seems never to have exceeded 33,000. It was Sherman's task by the rapidity of his movements to prevent a very formidable concentration against him. Johnston on the other hand must hinder if he could Sherman's junction with Schofield.

Just before that junction took place he narrowly missed dealing a considerable blow to Sherman's army at the battle of Bentonville in the heart of North Carolina, but had in the end to withdraw within an entrenched position where Sherman would not attack him, but which upon the arrival of Schofield he was forced to abandon. On March 23, 1865, Sherman took possession of the town and railway junction of Goldsborough between Raleigh and New Berne. From Savannah to Goldsborough he had led his army 425 miles in fifty days, amid disadvantages of ground and of weather which had called forth both extraordinary endurance and mechanical skill on the part of his men. He lay now 140 miles south of Petersburg by the railway. The port of New Berne to the east of him on the estuary of the Neuse gave him a sure base of supplies, and would enable him quickly to move his army by sea to Petersburg and Richmond if Grant should so decide. The direction in which Johnston would now fall back lay inland up the Neuse Valley, also along a railway, towards Greensborough, some 150 miles south-west of Petersburg; Greensborough was connected by another railway with Petersburg and Richmond, and along this line Lee might attempt to retire and join him.

All this time whatever designs Lee had of leaving Richmond were suspended because the roads in that weather were too bad for his transport; and, while of necessity he waited, his possible openings narrowed. Philip Sheridan had now received the coveted rank of Major-General, which McClellan had resigned on the day on which he was defeated for the Presidency. The North delighted to find in his achievements the dashing quality which appeals to civilian imagination, and Grant now had in him, as well as in Sherman, a lieutenant who would faithfully make his chief's purposes his own, and who would execute them with independent decision. The cold, in which his horses suffered, had driven Sheridan into winter quarters, but on February 27 he was able to start up the Shenandoah Valley again with 10,000 cavalry. Most of the Confederate cavalry under Early had now been dispersed, mainly for want of forage in the desolated valley; the rest were now dispersed by Sheridan, and the greater part of Early's small force of infantry with all his artillery were captured. There was a garrison in Lynchburg, 80 or 90 miles west of Richmond, which though strong enough to prevent Sheridan's cavalry from capturing that place was not otherwise of account; but there was no Confederate force in the field except Johnston's men near enough to co-operate with Lee; only some small and distant armies, hundreds of miles away with the railway communication between them and the East destroyed. Sheridan now broke up the railway and canal communication on the north-west side of Richmond. He was to have gone on south and eventually joined Sherman if he could; but, finding himself stopped for the time by floods in the upper valley of the James, he rode past the north of Richmond, and on March 19 joined Grant, to put his cavalry and brains at his service when Grant judged that the moment for his final effort had come.

On March 4, 1865, Abraham Lincoln took office for the second time as President of the United. States. There was one new and striking feature in the simple ceremonial, the presence of a battalion of negro troops in his escort. This time, though he would say no sanguine word, it cannot have been a long continuance of war that filled his thoughts, but the scarcely less difficult though far happier task of restoring the fabric of peaceful society in the conquered South. His difficulties were now likely to come from the North no less than the South. Tentative proposals which he had once or twice made suggest the spirit in which he would have felt his way along this new path. In the Inaugural address which he now delivered that spirit is none the less perceptible because he spoke of the past. The little speech at Gettysburg, with its singular perfection of form, and the "Second Inaugural" are the chief outstanding examples of his peculiar oratorical power. The comparative rank of his oratory need not be discussed, for at any rate it was individual and unlike that of most other great speakers in history, though perhaps more like that of some great speeches in drama.

But there is a point of some moment in which the Second Inaugural does invite a comment, and a comment which should be quite explicit. Probably no other speech of a modern statesman uses so unreservedly the language of intense religious feeling. The occasion made it natural; neither the thought nor the words are in any way conventional; no sensible reader now could entertain a suspicion that the orator spoke to the heart of the people but did not speak from his own heart. But an old Illinois attorney, who thought he knew the real Lincoln behind the President, might have wondered whether the real Lincoln spoke here.

For Lincoln's religion, like everything else in his character, became, when he was famous, a stock subject of discussion among his old associates. Many said "he was a Christian but did not know it." Some hinted, with an air of great sagacity, that "so far from his being a Christian or a religious man, the less said about it the better." In early manhood he broke away for ever from the scheme of Christian theology which was probably more or less common to the very various Churches which surrounded him. He had avowed this sweeping denial with a freedom which pained some friends, perhaps rather by its rashness than by its impiety, and he was apt to regard the procedure of theologians as a blasphemous twisting of the words of Christ. He rejected that belief in miracles and in the literally inspired accuracy of the Bible narrative which was no doubt held as fundamental by all these Churches. He rejected no less any attempt to substitute for this foundation the belief in any priestly authority or in the authority of any formal and earthly society called the Church. With this total independence of the expressed creeds of his neighbours he still went and took his boys to Presbyterian public worship – their mother was an Episcopalian and his own parents had been Baptists. He loved the Bible and knew it intimately – he is said also by the way to have stored in his memory a large number of hymns. In the year before his death he wrote to Speed:

"I am profitably engaged in reading the Bible. Take all of this book upon reason that you can and the balance upon faith and you will live and die a better man." It was not so much the Old Testament as the New Testament and what he called "the true spirit of Christ" that he loved especially, and took with all possible seriousness as the rule of life. His theology, in the narrower sense, may be said to have been limited to an intense belief in a vast and over-ruling Providence – the lighter forms of superstitious feelings which he is known to have had in common with most frontiersmen were apparently of no importance in his life. And this Providence, darkly spoken of, was certainly conceived by him as intimately and kindly related to his own life. In his Presidential candidature, when he owned to some one that the opposition of clergymen hurt him deeply, he is said to have confessed to being no Christian and to have continued, "I know that there is a God and that He hates injustice and slavery. I see the storm coming and I know that His hand is in it. If He has a place and work for me, and I think He has, I believe I am ready. I am nothing, but truth is everything; I know I am right because I know that liberty is right, for Christ teaches it, and Christ is God. I have told them that a house divided against itself cannot stand, and Christ and reason say the same, and they will find it so." When old acquaintances said that he had no religion they based their opinion on such remarks as that the God, of whom he had just been speaking solemnly, was "not a person." It would be unprofitable to enquire what he, and many others, meant by this expression, but, later at any rate, this "impersonal" power was one with which he could hold commune. His robust intellect, impatient of unproved assertion, was unlikely to rest in the common assumption that things dimly seen may be treated as not being there. So humorous a man was also unlikely to be too conceited to say his prayers. At any rate he said them; said them intently; valued the fact that others prayed for him and for the nation; and, as in official Proclamations (concerning days of national religious observance) he could wield, like no other modern writer, the language of the Prayer Book, so he would speak of prayer without the smallest embarrassment in talk with a general or a statesman. It is possible that this was a development of later years. Lincoln did not, like most of us, arrest his growth. To Mrs. Lincoln it seemed that with the death of their child, Willie, a change came over his whole religious outlook. It well might; and since that grief, which came while his troubles were beginning, much else had come to Lincoln; and now through four years of unsurpassed trial his capacity had steadily grown, and his delicate fairness, his pitifulness, his patience, his modesty had grown therewith. Here is one of the few speeches ever delivered by a great man at the crisis of his fate on the sort of occasion which a tragedian telling his story would have devised for him. This man had stood alone in the dark. He had done justice; he had loved mercy; he had walked humbly with his God. The reader to whom religious utterance makes little appeal will not suppose that his imaginative words stand for no real experience. The reader whose piety knows no questions will not be pained to think that this man had professed no faith.

He said, "Fellow Countrymen: At this second appearance to take the oath of the Presidential office, there is less occasion for an extended address than there was at the first. Then a statement, somewhat in detail, of a course to be pursued, seemed fitting and proper. Now, at the expiration of four years, during which public declarations have been constantly called forth on every point and phase of the great contest which still absorbs the energies and engrosses the attention of the nation, little that is new could be presented. The progress of our arms, upon which all else chiefly depends, is as well known to the public as to myself; and it is, I trust, reasonably satisfactory and encouraging to all. With high hope for the future, no prediction in regard to it is ventured.

"On the occasion corresponding to this four years ago, all thoughts were anxiously directed to an impending civil war. All dreaded it—all sought to avert it. While the inaugural address was being delivered from this place, devoted altogether to saving the Union without war, insurgent agents were in the city seeking to destroy it without war—seeking to dissolve the Union and divide effects, by negotiation. Both parties deprecated war; but one of them would make war rather than let the nation survive; and the other would accept war rather than let it perish. And the war came.

"One-eighth of the whole population were coloured slaves, not distributed generally over the Union, but localised in the Southern part of it. These slaves constituted a peculiar and powerful interest. All knew that this interest was, somehow, the cause of the war. To strengthen, perpetuate, and extend this interest was the object for which the insurgents would rend the Union, even by war; while the Government claimed no right to do more than to restrict the territorial enlargement of it. Neither party expected for the war the magnitude or the duration which it has already attained. Neither expected that the cause of the conflict might cease with, or even before, the conflict itself should cease. Each looked for an easier triumph, and a result less fundamental and astounding. Both read the same Bible, and pray to the same God; and each invokes His aid against the other. It may seem strange that any men should dare to ask a just God's assistance in wringing their bread from the sweat of other men's faces; but let us judge not, that we be not judged. The prayers of both could not be answered—that of neither has been answered fully. The Almighty has His own purposes. 'Woe unto the world because of offenses! for it must needs be that offenses come; but woe to that man by whom the offense cometh.' If we shall suppose that American slavery is one of those offenses, which, in the providence of God, must needs come, but which, having continued through His appointed time, He now wills to remove, and that He gives to both North and South this terrible war, as the woe due to those by whom the offense came, shall we discern therein any departure from those divine attributes which the believers in a living God always ascribe to Him? Fondly do we hope—fervently do we pray—that this mighty scourge of war may speedily pass away. Yet, if God wills that it continue until all the wealth piled by the bondman's two hundred and fifty years of unrequited toil shall be sunk, and until every drop of blood drawn with the lash shall be paid with another drawn with the sword, as was said three thousand years ago, so still it must be said, 'The judgments of the Lord are true and righteous altogether.'

"With malice toward none; with charity for all; with firmness in the right, as God gives us to see the right, let us strive on to finish the work we are in; to bind up the nation's wounds, to care for him who shall have borne the battle, and for his widow, and his orphan—to do all which may achieve and cherish a just and lasting peace among ourselves, and with all nations."

Lincoln's own commentary may follow upon his speech:

"March 15, 1865. Dear Mr. Weed,—Every one likes a little compliment. Thank you for yours on my little notification speech and on the recent inaugural address. I expect the latter to wear as well as—perhaps better than—anything I have produced; but I believe it is not immediately popular. Men are not flattered by being shown that there has been a difference of purpose between the Almighty and them. To deny it however in this case is to deny that there is a God governing the world. It is a truth which I thought needed to be told, and, as whatever of humiliation there is in it falls most directly on myself, I thought others might afford for me to tell it.

"Truly yours,

"A. LINCOLN."

On March 20, 1865, a period of bright sunshine seems to have begun in Lincoln's life. Robert Lincoln had some time before finished his course at Harvard, and his father had written to Grant modestly asking him if he could suggest the way, accordant with discipline and good example, in which the young man could best see something of military life. Grant immediately had him on to his staff, with a commission as captain, and now Grant invited Lincoln to come to his headquarters for a holiday visit. There was much in it besides holiday, for Grant was rapidly maturing his plans for the great event and wanted Lincoln near.

Moreover Sheridan had just arrived, and while Lincoln was there Sherman came from Goldsborough with Admiral Porter for consultation as to Sherman's next move. Peremptory as he was in any necessary political instructions, Lincoln was now happy to say nothing of military matters, beyond expressing his earnest desire that the final overmastering of the Confederate armies should be accomplished with the least further bloodshed possible, and indulging the curiosity that any other guest might have shown. A letter home to Mrs. Lincoln betrays the interest with which he heard heavy firing quite near, which seemed to him a great battle, but did not excite those who knew. Then there were rides in the country with Grant's staff. Lincoln in his tall hat and frock coat was a marked and curious figure on a horse. He had once, by the way, insisted on riding with Butler, catechising him with remorseless chaff on engineering matters and forbidding his chief engineer to prompt him, along six miles of cheering Northern troops within easy sight and shot of the Confederate soldiers to whom his hat and coat identified him. But, however odd a figure, he impressed Grant's officers as a good and bold horseman. Then, after Sherman's arrival, there evidently was no end of talk. Sherman was at first amused by the President's anxiety as to whether his army was quite safe without him at Goldsborough; but that keen-witted soldier soon received, as he has said, an impression both of goodness and of greatness such as no other man ever gave him.

What especially remained on Sherman's and on Porter's mind was the recollection of Lincoln's over-powering desire for mercy and for conciliation with the conquered. Indeed Sherman blundered later in the terms he first accepted from Johnston; for he did not see that Lincoln's clemency for Southern leaders and desire for the welfare of the South included no mercy at all for the political principle of the Confederacy. Grant was not exposed to any such mistake, for a week or two before Lee had made overtures to him for some sort of conference and Lincoln had instantly forbidden him to confer with Lee for any purpose but that of his unconditional surrender. What, apart from the reconstruction of Southern life and institutions, was in part weighing with Lincoln was the question of punishments for rebellion. By Act of Congress the holders of high political and military office in the South were liable as traitors, and there was now talk of hanging in the North. Later events showed that a very different sentiment would make itself heard when the victory came; but Lincoln was much concerned. To some one who spoke to him of this matter he exclaimed, "What have I to do with you, ye sons of Zeruiah, that ye should this day be adversaries unto me? Shall there any man be put to death this day in Israel?" There can be no doubt that the prerogative of mercy would have been vigorously used in his hands, but he did not wish for a conflict on this matter at all; and Grant was taught, in a parable about a teetotal Irishman who forgave being served with liquor unbeknownst to himself, that zeal in capturing Jefferson Davis and his colleagues was not expected of him.

While Lincoln was at Grant's headquarters at City Point, Lee, hoping to recover the use of the roads to the south-west, endeavoured to cause a diversion of the besiegers' strength by a sortie on his east front. It failed and gave the besiegers a further point of vantage. On April 1 Sheridan was sent far round the south of Lee's lines, and in a battle at a point called Five Forks established himself in possession of the railway running due west from Petersburg. The defences were weakest on this side, and to prevent the entrance of the enemy there Lee was bound to withdraw troops from other quarters. On the two following days Grant's army delivered assaults at several points on the east side of the Petersburg defences, penetrating the outer lines and pushing on against the inner fortifications of the town.

On Sunday, April 2, Jefferson Davis received in church word

from Lee to make instant preparation for departure, as Petersburg could not be held beyond that night and Richmond must fall immediately. That night the Confederate Government left the capital, and Lee's evacuation of the fortress began the next day. Lincoln was sent for. He came by sea, and to the astonishment and alarm of the naval officers made his way at once to Richmond with entirely insufficient escort. There he strolled about, hand in hand with his little son Tad, greeted by exultant negroes, and stared at by angry or curious Confederates, while he visited the former prison of the Northern prisoners and other places of more pleasant attraction without receiving any annoyance from the inhabitants. He had an interesting talk with Campbell, formerly a Supreme Court judge, and a few weeks back one of Davis' commissioners at Hampton Roads. Campbell obtained permission to convene a meeting of the members of the Virginia Legislature with a view to speedier surrender by Lee's army. But the permission was revoked, for he somewhat clumsily mistook its terms, and, moreover, the object in view had meantime been accomplished.

Jefferson Davis was then making his way with his ministers to Johnston's army. When they arrived he and they held council with Johnston and Beauregard. He would issue a Proclamation which would raise him many soldiers and he would "whip them yet." No one answered him. At last he asked the opinion of Johnston, who bluntly undeceived him as to facts, and told him that further resistance would be a crime, and got his permission to treat with Sherman, while the fallen Confederate President escaped further south.

Lee's object was to make his way along the north side of the Appomattox River, which flows east through Petersburg to the James estuary, and at a certain point strike southwards towards Johnston's army. He fought for his escape with all his old daring and skill, while hardly less vigorous and skilful efforts were made not only to pursue, but to surround him. Grant in his pursuit sent letters of courteous entreaty that he would surrender and spare further slaughter. Northern cavalry got ahead of Lee, tearing up the railway lines he had hoped to use and blocking possible mountain passes; and his supply trains were being cut off. After a long running fight and one last fierce battle on April 6, at a place called Sailor's Creek, Lee found himself on April 9 at Appomattox Court House, some seventy miles west of Petersburg, surrounded beyond hope of escape.

On that day he and Grant with their staffs met in a neighbouring farmhouse. Those present recalled afterwards the contrast of the stately Lee and the plain, ill-dressed Grant arriving mud-splashed in his haste. Lee greeted Meade as an old acquaintance and remarked how grey he had grown with years.

Meade gracefully replied that Lee and not age was responsible for that. Grant had started "quite jubilant" on the news that Lee was ready to surrender, but in presence of "the downfall of a foe who had fought so long and valiantly" he fell into sadness. Pleasant "talk of old army times" followed, and he had almost forgotten, as he declares, the business in hand, when Lee asked him on what terms he would accept surrender.

Grant sat down and wrote, not knowing when he began what he should go on to write. As he wrote he thought of the handsome sword Lee carried. Instantly he added to his terms permission for every Southern officer to keep his sword and his horse.

Lee read the paper and when he came to that point was visibly moved. He gauged his man, and he ventured to ask something more. He thought, he said, Grant might not know that the Confederate cavalry troopers owned their own horses. Grant said they would be badly wanted on the farms and added a further concession accordingly. "This will have the best possible effect on the men," said Lee. "It will do much towards conciliating our people." Grant included also in his written terms words of general pardon to Confederate officers for their treason.

This was an inadvertent breach, perhaps, of Lincoln's orders, but it was one which met with no objection. Lee retired into civil life and devoted himself thereafter to his neighbours' service as head of a college in Virginia—much respected, very free with alms to old soldiers and not much caring whether they had fought for the South or for the North. Grant did not wait to set foot in the capital which he had conquered, but, the main business being over, posted off with all haste to see his son settled in at school.

Lincoln remained at City Point till April 8, when he started back by steamer. Those who were with him on the two days' voyage told afterwards of the happy talk, as of a quiet family party rejoicing in the return of peace. Somebody said that Jefferson Davis really ought to be hanged. The reply came in the quotation that he might almost have expected, "Judge not, that ye be not judged." On the second day, Sunday, the President read to them parts of "Macbeth." Sumner, who was one of them, recalled that he read twice over the lines,

> "Duncan is in his grave;
>
> After life's fitful fever he sleeps well;
>
> Treason has done his worst; nor steel, nor poison,
>
> Malice domestic, foreign levy, nothing
>
> Can touch him further."

On the Tuesday, April 11, a triumphant crowd came to the White House to greet Lincoln. He made them a speech, carefully prepared in substance rather than in form, dealing with the question of reconstruction in the South, with special reference to what was already in progress in Louisiana. The precise points of controversy that arose in this regard hardly matter now.

Lincoln disclaimed any wish to insist pedantically upon any detailed plan of his; but he declared his wish equally to keep clear of any merely pedantic points of controversy with any in the South who were loyally striving to revive State Government with acceptance of the Union and without slavery; and he urged that genuine though small beginnings should be encouraged. He regretted that in Louisiana his wish for the enfranchisement of educated negroes and of negro soldiers had not been followed; but as the freedom of the negroes was unreservedly accepted, as provision was made for them in the public schools, and the new State constitution allowed the Legislature to enfranchise them, there was clear gain. "Concede that the new government of Louisiana is only to what it should be as the egg is to the fowl, we shall sooner have the fowl by hatching the egg than by smashing it. What has been said of Louisiana will apply generally to other States. So new and unprecedented," he ended, "is the whole case that no exclusive and inflexible plan can safely be prescribed as to details and collaterals.

Such exclusive and inflexible plan would surely become a new entanglement. Important principles may and must be inflexible. In the present situation, as the phrase goes, it may be my duty to make some new announcement to the people of the South. I am considering, and shall not fail to act when satisfied that action will be proper." A full generation has had cause to lament that that announcement was never to be made.

On Good Friday, April 14, 1865, with solemn religious service the Union flag was hoisted again on Fort Sumter by General Anderson, its old defender. On that morning there was a Cabinet Council in Washington. Seward was absent, in bed with an injury from a carriage accident. Grant was there a little anxious to get news from Sherman. Lincoln was in a happy mood. He had earlier that morning enjoyed greatly a talk with Robert Lincoln about the young man's new experience of soldiering.

He now told Grant and the Cabinet that good news was coming from Sherman. He knew it, he said, for last night he had dreamed a dream, which had come to him several times before. In this dream, whenever it came, he was sailing in a ship of a peculiar build, indescribable but always the same, and being borne on it with great speed towards a dark and undefined shore. He had always dreamed this before victory. He dreamed it before Antietam, before Murfreesborough, before Gettysburg, before

Vicksburg. Grant observed bluntly that Murfreesborough had not been a victory, or of any consequence anyway. Lincoln persisted on this topic undeterred. After some lesser business they discussed the reconstruction of the South. Lincoln rejoiced that Congress had adjourned and the "disturbing element" in it could not hinder the work.

Before it met again, "if we are wise and discreet we shall re-animate the States and get their governments in successful operation, with order prevailing and the Union re-established." Lastly, there was talk of the treatment of rebels and of the demand that had been heard for "persecution" and "bloody work." "No one need expect me," said Lincoln, "to take any part in hanging or killing these men, even the worst of them. Frighten them out of the country, open the gates, let down the bars, scare them off." "Shoo," he added, throwing up his large hands like a man scaring sheep. "We must extinguish our resentments if we expect harmony and union.

There is too much of the desire on the part of some of our very good friends to be masters, to interfere with and dictate to those States, to treat the people not as fellow citizens; there is too little respect for their rights. I do not sympathise in these feelings." Such was the tenor of his last recorded utterance on public affairs.

In the afternoon Mr. and Mrs. Lincoln drove together and he talked to her with keen pleasure of the life they would live when the Presidency was over. That night Mr. and Mrs. Lincoln went to the theatre, for the day was not observed as in England. The Grants were to have been with them, but changed their minds and left Washington that day, so a young officer, Major Rathbone, and the lady engaged to him, both of them thereafter ill-fated, came instead.

The theatre was crowded; many officers returned from the war were there and eager to see Lincoln. The play was "Our American Cousin," a play in which the part of Lord Dundreary was afterwards developed and made famous. Some time after 10 o'clock, at a point in the play which it is said no person present could afterwards remember, a shot was heard in the theatre and Abraham Lincoln fell forward upon the front of the box unconscious and dying. A wild-looking man, who had entered the box unobserved and had done his work, was seen to strike with a knife at Major Rathbone, who tried to seize him. Then he jumped from the box to the stage; he caught a spur in the drapery and fell, breaking the small bone of his leg. He rose, shouted "Sic semper tyrannis," the motto of Virginia, disappeared behind the scenes, mounted a horse that was in waiting at the stage door, and rode away.

This was John Wilkes Booth, brother of a famous actor then playing "Hamlet" in Boston. He was an actor too, and an athletic and daring youth. In him that peculiarly ferocious political passion which occasionally showed itself among Southerners was further inflamed by brandy and by that ranting mode of thought which the stage develops in some few. He was the leader of a conspiracy which aimed at compassing the deaths of others besides Lincoln. Andrew Johnson, the Vice-President, was to die.

So was Seward. That same night one of the conspirators, a gigantic boy of feeble mind, gained entrance to Seward's house and wounded three people, including Seward himself, who was lying already injured in bed and received four or five wounds. Neither he nor the others died. The weak-minded or mad boy, another man, whose offense consisted in having been asked to kill Johnson and refused to do so, and another alleged conspirator, a woman, were hanged after a court-martial whose proceedings did credit neither to the new President nor to others concerned. Booth himself, after many adventures, was shot in a barn in which he stood at bay and which had been set on fire by the soldiers pursuing him. During his flight he is said to have felt much aggrieved that men did not praise him as they had praised Brutus and Cassius.

There were then in the South many broken and many permanently embittered men, indeed the temper which would be glad at

Lincoln's death could be found here and there and notably among the partisans of the South in Washington. But, if it be wondered what measure of sympathy there was for Booth's dark deed, an answer lies in the fact that the murder of Lincoln would at no time have been difficult for a brave man. Fair blows were now as powerless as foul to arrest the end.

On the very morning when Lincoln and Grant at the Cabinet had been telling of their hopes and fears for Sherman, Sherman himself at Raleigh in North Carolina had received and answered a letter from Johnston opening negotiations for a peaceful surrender. Three days later he was starting by rail for Greensborough when word came to him from the telegraph operator that an important message was upon the wire.

He went to the telegraph box and heard it. Then he swore the telegraph operator to secrecy, for he feared that some provocation might lead to terrible disorders in Raleigh, if his army, flushed with triumph, were to learn, before his return in peace, the news that for many days after hushed their accustomed songs and shouts and cheering into a silence which was long remembered. He went off to meet Johnston and requested to be with him alone in a farmhouse near. There he told him of the murder of Lincoln. "The perspiration came out in large drops on Johnston's forehead," says Sherman, who watched him closely.

He exclaimed that it was a disgrace to the age. Then he asked to know whether Sherman attributed the crime to the Confederate authorities. Sherman could assure him that no one dreamed of such a suspicion against men like him and General Lee; but he added that he was not so sure of "Jefferson Davis and men of that stripe." Then followed some delay, through a mistake of Sherman's which the authorities in Washington reversed, but in a few days all was settled and the whole of the forces under Johnston's command laid down their arms. Twenty years later, as an old man and infirm, their leader left his Southern home to be present at Sherman's funeral, where he caught a chill from which he died soon after. Jefferson Davis was captured on May

10, near the borders of Florida. He was, not without plausible grounds but quite unjustly, suspected in regard to the murder, and he suffered imprisonment for some time till President Andrew Johnson released him when the evidence against him had been seen to be worthless. He lived many years in Mississippi and wrote memoirs, in which may be found the fullest legal argument for the great Secession, his own view of his quarrels with Joseph Johnston, and much besides. Amongst other things he tells how when they heard the news of Lincoln's murder some troops cheered, but he was truly sorry for the reason that Andrew Johnson was more hostile to the cause than Lincoln. It is disappointing to think, of one who played a memorable part in history with much determination, that in this reminiscence he sized his stature as a man fairly accurately. After several other surrenders of Southern towns and small scattered forces, the Confederate General Kirby Smith, in Texas, surrendered to General Canby, Banks' successor, on May 26, and after four years and forty-four days armed resistance to the Union was at an end.

On the night of Good Friday, Abraham Lincoln had been carried still unconscious to a house near the theatre. His sons and other friends were summoned. He never regained consciousness. "A look of unspeakable peace," say his secretaries who were there, "came over his worn features." At 7.22 on the morning of April 15, Stanton, watching him more closely than the rest, told them what had passed in the words, "Now he belongs to the ages."

The mourning of a nation, voiced to later times by some of the best lines of more than one of its poets, and deeper and more prevailing for the lack of comprehension which some had shown him before, followed his body in its slow progress—stopping at Baltimore, where once his life had been threatened, for the homage of vast crowds; stopping at New York, where among the huge assembly old General Scott came to bid him affectionate farewell; stopping at other cities for the tribute of reverent multitudes—to Springfield, his home of so many years, where, on May 4, 1865, it was laid to rest.

After the burial service the "Second Inaugural" was read over his grave, nor could better words than his own have been chosen to honour one who "with malice toward none, with charity toward all, with firmness in the right as God gave him to see the right, had striven on to finish the work that he was in." In England, apart from more formal tokens of a late-learnt regard and an unfeigned regret, Punch embodied in verse of rare felicity the manly contrition of its editor for ignorant derision in past years; and Queen Victoria symbolised best of all, and most acceptably to Americans, the feeling of her people when she wrote to Mrs. Lincoln "as a widow to a widow." Nor, though the transactions in which he bore his part were but little understood in this country till they were half forgotten, has tradition ever failed to give him, by just instinct, his rank with the greatest of our race.

Many great deeds had been done in the war. The greatest was the keeping of the North together in an enterprise so arduous, and an enterprise for objects so confusedly related as the Union and freedom. Abraham Lincoln did this; nobody else could have done it; to do it he bore on his sole shoulders such a weight of care and pain as few other men have borne. When it was over it seemed to the people that he had all along been thinking their real thoughts for them; but they knew that this was because he had fearlessly thought for himself. He had been able to save the nation, partly because he saw that unity was not to be sought by the way of base concession.

He had been able to free the slaves, partly because he would not hasten to this object at the sacrifice of what he thought a larger purpose. This most unrelenting enemy to the project of the Confederacy was the one man who had quite purged his heart and mind from hatred or even anger towards his fellow-countrymen of the South. That fact came to be seen in the South too, and generations in America are likely to remember it when all other features of his statecraft have grown indistinct.